Professional Development
with Visio 2000

David A. Edson

A Division of Macmillan USA
201 West 103rd St., Indianapolis, Indiana, 46290 USA

EXECUTIVE EDITOR
Gregory Croy

AQUISITIONS EDITOR
Chris Webb

DEVELOPMENT EDITOR
Matt Purcell

TECHNICAL EDITOR
Robert Zigon

MANAGING EDITOR
Lisa Wilson

PRODUCTION
D&G Limited, LLC

COVER DESIGNER
Anne Jones

BOOK DESIGNER
Anne Jones

Overview

Contents

3   Modifying Visio SmartShape Symbols and Groups of Symbols   67

About the Author

David A. Edson is the Visio senior technical evangelist for Visio Corporation. He was trained as an architect and holds degrees in architecture and architectural history. Since 1985, Dave has been involved in the CADD industry as both a third-party developer to Autodesk and an independent consultant. He first began using Visio with its introduction in 1992, utilizing it as a tool for software development.

For 10 years, Dave worked as a custom programming manager in the field of computer-aided design and drafting, with a focus on architectural-based products and custom solutions. Dave has spent the past several years traveling all over the world training other developers in the use of Visio as a development and solutions platform and evangelizing the use of objects and object models as building blocks to robust software solutions.

Dave has been a featured speaker at Microsoft Tech-Ed, both in the United States and Europe, as well as at Advisor Dev-Con, MOVS, and Microsoft Technical Briefings. Dave has also been an author and columnist for *SmartPages*, *Technical Design Solutions*, Design-Drawing.com, *VBPJ*, *Microsoft Office and VBA Development*, *Cadence*, *Cadylist*, and *AutoCAD Tech Journal*.

Getting in Touch with Me

It seems that, as each day passes, the world becomes a smaller and better-connected place in which to live. Through the marvels of today's electronic communications, you can pop me a note at the speed of bits and bytes across the Web of email. I truly enjoy getting your feedback, constructive criticism, and praise, when justly due. I can be reached at

```
davide@visio.com
```

Additionally, I heartily encourage you to browse (or surf, if that's your style) the Visio Developer Network at

```
http://www.visio.com/vdn
```

Dedication

But it's not her air, her form, her face,

Though matching beauty's fabled Queen;

'Tis the mind that shines in ev'ry grace,

An' chiefly in her rogueish een.

—*From the early poems (1774–1784) of Robert Burns*

With pride and gratitude unbounded, I dedicate this to that lass.

Acknowledgments

Writing a book is a labor of love, if you will. Your life becomes confined to your bailiwick and your keyboard, monitor, and mouse. As such, you tend to forget that, even though writing seems to be a solitary endeavor, it is truly a team accomplishment.

To that end, I would like to take a moment to thank acquisitions editor Chris Webb, development editor Matt Purcell, and all the folks at Macmillan for their huge effort in seeing this project through. I would also like to thank, for their contributions, more folks at Visio than I can begin to list. Most notably, the Solutions Marketing and Consulting group (I still refuse to refer to you as *SMAC*), the development teams, and the Documentation and User Education groups. Without them, this book truly would never have come to be. An additional and very special thanks goes to Dr. Mark Davison, Ph.D., who saw a wild, untamed, and unabashed Scotsman and perceived that he had much more in him than just random consulting and training.

A doff o' the bonnet goes out as well to every single Visio user and, more importantly, to each and every Visio Solutions Partner, independent Visio developer, and corporate solution developer utilizing Visio software. You are the folk who make writing a book like this truly my raison d'être.

Preface

Communication involves the transfer of information from one party to another and back again. Originally, communication was, in fact, graphics based. Cave drawings are a classic illustration of this. Later, language was developed and codified. Slowly, words and numbers began to replace images as a communications mechanism. But through it all, we still remain inherently graphic communicators and thinkers. Look into any board room or corporate meeting room. You will find people communicating by writing both words and pictures on white boards and flip charts. Far too often, the task of creating intelligible graphics is somehow lost in the transition between the thought and the pen. This is how Visio came to be. Visio is the tool that enables knowledge workers and makes their communication lucid and powerful.

There comes a time in the growth of a software company like Visio when the acceptance of the software begins to transition beyond the selling of individual boxes and marches forward to mission-critical usage deployed across every enterprise desktop. That transition does not automatically come about. It requires that the corporate developers and independent software consultants not only adopt the software for their daily use and view the software as a "cannot live without" tool in their work, but also extend the software and make it become the development platform of choice for their enterprisewide solutions. Visio is beginning to take on this new and expanded role in the corporate enterprise.

It is books like David Edson's *Professional Development with Visio 2000* that forward this acceptance. This book takes the Visio user on a journey from the basics of understanding the Visio ShapeSheet paradigm through to Automation application development using ActiveX and Visual Basic for Applications. Dave assists developers, both novice and professional alike, in understanding how to develop high-quality, meaningful solutions with Visio as their development platform of choice. Dave has spent countless hours in front of Visio developers and users as a lecturer, an instructor, and as the Visio senior technical evangelist, speaking at developer conferences worldwide.

I encourage you to take the time to work your way through this book. Begin with the fundamentals. Learn the power of the ShapeSheet environment. Then, begin to extend your expertise with Automation development. Use Visio's internal VBA environment. Have fun learning how to solve your daily enterprise challenges. When you have completed the book, keep it at hand as a quality reference for your development needs.

Jeremy Jaech
President, Founder, and CEO
Visio Corporation

Introduction

Epistle to Davie

The honest heart that's free frae a'
Intended fraud or guile,
However Fortune kick the ba',
Has ay some cause to smile;

—Robert Burns, January 1785

Visio. When most folks hear that word or are asked, "Do you know about Visio?," they respond, "Oh, yes, Visio. Isn't that the program for making those flow charts and org charts?" Well, yes, Visio is indeed a flow-charting and org-charting tool—but it is much more. Visio is a graphics application that joins graphical symbology and images with data from many data sources and produces diagrams that convey information in a clear format that is highly useful. This sounds grand, but are the solutions contained in the box and listed in the associated copy all there is to Visio? Actually, there is much more to Visio! Brilliant solutions can be accomplished if the user or developer is willing to work just a small distance "beyond the box," which is why you have chosen this book in the first place, isn't it?

What's New in Visio 2000 for Developers

For the shape developer, there are now *cross-container references*. This new feature allows Visio ShapeSheet formulas to reference any cell in a document, which includes cells in pages, masters, styles, and the document ShapeSheet. There are now *rotating foreign objects*. This capability allows the creation of complex, multiformat shapes to be used in places where they have to be rotated. Using bitmaps, metafiles, and OLE objects for Visio shapes that do not have to exhibit smart behavior can increase the performance of your solution.

In Visio 2000, groups can now exhibit the following behavior:

- Group shapes may contain text and/or geometry.
- There are now three distinct group selection modes (group only, group first, member first).
- Snap and glue operations will selectively target group member shapes.
- There is complete mouse editing of subselected shapes (move, size, rotate, and so on).
- There are direct deletions of subselected shapes.

These enhancements allow Visio shape developers more control over the group's shape and subshape behavior.

For the solution developer producing drawings, there are improved *undo Automation* capabilities. The new undo capabilities for Visio 2000 give the Visio solution developer more control over how his or her add-ons work with the Undo Manager.

Visio 2000 includes new *Automation methods and events*. These new methods and events add to the underlying object model to provide easier access and more complete control of the Visio drawing model.

New *Automation objects* include hyperlinks. The Hyperlinks object represents a collection of hyperlink objects. The MasterShortCut object is simply another kind of Stencil object. MasterShortCuts look and behave very much like a master in Visio but are only a reference to a master that may reside in a completely different Stencil.

Visio 2000 now has the capability to access cells within masters, styles, the document ShapeSheet, and other pages.

GETVAL and GETREF functions allow a ShapeSheet cell to see either the value or a formula in any other cell.

New ShapeSheet cells include new group shape cells, new shape cells, and new page cells.

Group behavior has been significantly enhanced. In Visio 2000, a group shape can now have geometry. You can add geometry to a group shape by selecting a drawing tool (Pencil, Freeform, Line, Arc, Rectangle, Ellipse), selecting the shape to add to, holding down the Ctrl+Shift keys, and gesturing in new geometry. You can also add a geometry section to a group via the group ShapeSheet window. In Visio 2000, the group shape now has the option to contain text. You can set and unset this option via the Behavior dialog box, Format, Behavior, or by setting the Group Properties text edit target cell, IsTextEditTarget, to either TRUE or FALSE.

Visio 2000 has three types of group selection behavior:

- Group only—No subselection
- Group first, then group member—Visio 5.0 behavior
- Group member first, then group—Direct selection of group members

You can set a group's selection mode via the Behavior dialog box, Format > Behavior, or by setting the Group Properties group selection mode cell, SelectMode, to one of the following values: 0 = Group Only, 1 = Group First, or 2 = Member First.

In Visio 2000, group shapes may contain visible components such as text or geometry. You can set a group's display via the Behavior dialog box, Format > Behavior, or by setting the Group Properties group data display cell, DisplayMode, to one of the following values: 0 = Hide, 1 = Behind member shapes, or 2 = In front of member shapes.

There are numerous *geometry functions* new in Visio 2000. These include

- POLYLINE
- NURBS
- LOCTOLOC
- LOCTOPAR
- ANGLETOLOC
- ANGLETOPAR

There are numerous *sheet property functions* new in Visio 2000. These include

- Name
- MasterName
- BkgPageName
- Data1, Data2, and Data3
- Type
- TypeDes
- ID
- FieldPicture

There are numerous *document property functions* new in Visio 2000. These include

- Directory
- Filename
- DocCreation
- DocLastPrint
- DocLastSave
- Creator
- Description
- Keywords
- Subject
- Title
- Manager
- Manager
- Category
- HyperlinkBase

The new *page tab control* in Visio provides a simple, intuitive means of managing drawing pages in the Visio environment. The page tab control is located along the bottom edge of the drawing window and resembles the paper index tabs that are attached to pages in a volume.

This new control offers a simple way to reorder and rename pages in Visio. To reorder pages, drag and drop a tab into its new position. You can rename a page by right-clicking a tab and selecting Rename from the right-click menu. The text in the tab will become selected, and a text caret will begin flashing at the end of the text. When this occurs, you may retype or edit the name in the tab.

Visio 2000 now offers the capability to "nudge" selected objects to the nearest snappable point or pixel. *Nudging* means to move a shape by tapping an arrow key while the shape is selected. In Visio, nudging shapes can be most useful when you're fine-tuning the position of your shape on the Visio drawing page.

When you use the navigation keys to nudge your selection, the shapes in your selection will automatically snap to the nearest snappable point, as defined by the *Snap and Glue dialog box*. You can dictate your Snap and Glue settings in the Snap and Glue dialog box by selecting Tools, Snap and Glue from the Visio menu. If you have to move your selection one pixel at a time, hold down the Shift key and use the navigation keys to move your shape, pixel by pixel. You can enable nudging in Visio by turning off the Scroll Lock.

The new modeless *Pan and Zoom window* was designed to help you quickly survey a diagram and dive down into the specific areas of interest. You can display the Pan and Zoom window from the menu by selecting View, Windows, Pan and Zoom. Depending on your personal preference, the Pan and Zoom window can anchor itself to one or two inner edges in your Visio drawing window, or it can float as a popup window. When anchored, the Pan and Zoom window can optionally slide out of view when the cursor leaves the window and then slide back into view when the cursor hovers over the collapsed window. When the window is floating, you can control the size and position of this window in your drawing.

The bold rectangle inside the Pan and Zoom window represents the current viewable area of the drawing window. To pan the drawing window to a new location, click and drag the rectangle to a new location on the page. You can zoom to a section of the drawing by clicking and dragging out a new view region, which will zoom the drawing window to fit the new rectangle.

The new *Document Explorer window* provides a central location where you can easily explore and manage the contents of your Visio document. You can display the Document Explorer by selecting View, Windows, Document Explorer from the Visio menu. Again, depending on your personal preference, the Document Explorer can anchor itself to one or two inner edges in the document window, or it can float as a popup window. (For more information on anchored and floating windows, see the preceding Pan and Zoom description.)

When you open the Document Explorer, you will find the contents of the document displayed in a hierarchical fashion. You can expand or collapse folders by double-clicking on the folder. The text of each item can be edited by single-clicking on the item and then hovering your cursor over the item to invoke the text editor.

Each item in the Document Explorer has a menu associated with it. To invoke this menu, right-click on the item you want to work.

The *Size and Position dialog* has been designed to include a new modeless window that helps you size and position shapes in an exact manner. You can display the new *Size and Position window* by selecting View, Windows, Size and Position from the Visio menu. Depending on your personal preference, the Size and Position window can anchor itself to one or two inner edges in your Visio drawing window, or it can float as a popup window.

Visio 2000 now includes a new modeless *Custom Properties window*. You can display the Custom Properties window by selecting View, Windows, Custom Properties from the Visio menu. Depending on your personal preference, the Custom Properties window can anchor itself to one or two inner edges in your Visio drawing window, or it can float as a popup window.

With the new *Custom Properties* window, you can select single or multiple shapes to display their custom properties in the modeless Custom Properties window. When a single shape is selected, the selected shape's properties and values are displayed in the window. When you select multiple shapes, only the custom properties common to the selected shapes are displayed in the Custom Properties widow. If the value of a custom property row has been visually truncated in the dialog box, hold your cursor over the value grid to see a ScreenTip that shows the entire contents of your value cell. You can also display a custom property row prompt by placing your cursor over the property description cell.

Shortcuts to masters are similar to file shortcuts in Windows. They look and behave very much like a master in Visio but are only a reference to a master that may reside in a completely different Stencil. There are a number of benefits to using shortcuts to masters rather than duplicating the original master. They include

- By referencing masters that appear in more than one Stencil, you can begin to create smaller Stencils.
- By referencing masters that appear in more than one Stencil, you can easily apply fixes and enhancements in just one place, rather than have to track down and update each duplicate copy.

Because each shortcut can contain its own "state data," which is applied to the shape at drop time, you can create several shortcuts to the same master and produce very different effects when dropped on the same page.

CommandBars are the fusion of toolbars, menu bars, and popup menus into a single control type. A CommandBar is a window that contains a series of buttons or other controls, such as combo boxes and edit fields. A CommandBar may be docked at the edge of a frame window, or it may float over the desktop. CommandBars can be in one of three styles:

- Toolbar style—Controls are arranged horizontally. Buttons are displayed *without* text, but *with* an icon.

- Menu bar style—Controls are arranged horizontally. Buttons are displayed *with* text, but *without* an icon.

- Popup menu style—Controls are arranged vertically. Buttons are displayed *with* text and *with* icons, if available.

In Visio 2000, you may now customize existing CommandBars or create new CommandBars with the help of a new Visio customization interface. To customize a CommandBar, right-click anywhere on a CommandBar object and select Customize to receive the customization dialog box. This new modeless dialog box provides a palette of controls that may be dragged and dropped onto the showing CommandBars. While you are in the Customize mode, you may also select which CommandBars are shown or hidden and create and name new CommandBars.

In Visio 2000, a shape's begin and end points can now have different line-end sizes. They can be set in the Format Line dialog; Format, Line from the menu; and in the Line Format section of the ShapeSheet window. The cell names for begin and end arrow sizes are *BeginArrowSize* and *EndArrowSize*.

To better support engineering, Visio 2000 now supports *multidimensional units*. Multidimensional units can be added to ShapeSheet formulas by using a caret (^) character after an explicit unit followed by an exponent. For example, 4in^2 would denote 4 square inches; a ShapeSheet formula such as 2 in * 6 in + 5in^2 would return 17in^2, or 17 square inches. The exponent sign can be represented by nothing, indicating a positive value, or a single minus (-) character, indicating a negative value.

To support the exchange of image data with other applications, the *Icon Editor* has been enhanced to use the standard Windows bitmap format. This new feature allows the Cut, Copy, and Paste Clipboard commands to interact with other Windows bitmaps.

What You Should Know Before Reading This Book

This book makes two basic presumptions. First, it presumes that you have at least a passing acquaintance with using the Visio user interface. You can "drag, drop, and pull-on-the-green-things." You can move SmartShape symbols around on a page and connect them as necessary to create simple connected diagrams. Second, it presumes that you have a...and here you will forgive the pun...*basic* understanding of Visual Basic and/or VBA within at least one Microsoft Office application: Word, Excel, Access, PowerPoint, or Outlook.

How This Book Is Organized

This book is organized into four general parts. Each is designed to assist you in your learning process when working with Visio solutions development.

Part I: Visio Development with ShapeSheets

The first chapter is designed to acquaint you with the Visio ShapeSheet and Automation paradigms. It introduces you to the Visio SmartShape symbols and their inherent ShapeSheets.

The next nine chapters effect your total immersion into the ShapeSheet programming environment. In these chapters, you will learn about virtually every cell in a Visio ShapeSheet. You will learn how to set and retrieve values and formulas and use them to reference and manipulate other cells. In this manner, you create specialized behavior that is the hallmark of SmartShape symbol development.

Part II: Visio ActiveX Development

The five chapters that follow the ShapeSheet development section deal with enhanced access to every aspect of the Visio environment through ActiveX Automation. This includes manipulating Visio SmartShape symbols, Visio pages and drawings, and even the Visio user interface.

Part III: Visio Development with Microsoft Office 2000 and Other VBA-Enabled Applications

In the last seven chapters, you will learn how to interact with other VBA-enabled applications, such as all the Microsoft Office 2000 applications—Excel, Access, Word, PowerPoint, and Outlook.

About the CD

This book comes with a companion CD-ROM that contains the following:

- A fully functional evaluation copy of Visio 2000 Professional Edition. This software is a time-expiring version of Visio that is identical to a full license version. It simply times out after 30 days.

- Every Visio 2000 drawing file used to create the examples in this book. You are free to open each drawing and use any of the SmartShape symbols and any code used in these diagrams. Remember that there is no such thing as stealing code here. It is "adaptive reuse"!

- Numerous other example files and whitepapers to assist you in your development efforts.

Visio Development with ShapeSheets

IN THIS PART

Solutions Development Theory

CHAPTER

1

IN THIS CHAPTER

One of the advantages of Visio development is that it is eminently scalable. By *scalable*, I mean that solutions can be built and delivered incrementally using any of the various developmental tools found within Visio, the Visio ShapeSheet environment, or an Automation interface such as C, C++, Visual Basic (VB), and Visio's own internal Visual Basic for Applications (VBA) environment.

You can start by working with the SmartShape symbols supplied by Visio. You can then begin to make small levels of customization by adding custom properties. With custom properties added, you can then use the built-in tools to generate reports in Excel, Access, or Word. You can write your own Automation interface as well. This will enable full interoperability between Visio and other VBA-enabled applications, such as Peachtree or Great Plains.

You can further your customization by adding the new customized SmartShape symbols to your own stencil and by distributing them as part of a template so that every new document your users create has your customization already available to them. Taking the customization further, you can create your own highly intelligent Visio SmartShape symbols by using a combination of Visio's native drawing tools and the robust ShapeSheet programming environment. This Excel-like ShapeSheet environment is intuitive and powerful. It allows you to create parametric SmartShape symbols that respond to user input, as well as data from external sources, as shown in Figure 1.1.

Going beyond the ShapeSheet programming environment, you can begin to tap in to the power of Visio's rich object model and use an Automation controller such as C, C++, VB, and VBA or even Delphi or Java to generate Visio diagrams automatically, add data to collections of Visio SmartShape symbols, query Visio diagrams, and extract data from them to interact real time with other Automation-enabled applications. These Automation solutions can be delivered piece by piece. Each small Automation and interoperability application can be delivered as part of a stencil or drawing in a template form and later incorporated with other solutions into larger members of the digital nervous system for enterprisewide solutions delivery.

Concepts: Design Versus Drafting

I feel it very important that I make a point here: Drawing with graphic primitives creates a picture, and drawing with objects creates a model. Drawing with graphic primitives is called *drafting*, and drawing with objects is called *designing*.

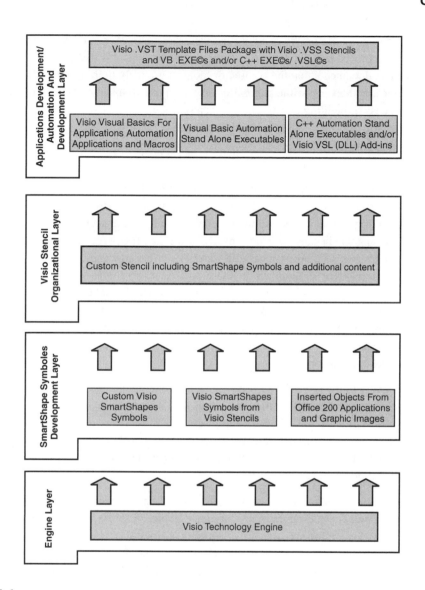

FIGURE 1.1

A model of a scalable Visio solution.

Here, I'm going to admit a bias—I was trained as an architect and tend to lean toward architectural examples and illustrations to drive a point home. Consider the example of a construction project, commercial or residential (it doesn't matter). When the architect draws up a set of drawings and prints them on blue-line paper, he creates what he refers to as construction documents. The building contractor who receives a set of these documents (drawings) takes many things for granted. He or she assumes that the drawings were put together by a person well versed in the procedures, methodologies, materials, and systems that go into the creation of a building. The documents that the contractor looks at are truly nothing more than blue lines, arcs, circles, and text on white paper. Because both the architect and contractor are educated in the process of building construction—because they both can speak the symbolic language shown on the drawings—they both assume that the circle with the big plus through it represents a ceiling light fixture. For the same reason, they both assume that the large S with the lines through it represents a light switch.

If the facts are truly analyzed, the contractor is heavily reliant on the symbolic representations shown on that set of papers. If something is not shown physically on the drawings, it can be only one of two things: either an omission or something left to interpretation. In the case of an omission, this means that because it is not physically on the drawing, it does not exist and is therefore not built. Imagine a house without a water heater because the heater does not exist on the drawing, or a warehouse without a warehouse door. Open to litigation? Absolutely. In the case of *left to interpretation*, this means that the contractor would make his or her own educated guess at what the architect had in mind. Imagine the lime-green living room because the contractor thought that the owner might like lime green instead of the pale putty wall color specifically requested by the owner. The cost for repainting would have to be born by someone. This is where lawsuits originate.

How does this apply to the typical enterprise problem? Imagine the network diagram with only pictures of each piece of network equipment. Imagine that the person creating this diagram used these pieces of clip art with lines to connect them. The resultant drawing might look like a proper network configuration, but in reality it would never work to create a workable and viable network. Hundreds of thousands, if not millions of dollars hang in the balance with improperly created documents.

Now imagine a network diagram created using objects for each piece of equipment required to put the network together. As each piece of equipment is placed in the drawing and connected, it would react as if it were the actual piece of equipment, identifying IP addresses, determining whether switches and hubs were properly placed and configured (see Figure 1.2). A significant savings in installation and configuration is therefore realized with each properly created network diagram.

Consider something as basic as an organizational chart. This simple diagram, if graphically analyzed, is nothing more than boxes connected with lines. However, if organizational diagram SmartShape symbol objects are used, when a subordinate SmartShape symbol is dropped on its manager SmartShape symbol, it is properly filled with the requisite information and correctly laid out within the structure of the corporate human resources infrastructure.

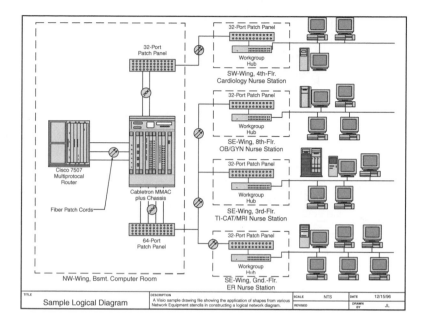

FIGURE 1.2

A typical network diagram.

Should a report have to be generated, the report does not reveal 600 boxes and 599 lines. Rather, it reports on each individual employee, his manager, the department to which he is assigned, his telephone extension, his IP address, and his email address. When an employee is added to the organization, these telephone, IP address, email address, and office number assignments are made, and the proper members of the organization's support staff are notified of the work required to get the new employee set up and immediately productive. Conversely, when an employee leaves the corporation, his resources are freed, and all the appropriate departments are notified: departments such as I.S. (Information Systems), Finance, Human Resources, and Facilities Management (see Figure 1.3).

As you can see, designing with objects creates intelligent documents that can be used and shared throughout the entire enterprise. In contrast, drawings of graphic primitives are little more than clip art open to interpretation and omissions and do little to advance the profitability and productivity of the corporate enterprise.

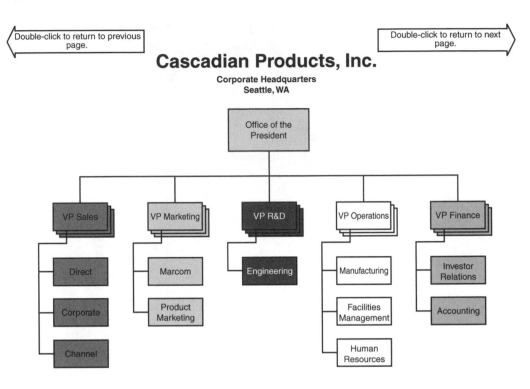

FIGURE 1.3

A typical organizational chart.

ShapeSheet Development

Most of the books you have purchased that proudly display the words *developer* or *development* in the title immediately throw you into a common programming language: C, C++, or VB. You expect to be able to create Automation applications by getting references to objects and manipulating them by their properties, methods, and events. Although this is fundamentally correct as it applies to Visio development, you should recognize that every SmartShape symbol, every page in a document, every document you create—even Visio, the application itself—is indeed an object. To fully exploit the objects in Visio, you must understand how the shape that you see graphically relates to its corresponding and underlying ShapeSheet and how those relate to the Visio Object Model hierarchy (see Figure 1.4). You will begin with ShapeSheet development.

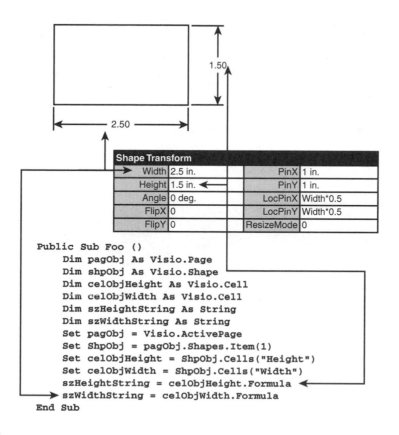

FIGURE 1.4.

The relationship among SmartShape symbols, ShapeSheet cells, and Automation programs.

The Visio ShapeSheet is, in its most basic form, an Excel-like spreadsheet replete with cells that can hold both values and simple or complex formulas that evaluate to given values. The greatest difference between the typical spreadsheet and a Visio ShapeSheet is that the ShapeSheet is broken down into discrete sections, each with its own title bar to assist the developer in understanding the purpose of that section. Cells in a given section control the appearance of or properties of unique aspects of the SmartShape symbol they reference.

Like a typical spreadsheet, the ShapeSheet can have any one cell reference another cell and, therefore, by these intercell references perform specific forms of parametric relationships (see Figure 1.5). For example, a SmartShape symbol can be specified via its ShapeSheet so that the height of the SmartShape symbol is always equal to half the width of that symbol. No matter how the user of the symbol attempts to adjust the width or height of the symbol through the user interface, the specific relationship between height and width will always be maintained.

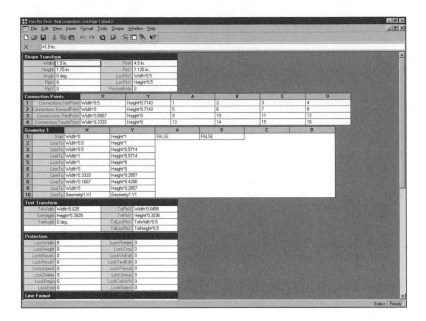

FIGURE 1.5

A Visio SmartShape symbol's ShapeSheet.

Moreover, any cell in any given SmartShape symbol can reference any cell in any other SmartShape symbol's ShapeSheet. This means that the user's manipulating SmartShape symbol A can produce direct and immediate effects on SmartShape symbol B.

ShapeSheet development often starts with launching the Visio ShapeSheet environment for a selected existing Visio shape dragged from a stencil. With the ShapeSheet environment open, the user or developer then manipulates the values and formulas in existing sections and cells and adds new sections to create even more complex relationships between cells and SmartShape symbols. When the newly customized Visio SmartShape symbol exhibits the proper behavior, it is then added to a new stencil and made available to not only the current drawing but also other drawings.

Before Automation development can take place, a solid understanding of the ShapeSheet's cells is required. Without this understanding, the your ability to fully exploit Automation interfaces is very limited.

Automation Development

Automation development doesn't simply begin where ShapeSheet development leaves off. It extends the power of ShapeSheet development and enriches solutions by creating applications with full programming constructs, such as loops and decisions. This power takes full advantage of all the elegant interactivity inherent in the ShapeSheet and SmartShape symbol environment and extends it with solution-specific programming to create a rich, user-friendly solution to enterprisewide challenges.

Automation development can be accomplished by any available OLE-compliant or COM-compliant Automation controller. This includes C, C++, VB, VBA, and Delphi, as well as others. For the purposes of this book, I will focus on both VB and VBA. This is not because I have a particular affinity with or proclivity toward these languages, but rather because these languages are highly approachable and can be rapidly learned. As an added bonus, because VBA is an integral part of Visio, you will not be required to purchase any other development tools to build your solutions; the tools are right there in the box! Moreover, Visio has done numerous benchmarks for Automation application speed, and in a large number of cases, solutions created in VBA are as fast as, if not faster than, the same solution created in C++. This is, in large part, due to VBA's running in-process with Visio rather than across process boundaries.

Remember, also, that hybrid solutions are available to the developer as well. This means that you can build applications in C++ or VB that call functionality in VBA for specific tasks. Keep in mind that you are the architect of the solution and you have a palette of tools at your command to orchestrate the solution you want to create. The language is less important than solving the challenge at hand.

A point that I will make again, and again, is that an Automation solution requires a quality object model to be effective at all. You can use VB to create beautiful data-entry dialogs and perform all the numeric transformations that you want, but if your application has no means of communicating with the objects in the host application—in this case, Visio—it is of very limited value. Visio contains a highly robust and very complete object model. Through this object model, you, as the solutions developer, can manipulate any aspect of Visio. By this, I mean that you can alter the visual properties and the behavior of any SmartShape symbol, as well as the data that underlie them. You can manipulate groups of SmartShape symbols, the page they exist on, the document they are contained in, and even any aspect of the user interface, such as menus, toolbars, status lines, and more.

Your Automation solution should be designed to make an environment focused so that the user of your solution is unencumbered by any extraneous information. The solution should focus on solving the challenge set forth in the development requirements and keep the user focused on interacting with only that which is applicable. If you do not want your users to be using the pencil tool to draw and create line and arc segments, which will become rudimentary SmartShape symbols, remove the pencil tool from the toolbar, and remove the commands to activate that tool from all menus. If you want to ensure that the user has only your predesignated stencils of SmartShape symbols and does not have access to other stencils, remove that capability from the user's environment as well. It is my considered opinion that your solutions should be based on a template file. As in Microsoft Word, where you create a new Word document based on a particular template, Visio provides you with the ability to create templates for your solutions. These templates can set, through Automation code, the parameters of the user interface that will be accessible to the user and can provide the collections of stencils required to use the solution. When the user chooses to use Visio to create a totally different diagram type, the full Visio user interface will be available to him or her for that diagram type. This is far preferable to strong-arming your users into only one user interface, which might greatly hinder their ability to create the additional diagrams that might be required for their particular job function.

The Contents of a Typical Visio Solution

Well, with all this said about the ShapeSheet and Automation development environments, what are the contents of a typical Visio solution? A Visio solution typically contains most, if not all, of the following items, shown in Figure 1.6:

- Stencils of master SmartShape symbols
- Templates to set the user interface and environment, as well as open the required stencils
- Add-ons and/or macros written with an Automaton controller
- Help
- Documentation
- Training

Your solution should provide stencils of Visio SmartShape symbols, both those that you have collected from other stencils, if necessary, and those that you have designed and created so that the user of your solution is not required to draw anything, if at all possible. Remember that Visio's paradigm is drag-and-drop assemblage of drawings instead of runtime drawing of individual features within a drawing. Carefully created SmartShape symbols with a high level of intelligence often make it unnecessary for the user to do anything more than drag symbols from a stencil, place them in a logical position on the page, fill in data items as custom properties, and then print the diagram. I will be discussing much, much more about stencils in future chapters. For now, keep in mind that you want to organise SmartShape symbols on stencils so that they are intuitive to find, are easy to access, and appear in a logical order, which makes them far more valuable than a warren of clip art in a very large directory with cryptic names.

As previously stated, template files can facilitate the creation of new diagrams based on the environment you predefine. Providing a template makes the usage of your solution much, much easier. The user has all the tools right at his or her hands and can generally create the required diagram type with little or no assistance the first time out!

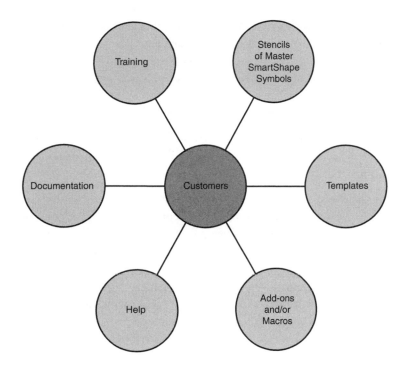

FIGURE 1.6

The contents of a typical Visio solution.

When a SmartShape symbol is dragged from a stencil and dropped onto a Visio drawing page, this triggers an event: the drop event. This event can be associated with code that you, the solution developer, create to automate a given task or draw information from the user or another data repository such as a SQL Server database. Your add-ons and/or macros are the extensions to the solution that give it that extra power to make it highly valuable to your users. Your solution can contain the code for this Automation directly inside the document based on the template using VBA, or it can call the code from an add-on residing in a directory known to the Visio environment. I will be speaking more in the section on ActiveX Automation about the structure of your Automation code and where it should live.

Covering the topic of help in and of itself would take up an entire book. I know that most solutions developers feel as if their solution is so well crafted that they should never have to include help. However, Visio has had the foresight to provide numerous methodologies for including help with your solutions. Help is available on every control handle in a Visio SmartShape symbol. Help is available via a right click on any Visio SmartShape symbol as well. Generally, all dialogs contain help systems as well. Custom properties contain prompt information to act as help. Each master SmartShape symbol on a stencil has a prompt on the status line, as well as available help.

There are numerous help authoring tools out there. Your choice of tool is independent of Visio, and I recommend that you use the tool that (a) best suits your development style and (b) is as close to your normal document creation style as possible. Help is one of those things that tends to get shunted to the very end of the development process. If you will discipline yourself to author your help as your development progresses and edit as necessary, your help will be of far greater benefit to your users than if you reserve it as a last-minute task.

Documentation tends to fall into the same category as help. Most developers think of it as someone else's task. They assume that the application is so well designed and implemented that the user can immediately use it without ever touching documentation.

If the user can do the wrong thing, he or she, in fact, will! It is in your best interest to provide well-written, quality, robust documentation for your application, no matter how small you feel the solution is. I know that every user of software fairly screams for documentation to be provided in hard copy and not just online. There is something quite comforting to them about the tactile sensation of thumbing through paper-based documentation. These are, in fact, the same folks who take that manual, thumb through it once, place it on the shelf, and never open it again. These are the same folks who call time and time again asking for technical support and, when asked whether they read about how to perform that specific task in the manual, will sheepishly and reluctantly tell you that they could not find it there, even though it was listed in 16-point bold text in the table of contents. Trust me here folks—provide documentation with your solutions!

Training is a bit of a variable issue. Presuming that your help and documentation systems are first-rate and that the scope of the application is small, training may not be a requirement. However, in world-class, very large solutions such as Visio's UML and ORM solutions, training for the end user will greatly increase the chances of your solution being deployed and, more importantly, implemented. Training can range from a quick, 20-minute, hands-on overview to a full-fledged, 5-day, in-depth course replete with training manuals and student exercises. The choice is yours. Base your training on the scope of your solution, and gear any training toward making your users as productive as possible as quickly as possible.

What, then, defines a good Visio solution? In a good Visio solution, the graphical objects (Visio SmartShape symbols) correspond to objects in the problem domain. By this, I mean that when a chair is dropped from a stencil and properly placed in a Visio architectural planning diagram, it should look, act, and behave as a chair would in an office. It would not be able to randomly resize; rather, it would be changed in size according to a strictly constrained menu of choices, most probably as selected from an associated database. It should be able to rotate, if a pedestal chair, via a rotation handle and be able to be placed at any angle via the normal rotational controls in Visio. Things like fabric, finish, and color should be inherent data properties of the chair SmartShape symbol. If the catalog item specifies that the chair has no arms, it should be graphically represented that way. If it is specified with arms, that should be its proper representation. The location and owner should be part of the data store for that chair as well.

In a good Visio solution, making the drawing or diagram builds the model. A drawing is a view of a model. A plan view drawing of an office space shows chairs, tables, computers, lamps, electrical outlets, light fixtures, doors, walls, and windows. The model is a listing or data warehousing of all the component parts that make up this office. Every item and its location, physical size, finish properties, ownership details, maintenance details, purchase price, amortization schedule, and much more are an inherent part of the model. The drawing that is presented and most probably printed is only a view into this model. It would be highly impractical to place all that information on the drawing, because this would result in so much visual clutter that the drawing would be unusable. The data should be accessible via database queries and reports, spreadsheets, and other reporting tools. After a model is constructed by assembling the drawing or diagram, other graphical views can be constructed automatically with an Automation add-on, and analysis and reporting can be done automatically as well.

In a good Visio solution, object (a Visio SmartShape symbol) behavior encourages correct graphical representation. In a diagram of an automobile assembly line, if the user attempted to place robotic units in a physical location that would cause the robotic arms to collide, and therefore cost the auto maker millions of dollars, the behavior of the SmartShape symbols should be such that they would relocate themselves to keep the minimum allowable clearance intact. If the distance was greater than optimal efficiency would dictate, the user placing the symbol should be alerted to the deficiency and allowed to correct it immediately, instead of the quarterly report for the assembly line showing diminished line capacity for the entire assembly line.

In a good Visio solution, manual override should always be allowed to create readable representations. Visio ships with an Organizational Charting Wizard, which reads data from an external source and, based on this data, creates an organizational chart diagram. If the organization in question is shallow and broad in nature, the diagram could well take up only half a page height, but span several pages in width. If the user is allowed to manipulate the position of the employee SmartShape symbols, he or she can compress the width of the diagram and still make the chart readable if the boxes are laid out in a staggered pattern instead of purely linearly.

There you have the basic theory of developing solutions in Visio. In the course of the next 26 chapters, you are going to roll up your sleeves and get your hands very dirty. You are going to begin by learning ShapeSheet development in depth. You will look at every section and generally every cell in a Visio ShapeSheet. You will learn about intercell references, as well as intershape references. You will learn how to create highly intelligent SmartShape symbols that behave as though they were their counterparts in the real environment. From there, you will look deeply into using the knowledge acquired from ShapeSheet development and apply it to

Automation development using Visio's highly robust object model. You will learn how to programmatically control every aspect of Visio via Automation. You will create drawings, add SmartShape symbols, place them on a page, connect them, add data to them, and extract information from them. You will print drawings, save drawings, open drawings, transfer information from drawings to Microsoft Office applications, draw information out of databases, and much, much more—all under Automation control using Visio's VBA as the Automation controller.

You will also look into how to package and deploy Visio solutions so that when you have finished creating your world-class application, the solution that solves all your enterprisewide challenges, you can get it smoothly deployed and have it running on every corporate desktop. In short, together we are going to make you a hero. A nice bit of work wrapped up in a Visio development book, is it not?

Lets get started!

An Introduction to ShapeSheet Programming

IN THIS CHAPTER

Visio often defines SmartShape symbols as having parametric behavior. Parametric behavior can be defined as being modifiable by the acquisition of a set of input values, that is, parameters. Now I realize that this sounds like a lot of prose to say nothing, but look at exactly what this means.

Beginning ShapeSheet Exploration

To illustrate this concept, you should have Visio up and running. If you are using Visio 5.0, begin a new drawing based on Blank Drawing.VST. If you are using Visio 2000, create a new drawing based on Basic Diagram. When you have a Visio drawing page open in front of you, select the Rectangle Tool button from the toolbar. Click, drag out, and release to create a rectangle of any indeterminate size. Make sure that the rectangle you have just created is selected. You will know this by the green things (selection handles) displayed around the SmartShape symbol.

Now, you are going to perform a task that should become so innately familiar to you that it becomes your development mantra: from the menus, select Window, Show ShapeSheet, Window, Tile. If the developer toolbar is visible, you can select the Show ShapeSheet button rather than use the menu methodology. This is identical in both Visio 5.0 and Visio 2000. You will be presented with two windows: the Visio Drawing Page window and the ShapeSheet window.

The Visio ShapeSheet is a spreadsheet-like interface very similar to Microsoft Excel. As an aside, when the very first version of Visio was being prototyped, the Visio development team cobbled an Excel spreadsheet to a primitive graphics display engine and proved that graphics could be controlled via a spreadsheet interface. To this day, it amazes me that when a person new to Visio inadvertently selects Window, Show ShapeSheet, she closes the window as rapidly as possible as if she had done something horribly wrong and exposed something that is taboo—this, from the same people who work with Microsoft Excel every day.

The primary difference between a typical spreadsheet and Visio's ShapeSheet is that we at Visio have broken down the spreadsheet into discrete sections, each with its own header to make it easier to understand what that section is used for. Additionally, each cell is labeled to make navigating and referencing these cells easier. Into these cells, you have the ability to enter information either as values, that is, numbers and distances or text, or as formulas similar to Excel's formula structure as shown in Figure 2.1.

In a moment, I am going to detail each section and each cell within that section. However, for the moment I want to direct you to the Height and Width cells in the Shape Transform section of the ShapeSheet. Make sure that the ShapeSheet window is active. Find the Shape Transform section. It should be the very top section within the ShapeSheet. Now, locate the Height and Width cells. These equate to the height and width of the bounding box around the rectangle you just created. From the menu, select View and then either Values or Formulas.

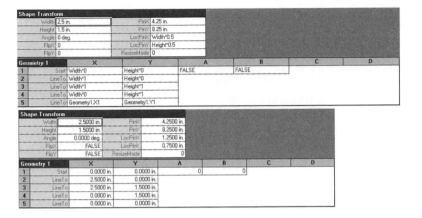

FIGURE 2.1

Viewing formulas versus viewing values.

Important Concept Number One

When you select Formulas, you are looking at the actual formula in the cell. When you select Values, you are looking at the evaluation of the formula.

Suppose that the value in the Width cell was 1.5 in.. Now, suppose that the formula in the Height cell was =Width * 0.5. The value in the Height cell would be 0.75 in. because the evaluation of the SmartShape symbol's width (1.5 in.) times a factor of 0.5 (Width * 0.5) equates to 0.75 in.. This is actually an intercell reference. I will discuss much more about this at the end of this chapter. For now, be sure that Formulas is selected as the viewing mode.

Try typing in a new formula in the Width cell. In Visio 5.0, click in the Width cell; then, click up into the editing line at the top of the window, just beneath the menus. Now, enter a new formula for the SmartShape symbol's width, say, 3.25 in.. Don't worry about placing an equal sign before the formula; just enter the number and press the Enter key. Notice that Visio took care of properly formatting the formula for you. Notice also that the width of the SmartShape symbol in the drawing window just changed as well. In Visio 2000, you can enter information directly into the cell in question without having to go up to the editing line.

Now, activate the drawing window. Click and hold the sizing handle at the center right of the rectangle. Drag it out or in to a new width and release. Notice how the formula and value in the Width cell of the ShapeSheet are also immediately updated to reflect the new size.

> ## Important Concept Number Two
>
> The values and formulas in the ShapeSheet and the physical size of the geometry are *not* two separate things; they are, in fact, two differing views of *exactly* the same data. One (the SmartShape symbol in the drawing window) is a graphical view, whereas the other (the ShapeSheet window) is a data view.

You entered a parameter in the ShapeSheet, and the SmartShape symbol responded accordingly. Et voilà! Parametric object at your service. As you progress through the rest of this chapter, and through the next eight that follow it, you will see much, much more that can be done to maximize the services of the Visio ShapeSheet engine and make your parametrically driven shapes highly intelligent.

Activate the ShapeSheet window. Click in the Height cell. Enter the formula = GUARD(Width * 0.5) and press Enter. Now, activate the drawing window. Again, click and hold the sizing handle at the center right of the rectangle. Drag it out or in to a new width and release. Notice how the height of the SmartShape symbol is exactly one-half the width. No matter how you attempt to resize the SmartShape symbol, via *any* sizing handle, the ratio of height to width always remains 1 to 2. This is because of the structure of the formula in the Height cell. You are looking at truly parametric behavior. The SmartShape symbol's height takes as its parameter the value passed to it from the width and multiples it by 0.5 (divides it by 2), and the GUARD() function that wraps the parameter prohibits it from being altered from the user interface.

Programming Parametric SmartShape Symbols

Take a look at one more example of parametric behavior in Visio SmartShape symbols. The premise is that if a SmartShape symbol ever becomes greater than two inches in width, the filled color of the SmartShape symbol should turn red; otherwise, the filled color should be green. To fully understand this process, you have to be aware of at least one more section in a Visio ShapeSheet, the Fill Format section, and more specifically, the FillForegnd cell. This cell controls the foreground color of the filled area of a SmartShape symbol.

As you did before, drag out a rectangle of indeterminate size. You might want to make its initial size around one and a half inches wide and one inch high. Now, as before, use the first mantra (Window, Show ShapeSheet, Window, Tile) to open the ShapeSheet for the rectangle. With the ShapeSheet window active, select View, Sections from the menu. When the dialog appears, click the All button. This displays all the available sections in the ShapeSheet of the currently selected SmartShape symbol.

Now, scroll down to the Fill Format section and locate the FillForegnd cell. Note that when the SmartShape symbol was created, the default color of one, or white, was entered here. The values in this cell equate to the palette of colors currently available to this drawing. You can see the palette and match the color number to the actual color by activating the drawing window and selecting Tools, Color Palette from the menu. Note that color two equates to red, and color three equates to green. Try entering either of these numbers in this cell. Note how the foreground color of the shape changes immediately upon accepting the value. As I told you before, you can enter either values or formulas into any ShapeSheet cell.

To make the rectangle SmartShape symbol behave as I just described, you will enter a custom formula into the FillForegnd cell. Here is the formula:

```
=GUARD(IF(Width > 2 in., 2, 3))
```

I have already briefly discussed the GUARD() function, but nested inside that GUARD() function is an IF() function. The IF() function has three mandatory arguments that must be passed to it. They are Text, True Result, and False Result. In plain English, the IF() statement, as used in the preceding formula, reads as follows: "If the evaluation of the formula in the Width cell is ever greater than two inches, then the value of the FillForegnd cell must evaluate to the color whose index is two (red); otherwise, the value of the FillForegnd Cell must evaluate to the color whose index is three (green)."

With this formula entered into the FillForegnd cell, activate the drawing window and adjust the width of the rectangle SmartShape symbol. Notice that as soon as you release the symbol, if its width is greater than two inches, it immediately turns red. If its width is less than or equal to two inches, it turns green—again, true parametric behavior (see Figure 2.2).

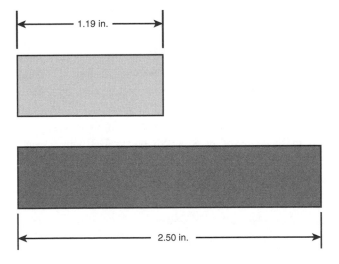

FIGURE 2.2

Shape color based on parametric formulas.

The text itself can be determined by the geometry of a shape. To illustrate this, create a rectangle shape. You will be creating lots and lots of simple SmartShape symbols based on rectangles to demonstrate certain fundamental points. Double-click on the SmartShape symbol as if you were going to edit its text. Now, type in the string Width = . Make sure that you leave the trailing space after the equal sign. Next, select Insert, Field from the menus.

When the dialog appears, in the first column select Geometry, in the second column select Width, and in the third column select 0 #/## units. Click OK. Now, click away from the shape and reselect it using your pointer tool. Change its width. Notice how the text on the SmartShape symbol reflects the true width of the symbol. The text is parametrically driven by the actual width of the SmartShape symbol.

Programming a Bar-Graph SmartShape Symbol

Have you ever wondered how bar graph shapes are created in Visio? This example shows another highly intelligent Visio SmartShape symbol that allows the user to enter a value directly onto the SmartShape symbol as text and have it directly control the width of the symbol. Here are the design goals: Create a Visio SmartShape symbol that adjusts its width according to the value entered on the face of the shape. Furthermore, the symbol should grow from left to right; that is, it should be anchored at the left side of the symbol, and all its growth should take place at the right edge of the symbol.

Another concept that I will discuss in far greater detail in a moment is the concept of the pin and local pin in a Visio SmartShape symbol. For the moment, suffice it to say that all movement in a SmartShape symbol takes place about the local pin. The cells that control this are the LocPinX and LocPinY cells. They are also found in the Shape Transform section.

First, using the rectangle tool, drag out a rectangle SmartShape symbol, and adjust its size so that it is one half inch high and one and a half inches wide. Using the "mantra," open the ShapeSheet and look at the Shape Transform section. Notice that, by default, the value of the LocPinX cell is =Width*0.5. This means that it is located at a point one-half the width of the symbol. You can identify this by activating the drawing window and selecting the rotation tool. Notice the dot directly in the center of the SmartShape symbol. This is controlled in its X position by the LocPinX cell and in its Y position by the LocPinY cell. Activate the ShapeSheet window and change the value of the LocPinX cell to =0. Note that the dot shifted to the left center of the symbol. Now, all growth will take place based on this point.

Locate the Width cell and enter the following formula:

```
=GUARD(MAX(EVALTEXT(TheText),0.125 in.))
```

Breaking this down from the inside out, you find a function named EVALTEXT(). This function has one mandatory argument. EVALTEXT() evaluates the text in the SmartShape symbol as if it were a formula and returns the result. If there is no text, the result is zero. If the text cannot be evaluated, the function returns an error. The Text argument refers to all the text contained in a shape's text block. This is a Visio keyword that refers to the entire quantity of text actively on the SmartShape symbol. Outside that, the function MAX() stipulates to use whichever argument is greater in the list of arguments. In this case, argument one is the evaluation of the EVALTEXT() function, and argument two is the value 0.125 in.. This was done so that if the SmartShape symbol contained no text at all, it would not collapse down to a width of 0 inches—because without it, the cell under EVALTEXT(TheText) and with no text set would pass 0 to the Width cell.

Look at the SmartShape symbol you have just created. It is now 0.5 inch high and 0.125 inch wide. Activate the drawing window. With the new custom SmartShape symbol selected, type in a value of 3 in.. Note how the symbol grows from left to right to a width of three inches. Because the SmartShape symbol is *evaluating* the text and passing that text's evaluation to the Width cell, you can actually enter calculations in the text. Try typing in 2.5 in. + 1.75 in.. Note that the SmartShape symbol is now exactly 4.25 in. wide. This is another great example of parametric behavior in a Visio SmartShape symbol.

Some things to remember about Visio SmartShape symbols as parametric objects are

- All object properties for the SmartShape symbol object (with the exception of the actual text on the shape) are stored in a spreadsheet that Visio calls the *ShapeSheet*.
- The ShapeSheet and the graphical object are two views of the same data.
- Visio implements all graphical interactions by changing values and formulas in the ShapeSheet.
- Text can be determined by formulas.
- SmartShape symbol geometry can be altered by changes in the text.

The Visio Smart Arrow Lab Exercise

Now, you have arrived at your first lab exercise. You are going to step through the creation of a Visio SmartShape symbol. This is no ordinary symbol. It is, in fact, the symbol that launched Visio and opened the world to this new graphics paradigm.

Here is a bit of history and observation. Assume that you are creating a presentation for your corporate officers. This is a very important presentation. The outcome of this presentation may well determine whether your next development project is funded. Keep in mind that two of the executives on the review panel graduated from the Acme Institute of Fine Arts and are very picky about the graphics in presentations.

You decided on your favorite onscreen presentation application. You are making a slide that shows how development dollars flow into research teams and then the research flows out to new products to be produced, which, in turn, flow out to revenues returned to the company. This *should* be wildly successful. However, when you placed an arrow in your slide to represent the flow, you noted that the arrowhead was exactly at a 45-degree angle. When you stretched the arrow to make it longer, the arrowhead distorted and now looks as if it were at about a 65-degree angle. All consistency is gone from the arrows in your presentation, and it looks as if it were created by "Presentations-R-Us" rather than by a crack graphics team.

This is exactly why Visio was created. Graphic objects should behave properly. When an arrow is stretched, the arrowhead should maintain its 45-degree angle, and all of the stretch should take place in the shaft of the arrow. Remember, I said that when Visio was first created, the developers hooked a spreadsheet to a graphics engine? This arrow example is, in fact, the example they used. Together, we are going to re-create a bit of Visio history and learn about SmartShape symbol behavior and development in the process.

Begin a new blank drawing in Visio. When you have the drawing page window active, select the line tool from the toolbar. For Visio 5.0 developers, this is found right there on your standard toolbar between the pencil tool and the rectangle tool. It looks like a diagonal line sloping up from lower left to upper right. For those of you using Visio 2000, you will find the same tool in the drop-down button set of drawing tools right next to the rectangle tool.

Before you begin drawing, here's a little tip about using the line tool. The sequence you are going to use is this: Click, drag over to the next position (letting the page's snap-to-grid assist you), and release at the next point. Click again exactly where you left off, repeat the drag, and release at the next point. Repeat the process until you have drawn the entire path around the arrow in sequence. When you are drawing that final line segment, make sure that you release directly over the top of the point where you began drawing your arrow symbol. If you do this correctly, your arrow symbol will automatically be filled in. If you make a mistake, you will have a bunch of lines. Remember that when you are not drawing, you generally want to select the pointer tool; when you are drawing, you have to select the proper drawing tool to assist you.

The arrow you are going to create is three inches from tail to tip. It is two inches from the top tip of the arrowhead to the bottom tip of the arrowhead. The shaft thickness is one inch.

Figure 2.3 shows exactly what your arrow symbol should look like.

Similar to what they say in that famous film about fighting evil in space, "Let the *grid* be with you." Use the grid to assist you in creating your arrow symbol. Using the line tool, begin by clicking a point on the drawing. Notice the rulers and use them to assist in determining the lengths of the dragging motion.

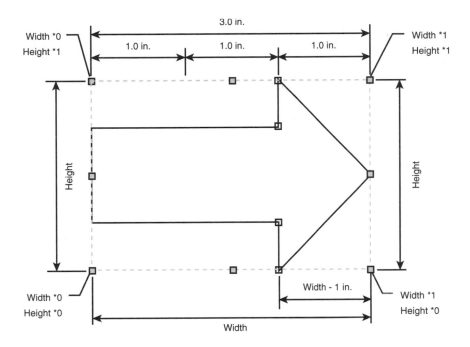

FIGURE 2.3

Layout dimensions for the arrow SmartShape symbol.

1. Drag to the right exactly 2 inches and release.

2. Click again, drag directly down exactly 0.5 inch, and release.

3. Click again and drag up and over to the right at exactly 45 degrees to a point one inch above and one inch over to the right of the point you just clicked, and release.

4. Click again, drag to a point exactly one inch up and one inch to the left of the point you just clicked, and release. This will be a 90 degree + 45 degree, or 135-degree, angle.

5. Click again, drag straight down to a point exactly 0.5 inch below the point you just clicked, and release.

6. Click again, drag directly to the left to a point exactly two inches to the left of the point you just clicked, and release.

7. Click one last time, drag exactly one inch down to the point where you started the entire sequence, and release. Your arrow symbol should be filled and should look like the arrow symbol in Figure 2.1.

Remember that users of Visio do not have to learn how to draw; they have only to assemble drawings from predrawn components. You, however, as a SmartShape symbol designer, must learn how to use the drawing tools to create basic SmartShape symbols to be accessed by your users. In future chapters, you will learn how to use Boolean operations to make your work even easier. However, for now you need to learn the basics.

Now, test the symbol you just created. No, do not touch that arrow!

Important Concept Number Three

Always test your work on a *copy* of the SmartShape symbol you just created, *never* the original. This way, you can go back and make corrections to the original and test the new changes only—without worrying about undoing the damage you might have done.

Switch to the pointer tool. Select the original, hold down the Ctrl key, and drag out a duplicate of the SmartShape symbol you just created. Pull on the sizing handle to adjust its width. Notice how the arrowhead distorts and the angle of the arrowhead changes as the arrow becomes longer or shorter. Not good behavior. Your executive board members would not be pleased. This is no better than—and is exactly the same as—the behavior that was exhibited in the presentation package tool you were using before. Okay, select the distorted copy and press the Delete key. The bad symbol is gone for good!

Select the original arrow symbol and open the ShapeSheet for the arrow. (Remember the mantra: Window, Show ShapeSheet, Window, Tile?) What you will do next is analyze why this bad behavior happened and how the arrow was constructed. Then, you will change some formulas to make the behavior work the way you intended.

You are going to be looking at two sections of the ShapeSheet: the Shape Transform section and the Geometry 1 section. In a moment, you will be analyzing these sections on a cell-by-cell basis, but for now, stay with me and take a look at what is going on in this particular arrow.

With the ShapeSheet window open, make sure that you can clearly see the entire arrow in the drawing window. You might have to zoom so that the arrow fills most of the drawing window. Here's a navigational tip for you. Visio provides four pan and zoom shortcuts to fine-tune what you are seeing. These work under all versions of Visio, from Visio 1.0 through Visio 2000. To zoom in, hold down Ctrl+Shift simultaneously and click with the left mouse button. You will zoom in centered on the mouse pointer location. The opposite, that is, zooming out, means holding down the Ctrl+Shift keys simultaneously and clicking the right mouse button. You will zoom out centered on the mouse pointer location. If you hold down Ctrl+Shift simultaneously and then click-drag-and-release a windowed area, you will zoom in to that windowed area.

If you hold down Ctrl+Shift simultaneously and right-click-and-drag the mouse pointer, the mouse pointer changes to a small hand, and you can pan around the drawing at the current zoom aspect ratio.

Make sure that you can see your arrow clearly, and activate the ShapeSheet window. Look at the Geometry 1 section of the ShapeSheet. For those of you using Visio 5.0, place your cursor in the row marked Start and the column marked X. For those of you using Visio 2000, place your cursor in the row marked MoveTo and the column marked X.

Notice that in the drawing window, a large black box appeared where you began drawing your arrow symbol. Notice that in the ShapeSheet, in the X cell, the formula states `Width*0`. In the Y cell, the formula states `Height*0.25`. Remember that for this particular SmartShape symbol, the coordinate system (it is a Cartesian coordinate system—remember Rene Descartes?) begins in the lower-left corner of the SmartShape symbol; X increases to the right, and Y increases upward. The bounding box is the basis for distance measurement. Therefore, the starting point for the geometry of this SmartShape symbol begins at a point that is the overall width of the shape times zero, or at the far left, and at a point that is the overall height of the shape times 0.25, or one-quarter the distance up the shape.

A Bit of History and Trivia

The black box that you see at a given vertex was designed under Visio 1.0 and code-named *Papa Smurf*. This was a very last-minute feature item in Visio 1.0, and the developer of this feature didn't want folks talking about it until it was released.

Now, either click in the next row down, or use the down arrow key on your keyboard to move down to the next row. Notice how the black box in the drawing window moved from the start point to the next vertex in the geometry path? Notice that the formula for the X cell states `Width*0.666`, and for the Y cell it states `Height*0.25`. Continue "walking" around the SmartShape symbol by moving down through each row. Notice that the final row's X cell states that the formula is `Geometry1.X1` and that the final row's Y cell states that the formula is `Geometry1.Y1`. These are what are known as *intercell references*. The final X cell is referencing itself back up to the Geometry1 section's X1 cell, or the first X row in the section. The final Y cell is referencing itself back up to the Geometry1 section's Y1 cell, or the first Y row in the section.

Here's some basic geometry for you now. Because the back edges of the arrowhead contain a formula stating that they must be located in X at a point that is always 0.666 times the total width, whenever the SmartShape symbol is stretched from its original proportions to a width greater than it is now, this point remains consistently at two-thirds the width, and the arrowhead therefore distorts. To avoid this behavior, you must alter the four X cell values for the four X cells that lie along the back edge of the arrowhead. Looking again at the arrow symbol, you can see that the back edge of the arrowhead is at a point exactly one inches to the left of the tip of the arrow. If that distance became fixed, when the arrow was stretched, these points would still remain exactly one inch to the left of the tip, and the arrowhead's angle would remain constant.

Find the first X row where the black box lies along the back edge of the arrowhead. This should be the X2 row. You are going to change the default formula from =Width*0.666 to =Width - 1 in.. Remember to either press the Enter key or click the green check on the edit line to accept the change you just made. You are setting this point in X to a point that is always at the width of the symbol less one inch.

You could enter this formula three more times, once for each additional row along the back edge of the arrow. However, because programmers are inherently lazy and I want to make this as easy as possible, I am going to show you a shortcut. Move your cursor to the next row at the back of the arrowhead. This should be the X3 row. Here's the trick. In this cell, click the equal sign (=) to clear the contents of the cell. Now, click in the X2 cell. Press the Enter key or click the green check to accept the change.

Notice how Visio filled in the intercell reference for you. The X3 cell should now hold the formula Geometry1.X2. Do this again for the X5 and X6 cells. Not only is this easier than a whole lot of typing, but intercell references are also, by nature, much more efficient because Visio's calculation engine only has to look at the cell X2 and recalculate it, as necessary. The three remaining cells simply reference that calculation and accept the value posted there.

Try out your new SmartShape symbol. Close the ShapeSheet window, and using the Ctrl key, drag out a duplicate of the arrow symbol. Adjust the width of the arrow, and note how all the growth takes place in the shaft and the arrowhead remains at a constant 45-degree angle. Exactly as advertised. I'm sure that you will notice that if you adjust the height of the symbol, all fixes seem to fly out the window. Don't despair. Later, you will make further changes to the arrow to correct this behavior and to make this SmartShape symbol even more intelligent. Oh, before you continue, save that arrow. You will want to have it around for the next lab exercise later in this chapter.

The Shape Transform Section of the ShapeSheet

On to the individual sections of the ShapeSheet. First, you are going to look in depth at every cell in the Shape Transform section of a Visio SmartShape symbol's ShapeSheet. The cells that are included are

- Width
- Height

- Angle
- FlipX
- FlipY
- PinX
- PinY
- LocPinX
- LocPinY
- ResizeMode

I'll take these cell by cell and work through all the important aspects of the cell and how it relates to other cells and affects the behavior of a given Visio SmartShape symbol.

Working with the dimensions of a SmartShape symbol

Width

Although the Width cell might seem obvious, it is very important that you understand its exact meaning. *Width* is the linear distance from the left side of a SmartShape symbol's bounding box to its right side. It is a number-unit pair; that is, it always is a number combined with units. If you enter a raw number without a unit assignment like in., or mm., Visio will assume that you mean to use Visio's internal units, which are definitively inches. Geometry in a given Visio SmartShape symbol can, and in many instances does, lapse outside the bounding box. Therefore, given Geometry cells can reference formulas such as =Width*-0.625. Width measurement always begins at the shape's left edge and proceeds to its right, presuming that the shape has not been *flipped* (mirrored) in X. Geometry X cells generally reference, by default, the Width cell in their formulae.

Height

Like the Width cell, the Height cell refers to the bounding box. *Height* is the linear distance from the bottomedge of a SmartShape symbol's bounding box to its top edge. It is a number-unit pair (always a number combined with units). If you enter a raw number without a unit assignment like in., or mm., Visio will assume that you mean to use Visio's internal units, which are definitively inches. Geometry in a given Visio SmartShape symbol can, and often does, lapse outside the bounding box. Height measurement always begins at the shape's bottom edge and proceeds to its top, presuming that the shape has not been flipped in Y. By default, Geometry Y cells generally reference the Height cell in their formulae.

Angle

The Angle cell in the Shape Transform section refers to the placement angle of the Visio SmartShape symbol relative to its parent. In the case of a SmartShape symbol on a page, the

SmartShape symbol's parent is the page itself. In the case of a SmartShape symbol within a group, the SmartShape symbol's parent is the group SmartShape symbol. Angle zero, that is zero degrees, is measured from the SmartShape symbol's pin and a point infinitely and directly to the right of the shape relative to the page. Effectively, angle zero is a horizontal line from left to right. Angles increase in a counter-clockwise direction from angle zero through 360 degrees. Angle behavior exhibits itself unusually if either the FlipX cell or the FlipY cell or both are set to a non-zero value. Rotation of a Visio SmartShape symbol always takes place about its pin and is reflected in the value set in the Angle cell. This might not be accurately apparent to the user if the shape has been flipped.

FlipX

The FlipX cell holds a Boolean value of True or False. Actually, the formula is a Boolean TRUE or FALSE; the value is either zero (which is the evaluation of FALSE) or non-zero (which is the evaluation of TRUE). The value sets whether a shape is flipped across its Y axis. Obviously, if TRUE, the symbol has been flipped; if FALSE, it has not.

FlipY

The FlipY cell holds a Boolean value of True or False. The formula is a Boolean TRUE or FALSE; the value is either 0 or non-zero, the evaluation of FALSE and TRUE, respectively. The value sets whether a shape is flipped, or mirrored, across its X axis. If TRUE, obviously the symbol has been flipped; if FALSE, it has not.

Understanding PinX, PinY, LocPinX, and LocPinY

The next four cells that I am going to discuss are all very closely related. They are in pairs; PinX and PinY are one pair, and LocPinX and LocPinY are another. It is very important that you understand the difference between the local pin and the pin.

To illustrate the difference, imagine that you hold in your hands two items: a pushpin and a round fiberboard beer pad or coaster. I'm sure that all you developers are very familiar with these items (or *visual aids*, as they say in the education biz)—if not with both, at least with the latter, because beer and development seem to go hand in hand. Now, imagine yourself to be standing in front of a large rectangular cork tack board. The board is the page in Visio, and the beer pad is a Visio SmartShape symbol. The pushpin is used to attach the beer pad to the tack board. When you push the pushpin through the beer pad and into the tack board, you make a small hole in the beer pad. You also make a small temporary hole in the tack board. The hole in the tack board can be measured in distance from the tack board's lower-left corner. Perhaps it is five inches to the right and four inches up. You can say that the pin is located at a point with a PinX of five inches and a PinY of four inches.

Now the beer pad has a hole in it that is exactly in the center of the beer pad. Presuming that the beer pad is four and a half inches in diameter, the bounding box for the beer-pad symbol is four and a half inches by four and a half inches. The width of the beer-pad symbol would be four and a half inches, and the height would be four and a half inches.

The pinhole, at the exact center would be at `Width*0.5` in X and `Height*0.5` in Y. The LocPinX would be `Width*0.5`, and the LocPinY would be `Height*0.5`. Pin coordinates are always expressed in their parent's coordinate system. Local pin coordinates are always expressed in their local coordinate system. Changing the LocPinX or LcPinY values does not affect the PinX or PinY values. In other words, if the pinhole in the beer pad were located left of center, the pin is still pressed into the tack board at the same place it was before. The beer pad has apparently shifted, but the pin's placement into the tack board has not.

In a Cartesian coordinate system, all coordinates are made up of a coordinate pair where X is the ordinate and Y is the abscissa.

PinX

The PinX is the X ordinate of the pin point expressed in the SmartShape symbol's parent coordinate system. All placement and rotation takes place about the point composed of this PinX and its associated PinY.

PinY

The PinY is the Y abscissa of the pin point expressed in the SmartShape symbol's parent coordinate system. All placement and rotation take place about the point composed of this PinY and its associated PinX.

LocPinX

The LocPinX is the X ordinate of the local pin point expressed in the SmartShape symbol's local coordinate system. All placement and rotation take place about the point composed of this LocPinX and its associated LocPinY. LocPinX formulas generally express, by default, some percentage or fractional amount of Width values for the given Visio SmartShape symbol.

LocPinY

The LocPinY is the Y abscissa of the local pin point expressed in the SmartShape symbol's local coordinate system. All placement and rotation take place about the point composed of this LocPinY and its associated LocPinX. By default, LocPinY formulas generally express some percentage or fractional amount of the Height values for the given Visio SmartShape symbol.

ResizeMode

The ResizeMode cell can validly contain only the three numeric values 1, 2, or 3. The value determines how the subject Visio SmartShape symbol will behave when it is included within a group SmartShape symbol when that symbol is resized. The list below details the valid settings:

- 0—The subshape will use whatever setting the group has been set to.
- 1—The subshape will reposition itself only and will not resize according to the resizing of the group shape.
- 2—The subshape will simply scale with the group shape.

All formulas and values in the Shape Transform section of a ShapeSheet are subject to being overwritten (*thrashed*, in highly technical terms) by differing operations that can be made with regard to the SmartShape symbol in question—such as being grouped and ungrouped, resized, repositioned, rotated, and/or changed from a 2D shape to a 1D shape and back. For this reason, if you want a specific formula or value to remain in a cell in this section, you must use the GUARD() function to protect its contents.

The Geometry Section of the ShapeSheet

The Geometry section of a Visio ShapeSheet is perhaps the most diverse and complex section available. It can contain many types of information. This depends on which base object classes are being used to make up the SmartShape symbol's geometry path. For example, a geometry path may contain both line and arc segments. Versions of Visio from Visio 1.0 to Visio 2000 have an increasing complexity available to them as new object classes have been introduced to the SmartShape symbol. Additionally, a given ShapeSheet may have one or more Geometry sections.

Things have changed enough in Visio 2000 from Visio 5.0 that I feel it necessary to address each separately. I'll go through the possible rows in a Visio 2000 Geometry section first. If you want to see the Visio 5.0 version, I've repeated the exercise in Appendix D, "Visio 5.0 ShapeSheet Cells," on the CD-ROM.

The Geometry Section of the ShapeSheet

The first row in a Visio 2000 Geometry section is always the Status Display row. This row contains four discrete cells. They are

- Geometry[n].NoFill
- Geometry[n].NoLine
- Geometry[n].NoShow
- Geometry[n].NoSnap

These cells determine the visibility and capability status of the current Geometry section.

Geometry[n].NoFill

This cell is *always* referenced under Visio 2000 as the *Geometry[n].NoFill cell*, where *[n]* is the number of the Geometry section. For compatibility with earlier versions of Visio, this cell can be referred to by either name (*Geometry[n].NoFill* or *Geometry[n].A0*). This cell indicates whether a shape can be filled. If TRUE (non-zero value), the shape's paths are open, so it cannot be filled. If FALSE (zero value), its paths are closed, so it can be filled. This is the first column in the Start row.

Geometry[n].NoLine

This cell is *always* referenced under Visio 2000 as the *Geometry[n].NoLine cell*, where *[n]* is the number of the Geometry section. There is no backward compatibility for this cell. This cell indicates whether a shape's line for this geometry path can be displayed. If TRUE (non-zero value), the shape's entire geometry path line is invisible, so it cannot be displayed. If FALSE (zero value), its path is visible, so it can be displayed. This is the second column in the Start row.

Geometry[n].NoShow

This cell is *always* referenced under Visio 2000 as the *Geometry[n].NoShow cell*, where *[n]* is the number of the Geometry section. For compatibility with earlier versions of Visio, this cell can be referred to by either name (*Geometry[n].NoShow* or *Geometry[n].B0*). This cell indicates whether a shape can be displayed. If TRUE (non-zero value), the shape's entire geometry path and fill are invisible, so it cannot be displayed. If FALSE (zero value), its paths are visible, so it can be displayed. This is the third column in the Start row.

Geometry[n].NoSnap

This cell is *always* referenced under Visio 5.0 as the *Geometry[n].NoSnap cell*, where *[n]* is the number of the Geometry section. There is no backward compatibility for this cell. This cell indicates whether a shape's line for this geometry path can be displayed. If TRUE (non-zero value), the shape's entire geometry path line cannot be snapped to. If FALSE (zero value), its path can be snapped to at its vertices. This is the fourth column in the Start row.

MoveTo Row

Following the Status Display row, the geometry section will always contain a MoveTo row. This row indicates the displacement distance in X and Y from the current Visio SmartShape symbol's Cartesian origin (lower left at X = 0 in., Y = 0 in.) to the point where the active geometry path begins. This row contains two discrete cells, X and Y.

X

This is the X ordinate of the coordinate pair that defines the beginning point of the geometry path. It is a united number and is always expressed in the SmartShape symbol's local coordinate system. This is the first column in the MoveTo row.

Y

This is the Y abscissa of the coordinate pair that defines the beginning point of the geometry path. It is a united number and is always expressed in the SmartShape symbol's local coordinate system. This is the second column in the Start row.

Additional Geometry Row Types

The Geometry section can also include these cells:

- LineTo
- EllipticalArcTo
- ArcTo
- PolyLineTo
- PolyArcTo
- NURBSTo
- SplineStart
- SplineKnot
- InfiniteLine
- Ellipse

From the MoveTo row—which, as I said before, defines the beginning of the geometry path—a series of [*xxx*]To (LineTo, ArcTo, EllipticalArcTo, PolyLineTo, PolyArcTo, NURBSTo, InfiniteLine, Ellipse or SplineStart and SplineKnot) rows make up the total coordinate path of the geometry section. You can think of this as a series of instructions for a pen to draw an object from the preceding point *to* the next defined point. Each row type has its own special parameters.

LineTo Row

A LineTo row has two cells: an X cell and a Y cell. These determine the X ordinate and the Y abscissa of the coordinate pair for the next point. The line segment (a straight vector) is generated from the last point *to* this new coordinate.

X

This is the X ordinate of the coordinate pair that defines the next point of the geometry path. It is a united number and is always expressed in the SmartShape symbol's local coordinate system. This is the first column in the LineTo row.

Y

This is the Y abscissa of the coordinate pair that defines the next point of the geometry path. It is a united number and is always expressed in the SmartShape symbol's local coordinate system. This is the second column in the LineTo row.

EllipticalArcTo Row

An elliptical arc is the basic and default arc type created by Visio. An EllipticalArcTo row consists of six columns that define the formation of the elliptical arc, its x and y coordinates, control points, angle of eccentricity, and ratio of major and minor axes of an elliptical arc. The X and Y cells define the ending point of the segment—the *To* point, if you will. The A, B, C, and D cells define the arc's structure.

X

This is the X ordinate of the coordinate pair that defines the next point of the geometry path as the ending point of the arc. It is a united number and is always expressed in the SmartShape symbol's local coordinate system. This is the first column in the EllipticalArcTo row.

Y

This is the Y abscissa of the coordinate pair that defines the next point of the geometry path as the ending point of the arc. It is a united number and is always expressed in the SmartShape symbol's local coordinate system. This is the second column in the EllipticalArcTo row.

A

This is the X ordinate of the coordinate pair that defines the control point of the geometry path through which the arc passes. It is a united number and is always expressed in the SmartShape symbol's local coordinate system. The control point is best located between the beginning and ending vertices of the arc. Otherwise, the arc may grow to an extreme size to pass through the control point, with unpredictable results. This is the third column in the EllipticalArcTo row.

B

This is the Y abscissa of the coordinate pair that defines the control point of the geometry path through which the arc passes. It is a united number and is always expressed in the SmartShape symbol's local coordinate system. The control point is best located between the beginning and ending vertices of the arc. Otherwise, the arc may grow to an extreme size to pass through the control point, with unpredictable results. This is the fourth column in the EllipticalArcTo row.

C

This cell contains the angle (expressed as a real number representing degrees) of the arc's major axis relative to angle zero for the drawing page. If the arc has not been rotated, this value is 0. This is the fifth column in the EllipticalArcTo row.

D

This cell contains the real number that is the ratio of the arc's major axis to its minor axis. Ordinarily, this value is greater than 1, representing a major axis that is longer than the minor axis. If this value is less than 1, the major axis is shorter than the minor axis. Setting this cell to a value less than or equal to 0 or greater than 1,000 can lead to unpredictable results. This is the sixth column in the EllipticalArcTo row.

ArcTo Row

An arc as defined by Visio is actually a circular arc and therefore a portion of a circle. When you first draw an arc in Visio, it is an elliptical arc, even if it is based on a circle. In the Geometry section, the arc is indicated by an EllipticalArcTo row. The eccentricity handles of an elliptical arc are based on its height and width, so the arc changes shape when you drag an eccentricity handle.

Select ArcTo as the new row type and click OK. To convert an elliptical arc to a circular arc, change the EllipticalArcTo to an ArcTo row, using the Change Row Type command. To do this, click in the row in question. Then, right-click and select Change Row Type from the context menu. Select ArcTo as the new row type, and click OK.

When you drag the beginning or ending vertex of a circular arc, the arc changes size but always remains the same portion of a circle. An ArcTo row consists of three columns that define the formation of the arc: its x and y coordinates and the arc's bow length. The X and Y cells define the ending point of the segment—the *To* point, if you will. The A cell defines the arc's structure.

X

This is the X ordinate of the coordinate pair that defines the next point of the geometry path as the ending point of the arc. It is a united number and is always expressed in the SmartShape symbol's local coordinate system. This is the first column in the ArcTo row.

Y

This is the Y abscissa of the coordinate pair that defines the next point of the geometry path as the ending point of the arc. It is a united number and is always expressed in the SmartShape symbol's local coordinate system. This is the second column in the ArcTo row.

A

This cell contains the distance as a united number from the arc's perpendicular bisector to the bow point, which is the point on the arc halfway between the arc's beginning vertex and ending vertex. This is the third column in the ArcTo row.

PolyLineTo Row

A PolyLineTo row has three cells: an X cell, a Y cell, and an A cell. These determine the X ordinate and the Y abscissa of the coordinate pair for the next point, as well as the polyline definition vector. The polyline segment (a complex vector) is generated from the last point *to* this new coordinate.

X

This is the X ordinate of the coordinate pair that defines the next point of the geometry path. It is a united number and is always expressed in the SmartShape symbol's local coordinate system. This is the first column in the PolyLineTo row.

Y

This is the Y abscissa of the coordinate pair that defines the next point of the geometry path. It is a united number and is always expressed in the SmartShape symbol's local coordinate system. This is the second column in the PolyLineTo row.

A

This cell is the definition of the Polyline curve. This is the third column in the PolyLineTo row.

PolyArcTo Row

A PolyArcTo row has four cells: an X cell, a Y cell, an A cell, and a B cell. These determine the X ordinate and the Y abscissa of the coordinate pair for the next point, as well as the polyline definition vector. The polyarc segment (a complex vector) is generated from the last point *to* this new coordinate.

X

This is the X ordinate of the coordinate pair that defines the next point of the geometry path. It is a united number and is always expressed in the SmartShape symbol's local coordinate system. This is the first column in the PolyArcTo row.

Y

This is the Y abscissa of the coordinate pair that defines the next point of the geometry path. It is a united number and is always expressed in the SmartShape symbol's local coordinate system. This is the second column in the PolyArcTo row.

A

This cell is the first definition of the Polyarc curve. This is the third column in the PolyArcTo row.

B

This cell is the second definition of the Polyarc curve. This is the fourth column in the PolyArcTo row.

NURBSTo Row

A NURBSTo row begins the NURBS (non-uniform rational B-spline) definition. The NURBSTo row must be preceded by another row type, such as a MoveTo, to indicate the first control point of the NURBS path. A NURBSTo row consists of seven columns that define the formation of the spline beginning and performance details.

X

This cell holds the X ordinate of the coordinate pair that defines the last control point of a non-uniform rational B-spline (NURBS). This is the first column in the NURBSTo row.

Y

This cell holds the Y abscissa of the coordinate pair that defines the last control point of a non-uniform rational B-spline (NURBS). This is the second column in the NURBSTo row.

A

This cell holds the second-to-the-last knot of the non-uniform rational B-spline (NURBS). This is the third column in the NURBSTo row.

B

This cell holds the last weight of the non-uniform rational B-spline (NURBS). This is the fourth column in the NURBSTo row.

C

This cell holds the first knot of the non-uniform rational B-spline (NURBS). This is the fifth column in the NURBSTo row.

D

This cell holds the first weight of the non-uniform rational B-spline (NURBS). This is the sixth column in the NURBSTo row.

E

This cell holds a non-uniform rational B-spline (NURBS) formula. This is the seventh column in the NURBSTo row.

SplineStart Row

A SplineStart row begins the spline definition. It is always followed by at least one and generally more SplineKnot rows. The SplineStart row must be preceded by another row type, such as a Start row or another LineTo, EllipticalArcTo, or ArcTo row, to indicate the first control point of the spline. A SplineStart row consists of six columns that define the formation of the spline beginning and performance details.

X

This is the X ordinate of the coordinate pair that defines the next point of the geometry path as the spline's second control point. It is a united number and is always expressed in the SmartShape symbol's local coordinate system. This is the first column in the SplineStart row.

Y

This is the Y abscissa of the coordinate pair that defines the next point of the geometry path as the spline's second control point. It is a united number and is always expressed in the SmartShape symbol's local coordinate system. This is the second column in the SplineStart row.

A

This cell specifies the position of the second knot on the spline. This is the third column in the SplineStart row.

B

This cell specifies the position of the first knot on the spline. This is the fourth column in the SplineStart row.

C

This cell specifies the position of the last knot on the spline. This is the fifth column in the SplineStart row.

D

This cell specifies the degree of the spline as an integer from 1 to 9. This is the sixth column in the SplineStart row.

SplineKnot Row

A SplineKnot row specifies the x and y coordinates of the spline knots. A SplineKnot row consists of three columns that define the formation of the spline knot and performance details.

X

This is the X ordinate of the coordinate pair that defines the next point of the geometry path as the spline's current control point. It is a united number and is always expressed in the SmartShape symbol's local coordinate system. This is the first column in the SplineKnot row.

Y

This is the Y abscissa of the coordinate pair that defines the next point of the geometry path as the spline's current control point. It is a united number and is always expressed in the SmartShape symbol's local coordinate system. This is the second column in the SplineKnot row.

A

This cell specifies the location of the third or greater spline knot. This is the third column in the SplineKnot row.

InfiniteLine Row

An InfiniteLine row defines a complete infinite line as a singular open Visio geometry path. An InfiniteLine row consists of four columns that define the formation of the infinite line, including its start and end points of its definition vertices.

X

This is the X ordinate of the coordinate pair that defines the begin definition point of the infinite line object. It is a united number and is always expressed in the SmartShape symbol's local coordinate system. This is the first column in the InfiniteLine row.

Y

This is the Y abscissa of the coordinate pair that defines the begin definition point of the infinite line object. It is a united number and is always expressed in the SmartShape symbol's local coordinate system. This is the second column in the InfiniteLine row.

A

This cell holds the X ordinate of a point on the infinite line, paired with the Y abscissa represented by the B cell. This is the third column in the InfiniteLine row.

B

This cell holds the Y abscissa of a point on the infinite line, paired with the X ordinate represented by the A cell. This is the fourth column in the InfiniteLine row.

Ellipse Row

An Ellipse row defines a complete ellipse as a singular closed Visio geometry path. An Ellipse row consists of six columns that define the formation of the ellipse, including its center and the end points of its major and minor axis.

X

This is the X ordinate of the coordinate pair that defines the center point of the ellipse object. It is a united number and is always expressed in the SmartShape symbol's local coordinate system. This is the first column in the Ellipse row.

Y

This is the Y abscissa of the coordinate pair that defines the center point of the ellipse object. It is a united number and is always expressed in the SmartShape symbol's local coordinate system. This is the second column in the Ellipse row.

A

This is the X ordinate of the coordinate pair that defines the end point of the major axis vector for the ellipse object. It is a united number and is always expressed in the SmartShape symbol's local coordinate system. This is the third column in the Ellipse row.

B

This is the Y abscissa of the coordinate pair that defines the end point of the major axis vector for the ellipse object. It is a united number and is always expressed in the SmartShape symbol's local coordinate system. This is the fourth column in the Ellipse row.

C

This is the X ordinate of the coordinate pair that defines the end point of the minor axis vector for the ellipse object. It is a united number and is always expressed in the SmartShape symbol's local coordinate system. This is the fifth column in the Ellipse row.

D

This is the Y abscissa of the coordinate pair that defines the end point of the minor axis vector for the ellipse object. It is a united number and is always expressed in the SmartShape symbol's local coordinate system. This is the sixth column in the Ellipse row.

A Smarter Arrow SmartShape Symbol

Now, I know that that is an incredible amount of information to digest. However, a thorough understanding of all the possibilities in both the Shape Transform and the Geometry sections will enable you to begin to create your own SmartShape symbols with much more confidence. It's time for another lab exercise. This will build on the smart arrow you completed in the first exercise in this chapter.

Remember how the arrow did not remain properly proportioned when you changed the height of the arrow, but did when you adjusted the width? This is due to the fact that you "hard-coded" in a number for the back edge of the arrowhead from the tip. As you all are aware, hard-coding is a definite no-no, and now you have seen the results of that type of behavior.

Take a look at your arrow again. Dig back in your memory and remember your basic trigonometry lessons. What needs to occur in height and width of a right triangle to ensure that the interior angle is exactly 45 degrees? Correct! The height and width must be exactly equal. If you look at the arrowhead, you can see that the distance in X from the tip of the arrow to the back of the arrowhead is exactly the same as the distance from the bottom of the bounding box for the arrow symbol to the tip of the arrow. In other words, from tip to arrowhead back is equal to half the height.

Therefore, instead of the X formula that you changed to read to =Width - 1 in., which is a hard-coded constant, you will place the formula =Width - Height/2 in the Geometry1.X2 cell. Because Visio understands that operator precedence and multiplication and division come before addition and subtraction, your formula works just fine. If you wanted to get very explicit about it, the formula could read =Width - (Height / 2) just as well. That one change in formula for that one cell took care of all four X values because you used intercell references.

See how these references save time and keystrokes? Now, try out your newly customized Visio SmartShape symbol arrow using a duplicate of the arrow. Remember to control-drag out a copy and test with that copy. Does it work as advertised? Great! However, you might have noticed that if you made your arrow too short, the shaft begins to "implode" into the arrow-head. This is not acceptable, either. To ensure that your arrow is truly world-class, go ahead and make just a few more modifications to the arrow.

At what point did the arrow begin to misbehave? Correct! When the width of the arrow became less than half the height. This is because your formulas for the back edge of the arrowhead now reference a function of height and no longer reference width at all! To correct the aberrant behavior, you can do one of several things to the formulas controlling the arrow symbol. You can ensure that the width of the symbol is *never* less than the height divided by two, or you can allow the symbol to distort if the width-less-than-half-height condition exists.

Let's attack the second of these two options first. Remember a while back, I showed you a MAX() function to use the greater of several values? You can use its companion MIN(), which uses the lesser of several values. Take a look at the following formula:

```
=Width - MIN(Height/2,Width)
```

This formula will place the back of the arrowhead at

```
Width - Height/2 OR Width - Width
```

Visually, this means that if the arrow is long, the function works just as advertised. However, if the arrow's width ever becomes less than Height/2, the arrowhead will simply be at the far left, and the shape will continue to distort until it is a flat vertical line when the width is zero.

This is well and good, but you should look at a method to keep the shape from ever being in a situation where the width is less than Height/2. In a little while, I will discuss in much greater detail the functionality of the UserDefined section of the ShapeSheet. For now, ensure that your ShapeSheet window is active, and select Insert, Sections from the menu. Check the User Defined item and click OK. A new UserDefined section has been added to your ShapeSheet. In the Value cell (under Visio 2000), enter the following formula:

```
=IF(Width<Height/2,SETF("Width",Height/2),0)
```

This reads in plain English: "If the width of the arrow symbol ever becomes less that half the height, then set the value of the Width cell to be half the height; otherwise, do nothing at all."

The SETF() function takes two arguments. The first is the *quoted* name of the cell whose value you want to change. The second is the value or formula you want to pass to it. You will learn even more about this function as you go along.

Whenever the SmartShape symbol is changed in position, size, or orientation, the cells in the ShapeSheet are re-evaluated. When this User Defined cell is evaluated, the statement makes sure that the improper condition is corrected, and the Visio SmartShape symbol performs perfectly!

As a final bit of polish, I would set the formula for the LocPinX to be =Width instead of Width*0.5. This will make the positional and rotational point for the arrow focused at the arrow's tip rather than in the center. There you have it! A perfectly designed arrow that you can be proud to show to that executive committee. Because it works so well, your next project is sure to be funded at, say, 160 percent!

The Scratch Section of the ShapeSheet

Long, long ago, in a galaxy far, far away, Visio created the SmartShape symbol, and with it, the ShapeSheet. In that ShapeSheet, Visio felt that it was necessary to be able to store intermediate calculations—especially because, at that time, the number of characters that could be placed in any given ShapeSheet cell was very limited. Users took to this storage facility and began to use it for an increasing number of purposes. Today, the Scratch section still exists, and because it does, I'm going to detail what a Scratch row is all about and how you can use it. Additionally, I will discuss some of the limitations inherent in a Scratch row and how these limitations can come back to bite you if you are not careful.

Scratch Row

A Scratch row is a repository for textual and numeric data. This data can be both formulas and values. A Scratch row consists of six columns divided into two distinct types. Cells X and Y are united cells. Cells A through D are non-united cells.

X

The X cell holds a united number or a formula that evaluates to a united number. It is a number-unit pair; that is, it always is a number combined with units. If you enter a raw number without a unit assignment like in., or mm., Visio will assume that you mean to use Visio's internal units, which are definitively inches. This is the first column in the Scratch row.

Y

The Y cell holds a united number or a formula that evaluates to a united number. It is a number-unit pair (always a number combined with units). If you enter a raw number without a unit assignment like in., or mm., Visio will assume that you mean to use Visio's internal units, which are definitively inches. This is the second column in the Scratch row.

A

The A cell holds any one of the following: a united number, a non-united number, a formula that evaluates to a united number, a formula that evaluates to a non-united number, a formula that evaluates to the Boolean TRUE or FALSE, or a string. This is the third column in the Scratch row.

B

The B cell holds any one of the following: a united number, a non-united number, a formula that evaluates to a united number, a formula that evaluates to a non-united number, a formula that evaluates to the Boolean TRUE or FALSE, or a string. This is the fourth column in the Scratch row.

C

The C cell holds any one of the following: a united number, a non-united number, a formula that evaluates to a united number, a formula that evaluates to a non-united number, a formula that evaluates to the Boolean TRUE or FALSE, or a string. This is the fifth column in the Scratch row.

D

The D cell holds any one of the following: a united number, a non-united number, a formula that evaluates to a united number, a formula that evaluates to a non-united number, a formula that evaluates to the Boolean TRUE or FALSE, or a string. This is the sixth column in the Scratch row.

Okay, why is it important to understand the distinction between storing unit-ed and non-unit–ed numbers in cells? Let's experiment a little bit and see what can happen when you play fast and loose with these cells.

Begin by dragging out a basic rectangle shape and opening its ShapeSheet. Remember the mantra? Grand! Now, with the ShapeSheet window active, select Insert, Sections from the menu. Check the Scratch box and click OK. You have now added a Scratch section to your ShapeSheet. To add another row to this section, simply click in the existing row. Conveniently, you can click in the X cell and then select Insert, Row or Insert, Row After from the menu. The difference between Row and Row After should be quite evident.

Okay, back to business. Remember that the X and Y cells must be united. The rest are not mandatory, although they *can* hold united numbers if you want. In the A cell, place the value 22 mm.; in the B cell, place the value 11 mm.. Now, in the X cell, place the formula =Scratch.A1/Scratch.B1. Select View, Values from the menu. Look what value is sitting in the X cell! 2 in.! How can Visio pull a lame stunt like this? The fault, dear reader, lies not in the software but in you! Here's the issue. In mathematics, when you divide a united number by a number with a unit, the units cancel, leaving you with a unitless number. The number that was returned by the evaluation of 22 mm. / 11 mm. was, in fact, 2. Just plain, simple 2. Now, I stated that the X cell must be united. Therefore, Visio looked at this number and said, "If you are not going to tell me what units to use, I'm going to use my own internal units—and those internal units happen to be inches! Therefore the number that resides in the cell is two inches, like it or not!"

All right, how can you avoid this abnormality? Take a look at this next formula:

```
=1mm.*(Scratch.A1/Scratch.B1)
```

The evaluation is 2 mm.—exactly what you needed! By taking the base unit as a constant with a multiplier of one and multiplying that unit times the non-united number, the result was a united number of the unit type of the first item, that is, mm..

Here is another example. In the A cell, place the value 2 mm.; in the B cell, place the value 5 mm.. Now, in the X cell place the formula =Scratch.A1*Scratch.B1. Select View, Values from the menu. Look what value is sitting in the X cell!! 0.3937 mm.! Wait a minute. I know that 2mm. times 5mm. equals 10sq.mm. What's going on here? Well, Visio understands strings, Visio understands unitless numbers (in the right places), and Visio also understands united numbers *as linear distances and measurements*. However, Visio *does not* understand square or cubic *volume*. A united number times a united number yields an area of volume, which Visio simply cannot deal with. Internally, Visio churns up a memory register number and tosses it back to the cell with the first unit it understood. Not pretty, indeed.

If you want to calculate a volume, convert the numbers to unitless, do the multiplication, and use the raw number as a raw number result in a unitless Scratch cell (A through D). Alternatively, play the uniting trick from before in the X or Y cell, and show it as a basic unit, not a volumetric unit. For an A through D cell, your formula could be

```
=(Scratch.A1/1 mm.)*(Scratch.B1/1 mm.)
```

This evaluates to 10.00.

For an X or Y cell, your formula could be

```
=1 mm.*((Scratch.A1/1 mm.)*(Scratch.B1/1 mm.))
```

This evaluates to 10.00 mm.

Another thing to remember (as I said before), FALSE evaluates to 0, and TRUE evaluates to non-zero. Therefore, 2*FALSE evaluates to 0, and 3*TRUE evaluates to—that's right—it evaluates to 3.

The User-Defined Cells Section of the ShapeSheet

Now Scratch cells were well and good, but as you have seen, they have their quirks, and they additionally have no means of storing what the heck the formula you had so carefully crafted was for. Six months or a year later when you, as a developer, would have looked at the ShapeSheet, you would have sat and stared at that formula and you would have had to spend much time attempting to suss out what you had intended by that obscure formula. Well, time advances and so did Visio. Visio created user-defined cells to make formula manipulation much easier, with the added advantage, as you saw a short while ago, of the user-defined cell being re-evaluated when changes took place in a Visio SmartShape symbol.

User-Defined Cells Row

A User-Defined Cells row is a repository for textual and numeric data. This data can be both formulas and values. A User-Defined Cells row consists of three columns divided into three distinct types. The first cell is the row name. The second is the value. The third is the prompt or comment.

Name

The Name cell is the leftmost cell in the row. By default, it is sequentially named, as in Row_1, then Row_2, and so on. The rows can be named in user-friendly names that assist the developer in understanding and referencing them. Remember that Scratch rows are strictly Scratch.X1 or Scratch.A18, and so on. This means that Scratch rows can be programmatically accessed by any application and erroneous information can be retrieved, if placed there by another application. User-Defined rows, because they can be uniquely named, are more difficult to erroneously reference and, given logical names, are easier to reference, as in User.Price_Data.

To rename a user-defined name cell, simply click in the name cell and enter a new name; then press Enter or click the green check. The names of user-defined name rows can be up to 31 characters and can contain no spaces—only letters, numbers, dashes, and underscores. This is the first column in the User-Defined row.

Value

The Value cell holds any one of the following: a united number, a non-united number, a formula that evaluates to a united number, a formula that evaluates to a non-united number, a formula that evaluates to the Boolean TRUE or FALSE, or a string. This is the second column in the User-Defined row.

Prompt

The Prompt cell holds a string, which is a comment to the developer about the usage of the formula or value in the Value cell. This is a descriptive prompt or comment for the user-defined cell. Visio automatically encloses the prompt text in quotation marks (" ") to indicate that it is a text string. If you type an equal sign (=) and omit the quotation marks, you can enter a formula in this cell that Visio evaluates.

The Controls Section of the ShapeSheet

Ah, control! It makes you think that you just might be in charge of something, right? Perhaps. In Visio terms, a control on a SmartShape symbol is yet another "green thing." Similar to a sizing handle, it is green, but dimmer. When you select a SmartShape symbol and then click-and-drag on a control handle, two things will become readily apparent. First, by pausing on the handle before clicking it, you will generally see a brief item of information displayed in a help box. This assists you in understanding what the control handle is for. Second, when you drag the control handle around, it manipulates some aspect of the SmartShape symbol: its physical geometry, its rotation, its size, the location of parts of the symbol, or other functional requirements. This is a very handy little function that Visio has given you as developers. In a moment, you are going to create a shape to exploit the features of the control handle, but first I'll explain each cell in the Controls row and detail its functionality.

The Controls Row in the ShapeSheet

There are eight cells in a Controls row.

X

The X cell holds the preset and later current position of the X ordinate, as a united number in local coordinates, for the location of the control handle. It is a number-unit pair; that is, it is always a number combined with units. If you enter a raw number without a unit assignment like in., or mm., Visio will assume that you mean to use Visio's internal units, which are definitively inches. This is the first column in the Controls row.

Y

The Y cell holds the preset and later current position of the X abscissa, as a united number in local coordinates, for the location of the control handle. It is a number-unit pair (always a number combined with units). If you enter a raw number without a unit assignment like in., or mm., Visio will assume that you mean to use Visio's internal units, which are definitively inches. This is the second column in the Controls row.

X Dynamics

The X Dynamics cell (always referred to as *Controls.Xdyn* if only one Controls row is present and *Controls.Xdyn[n]* for the second or more, if more than one Controls row is present) holds the preset root of movement position of the X ordinate, as a united number in local coordinates, for the location base vector from which the control handle is moved. It is a number-unit pair; that is, it always is a number combined with units. If you enter a raw number without a unit assignment like in., or mm., Visio will assume that you mean to use Visio's internal units, which are definitively inches. This is the third column in the Controls row.

Y Dynamics

The Y Dynamics cell (always referred to as *Controls.Ydyn* if only one Controls row is present and *Controls.Ydyn[n]* for the second or more, if more than one Controls row is present) holds the preset root of movement position of the X abscissa, as a united number in local coordinates, for the location base vector from which the control handle is moved. It is a number-unit pair (always a number combined with units). If you enter a raw number without a unit assignment like in., or mm., Visio will assume that you mean to use Visio's internal units, which are definitively inches. This is the fourth column in the Controls row.

X Behavior

The cell holds the integer value that defines how the X ordinate (always referred to as *Controls.XCon* if only one Controls row is present and *Controls.XCon[n]* for the second or more, if more than one Controls row is present) of the control handle behaves when the control handle is moved. The valid range of integers for this cell is 0 through 9, as shown in Table 2.1.

TABLE 2.1   ControlsX Constraint Values

Value	Behavior	Definition
0	Proportional	The control handle can be moved, and it also moves in proportion with the shape when it is stretched.
1	Proportional locked	The control handle moves in proportion with the shape, but the control handle itself cannot be moved.
2	Offset from left edge	The control handle is offset a constant distance from the left side of the shape.
3	Offset from center	The control handle is offset a constant distance from the center of the shape.
4	Offset from right edge	The control handle is offset a constant distance from the right side of the shape.
5	Proportional, hidden	Same as 0, but the control handle is not visible.
6	Proportional locked, hidden	Same as 1, but the control handle is not visible.
7	Offset from left edge, hidden	Same as 2, but the control handle is not visible.
8	Offset from center, hidden	Same as 3, but the control handle is not visible.
9	Offset from right edge, hidden	Same as 4, but the control handle is not visible.

This is the fifth column in the Controls row.

Y Behavior

The cell holds the integer value that defines how the Y abscissa (always referred to as *Controls.YCon* if only one Controls row is present and *Controls.YCon[n]* for the second or more, if more than one Controls row is present) of the control handle behaves when the control handle is moved. The valid range of integers for this cell is 0 through 9, as shown in Table 2.2.

TABLE 2.2   ControlsY Constraint Values

Value	Behavior	Definition
0	Proportional	The control handle can be moved, and it also moves in proportion with the shape when it is stretched.
1	Proportional locked	The control handle moves in proportion with the shape, but the control handle itself cannot be moved.
2	Offset from bottom edge	The control handle is offset a constant distance from the bottom of the shape.
3	Offset from center	The control handle is offset a constant distance from the center of the shape.

Value	Behavior	Definition
4	Offset from top edge	The control handle is offset a constant distance from the top of the shape.
5	Proportional, hidden	Same as 0, but the control handle is not visible.
6	Proportional locked, hidden	Same as 1, but the control handle is not visible.
7	Offset from left edge, hidden	Same as 2, but the control handle is not visible.
8	Offset from center, hidden	Same as 3, but the control handle is not visible.
9	Offset from right edge, hidden	Same as 4, but the control handle is not visible.

This is the sixth column in the Controls row.

Can Glue

The cell (always referred to as *Controls.CanGlue* if only one Controls row is present and *Controls.CanGlue[n]* for the second or more, if more than one Controls row is present) holds the Boolean value FALSE or TRUE (zero or non-zero) that defines whether a control handle can glue to another Visio SmartShape symbol's valid glue-able connection point or point of geometry. Note that there are limitations to this feature. If either the X Behavior or the Y Behavior has been locked in any manner, this acts the same as setting the Can Glue's value to TRUE or non-zero. This is the seventh column in the Controls row.

Tip

The cell (always referred to as *Controls.Prompt* if only one Controls row is present and *Controls.Prompt[n]* for the second or more, if more than one Controls row is present) holds an informative text string that appears as a help box or ToolTip when the user of the SmartShape symbol containing the control handle rests the mouse pointer over the control handle. Visio automatically encloses the tip string in quotation marks in the cell, but the quotation marks are not displayed in the ToolTip. Note that if the string within the Tip cell is a valid formula and not enclosed in quotes, the Tip will display the evaluation of the formula. Quoted information and formulae may be concatenated via the Basic concatenation operator, the ampersand (&), to make complex strings as follows:

```
="The Handle's X position is: " & Controls.X1
```

This is the eighth column in the Controls row.

Creating an Indicator SmartShape Symbol

Now you have more information in your tool set of knowledge, and you should be able to do brilliantly on the next lab exercise. I'm going to put you through your paces here. You are going to implement much of what you already know and just a little more to make this next

Visio SmartShape symbol. The symbol you are going to create is an Indicator symbol. The symbol is adjustable in both height and width. Adjustment in width displays the width as a real unitless number above the symbol as text on the symbol It is an indicator of quantity. The symbol includes an adjustable pointer that displays the percent completed or the percent along the indication path as a ToolTip to the control handle. The position of the indicator is adjustable via two control handles. The symbol does not distort when adjusted in any manner. Sound like a lot to tackle? It is, but I'm sure that you are up to the challenge.

When you are finished, your indicator will look like Figure 2.4.

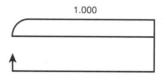

FIGURE 2.4

The indicator SmartShape symbol.

Begin a new blank Visio drawing. Zoom in to an area about three inches width and height. Using the arc tool, draw out an arc, moving up and right 1/8 of an inch. Do not deselect, but change to your line tool, and draw a horizontal line from the end of the arc to a point that is 7/8 of an inch. directly to the right of the end of the arc. Draw the next line segment directly down 1/8 of an inch. Draw the next line segment exactly one inch. to the left, which is back to the beginning of the arc. Great! Your figure should look like a rectangle with its upper-left corner rounded to a quarter circle. Your symbol should be filled. Here is where the magic begins.

Open the ShapeSheet for your new custom SmartShape symbol. Look at the Geometry section. You will see the row for the elliptical arc as the first row after the Start row (Visio 5.0) or the MoveTo row (Visio 2000). The first thing you want to accomplish is changing the elliptical arc into a circular arc. The reason you want this to happen is that when you stretch the shape, you want the arc to remain as a quarter circle at all times.

To do this, simply click in the X cell of the Elliptical Arc row. Right-click and select Change Row Type from the context menu. Click ArcTo as the new row type and click OK. Your row should now be an arc type instead of an elliptical arc. Note how the X cell refers to width and the Y cell refers to height. You want to ensure that the arc will enlarge or shrink only when the height is altered. Therefore, you have to make sure that the formulas in both the X and Y cells refer to what? Correct. Height.

Note that the Y cell has a formula that states =Height*1. What is height times one? Exactly right again. Height*1=Height. Therefore, to help Visio avoid having to recalculate height times one every time, there is a change to the symbol, you will change the formula in the cell to read =Height.

Now, you want the arc to always remain a quarter circle. As you know from your basic geometry lessons, the distance from the start of a circular arc to the center of the defined circle must be equal to the distance from the end of the circular arc to the center of the defined circle. Therefore, you can change the formula in the X cell to read =Height as well. This means that only when the symbol is changed in height will the arc change, not when its width is adjusted.

As you did with the preceding row, you are going to optimize the formulae in the next row: the LineTo row. Where it states =Width*1, you will change that to =Width. Where it states =Height*1, you will change that to =Height. This is the line from the end of the arc to the upper-right corner of the symbol. In the next row, you have to optimize the formulae as well. Here, the X cell should also be =Width. The Y cell currently reads =Height*0. Height times zero equals zero, so you can optimize the formula to be 0 here. Wherever you can optimize formulae, you should always perform this task because it makes the performance of the symbol that much better. The last row refers back to its point of origin, so you can leave that as is.

All right, you have optimized the general symbol to make it perform properly and efficiently. But what about the pointer portion of your symbol? Remember that you are currently at the lower-left corner of your symbol. Think of yourself as a plotter who must draw this symbol. To make the next set of lines required to display the pointer, you will have to draw a line over to the right, then down, then back to the left, and finally, a short distance up again. That is exactly what you are going to do.

Place your cursor in the X cell of the last LineTo row—the row that states =Geometry1.X1 as its formula. Now select Insert, Row After from the menu. Notice how a new row is added after the row you were just planted in. Do this again three more times. You should now have exactly four more rows following what *was* the final row. All of the X cell formulae read =Width*0 and all of the Y cell formulae read =Height*0. This is the default when you build new rows through the ShapeSheet.

You are now going to alter the formulae for these four rows to make your new pointer components display properly. Remember the path I just described as if you were the plotter? Set the first X cell in the first new row to have the formula =Width. That will move it over to the symbol's right. Set its Y cell to have the formula =0. That keeps it at the bottom of the symbol.

In the next row, you must go down in motion, so you will set its X cell to be =Width to keep it at the right and set the Y cell to be =Height*-2 to send it down twice the height of the symbol. You are going to alter this more later, but for now, this will make it easier to visualize.

In the third new row, you want to go back to the left again, so you set the X cell to =0 because you want width times zero, but optimized. For the Y cell, you want it to be the same as the Y cell above, so you can use the formula =Geometry1.Y7. Finally, you want to go up a little, so you will set the last new X cell to be =0 to keep it at the left and the last new Y cell to be =Geometry1.Y7+Height to go up slightly.

One last thing. You want a pointer arrow at the end of your pointer. Activate the drawing window. With the symbol selected, select Format, Line from the menus. Set the line end to be an arrowhead style (number 6) and its size to be small. Notice how only the open-ended line segment took the new style. Anywhere you have a closed path, the end styles do not apply. Additionally, you have not altered the begin style for the line, so you are not making any changes there.

Now, test out your new symbol on a duplicate. Control-drag out a copy of the SmartShape symbol. If you alter the symbol's width, see how the arc remains constant. If you alter the width, see how the arc properly grows as a quarter circle? This is brilliant! However, the pointer part is worthless! You must dig back into the ShapeSheet and add control handles to make this work.

Delete your duplicate. Select your original symbol and open its ShapeSheet. With the ShapeSheet window active, select Insert, Sections from the menu. Add a Controls section to the ShapeSheet. Add one additional Controls row to the new section. You do this by clicking in the X cell of the new Controls section's first row and selecting Insert, Row. You should now have two Controls rows. Notice how they are both located at the lower-left corner of the symbol. Their X cells read =Width*0, and their Y cells read =Height*0.

The first control handle is going to be used to control the left-to-right movement of the pointer arrow. The second control handle is going to be used to control the vertical position of the indicator arm.

Start with the first Controls row. As a default position, you will leave the pointer at the far left. Therefore, the X cell will read =0, and the Y cell will read =GUARD(Geometry1.Y9. This ensures that the pointer will always stay affixed to the end of the pointer arrow. Notice how the Xdynamics and Ydynamics are set to refer to the positions in the X and Y cells of the Controls row. You will let this remain the default behavior because it will track how the user alters the pointer position from its last placement.

In the Xbehavior cell, you want the user to be able to slide the pointer left and right, so you give the user free control by setting its value to =0—not exactly. You actually set it to =2 because when the shape is stretched, you want the pointer to remain a constant distance from the left during the stretching. For the Ybehavior, however, you do not want the control handle to move up or down at all. Therefore, you set the Ybehavior to =1 for Locked.

CanGlue is FALSE because you do not want the pointer to glue to anything. The Tip cell is a special case. Remember how you said that this cell could contain both static text and formulas that could be evaluated? I'm going to take advantage of this behavior and add the following formula to the Tip cell:

```
="Percent Complete = "&((Controls.X1*100)/Width)&" %"
```

This will display the Percent Complete = followed by the calculation of the percentage the pointer is from the right, followed by the percent sign (%). Remember your basic algebra here. If you take the width of the shape as 100% and the position of the control handle as X% and cross-multiply, then X equals the quantity of the control handle position times 100 divided by the width. Each time the user rests his or her pointer over the control handle, the handle's tip will display something like this:

```
Percent complete = 34.875 %
```

Pretty slick, right?

Now, to wire the geometry of the pointer to the control handle, you must set a few intercell references. In the X cells of both Geometry rows eight and nine, you set the formulas to read =Controls1.X1. This ensures that the X position of both these line-end segments will follow the control handle.

The second control handle is designed to adjust the vertical position of the pointer arm—the long line that goes from right to left under the symbol. The X cell for this control row can initially be set to be halfway across the symbol so that it is centered. However, you want to ensure that it *always* remains at the center of the line segment. To facilitate this, you place the following formula in the X cell of the second control handle row:

```
=GUARD(Width-((Width-Controls.X1)/2))
```

This takes the distance from the far right to the current position of the control handle, divides it by 2 to find its midpoint, and then subtracts that from the total width to set its X position. The Y cell has the initial formula =Height*-2. Because this will be moving, you will let this sort itself out later.

Xdynamics and Ydynamice are just like the row above. Xbehavior must be locked because you do not want the user to be relocating the control from where you so carefully placed it. Therefore, the Xbehavior should read =1. The YBehavior can be truly mobile, so its formula can read =0. CanGlue is as above, FALSE, and the Tip can read Adjust Indicator Depth.

Let's wire the last few cells to the second control handle. Both rows 7 and 8 in Y should be connected to the Y position of the control handle. Therefore, Geometry1.Y7 and Geometry1.Y8 should have formulas that state =Controls.Y2. The position of the very tip of the indicator arm should still be above the horizontal member, so the formula for the Geometry1.Y9 cell should be =Controls.Y2+Height.

Two more bits of business to take care of. You want the actual width of the symbol to show up as text on the symbol itself. Furthermore, you want the text to be above the symbol. Activate the drawing window and double-click on the symbol as if to edit the text. Select Insert, Field from the menu. In the first column, select Geometry; in the second column, select Width; and in the third column, select 0.000 as the units. Accept the settings and click off the symbol. By not displaying the units, they can mean anything from days, to years, to degrees, to pound sterling.

You must now move the text off and above the symbol. To do this, select the text rotation tool from the toolbar. It looks like a circular arrow with the letter *A* inside it. In Visio 5.0, it is on the face of the toolbar; in Visio 2000, it is located under the A button. Move your cursor over the text itself. Notice how the cursor symbol changes to two small boxes? More about this later, but for now, simply click-and-drag the text and slip it farther up until it is just above the symbol.

There you have your complete indicator shape. As always, test it out on a duplicate of the symbol, and save your work. A completed version of this indicator shape is located on the companion CD-ROM at the back of this book.

The Connection Points Section of the ShapeSheet

When you glue a 1D shape such as a dynamic connector to a 2D SmartShape symbol such as a Flowchart symbol, you normally glue the endpoint of the 1D to a small blue *X* on the 2D SmartShape symbol. These small blue *X*s, are, in fact, the visual indicators of connection points. Each time glue is made, a connection point (if it does not already exist) is created by Visio. These are indicated in the Connection Points section of the ShapeSheet.

Connection Points Row

By default under Visio 2000, a Connection Points row has five columns.

Visio 5.0 Connection Points Cells

X

This is the X ordinate of the coordinate pair that defines the location of the connection point. It is a unit-ed number and is always expressed in the SmartShape symbol's local coordinate system. This is the first column in the Connection Points row.

Y

This is the Y abscissa of the coordinate pair that defines the location of the connection point. It is a unit-ed number and is always expressed in the SmartShape symbol's local coordinate system. This is the second column in the Connection Points row.

Variable Connection Point Row Cells

Under Visio 5.0 and forward, there is an expansion capability within Connection Points rows. Five additional cells can be added to the row: a name cells and four comment or data repository cells (A through D). These cells are made available by right-clicking the row and selecting Change, Row Type from the context menu. The additional cells are detailed as follows.

Named Row

This is the named cell that defines the unique identifier for the connection point. When used for the first time, in the first Connection Points row, it must be given a valid name, similar to a User-Defined row. The additional restriction is that it cannot be named *A*, *B*, *C*, or *D* because these would conflict with the comment cells to follow. Uniquely identifying the row gives the developer the ability to test for the validity of connections. This becomes the new first column in the Connection Points row and increments the column number of all columns to follow.

A

This cell accepts a text string as a comment or data repository cell. Versions before Visio 5.0 do not recognize this cell. When saved in versions before Visio 5.0, any information in this cell is lost. This becomes the new fourth column in the Connection Points row.

B

This cell accepts a text string as a comment or data repository cell. Versions before Visio 5.0 do not recognize this cell. When saved in versions before Visio 5.0, any information in this cell is lost. This becomes the new fifth column in the Connection Points row.

C

This cell accepts a text string as a comment or data repository cell. Versions before Visio 5.0 do not recognize this cell. When saved in versions before Visio 5.0, any information in this cell is lost. This becomes the new sixth column in the Connection Points row.

D

This cell accepts a text string as a comment or data repository cell. Versions before Visio 5.0 do not recognize this cell. When saved in versions before Visio 5.0, any information in this cell is lost. This becomes the new seventh column in the Connection Points row.

Alternate Connections Cells

X

This is the X ordinate of the coordinate pair that defines the location of the connection point. It is a united number and is always expressed in the SmartShape symbol's local coordinate system. This is the first column in the Connection Points row.

Y

This is the Y abscissa of the coordinate pair that defines the location of the connection point. It is a united number and is always expressed in the SmartShape symbol's local coordinate system. This is the second column in the Connection Points row.

DirX/A

This is the X ordinate of the coordinate pair that defines the location of the direction vector for the connection point. It is a united number and is always expressed in the SmartShape symbol's local coordinate system. For backward compatibility with Visio 5.0, this cell also accepts a text string as a comment or data repository cell. Versions before Visio 5.0 do not recognize this cell. When saved in versions before Visio 5.0, any information in this cell is lost. This is the third column in the Connection Points row.

DirY/B

This is the Y abscissa of the coordinate pair that defines the location of the direction vector for the connection point. It is a united number and is always expressed in the SmartShape symbol's local coordinate system. For backward compatibility with Visio 5.0, this cell also accepts a text string as a comment or data repository cell. Versions before Visio 5.0 do not recognize this cell. When saved in versions before Visio 5.0, any information in this cell is lost. This is the fourth column in the Connection Points row.

Type/C

This is the integer value that defines the connection type for the connection point. There are three valid values for this cell: 0, which is an in type, 1, which is an out type, and 2, which is an in and out type. For backward compatibility with Visio 5.0, this cell also accepts a text string as a comment or data repository cell. Versions before Visio 5.0 do not recognize this cell. When saved in versions before Visio 5.0, any information in this cell is lost. This is the fifth column in the Connection Points row.

Selectable Alternate Connections Cells

Under Visio 2000, there is an expansion capability within Connection Points rows. Two additional columns can be added to the row: a name column and one comment or data repository column (D). These cells are made available by right-clicking the row and selecting Change, Row Type from the context menu. The additional cells are detailed as follows.

Named Row

This is the named cell that defines the unique identifier for the connection point. When used for the first time, in the first Connection Points row, it must be given a valid name, similar to a User-Defined row. The additional restriction is that it cannot be named *A*, *B*, *C*, or *D* because these would conflict with the comment/direction and gender cells that precede it. Uniquely identifying the row gives the developer the ability to test for the validity of connections. This becomes the new first column in the Connection Points row and increments the column number of all columns to follow.

D

This cell accepts a text string as a comment or data repository cell. Versions before Visio 5.0 do not recognize this cell. When saved in versions before Visio 5.0, any information in this cell is lost. This becomes the new seventh column in the Connection Points row.

In Visio 2000 A, B, and C are used for connection point directional information and gender of the connection point (type). If we choose to change the row type, any information you had set in those cells is lost forever! So if you've spent a great deal of time setting up the connection points to attach at a 45 deg angle with the type of two (inward/outward) then that information would be totally destroyed when you switch the row type.

In many Visio solutions, it is necessary to ascertain whether the user has connected a 1D SmartShape symbol to the proper connection point on a 2D SmartShape symbol. An example of this is a wiring diagram in which specific pieces of electronics equipment are being connected to others via cables. A 220-volt AC output on equipment item A cannot be validly connected to a 12-volt DC input on another. This would destroy equipment item B. By creating an Automation application that takes maximum advantage of named and data-rich connections, it is possible to determine improper connections and take appropriate actions.

Intercell References

Before I end this chapter and move on to more complex issues, I want to take a moment to further discuss intercell references. You have already made use of intercell references when you created your smart arrow symbol, as well as your indicator symbol. Intercell references lend a great additional power to the ShapeSheet development environment. They assist in optimization of SmartShape symbols, as well as make it much faster and easier to create the custom symbols. However, the intercell references must be utilized properly. Whereas it is very good for Geometry1.X2, Geometry1.X3, Geometry1.X4, and Geometry1.X5 all to reference Geometry1.X1, because this optimizes the formulae and limits the required number of recalculations, it is not only bad form but also counterproductive to have Geometry1.X4 reference Geometry1.X3, which references Geometry1.X2, which, in turn, references Geometry1.X1. These "chained" references actually slow down the recalculation engine and decrease the efficiency of any given SmartShape symbol.

Summary

You have learned a lot in this chapter. You now know all the functionality of the Shape Transform, Geometry, Scratch, User-Defined, Controls, and Connection Points sections of the ShapeSheet. You have learned how to use intercell references to create custom SmartShape symbols that conform to intelligent behavior rather than to simply "rubber-sheet" stretch behavior.

In the next chapter, you will look at how you can further modify a SmartShape symbol's behavior, as well as the behavior of groups of SmartShape symbols, through these additional sections of the ShapeSheet:

- The Protection section
- The Miscellaneous section
- The Line, Fill, Character, Paragraph, and Text Block Format sections
- The Visio 2000 Shape Layout section

I will discuss Inter-Shape and Inner-Shape references, as well as Boolean operations to assist in the creation and modification of SmartShape symbols. Take a short, but well-deserved break, and we'll meet right here again, caffeine in hand, to get back to the fun task of learning Visio ShapeSheet and Automation development.

Modifying Visio SmartShape Symbols and Groups of Symbols

IN THIS CHAPTER

As I stated earlier, certain actions a user or a developer can take can actually eradicate formulas and change values in a SmartShape symbol's ShapeSheet. We also looked at the GUARD() function as one method of working around this issue. Another method for ensuring that custom SmartShape symbols behave the way they were intended to is setting values in the Protection section of the ShapeSheet. In both Visio 5.0 and Visio 2000, there are 16 cells in the Protection section. They are

- LockWidth
- LockHeight
- LockMoveX
- LockMoveY
- LockAspect
- LockDelete
- LockBegin
- LockEnd
- LockRotate
- LockCrop
- LockVtxEdit
- LockTextEdit
- LockFormat
- LockGroup
- LockCalcWH
- LockSelect

Protecton Section Settings

All of these cells are Boolean FALSE or TRUE (zero or non-zero) values. Cell by cell, I'll work through all the important aspects of each cell and how it relates to other cells and affects the behavior of a given Visio SmartShape symbol. When you are beginning to learn how each of these cells function, have a Rectangle Visio SmartShape symbol that has been converted to a 1D symbol (by selecting Format, Behavior from the menu and selecting the 1D radio button, and then clicking OK) and a Line Visio SmartShape symbol at your disposal in the drawing window. Be ready to open the appropriate 2D (rectangle), 1D (rectangle), or 1D (line) symbol's ShapeSheet and as you change these settings to interact with the symbol. See for yourself how the change in setting affects the behavior of the symbol. Some settings will become readily apparent via visual clues or by diminished ability—others are much more subtle.

> **Important Concept Number Four**
>
> The Protection section settings protect ONLY against changes instituted from the user interface by the user. Via the ShapeSheet or through Automation, any cell's settings can still be manipulated.

LockWidth

This applies to both 1D and 2D symbols. In a 1D symbol, small padlocks appear and replace the sizing handles at both the beginning and endpoints of the 1D symbol if the value is set to TRUE (non-zero). This prohibits the user from changing the width of the symbol through the user interface. In a 2D symbol, small padlocks appear and replace the sizing handles at the four corners and two sides of the symbol if the value is set to TRUE (non-zero). This also prohibits the user from changing the width of the symbol through the user interface. If the value is set to FALSE (zero), the symbol in both 1D and 2D cases behaves as appropriate.

LockHeight

This applies to both 1D and 2D symbols. In a 1D symbol, if the value is set to TRUE (non-zero), you will find that the sizing handles simply disappear in the 1D symbol. This prohibits the user from changing the width of the symbol through the user interface. This is apparent in symbols where the symbol was initially a 2D symbol and was changed to a 1D symbol by activating the Drawing window, selecting the 2D symbol, and then selecting Format, Behavior from the menu. The 2D symbol is converted to an 1D symbol. In the case of a line, where the symbol has no height, the setting of LockHeight is both not obvious and generally not applicable. In a 2D symbol, small padlocks appear and replace the sizing handles at the four corners and at the top and bottom of the symbol if the value is set to TRUE. This also prohibits the user from changing the width of the symbol through the user interface. If the value is set to FALSE (zero), the symbol in both 1D and 2D cases behaves as appropriate.

LockMoveX

This applies to both 1D and 2D symbols. In a 1D symbol, all X axis movement is prohibited from the user interface. In a 2D symbol, if the value is set to TRUE, you will find that it is impossible to move the symbol in the X axis from the user interface. If the value is set to FALSE, the symbol in both 1D and 2D cases behaves as appropriate.

LockMoveY

This applies to both 1D and 2D symbols. In a 1D symbol, all Y axis movement is prohibited from the user interface. In a 2D symbol, it is impossible to move the symbol in the Y axis from the user interface if the value is set to TRUE. If the value is set to FALSE, the symbol in both 1D and 2D cases behaves as appropriate.

LockAspect

This applies to 2D symbols only. In a 2D symbol, if the value is set to TRUE, the ratio as it exists between height and width at the time this value is set to TRUE (non-zero) becomes fixed. No user interface changes take place. However, if the user attempts to adjust the symbol in either height or width alone, the symbol will maintain its aspect ratio between height and width. If the value is set to FALSE, the symbol behaves as appropriate.

LockDelete

This applies to both 1D and 2D symbols. If the value is set to TRUE, the user will not be able to delete the symbol from the user interface. If the value is set to FALSE, the symbol in both 1D and 2D cases behaves as appropriate.

LockBegin

This applies to 1D symbols only. If the value is set to TRUE, the beginning point of any 1D symbol may not be altered by the user through the user interface. If the value is set to FALSE, the symbol behaves as appropriate.

LockEnd

This applies to 1D symbols only. If the value is set to TRUE, the end point of any 1D symbol may not be altered by the user through the user interface. If the value is set to FALSE, the symbol behaves as appropriate.

LockRotate

This applies to both 1D and 2D symbols. If the value is set to TRUE in 2D symbols, padlocks will appear at all four corners and at the pin point when the user selects the Rotation tool from the Toolbar. This prohibits the user from rotating the symbol from the user interface. If the value is set to TRUE, in 1D symbols, padlocks appear at the begin and end points of the symbol when the user selects the Rotation tool from the toolbar. This prohibits the user from rotating the symbol from the user interface. If the value is set to FALSE, the symbol in both 1D and 2D cases behaves as appropriate.

LockCrop

This applies to 2D symbols containing imported images only. If the value is set to TRUE (non-zero) and the user selects the Crop tool from the toolbar, padlocks will appear at all sizing handle points on the symbol. This prohibits the user from cropping the symbol in any manner from the user interface. However, this does not prohibit the user from relocating the image to any point within the symbol using the Crop tool's pan capabilities. If the value is set to FALSE, the symbol behaves as appropriate.

LockVtxEdit

This applies to both 1D and 2D symbols. If the value is set to TRUE and the user selects any of the basic drawing and editing tools, the pencil tool, the line tool, the arc tool, or the freeform tool, padlocks appear at every vertex. This prohibits the user from altering any vertex from the user interface. If the value is set to FALSE, the symbol in both 1D and 2D cases behaves as appropriate.

LockTextEdit

This applies to both 1D and 2D symbols. If the value is set to TRUE (non-zero), the user is prohibited from entering or editing any text associated with a symbol from the user interface. A warning dialog will appear telling the user that protection features prohibit this action. This does not affect text already associated with the symbol nor the performance of any text field already associated with the symbol. If the value is set to FALSE (zero), the symbol in both 1D and 2D cases behaves as appropriate.

LockFormat

This applies to both 1D and 2D symbols. If the value is set to TRUE, the user will be prohibited from making any changes to the symbol's line, fill, or text formatting. Additionally, the user will be prohibited from the application of any style. A warning dialog will appear telling the user that protection features prohibit this action. This restricts all formatting changes from the user interface. If the value is set to FALSE, the symbol in both 1D and 2D cases behaves as appropriate.

LockGroup

This applies to both 1D and 2D symbols that are group symbols (created by selecting Shape, Grouping, Group). If the value is set to TRUE for a group symbol, any attempt by the user to add a symbol to the group or remove a symbol from the group will either result in the inability to select the context menu item or will result in a dialog box warning that protection features prohibit this action. If the value is set to FALSE, the symbol in both 1D and 2D cases behaves as appropriate.

3

MODIFYING VISIO
SMARTSHAPE
SYMBOLS

LockCalcWH

This applies to both 1D and 2D symbols. If the value is set to TRUE, the addition of any geometry to the symbol via the ShapeSheet or the movement of any geometry via the user interface or by association with a Control Handle will not affect the size and aspect ration of the symbol's bounding box. If the value is set to FALSE (zero), the symbol in both 1D and 2D cases behaves as appropriate.

LockSelect

This applies to both 1D and 2D symbols. If the value is set to TRUE (non-zero) and the user attempts to select the symbol from the User Interface, the symbol can not be selected. NOTE: This can take place ONLY after the following two steps have been accomplished. First, the LockSelect cell must be set to a value of TRUE. Second, the user of the drawing must select Tools, Protect Document from the menus. In Visio 2000, you do this by showing the Drawing Explorer (View, Windows, Drawing Explorer), right-mouse clicking the document name in the tree view, and selecting Protect Document.

Then the user must enter a password into the password field and check the Shapes check box, and then click the OK button. Afterward, the symbol can not be selected again for the life of the drawing unless the user selects Tools, Unprotect Document from the menu and enters the correct password.

Important Concept Number Five

Visio uses the same password protection mechanisms that Microsoft Office uses. This is highly secure. If you forget your password, nothing short of contacting Visio to have the document opened while running a debug version of Visio from within the development core will unprotect the document and allow you to access the protected symbol(s). If the value is set to FALSE, the symbol in both 1D and 2D cases behaves as appropriate.

Those are the features of the Protection section of the ShapeSheet. There's a lot there—using all the features available can add lots of power and polish to the SmartShape symbols that you design. I'll lead you through another lab exercise in a little bit, but before I do, I want to guide you through the Miscellaneous section of the ShapeSheet.

The Miscellaneous Section of the ShapeSheet

The Miscellaneous section of the ShapeSheet is a bit of a catch-all. It is designed to hold information that does not fit neatly into other sections. Under Visio 5.0, this section consists of eight cells. They are NoObjHandles, NoCtlHandles, NoAlignBox, DynFeedback, ObjInteract, UpdateAlignBox, NonPrinting, HideText, ObjType, and ObjBehavior.

In Visio 5.0, this section included ObjInteract and ObjBehavior cells. In Visio 2000, the behavior in the ObjInteract cell has been mapped to the following cells: ShapeFixedCode, ShapePermeableX, ShapePermeableY, and ShapePermeablePlace. The behavior in the ObjBehavior cell has been mapped to the ConFixedCode and ShapeRouteStyle cells.

Under Visio 20000 this section consists of eleven cells. They are

- Comment
- DynFeedback
- HideText
- IsDropSource
- NoAlignBox
- NoCtlHandles
- NoLiveDynamics
- NonPrinting
- NoObjHandles
- ObjType
- UpdateAlignBox

I'll detail these cells one at a time. With each, I will let you know how it is applicable to any particular version and how backwards-compatibility is handled.

NoObjHandles

This cell appears in both Visio 5.0 and Visio 2000. This cell holds Boolean FALSE or TRUE (zero or non-zero) values. It controls the display of the selection handles (in 1D symbols the small bright green boxes at the endpoints, in 2D symbols the small bright green squares at the 4 corners and 4 midpoints of the bounding box for the symbol) for the selected SmartShape symbol. If the value is set to TRUE, the selection handles will not be displayed when the subject SmartShape symbol is selected. If the value is set to FALSE, the symbol behaves as appropriate.

NoCtlHandles

This cell appears in both Visio 5.0 and Visio 2000. This cell holds Boolean FALSE or TRUE (zero or non-zero) values. It controls the display of the control handles (the dark green small squares) for the selected SmartShape symbol. If the value is set to TRUE, the control handles will not be displayed when the subject SmartShape symbol is selected. If the value is set to FALSE, the symbol behaves as appropriate.

NoAlignBox

This cell appears in both Visio 5.0 and Visio 2000. This cell holds Boolean FALSE or TRUE (zero or non-zero) values. It controls the display of the Alignment box (the green dashed line defining the bounding box for the symbol) for the selected SmartShape symbol. If the value is set to TRUE, the Alignment box will not be displayed when the subject SmartShape symbol is selected. If the value is set to FALSE (zero), the symbol behaves as appropriate.

DynFeedback

This cell appears in both Visio 5.0 and Visio 2000. This cell holds the integer value controlling the visual feedback that is provided to the user when a Visio Connector SmartShape symbol is dragged about on the drawing page. When the mouse button is released, the resulting behavior of the Connector symbol is not affected by this setting. Visio Routable Connector SmartShape symbols are not affected by this setting whatsoever. The valid values are as follows:

0   The connector remains straight (no legs)

1   The connector shows three legs when dragged

2   The connector shows five legs when dragged

ObjInteract

This cell appears in Visio 5.0 only. This cell applies to the interaction of placeable or routable Visio SmartShape symbols in a connected diagram. Two valid values exist for this cell; No Formula and the integer zero, which indicates the use of an interaction style for a placeable or routable SmartShape symbol. For a placeable or routable shape in Visio 5.0, the value of this cell should be set to zero; non-zero values will cause unpredictable behavior.

UpdateAlignBox

This cell appears in both Visio 5.0 and Visio 2000. This cell holds Boolean FALSE or TRUE (zero or non-zero) values. It controls the recalculation of the Alignment box (the green dashed line defining the bounding box for the symbol) for the selected SmartShape symbol whenever a control handle (the dark green small square) for the selected SmartShape symbol is moved. If the value is set to TRUE, the Alignment box will be updated when the subject SmartShape symbol's control handle is moved. If the value is set to FALSE, the symbol behaves as appropriate.

NonPrinting

This cell appears in both Visio 5.0 and Visio 2000. This cell holds Boolean FALSE or TRUE (zero or non-zero) values. It controls whether the selected SmartShape symbol will print. If the value is set to TRUE, the SmartShape symbol will not print but will still be displayed. If the value is set to FALSE, the symbol behaves as appropriate.

HideText

This cell appears in both Visio 5.0 and Visio 2000. This cell holds Boolean FALSE or TRUE (zero or non-zero) values. It controls whether the text of the subject SmartShape symbol will be visible onscreen and in print. If the value is set to TRUE, the SmartShape symbol's text will not be displayed nor will it print. The user or developer can view text, edit properties, and apply styles to the text in the text block, although the changes will not appear until The HideText value is returned to FALSE (zero). If the value is set to FALSE (zero), the symbol behaves as appropriate.

ObjType

This cell appears in both Visio 5.0 and Visio 2000. This cell is valid in a diagram that uses automatic layout with objects that may be placeable or routable. This cell holds the integer value determining the placability of the SmartShape symbol depending upon its context. By default, ObjType is set to No Formula for a shape, which evaluates to 0, meaning that Visio determines whether the shape can be placeable depending on its context. For example, if you draw a simple rectangle, the value of its ObjType cell is 0. If you then use the Connect Shapes command or the Dynamic Connector tool to connect the rectangle to another shape, Visio resets the value of the rectangle's ObjType cell to 1 (placeable). The valid values are as follows:

No Formula	*Not a placeable nor routable object.*
0	Visio determines based upon the drawing context.
1	The shape is placeable.
2	The shape is routable.
3	Currently unassigned.
4	The shape is not placeable, not routable.

ObjBehavior

This cell appears in Visio 5.0 only. This cell is valid in a diagram that uses automatic layout with objects that may be placeable or routable. This cell holds the integer value determining the behavior of the SmartShape symbol in a connected diagram. The valid values are as follows:

No Formula	*Not a placeable nor routable object.*
0	Use the behavior that has been set for the page.
1	Create right angle connections.
2	Create straight connections.
5	Create a flowchart with north-south orientation.
6	Create a flowchart with west-east orientation.
7	Create a tree diagram with north-south orientation.
8	Create a tree diagram with west-east orientation.

Comment

This cell appears in Visio 2000 only. The Comment cell contains ASCII characters as a string for the subject Visio SmartShape symbol. The Comment may also be accessed by the Visio 2000 Comment dialog box.

IsDropSource

This cell appears in Visio 2000 only. This cell holds Boolean FALSE or TRUE (zero or non-zero) values. It controls whether a Visio SmartShape symbol may be added to a group by dragging it into the Group SmartShape symbol. If the value is set to TRUE (non-zero), a Visio SmartShape symbol may be added to a group by dragging it into the Group SmartShape symbol. If the value is set to FALSE, the symbol behaves as appropriate and this functionality is disabled. You should note that in addition to enabling this behavior for a shape, you must also enable a group to accept shapes that are dragged into it. To do so, select the group, select Format, Behavior from the menu, and then check Accept Dropped Shapes. This value is stored in the IsDropTarget cell in the Group Properties section.

NoLiveDynamics

This cell appears in Visio 2000 only. This cell holds Boolean FALSE or TRUE (zero or non-zero) values. It controls whether a Visio SmartShape symbol dynamically resizes or rotates whenever the user interacts with it via its sizing handles or its control handle(s). If the value is set to TRUE (non-zero), the SmartShape symbol will not dynamically update under user interaction. Additionally, a selection box will be visible. If the value is set to FALSE, the symbol behaves as appropriate and the dynamic interaction functionality is enabled.

You should now feel very well armed to go out and tackle some serious ShapeSheet development tasks. By combining the knowledge you have gained through understanding the Shape Transform, Geometry, Scratch, User-Defined, Controls, and Connection Points sections with the Protection and Miscellaneous sections, you should be able to develop SmartShape symbols that behave in a highly intelligent manner. Let's test this out a bit. We'll work on our next lab exercise: a Visio Telescope SmartShape symbol. I've included a beginning for this symbol on the CD-ROM that accompanies this book. This assists you by eliminating the need to first physically drag out and properly size and locate the eleven basic Visio Rectangle SmartShape symbols that comprise the custom telescope symbol we will create.

Before we dive further into this exercise, I want to make you aware of an additional feature within Visio. As you create new basic SmartShape symbols using the drawing tools within Visio, Visio automatically tracks them and assigns unique numbers to them. These unique naming assignments can be viewed by selecting Format, Special from the menu. Notice that the dialog box that appears has two fields of interest to us here: ID and Name. We will be discussing other fields later, but for now I'm going to focus on these two. The ID field displays the unique identifier integer for this symbol. These are assigned sequentially each time a symbol is added, either by using the drawing tools or by dragging from a stencil. The Name field, by default, shows the word "Sheet," followed by the same sequence number. Therefore the first symbol on a page would "Sheet.1," the next "Sheet.2," and so on. You are free to change the Name field to suit your own, and your user's needs. Overwrite the Name field and click the OK button.

Why is this unique naming feature valuable? I'll go in to much more detail later. For now, think of it as something to assist you in remembering the component parts of an assembly when you build complex symbols such as this telescope.

After you have the telescope drawing open in front of you, look at each ShapeSheet for each of the eleven rectangles in the drawing. There is a second telescope drawing in the Chapter 3, "Modifying Visio SmartShape Symbols and Groups of Symbols," directory on the CD as well. Go ahead and open that drawing as well. In addition to the second being "cosmetically prettier" than the first, lots of work has been done to each of the ShapeSheets to build the overall solution.

Functionally, when the telescope is selected, the user should be able to collapse and expand the sections of the telescope. When the sections of the telescope are collapsed and expanded the telescope symbol should look and behave as a real telescope would. In other words, each of the end caps should always remain attached to the opposite ends of the telescope sections. When the center section is slid into the left section, the right section should remain attached. The center section should never be allowed to slide farther in nor farther out than its proper length would allow. The same parameters are true for the right section.

To facilitate this, I have used control handles as the movement mechanisms for the sections. I have removed the user's ability to resize and move the sections through the User Interface, save through the use of the control handles. In the "finished" drawing, click the center section. Rest your mouse cursor over its control handle. See how the tip assists you? Try sliding the control handle left and right. See how the entire telescope behaves properly? Do the same with the right section. Note how the three telescope sections interact.

As a means of explaining what I have done, and what you need to do to make the first telescope look and behave like the second, I am going to display each of the Shape Transform, Geometry, Controls, Protection, User-Defined, and Miscellaneous sections of the shapes both "before" and "after." With each "before" and "after" displayed, I will discuss why each change was made and how it affected the overall telescope's performance.

Ready? Let's get started.

Let's map the ShapeSheets between the telescopeshape_started and the telescopeshape_finished drawings:

Sheet.1	= Tube1	= the front main (left) tube
Sheet.2	= Tube2	= the center (center) tube
Sheet.3	= Tube3	= the rear (right) tube
Sheet.4	= EyeCap	= the far right "ring"
Sheet.5	= ViewCap	= the far left "ring"
Sheet.6	= ScopePlate	= the plate attached to Tube1
Sheet.7	= Pivot	= the assembly hinge point
Sheet.8	= LegPlate	= the plate below the pivot
Sheet.9	= Leg2	= the center leg
Sheet.10	= Leg1	= the left leg
Sheet.11	= Leg3	= the right leg

Tables 3.1 and 3.2 will help you in understanding the ShapeSheets and their respective sections as they are listed.

TABLE 3.1 SHAPESHEET: SHEET.1

Cell	Value	Formula
Width	2.0000 in.	2 inches
Height	0.5000 in.	0.5 inches
Angle	0.0000 deg.	0 degrees
PinX	3.0000 in.	3 inches
PinY	8.2500 in.	8.25 inches
LocPinX	1.0000 in.	Width*0.5
LocPinY	0.2500 in.	Height*0.5
FlipX	FALSE	FALSE
FlipY	FALSE	FALSE
ResizeMode	0	0

TABLE 3.2 SHAPESHEET : TUBE1 SHEET.1

Cell	Value	Formula
Width	2.0000 in.	GUARD(2 inches)
Height	0.5000 in.	GUARD(0.5 inches)
Angle	0.0000 deg.	GUARD(0 degrees)
PinX	3.5625 in.	GUARD(Pivot!PinX)
PinY	7.8750 in.	GUARD(Pivot!PinY)
LocPinX	1.5626 in.	GUARD(Width*0.7813)
LocPinY	-0.1250 in.	GUARD(Height*-0.25)
FlipX	FALSE	GUARD(FALSE)
FlipY	FALSE	GUARD(FALSE)
ResizeMode	0	0

In both the height and width cells, we GUARD() the values that reside there. This prohibits the main tube section from being resized by the user. The Angle is guarded as well: This keeps the telescope level. (Improvements later can make the telescope tilt, in which case we will need to revisit this cell.) The PinX and PinY have strange formulas in them. We already understand the GUARD() function, but what is the reference with the exclamation point (referred to as a bang in programmer's parlance) in it? This is an intershape reference. I will be discussing this further later in the book. For now, understand that the notation works this way:

```
[Shape Name or Identifier][!][CellName]
```

where Shape Name or Identifier is as we discussed above for the TARGET or referenced symbol. The bang (!) is the separator between the shape name and the cell name. CellName is name of the cell being referenced. This is an expansion of the same theory that we used for intercell references.

In this symbol, we are referencing the PinX and PinY of the Pivot symbol. We will use this as the "common denominator" for the entire telescope so later we can simply pick up and move the telescope by its Pivot piece just as we would in the real world. We are setting the LocPinX and LocPinY to place them in a position in relationship to the Pivot shape as well. Finally, we GUARD() the FlipX and FlipY to prohibit the symbol from being flipped because we would not be able to do this in the real world independently of the overall telescope.

```
SHAPESHEET : SHEET.1
Start Section : USER DEFINED CELLS
End Section : USER DEFINED CELLS (CELLS TOTAL : 0)
SHAPESHEET : TUBE1 SHEET.1
```

```
Start Section : USER DEFINED CELLS
End Section : USER DEFINED CELLS (CELLS TOTAL : 0)
```

For the Tube1 symbol, no changes were made to the User-Defined section. In fact, no User-Defined section was added to the symbol.

```
SHAPESHEET : SHEET.1
Start Section : CONTROLS
End Section : CONTROLS (CELLS TOTAL : 0)
SHAPESHEET : TUBE1 SHEET.1
Start Section : CONTROLS
End Section : CONTROLS (CELLS TOTAL : 0)
```

For the Tube1 symbol, no changes were made to the Controls section. In fact, no Controls section was added to the symbol (see Tables 3.3 and 3.4).

TABLE 3.3   SHAPESHEET : SHEET.1

Cell	Value	Formula
Geometry1.NoFill(Component)	FALSE	FALSE
Geometry1.NoLine(Component)	FALSE	FALSE
Geometry1.NoShow(Component)	FALSE	FALSE
Geometry1.NoSnap(Component)	FALSE	FALSE
Geometry1.X1(Move To)	0.0000 in.	Width*0
Geometry1.Y1(Move To)	0.0000 in.	Height*0
Geometry1.X2(Line To)	2.0000 in.	Width*1
Geometry1.Y2(Line To)	0.0000 in.	Height*0
Geometry1.X3(Line To)	2.0000 in.	Width*1
Geometry1.Y3(Line To)	0.5000 in.	Height*1
Geometry1.X4(Line To)	0.0000 in.	Width*0
Geometry1.Y4(Line To)	0.5000 in.	Height*1
Geometry1.X5(Line To)	0.0000 in.	Geometry1.X1
Geometry1.Y5(Line To)	0.0000 in.	Geometry1.Y1
End Section : GEOMETRY (CELLS TOTAL : 14)		

TABLE 3.4 SHAPESHEET : TUBE1 SHEET.1

Cell	Value	Formula
Geometry1.NoFill(Component)	FALSE	FALSE
Geometry1.NoLine(Component)	FALSE	FALSE
Geometry1.NoShow(Component)	FALSE	FALSE
Geometry1.NoSnap(Component)	FALSE	FALSE
Geometry1.X1(Move To)	0.0000 in.	Width*0
Geometry1.Y1(Move To)	0.0000 in.	Height*0
Geometry1.X2(Line To)	2.0000 in.	Width*1
Geometry1.Y2(Line To)	0.0000 in.	Height*0
Geometry1.X3(Line To)	2.0000 in.	Width*1
Geometry1.Y3(Line To)	0.5000 in.	Height*1
Geometry1.X4(Line To)	0.0000 in.	Width*0
Geometry1.Y4(Line To)	0.5000 in.	Height*1
Geometry1.X5(Line To)	0.0000 in.	Geometry1.X1
Geometry1.Y5(Line To)	0.0000 in.	Geometry1.Y1

For the Tube1 symbol, no changes were made to the Geometry section (see Table 3.5).

TABLE 3.5 SHAPESHEET : SHEET.1

Cell	Value	Formula
LockWidth	0	0
LockHeight	0	0
LockAspect	0	0
LockMoveX	0	0
LockMoveY	0	0
LockRotate	0	0
LockBegin	0	0
LockEnd	0	0
LockDelete	0	0
LockSelect	0	0
LockFormat	0	0
LockTextEdit	0	0

3

**MODIFYING VISIO
SMARTSHAPE
SYMBOLS**

continues

TABLE 3.5 Continued

Cell	Value	Formula
LockVtxEdit	0	0
LockCrop	0	0
LockGroup	0	0
LockCalcWH	0	0

End Section : PROTECTION (CELLS TOTAL : 16)

SHAPESHEET : TUBE1 SHEET.1

Start Section : PROTECTION

Cell	Value	Formula
LockWidth	1	1
LockHeight	1	1
LockAspect	1	1
LockMoveX	1	1
LockMoveY	1	1
LockRotate	0	0
LockBegin	0	0
LockEnd	0	0
LockDelete	1	1
LockSelect	0	0
LockFormat	1	1
LockTextEdit	0	0
LockVtxEdit	1	1
LockCrop	0	0
LockGroup	0	0
LockCalcWH	1	1

End Section : PROTECTION
(CELLS TOTAL : 16)

In the Protection section, we locked down the symbol in its ability to be resized, moved, deleted, formatted, have its vertices edited, or its bounding box size recalculated.

SHAPESHEET : SHEET.1

Start Section : MISCELLANEOUS

Cell	Value	Formula
NoObjHandles	FALSE	FALSE
NoCtlHandles	FALSE	FALSE
NoAlignBox	FALSE	FALSE
NonPrinting	FALSE	FALSE
HideText	FALSE	FALSE
UpdateAlignBox	FALSE	FALSE
DynFeedback	0	0
NoLiveDynamics	FALSE	FALSE
ObjType	0	0
IsDropSource	FALSE	FALSE
Comment	No Formula	No Formula

End Section :
MISCELLANEOUS
(CELLS TOTAL : 11)

SHAPESHEET : TUBE1 SHEET.1

Start Section : MISCELLANEOUS

Cell	Value	Formula
NoObjHandles	TRUE	TRUE
NoCtlHandles	TRUE	TRUE
NoAlignBox	TRUE	TRUE
NonPrinting	FALSE	FALSE
HideText	FALSE	FALSE
UpdateAlignBox	FALSE	FALSE
DynFeedback	0	0
NoLiveDynamics	FALSE	FALSE
ObjType	0	0
IsDropSource	FALSE	FALSE
Comment	No Formula	No Formula

End Section : MISCELLANEOUS
(CELLS TOTAL : 11)

3

MODIFYING VISIO
SMARTSHAPE
SYMBOLS

In the Miscellaneous section, we turned off the Sizing Handles so the padlocks would not show and turned off the bounding box so the user would have no sense of selecting the symbol. This assists the user in selecting only the symbols with which she is supposed to interact.

SHAPESHEET : SHEET.1

Start Section : FILLFORMAT

Cell	*Value*	*Formula*
FillPattern	1	1
ShdwPattern	0	0
FillForegnd	1	1
ShdwForegnd	0	0
FillBkgnd	0	0
ShdwBkgnd	1	1

End Section :
FILLFORMAT
(CELLS TOTAL : 6)

SHAPESHEET : TUBE1 SHEET.1

Start Section : FILLFORMAT

Cell	*Value*	*Formula*
FillPattern	29	29
ShdwPattern	0	0
FillForegnd	5	5
ShdwForegnd	0	0
FillBkgnd	11	11
ShdwBkgnd	1	1

End Section : FILLFORMAT
(CELLS TOTAL : 6)

Finally, in the FillFormat section (a section we will be covering in detail a little later in the book), we changed the fill pattern to be a gradient fill from center in fill color at center to fill background color at the top and bottom (pattern 29). This essentially goes from dim yellow to bright yellow back to dim yellow as you go from Top to Bottom. We set the fill foreground color to 5, which is bright yellow, and the fill background color to 11, which is dim yellow. This gives the illusion of three-dimensionality and a "tubular" shape.

SHAPESHEET : SHEET.2

Start Section : SHAPE TRANSFORM

Cell	Value	Formula
Width	1.0000 in.	1 inches
Height	0.3750 in.	0.375 inches
Angle	0.0000 deg.	0 degrees
PinX	4.5000 in.	4.5 inches
PinY	8.2500 in.	8.25 inches
LocPinX	0.5000 in.	Width*0.5
LocPinY	0.1875 in.	Height*0.5
FlipX	FALSE	FALSE
FlipY	FALSE	FALSE
ResizeMode	0	0

End Section :
SHAPE TRANSFORM
(CELLS TOTAL : 10)

SHAPESHEET : TUBE2 SHEET.2

Start Section : SHAPE
TRANSFORM

Cell	Value	Formula
Width	1.0000 in.	GUARD(1 inches)
Height	0.3750 in.	GUARD(0.375 inches)
Angle	0.0000 deg.	GUARD(0 degrees)
PinX	4.0000 in.	GUARD(Tube1!PinX+(7 inches/16 inches))
PinY	8.2500 in.	GUARD(Pivot!PinY+0.375 inches)
LocPinX	0.0000 in.	GUARD(0 inches)
LocPinY	0.1875 in.	GUARD(Height*0.5)
FlipX	FALSE	GUARD(FALSE)
FlipY	FALSE	GUARD(FALSE)
ResizeMode	0	0

End Section : SHAPE TRANSFORM
(CELLS TOTAL : 10)

3

MODIFYING VISIO SMARTSHAPE SYMBOLS

Note here that we have guarded the height, width, Angle FlipX, and FlipY cells as we did before. The LocPinX has been set to the far left of the symbol and the LocPinY has been kept at the midpoint of the height. These cells have also been guarded. The PinX cell contains a formula that references the Tube1 symbol and adds to it a distance of 7/16 of an inch. The PinY cell contains a reference to the Pivot symbol and exists above it a distance of 0.375 of an inch. These formulas are guarded as well. By referencing other symbol's cells, we lock the behavior of the symbol to use the spatial requirements of the referenced symbol. This sets up a correspondence so when the Pivot symbol is moved, the referring symbol, in this case the Tube2 Symbol, moves along with it.

SHAPESHEET : SHEET.2

Start Section : USER DEFINED CELLS

End Section : USER DEFINED CELLS (CELLS TOTAL : 0)

SHAPESHEET : TUBE2 SHEET.2

Start Section : USER DEFINED CELLS

Cell	Value	Formula
User.MinimumCollapse	0.0000	IF(Controls.X1<=1 inches* (1 inches/16 inches),SETF ("Controls.X1",1 inches* (1 inches/16 inches)),0)
User.MinimumCollapse.Prompt	Minimum width allowable for the tube	Minimum width allowable for the tube
User.MaximumStretch	0.0000	IF(Controls.X1,1 inches, SETF("Controls.X1",1 inches),0)
User.MaximumStretch.Prompt	Maximum width allowable for the tube	Maximum width allowable for the tube

End Section : USER DEFINED CELLS (CELLS TOTAL : 4)

For this symbol, we have added a user-defined section to the ShapeSheet. Notice that there are two rows in the user-defined section. The first is to control the minimum width to which we will allow the shape to collapse, the second row controls the maximum width to which we will allow the symbol to be "stretched." Remember that this tube, tube2, is a tube that slides into Tube1. It was manufactured at a specific length and cannot simply grow or shrink in size. It "slides" into and out of the Tube1 symbol. It's length (width) is fixed at 1 inch. Therefore the formula for the first row, loosely translated into English, states that if the control handle that has been added to the symbol ever gets to a point that is less than or equal to 1/16 of an inch from the left edge of the symbol, we will force the handle to be relocated to the point that is indeed 1/16 of an inch from the left of the symbol. The formula for the second row, loosely translated into English, states that if the control handle that has been added to the symbol ever gets to a point that is greater than one inch from the left edge of the symbol (which is its designed original width), we will force the handle to be relocated to the point that is indeed one inch from the left of the symbol.

SHAPESHEET : SHEET.2

Start Section : CONTROLS

End Section : CONTROLS (CELLS TOTAL : 0)

SHAPESHEET : TUBE2 SHEET.2

Start Section : CONTROLS

Cell	Value	Formula
Controls.X1	1.0000 in.	width*1
Controls.Y1	0.1875 in.	Height*0.5
Controls.XDyn	0.0000 in.	0 inches
Controls.YDyn	0.1875 in.	Height*0.5
Controls.XCon	0	0
Controls.YCon	1	1
Controls.CanGlue	FALSE	FALSE
Controls.Prompt	Adjust the length of Tube Section #2	Adjust the length of Tube Section #2

End Section : CONTROLS
(CELLS TOTAL : 8)

Here we establish a control handle and initially place it at the center-right of the symbol. We determine that the root point for its movement will be at the center-left of the symbol. We restrict the movement of the control handle in the Y direction so it can only be moved in the X axis. Remember that the user-defined cells limit the minimum and maximum travel for this control handle. We determine that the control handle will not glue to anything and we establish a prompt for the control handle so when the user pauses his mouse cursor over the control handle it will display a message stating that his handle adjusts the length of tube section number two.

SHAPESHEET : SHEET.2

Start Section : GEOMETRY

Cell	Value	Formula
Geometry1.NoFill(Component)	FALSE	FALSE
Geometry1.NoLine(Component)	FALSE	FALSE
Geometry1.NoShow(Component)	FALSE	FALSE
Geometry1.NoSnap(Component)	FALSE	FALSE
Geometry1.X1(Move To)	0.0000 in.	Width*0
Geometry1.Y1(Move To)	0.0000 in.	Height*0
Geometry1.X2(Line To)	1.0000 in.	Width*1
Geometry1.Y2(Line To)	0.0000 in.	Height*0
Geometry1.X3(Line To)	1.0000 in.	Width*1
Geometry1.Y3(Line To)	0.3750 in.	Height*1
Geometry1.X4(Line To)	0.0000 in.	Width*0
Geometry1.Y4(Line To)	0.3750 in.	Height*1
Geometry1.X5(Line To)	0.0000 in.	Geometry1.X1
Geometry1.Y5(Line To)	0.0000 in.	Geometry1.Y1

End Section : GEOMETRY
(CELLS TOTAL : 14)

SHAPESHEET : TUBE2 SHEET.2

Start Section : GEOMETRY

Cell	Value	Formula
Geometry1.NoFill(Component)	FALSE	FALSE
Geometry1.NoLine(Component)	FALSE	FALSE
Geometry1.NoShow(Component)	FALSE	FALSE
Geometry1.NoSnap(Component)	FALSE	FALSE
Geometry1.X1(Move To)	0.0000 in.	Width*0
Geometry1.Y1(Move To)	0.0000 in.	Height*0
Geometry1.X2(Line To)	1.0000 in.	MAX(Controls.X1,1 inches* (1 inches/16 inches))
Geometry1.Y2(Line To)	0.0000 in.	Height*0
Geometry1.X3(Line To)	1.0000 in.	MAX(Controls.X1,1 inches* (1 inches/16 inches))

Cell	Value	Formula
Geometry1.Y3(Line To)	0.3750 in.	Height*1
Geometry1.X4(Line To)	0.0000 in.	Width*0
Geometry1.Y4(Line To)	0.3750 in.	Height*1
Geometry1.X5(Line To)	0.0000 in.	Geometry1.X1
Geometry1.Y5(Line To)	0.0000 in.	Geometry1.Y1
End Section : GEOMETRY (CELLS TOTAL : 14)		

Notice how the X cells for the right edge of the symbol are now referencing the control handle. As you now know, this means that when the control handle is adjusted, the Geometry follows. This effectively makes the tube length (the "width" of the symbol) adjustable via the control handle on the symbol.

SHAPESHEET : SHEET.2

Start Section : PROTECTION

Cell	Value	Formula
LockWidth	0	0
LockHeight	0	0
LockAspect	0	0
LockMoveX	0	0
LockMoveY	0	0
LockRotate	0	0
LockBegin	0	0
LockEnd	0	0
LockDelete	0	0
LockSelect	0	0
LockFormat	0	0
LockTextEdit	0	0
LockVtxEdit	0	0
LockCrop	0	0
LockGroup	0	0
LockCalcWH	0	0
End Section : PROTECTION (CELLS TOTAL : 16)		

SHAPESHEET : TUBE2 SHEET.2

Start Section : PROTECTION

Cell	Value	Formula
LockWidth	1	1
LockHeight	1	1
LockAspect	0	0
LockMoveX	0	0
LockMoveY	0	0
LockRotate	0	0
LockBegin	0	0
LockEnd	0	0
LockDelete	0	0
LockSelect	0	0
LockFormat	0	0
LockTextEdit	0	0
LockVtxEdit	0	0
LockCrop	0	0
LockGroup	0	0
LockCalcWH	0	0

End Section : PROTECTION
(CELLS TOTAL : 16)

The Protection cells for this symbol have been set so the user cannot adjust the height or width via the User Interface. By this means, only the control handle may be used to adjust the symbol.

ShapeSheet : SHEET.2

Start Section : MISCELLANEOUS

Cell	Value	Formula
NoObjHandles	FALSE	FALSE
NoCtlHandles	FALSE	FALSE
NoAlignBox	FALSE	FALSE
NonPrinting	FALSE	FALSE
HideText	FALSE	FALSE

Cell	Value	Formula
UpdateAlignBox	FALSE	FALSE
DynFeedback	0	0
NoLiveDynamics	FALSE	FALSE
ObjType	0	0
IsDropSource	FALSE	FALSE
Comment	No Formula	No Formula
End Section : MISCELLANEOUS (CELLS TOTAL : 11)		
SHAPESHEET : TUBE2 SHEET.2		
Start Section : MISCELLANEOUS		

Cell	Value	Formula
NoObjHandles	TRUE	TRUE
NoCtlHandles	FALSE	FALSE
NoAlignBox	TRUE	TRUE
NonPrinting	FALSE	FALSE
HideText	FALSE	FALSE
UpdateAlignBox	FALSE	FALSE
DynFeedback	0	0
NoLiveDynamics	FALSE	FALSE
ObjType	0	0
IsDropSource	FALSE	FALSE
Comment	No Formula	No Formula
End Section : MISCELLANEOUS (CELLS TOTAL : 11)		

3

MODIFYING VISIO SMARTSHAPE SYMBOLS

In the Miscellaneous section, we have turned off the Object (Sizing) handles. This eliminates the visual padlocks from the symbol. We have also turned off the Align box (the bounding box) for the symbol. This makes a very "clean" interface for the user to interact with. Though the interface is not a "typical" Visio interface with sizing handles and bounding boxes, it is quite intuitive because of the tip on the control handle and the user's own experience with opening and closing telescopes in the past.

SHAPESHEET : SHEET.2

Start Section : FILLFORMAT

Cell	Value	Formula
FillPattern	1	1
ShdwPattern	0	0
FillForegnd	1	1
ShdwForegnd	0	0
FillBkgnd	0	0
ShdwBkgnd	1	1

End Section : FILLFORMAT
(CELLS TOTAL : 6)

SHAPESHEET : TUBE2
SHEET.2

Start Section :
FILLFORMAT

Cell	Value	Formula
FillPattern	29	29
ShdwPattern	0	0
FillForegnd	5	5
ShdwForegnd	0	0
FillBkgnd	11	11
ShdwBkgnd	1	1

End Section : FILLFORMAT
(CELLS TOTAL : 6)

Here we have adjusted the fill colors for the symbol identically to those of Tube1.

For the sake of brevity and because I am sure that you can easily open the additional nine ShapeSheets, I will not list the ShapeSheet cells for the other SmartShape symbols here. But I would encourage you to do this at your leisure.

The Diverse Format Sections of the ShapeSheet

There are actually several "Format" sections in a Visio ShapeSheet. They include the Line Format, Fill Format, Character, Paragraph, and Text Block Format sections. I'll take you through them section by section, cell by cell. When we are through, you will know more than you ever thought possible about how the visual qualities of a Visio SmartShape symbol can be manipulated (and you thought all you could do was make flowchart boxes…).

Line Format Section

The Line Format Section of the ShapeSheet controls many aspects of a Visio SmartShape symbol's line. This is the line that is the Geometry path(s) for the symbol. It includes such diverse formatting information as line weight, color, line type, begin arrow or symbol types, end arrow or symbol types, and line cap style. This section consists of eight cells. They are

Line Pattern

Line Weight

Line Color

Line Cap

Begin Arrow

End Arrow

Arrow Size

Rounding

I'll detail these cells one at a time.

Line Pattern

This cell contains the integer value for the line pattern of the SmartShape symbol. The listing of the available line patterns is found by activating the drawing window and selecting Format, Line from the menu. The drop-down list of line types indicates the visual style as well as the index number. The valid integer values are

0	No line pattern
1	Solid
2–23	Assorted line patterns that correspond to indexed entries in the Line dialog box.

Note: To specify a custom line pattern, use the USE function in this cell.

Line Weight

This cell contains the integer or real number plus units that indicate the line weight of the SmartShape symbol. If a unit of measure is not entered, the unit of measure for text specified in the Options dialog box will be used. The line weight is independent of the scale of the drawing. If the drawing is scaled, the line weight remains the same.

Line Color

This cell contains the integer value that specifies the line color of the SmartShape symbol. It is identified by the number assigned to that color in the Color Palette dialog box. To see this, select Tools, Color Palette from the menu. Valid color numbers range from 0 to 23. A value of 24 or higher may be entered if a custom color has been created via the Color Palette dialog box. A number above 23 indicates a custom color that Visio specifies as a formula containing the RGB function.

Line Cap

This cell contains an integer value from zero through one, which indicates whether a line has rounded or square line caps. The valid integer values are as follows:

0	Rounded ends
1	Square ends

Begin Arrow

This cell contains an integer value, which indicates whether a line has an arrowhead or other line end format at its first vertex. Valid integers are from 0 through 45. The size of the arrowhead is set in the ArrowSize cell.

0	No arrowhead
1–45	Assorted arrowhead styles that correspond to indexed entries in the Line dialog box.

NOTE: To specify a custom line end, use the USE function in this cell.

End Arrow

This cell contains an integer value, which indicates whether a line has an arrowhead or other line end format at its last vertex. Valid integers are from 0 through 45 . The size of the arrowhead is set in the ArrowSize cell.

0	No arrowhead
1–45	Assorted arrowhead styles that correspond to indexed entries in the Line dialog box

NOTE: To specify a custom line end, use the USE function in this cell.

Arrow Size

This cell contains an integer value, which indicates the size of the arrowhead set in BeginArrow and EndArrow. Valid integer values are listed below:

0	Very small
1	Small
2	Medium
3	Large
4	Extra large

5	Jumbo
6	Colossal

Rounding

This cell contains unit-ed number that indicates the radius of the rounding circular segment applied where two straight line segments of a given SmartShape symbol meet. If no units are specified, Visio will assume the internal default, which is inches.

Fill Format Section

A ShapeSheet's Fill Format section contains cells that describe all aspects of the subject Visio SmartShape symbol's formatting with regard to its filled area and applied (if specified) drop shadow. The filled area aspects include the foreground color, the background color, and the pattern. The drop shadow aspects include the foreground color, the background color, and the pattern. The Fill Format section consists of six cells. They are

- FillBkgnd
- FillForegnd
- FillPattern
- ShdwBkgnd
- ShdwForegnd
- ShdwPattern

I'll detail these cells one at a time.

FillBkgnd

This cell contains the integer value that specifies the background color of the SmartShape symbol. It is identified by the number assigned to that color in the Color Palette dialog box. To see this, select Tools, Color Palette from the menu. Valid color numbers range from 0 to 23. A value of 24 or higher may be entered if a custom color has been created via the Color Palette dialog box. A number higher than 23 indicates a custom color that Visio specifies as a formula containing the RGB function.

FillForegnd

This cell contains the integer value that specifies the foreground color of the SmartShape symbol. It is identified by the number assigned to that color in the Color Palette dialog box. This can be seen by selecting Tools, Color Palette from the menu. Valid color numbers range from 0 to 23. A value of 24 or higher may be entered if a custom color has been created via the Color Palette dialog box. A number higher than 23 indicates a custom color that Visio specifies as a formula containing the RGB function.

FillPattern

This cell contains the integer value that specifies the fill pattern for the SmartShape symbol. Valid integer values for the FillPattern are

0   None (transparent fill)

1   Solid foreground color

2–40   Assorted fill patterns that correspond to indexed entries in the Fill dialog box

NOTE: To specify a custom fill pattern, use the USE function in this cell.

NOTE: The Geometry Section's "A" or NoFill Cell controls whether a given Geometry section has the capability of being filled. The FillPattern cell, when set to a value of zero, makes the pattern "transparent" or effectively "none" for the entire SmartShape symbol.

ShdwBkgnd

This cell contains the integer value that specifies the background color for the drop shadow fill pattern of the SmartShape symbol. It is identified by the number assigned to that color in the Color Palette dialog box. This can be seen by selecting Tools, Color Palette from the menu. Valid color numbers range from 0 to 23. A value of 24 or higher may be entered if a custom color has been created via the Color Palette dialog box. A number higher than 23 indicates a custom color that Visio specifies as a formula containing the RGB function.

ShdwForegnd

This cell contains the integer value that specifies the foreground color for the drop shadow fill pattern of the SmartShape symbol. It is identified by the number assigned to that color in the Color Palette dialog box. This can be seen by selecting Tools, Color Palette from the menu. Valid color numbers range from 0 to 23. A value of 24 or higher may be entered if a custom color has been created via the Color Palette dialog box. A number higher than 23 indicates a custom color that Visio specifies as a formula containing the RGB function.

ShdwPattern

This cell contains the integer value that specifies the fill pattern for the drop shadow of the SmartShape symbol. Valid integer values for the FillPattern are

0   None (transparent fill)

1   Solid foreground color

2–40   Assorted fill patterns that correspond to indexed entries in the Fill dialog box

NOTE: To specify a custom fill pattern, use the USE function in this cell.

Character Section

The Character section of a subject SmartShape symbol's ShapeSheet indicates the formatting attributes for the SmartShape symbol's text, including the font, the color, the text style, the case association, the position relative to the baseline of the text string, and the point size to be used as the base text size for the text string. The Character section consists of six cells. They are

- Case
- Color
- Font
- Pos
- Size
- Style

I'll detail these cells one at a time. In addition, Visio 2000 adds these cells:

- Scale
- Spacing
- Strikethru
- DoubleULine
- Overline
- Perpendicular

Case

This cell contains the integer value that controls the case of a shape's text. All capbolds and initial capitals do not change the appearance of text that was entered in all capital letters. The text must be entered in lowercase letters for these options to show an effect. The valid range of integers is from zero through two. The value descriptions are as follows:

0	Normal case
1	All capital (uppercase) letters
2	Initial capital letters only

Color

This cell contains the integer value that specifies the text color of the SmartShape symbol. It is identified by the number assigned to that color in the Color Palette dialog box. This can be seen by selecting Tools, Color Palette from the menu. Valid color numbers range from 0 to 23. A value of 24 or higher may be entered if a custom color has been created via the Color Palette dialog box. A number higher than 23 indicates a custom color that Visio specifies as a formula containing the RGB function.

Font

This cell contains the integer value that specifies the number of the font used to format the text. Font numbers vary according to the fonts installed on your system. The number 0 represents the default font, which is Arial, unless you change the default font in the VISIO.INI file under Visio 5.0 or in the Windows Registry under Visio 2000. Via automation, you can query each font number in the Fonts collection and obtain the font name associated with that font number index.

Pos

This cell contains the integer value that specifies the position of the shape's text relative to the baseline. The valid range of integers is from zero through two. The value descriptions are as follows:

0	Normal position
1	Superscript
2	Subscript

Size

This cell contains the number-unit pair value, which specifies the size of the text in the shape's text block, in the default units for text set in the Options dialog box. The text's size is independent of the scale of the drawing. If the drawing is scaled, the text size remains the same. Any valid unit may be used as the unit portion of the number-unit pair. If no unit is specified, Visio will assume internal units, which are inches.

Style

This cell contains the Boolean value that shows the character formatting applied to the text in the shape's text block. The value represents a binary number in which each bit indicates a character style. The bits are as follows:

Bit 8 = small caps
Bit 4 = Underline
Bit 2 = Italic
Bit 1 = Bold

As an example, a value of three represents text formatted in both italic and bold. If the value of Style is zero, the text is plain or unformatted.

To test for a particular format, use the Boolean functions `BITAND( )`, `BITNOT( )`, `BITOR( )`, or `BITXOR( )`.

Paragraph Section

The Paragraph section of a Visio ShapeSheet shows the paragraph formatting attributes for the selected Visio SmartShape symbol's text, including indents, line spacing, and horizontal alignment of paragraphs. The Paragraph section consists of seven cells. They are

- HAlign
- IndFirst
- IndLeft
- IndRight
- SpAfter
- SpBefore
- SpLine

I'll detail these cells one at a time. In addition, Visio 2000 adds these cells:

- Bullet
- BulletString

Halign

This cell contains the integer value, which specifies the horizontal alignment of text in the shape's text block. This cell can also be referred to as Para.HorzAlign. If you create a cell reference in a formula by clicking this cell, Visio inserts the name Para.HorzAlign. HAlign can have a values of zero through four. The value descriptions are as follows:

0	Left align
1	Center
2	Right align
3	Justify
4	Force justify

Justify adds space between words in every line except the last line of the paragraph to make both the left and right sides of text flush with the margins. Force justify justifies every line in the paragraph, including the last.

IndFirst

This cell contains the unit-ed distance. The first line of each paragraph in the shape's text block is indented from the left indent of the paragraph. This value is independent of the scale of the drawing. If the drawing is scaled, the first line indent remains the same.

IndLeft

This cell contains the unit-ed distance. All lines of text in each paragraph are indented from the left margin of the text block. This value is independent of the scale of the drawing. If the drawing is scaled, the left indent remains the same.

IndRight

This cell contains the unit-ed distance. All lines of text in each paragraph are indented from the right margin of the text block. This value is independent of the scale of the drawing. If the drawing is scaled, the right indent remains the same.

SpAfter

This cell contains the unit-ed distance that is the amount of space inserted after each paragraph in the shape's text block in addition to any space from SpLine and, if it is the first paragraph in a text block, BottomMargin. This value is independent of the scale of the drawing. If the drawing is scaled, the Space After setting remains the same.

SpBefore

This cell contains the unit-ed distance that is the amount of space inserted before each paragraph in the shape's text block, in addition to any space from SpLine and, if it is the first paragraph in a text block, TopMargin. This value is independent of the scale of the drawing. If the drawing is scaled, the Space Before setting remains the same.

SpLine

This cell contains the real number that is the distance between one line of text and the next, expressed as a percentage, where 100% is the height of a text line. SpLine have these valid values:

>0	Absolute spacing, regardless of type size
=0	Set solid (spacing=100% of type size)
<0	A percentage of type size (for example, -120% yields 120% spacing)

If SpLine is less than 100%, lines of text overlap. This value is independent of the scale of the drawing. If the drawing is scaled, the line spacing remains the same.

The Paragraph section does not include cells for tab settings. To set tabs for a shape's text under Visio 5.0, use the Text command. In Visio 2000, refer to the Tabs section of the ShapeSheet.

Tabs Section

This section applies to Visio 2000 only. This section consists of a maximum of 120 cells. The Tabs section contains cells for shapes or styles that control tab stop position and alignment.

When you set tab stops for specific characters, a new row is added to the Visio SmartShape symbol's Tabs Section for the selected symbol. The name of the row represents the number of characters the tab stop contains. There are two cell types in the Tabs section row: Alignment and Position.

Alignment

This cell contains the integer value that is the type of the tab alignment. The valid range of integers is from zero to three. The value descriptions are as follows:

0	Left
1	Center
2	Right
3	Decimal

Position

This cell contains the integer that specifies the position of a tab stop. The tab position is independent of the scale of the drawing. If the drawing is scaled, the line weight remains the same.

Text Block Format Section

The Text Block Format section shows the alignment and margins of text in a Visio SmartShape symbol's text block. The Text Block Format section consists of six cells. They are

- BottomMargin
- LeftMargin
- RightMargin
- TextBkgnd
- TopMargin
- VerticalAlign

I'll detail these cells one at a time. Visio 2000 adds these additional cells.

- DefaultTabStop
- TextDirection

BottomMargin

This cell contains the unit-ed distance that is the distance between the bottom border of the text block and the last line of text it contains. The default is 0.1 inch. This value is independent of the scale of the drawing. If the drawing is scaled, the bottom margin remains the same.

LeftMargin

This cell contains the unit-ed distance that is the distance between the left border of the text block and the text it contains. The default is 0.1 inch. This value is independent of the scale of the drawing. If the drawing is scaled, the left margin remains the same.

RightMargin

This cell contains the unit-ed distance that is the distance between the right border of the text block and the text it contains. This value is independent of the scale of the drawing. If the drawing is scaled, the right margin remains the same.

TextBkgnd

This cell contains the integer value that specifies the text background color of the SmartShape symbol. TextBkgnd can have any value identified by the number assigned to that color in the Color Palette dialog box. This can be seen by selecting Tools, Color Palette from the menu. Valid color numbers range from 0 to 23, or 255 (0 and 255 indicate a transparent text background). To select a color value, add one to the value displayed in the Color Palette dialog box.

TopMargin

This cell contains the unit-ed distance that is the distance between the top border of the text block and the first line of text it contains. The default is 0.1 of an inch. This value is independent of the scale of the drawing. If the drawing is scaled, the top margin remains the same.

VerticalAlign

This cell contains the integer value that is the vertical alignment of text within the text block. The VerticalAlign cell has three valid values. They are

0	Top
1	Middle
2	Bottom

The Shape Layout Section of the ShapeSheet

The Shape Layout Section of a ShapeSheet is applicable to Visio 2000 SmartShape symbols only. The section contains cells that control shape placement and connector routing settings. You can also set the values of the shape-specific cells in this section by using the Placement dialog box. You can set the values of the connector-specific cells in this section by using the Connector dialog box. This section consists of 11 cells. They are

- ConFixedCode
- ConLineJumpCode
- ConLineJumpDirX

- ConLineJumpDirY
- ConLineJumpStyle
- ShapeFixedCode
- ShapePermiablePlace
- ShapePermiableX
- ShapePermiableY
- ShapePlowCode
- ShapeRouteStyle

I'll detail these cells one at a time.

ConFixedCode

This cell contains the integer value that determines when a connector reroutes. The ConFixedCode cell has four valid values. They are

0	Reroute Freely
1	Reroute as needed (manual reroute)
2	Never reroute
3	Reroute on crossover

ConLineJumpCode

The ConLineJumpCode cell determines when a connector jumps. The ConLineJumpCode cell has five valid values. They are

0	As page specifies; choose File, Page Setup, and then click the Layout & Routing tab to see the page specifications.
1	Never
2	Always
3	Other connector jumps
4	Neither connector jumps

ConLineJumpDirX

The ConLineJumpDirX cell determines the line jump direction for line jumps occurring on a horizontal dynamic connector. The ConLineJumpDirX cell has three valid values. They are

0	Page default
1	Up
2	Down

> **NOTE**
>
> To set the default horizontal direction for all connector jumps on a page, use the PageLineJumpDirX cell in the Page Layout section.

ConLineJumpDirY

The ConLineJumpDirY cell determines the line jump direction for line jumps occurring on a vertical dynamic connector. The ConLineJumpDirY cell has three valid values. They are

0	Page default
1	Left
2	Right

> **NOTE**
>
> To set the default vertical direction for all connector jumps on a page, use the PageLineJumpDirY cell in the Page Layout section.

ConLineJumpStyle

The ConLineJumpStyle cell determines the line jump style for line jumps on a dynamic connector. The ConLineJumpStyle cell has nine valid values. They are

0	Page Default
1	Arc
2	Gap
3	Square
4	2 sides
5	3 sides
6	4 sides
7	5 sides
8	6 sides
9	7 sides

> **NOTE**
>
> To set the default style for all connector jumps on a page, use the LineJumpStyle cell in the Page Layout section.

ShapeFixedCode

The ShapeFixedCode cell specifies placement behavior for a placeable shape. The ShapeFixedCode cell has three valid values. They are

1	Don't move this shape when shapes are laid out automatically using the Lay Out Shapes command.
2	Don't move this shape when other placeable shapes are placed on or near it.
128	Don't glue to the perimeter of this shape. Glue to the shape's alignment box instead.

You can set any combination of these values for this cell. For example, you can enter the value three. This eliminates movement when you lay out shapes with the Lay Out Shapes command and when other placeable shapes are placed on or near the shape.

> **NOTE**
>
> In Visio 5.0, you set this behavior using the ObjInteract cell in the Miscellaneous section.

ShapePermeablePlace

The ShapePermeablePlace cell contains the Boolean FALSE or TRUE value that determines whether placeable shapes can be placed on top of a shape when laying out shapes using the Lay Out Shapes command. Set the value of this cell to TRUE to allow shapes to be placed on top of a shape or to FALSE to disallow this behavior.

> **NOTE**
>
> In Visio 5.0, you set this behavior using the ObjInteract cell in the Miscellaneous section.

ShapePermeableX

The ShapePermeableX cell contains the Boolean FALSE or TRUE value that determines whether a connector can route horizontally through a shape. Set the value of this cell to TRUE to enable connectors to route horizontally through a shape or to FALSE to disable this behavior.

> **NOTE**
>
> In Visio 5.0, you set this behavior using the ObjInteract cell in the Miscellaneous section.

ShapePermeableY

The ShapePermeableY cell contains the Boolean FALSE or TRUE value that determines whether a connector can route vertically through a shape. Set the value of this cell to TRUE to allow connectors to route vertically through a shape or to FALSE to disallow this behavior.

> **NOTE**
>
> In Visio 5.0, you set this behavior using the ObjInteract cell in the Miscellaneous section.

ShapePlowCode

The ShapePlowCode cell determines whether this placeable shape moves away when you drop another placeable shape near this shape on the drawing page. The ShapePlowCode cell has three valid values. They are

0	Plow as page specifies
1	Plow no shapes
2	Plow every shape

To set this behavior for all the shapes on the drawing page, use the PlowCode cell in the Page Layout section.

ShapeRouteStyle

The RouteStyle cell determines the routing style and direction for a connector on the drawing page. The ShapeRouteStyle cell has twenty-three valid values as shown in Table 3.6.

TABLE 3.6 ShapeRouteStyle Cell Values

Value	Routing Style	Direction
0	Default; right angle	None
1	Right angle	None
2	Straight	None
3	Organization chart	Top to bottom
4	Organization chart	Left to right
5	Flowchart	Top to bottom
6	Flowchart	Left to right
7	Tree	Top to bottom
8	Tree	Left to right
9	Network	None
10	Organization chart	Bottom to top
11	Organization chart	Right to left
12	Flowchart	Bottom to top
13	Flowchart	Right to left
14	Tree	Bottom to top
15	Tree	Right to left
16	Center to center	None
17	Simple	Top to bottom
18	Simple	Left to right
19	Simple	Bottom to top
20	Simple	Right to left
21	Simple Horizontal-Vertical	None
22	Simple Vertical-Horizontal	None

3

MODIFYING VISIO SMARTSHAPE SYMBOLS

To set this behavior for all the connectors on a page, use the RouteStyle cell in the Page Layout section.

NOTE

In Visio 5.0, you set this behavior using the ObjBehavior cell in the Miscellaneous section.

I know this was a lot of information to digest and plow through. We've taken a look at lots of pure formatting section material. Some of it you will use in the future as you manipulate your SmartShape symbols programmatically; some of it you will use when you are performing an analysis of other symbols created by other developers. The telescope symbol that we built a wee while back used some of this to create the tubular look to the elements of the telescope and stand.

Next I want to discuss how SmartShape symbols can be associated with each other in a manner known as Grouping. Additionally, we will look at what happens to symbols when they are grouped.

Grouping of SmartShapes Symbols

As you looked at each symbol that comprised the telescope, you noted that each of the symbol's PinX and PinY were using intershape references to create an association between them. Sometimes this is practical, but it can be cumbersome at other times. Another mechanism for associating symbols is grouping them. In order to illustrate this; let's create two rectangles. The size does not matter. In the first rectangle, type the words "Symbol-A." In the second, type in the words "Symbol-B." Make sure your pointer tool is selected. Select both symbols. Do this by selecting one of the symbols (its sizing handles turn on and are green), and then holding down Shift and selecting the other (its sizing handles turn on and are cyan). Now release Shift, hold down Ctrl, and drag out a new copy of both symbols. Grand!

If the two new rectangles are not already selected, select them both and then select Shape, Grouping, Group from the menus. Notice how what were two distinct and separate symbols has become for all intents and purposes a single symbol. The sizing handles are around the entire bounded area of both of the former individual symbols. With the new symbol selected, begin entering text onto the symbol. Which former symbol seemed to accept the text? The answer is the "top-most" in the "z-order." This means that when you create two symbols, each symbol as it is created is at the top of the z-ordering stack. You can, of course, change their order by selecting Shape, Bring Forward; Shape, Bring to Front; Shape, Send Backward; or Shape, Send to Back from the menu for any symbol. The order that they exist in will be their order within the new Group SmartShape symbol.

Important Concept Number Six

When SmartShape symbols are associated within a group by selecting Shape, Grouping, Group, a *new* SmartShape symbol is created. This new group symbol acts as a "shell" around all of the symbols within the group. Under Visio 5.0, any connection points that may have been created on any symbol within the group will *not* be available at the Group level. Under Visio 2000, the connection points *do* appear and *are* usable at the group "shell" level. Under Visio 5.0, the group symbol has no text block of its own but instead uses the text block of the top-most symbol in "z-order" within the group. Under Visio 2000, the group symbol has its own text block. This is in addition to the text blocks for each one of the sub-symbols within the group symbol. The behavior can be switched back to 5.0 style by selecting Format, Behavior and unchecking the Edit Text of Group check box.

Remember the ResizeMode cell in the Shape Transform Section of the ShapeSheet? Here is where it comes into play. Carefully reread the section covering it and be sure you understand it. When you are designing grouped symbols, you need to ensure that the component parts of the new group symbol behave as the user would expect. You may need to customise the behavior of certain Geometry cells to obtain the results you desire.

Remember the LockCalcWH cell in the Protection section of the ShapeSheet? This determined whether the bounding box would be updated, that is, grow or shrink, depending on factors such as the adding or removing symbols from a group. Let's try the following experiment:

Create a SmartShape symbol that is exactly 1 inch in both height and width. Duplicate that symbol by Ctrl-dragging out a copy. Make a group out of each symbol by selecting Shape, Grouping, Group from the menu. (Yes…a group can still be a group, even if it has only one member within the group.) For one of the new group symbols, open its ShapeSheet and set the LockCalcWH cell to TRUE. Close the ShapeSheet. Now create a new rectangle that is 0.5 inch wide by 2 inches tall. Duplicate that new tall thin rectangle. Place the tall thin rectangles directly over each of the group symbols. Select the group that has NOT had the LockCalcWH cell altered. Shift-select one of the new tall thin rectangles. Now select Shape, Grouping, Add to Group from the menu. Note how the bounding box changed to accommodate the new limitations of all of the Geometry. Try this again with the other group and the second tall thin rectangle. Note how the group's bounding box remains constant and the new member of the group is allowed to lapse outside of the bounding box. This is important to remember: You can define the boundaries for your SmartShape symbols to be any size that you choose. You need to set them at a size that makes the most sense to the user of your symbols.

We have not yet discussed the adding of Custom Properties to SmartShape symbols. When we do, you will need to keep in mind that under Visio 5.0, a symbol with custom properties that becomes part of a group symbol loses the access to the properties through the user interface. The user will no longer be able to access them by selecting the group, right-clicking and selecting Shape, Custom Properties from the context menu. Under Visio 2000, the properties are available by sub-selecting the component symbol within the group.

Intershape and Innershape References

We have already seen how any ShapeSheet cell can reference any other cell in the same ShapeSheet. We do this by making a direct reference to that cell's name. For example, if the value to be used for the width of a given SmartShape symbol is to be taken from a user-defined cell and the user-defined cell is named MyWidth, the formula in the ShapeSheet's Width would be =GUARD(MyWidth). We have also seen that any Visio SmartShape symbol can reference another by using intershape references. If the height of a symbol called Sheet.2 must always be equal to the height of a symbol called Sheet.1, the height cell in the ShapeSheet for Sheet.2 would contain the formula =GUARD(Sheet.1!Height). We see that the exclamation point (!) is the separator between the SmartShape symbol name and the cell referenced in the referred to SmartShape symbol's ShapeSheet.

Under Visio 2000, this intershape referencing can be extended to be called cross-container references. The Syntax is slightly different when you rise beyond the intershape level to go across pages. Let's take the example of a basic rectangle SmartShape symbol whose name is Sheet.1 on Page-1, and another basic rectangle SmartShape symbol whose name is Sheet.2 on Page-2. If we wanted to have the fill foreground color of Sheet.1 on Page-1 controlled by the fill foreground color of Sheet.2 on Page-2, Sheet.1's FillForegnd cell in its ShapeSheet would contain the formula =GUARD(pages[Page-2]!Sheet.2!FillForegnd). Notice how the page reference takes on the form of the keyword pages followed by an opening square bracket, the name of the page to be referenced, a closing square bracket, and then the exclamation point as a separator. This is followed by the normal inter-shape reference structure.

A while ago, I told you that any SmartShape symbol could be given a more user-friendly name by selecting the SmartShape symbol to be referenced, and then selecting Format, Special from the menu. Changing the Name property and then clicking the OK button then assigns the friendly name to the symbol. However, when we are dealing with intershape references and, even more importantly, when we are dealing with cross-container references, you MUST reference the target symbol by its Sheet.[n] name rather than its friendly name. Here is the general rule to follow: When the reference you are attempting to make is at exactly the same scoping level, for example, two symbols on the same page, you may use the friendly names. When a reference is made across any scoping boundary such as a symbol within a group referencing its parent (the group) or another symbol on the page, the reference must be made by its Sheet.[n] reference style.

Take a look at Figure 3.1.

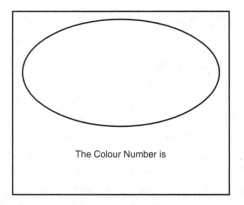

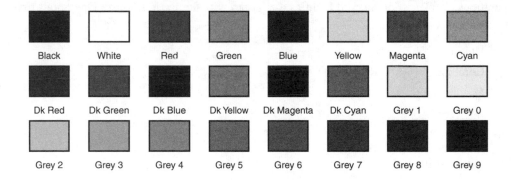

FIGURE 3.1
Color scheme diagram.

This is a screen shot of a Visio diagram I have included on the companion CD. By double-clicking any one of the 23 color blocks, you can change the color of the ellipse contained within the group at the top of the page. This uses an intershape reference at a differing scoping level and makes use of the SETF() function that we spoke of earlier. Note the general form of the formula contained in each color block of SmartShape symbol's Shape in the Events section in the EventDblClick cell. The formula looks like =SETF("Sheet.[n]!FillForegnd", [x]), where *n* is the number of the ellipse shape contained within the group and *x* is the actual color number. An even better formula is =SETF("Sheet.[n]!FillForegnd",FillForegnd) because the current symbol's FollForegnd cell can read the value from itself and use that to pass to the target referenced symbol.

Here's our next Lab Exercise. Load the demonstration file from the CD and open the ShapeSheet for a color block and study the references. Continue by poking about all the other aspects of this sample drawing and try to understand how all of the functionality works. Everything that you need to know is there in the materials that we have already covered.

Boolean Operations

Users of Visio solutions really need to know only a small amount of the Visio functionality to be able to effective create and query highly intelligent Visio diagrams. "Drag and drop and pull on the green things" is the phrase we banty about. However, you, as the *developer* of the solution, must know how to draw with Visio in order to create intelligent SmartShape symbols. You must be able to use the Line tool, the Arc tool, the Ellipse tool, the Rectangle tool, the Freeform tool, the Pencil tool, and more. These are the basic drawing tools of Visio. Often you will want to create complex boundary paths. It would be nice to have a set of tools available to make the pure creation of that geometry easier. This is why Visio presents you with the Boolean operation tools. All of these tools are accessible via selection Shape, Operations from the menus. I am going to classify these into three general categories: Basic Boolean Operations, Boolean Editing, and Utilities. Let's start with the Basic Boolean Operations first. The operations are

- Union
- Combine
- Fragment
- Intersect
- Subtract

I'll detail these for you.

Important Concept Number Seven

When you perform any of the following Basic Boolean Operations, you will destroy the former individual SmartShape symbols and create an entirely new SmartShape symbol from the resultant operation. Any smart formulas you had entered into any cell will be destroyed in the process. Use Boolean operations *before* you add intelligence to your symbols. Any Custom Properties, Scratch, User-Defined or Connection Point cells you may have added to a given symbol will be destroyed as well.

Union

A Boolean Union takes two or more SmartShape symbols and analyzes the total filled areas that overlap. It then creates a new SmartShape symbol that is the total area shared by the former symbols. The selection order in providing the selection set of symbols to be used in this operation is highly important. The first symbol selected provides the content for all Text, Line, and Fill styles as well as all Formatting options. For the before and after operations, see Figure 3.2.

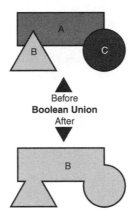

FIGURE 3.2
Boolean union operation.

Combine

A Boolean Combine takes two or more SmartShape symbols and combines them into one new SmartShape symbol. In the process, it generates a new Geometry section for the Geometry path of each of the former symbols. Wherever two Geometry paths overlap, the fill between them will be negated and that area will be "transparent" (contain no fill). The selection order in providing the selection set of symbols to be used in this operation is highly important. The first symbol selected provides the content for all Text, Line, and Fill styles, as well as all Formatting options. For the before and after operations, see Figure 3.3.

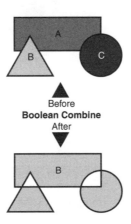

FIGURE 3.3
Boolean combine operation.

3

MODIFYING VISIO
SMARTSHAPE
SYMBOLS

Fragment

A Boolean Fragment takes two or more SmartShape symbols and performs an analysis on them. Wherever Geometry paths overlap and create a unique new bounded area, a new SmartShape symbol is generated. Wherever Geometry paths overlap and leave a portion of the Geometry isolated, a new SmartShape symbol is generated. Therefore, in three overlapping circles where the three share a common overlapping core and adjacent circles share overlapping areas as well, seven new SmartShape symbols are created as a result of the Boolean Fragment. (Additionally (this is not documented folks), if you have four distinct lines that cross over each other to enclose a bounded area, a Boolean Fragment operation will create a new SmartShape symbol from the bounded area and trim off the "tails," leaving you with a new filled polygon SmartShape symbol). The selection order in providing the selection set of symbols to be used in this operation is highly important. The first symbol selected provides the content for all Text, Line, and Fill styles as well as all Formatting options. For the before and after operations, see Figure 3.4.

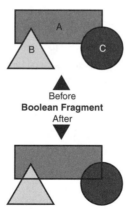

FIGURE 3.4

Boolean fragment operation.

Intersect

A Boolean Intersect takes two or more SmartShape symbols and performs an analysis on them. It looks for the areas in the selection set that are common to ALL of the symbols. With only the commonly shared filled areas, Intersect creates a new SmartShape symbol and destroys all of the former symbols. This leaves a new unique SmartShape symbol representing the intersection of the former symbols. The selection order in providing the selection set of symbols to be used in this operation is highly important. The first symbol selected provides the content for all Text, Line, and Fill styles as well as all Formatting options. For the before and after operations, see Figure 3.5.

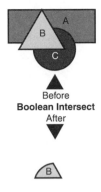

FIGURE 3.5

Boolean intersect operation.

Subtract

A Boolean Subtract takes two or more SmartShape symbols and subtracts the filled areas of the second and remaining symbols from the filled area of the first symbol. Subtract then destroys all of the former symbols and creates a new SmartShape symbol that represents the remainder area. The selection order in providing the selection set of symbols to be used in this operation is highly important. The first symbol is the area to be subtracted from, and the remaining symbols are the areas to be subtracted. The first symbol selected provides the content for all Text, Line, and Fill styles as well as all Formatting options. For the before and after operations, see Figure 3.6.

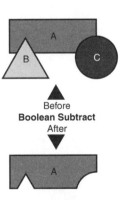

FIGURE 3.6

Boolean subtract operation.

We'll look at the Boolean editing operations next. The operations are

- Join
- Trim
- Offset...

I'll detail these for you.

Join

A Boolean Join takes two or more SmartShape symbols and joins them into a single new SmartShape symbol with a separate Geometry section for each former symbol. It then destroys the former symbols. This is similar to a Combine. However, the Join operation is used for non-closed geometry path symbols such as line segments and arcs. The first symbol selected provides the content for all Text, Line, and Fill styles as well as all Formatting options. For the before and after operations, see Figure 3.7.

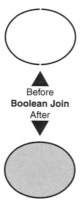

FIGURE 3.7

Boolean join operation.

Trim

A Boolean Trim takes two or more SmartShape symbols and trims them at the intersection point of each Geometry path crossing. The Trim then creates entirely new SmartShape symbols for each discrete new line or arc segment, destroying the former symbols. This is similar to the Fragment. However, the Trim operation is used for non-closed geometry path symbols such as line segments and arcs. The first symbol selected provides the content for all Text, Line, and Fill styles, as well as all Formatting options. For the before and after operations, see Figure 3.8.

FIGURE 3.8
Boolean trim operation.

Offset...

A Boolean Offset operation takes an open or closed path SmartShape symbols and analyzes the path. It then creates two new SmartShape symbols based on the offset distance a user types in the dialog box and offsets the path to both sides. This operation leaves the original SmartShape symbol intact and creates two entirely new SmartShape symbols as well. In the case of closed Geometry paths, the resulting new symbols will have their FillPattern cell in the Fill Format section of their ShapeSheet set to a value of zero, and the symbol will not be filled. Simply set the FillPattern to a value of one to see the fill in the new SmartShape symbols. The symbol selected as the base provides the content for all Text, Line, and Fill styles, as well as all Formatting options. For the before and after operations, see Figure 3.9.

3

MODIFYING VISIO
SMARTSHAPE
SYMBOLS

FIGURE 3.9
Boolean offset operation.

The final set of operations, the Utilities, contains

- Fit Curve
- Custom Fit…
- Reverse Ends
- Update Alignment Box

I'll detail these for you.

Fit Curve

A Boolean Fit Curve analyzes the selected SmartShape symbol and reduces the number of Geometry rows in the ShapeSheet by converting rows to the appropriate Spline, Arc, and Line segments. It changes the rows within the Geometry section but does not alter the remainder of the ShapeSheet.

Custom Fit…

A Boolean Custom Fit Curve analyzes the selected SmartShape symbol and reduces the number of Geometry rows in the ShapeSheet by converting rows to the appropriate Spline, Arc, and Line segments. It utilizes a dialog box that allows the user to specify the recognition of Periodic Splines, Circular Arcs, and Cusps and Bumps. It also allows for the specification of Error tolerance. It changes the rows within the Geometry section but does not alter the remainder of the ShapeSheet.

Reverse Ends

The Reverse Ends utility analyzes a selected Line segment and reverses the begin point and end point for the Line segment.

Update Alignment Box

If a SmartShape symbol has been created and the Protection section in that symbol's ShapeSheet has set the LockCalkWH to TRUE, geometry can be relocated outside the boundary box. If the LockCalcWH has been set to FALSE and geometry exists outside the sizing box for the symbol, selecting Update Alignment box analyzes the symbol and recalculates the boundary box at the total extents of the symbol.

You now have the tools you need to create your own highly complex Geometry paths without having to labor over the creation. Remember to use these tools *before* you begin adding intelligence to your symbols.

In the next chapter, we will discuss Master SmartShape symbols; that is, symbols that are accessible to many drawings and are highly reusable. We will look carefully at Visio Stencils and how they function, how to create custom Stencils, and all of the perameters controlling them. We will look at what happens when you instance a Master SmartShape symbol into a Visio diagram and study in depth the concepts of Inheritance and Local Formatting. Finally, we will also learn how to create Template files so new diagrams can be easily created based on a totally controlled environment.

SmartShape Symbol Reuse

IN THIS CHAPTER

All right—time for a little breather from working within Visio's ShapeSheet environment. I want to take a wee bit of time to discuss the concept of Master SmartShape symbols and what they can give both you as a developer and to your end-users of Visio.

First, let's define exactly what a Master Shape is. A Master Shape is a Visio SmartShape symbol that resides on either a Visio diagram's local stencil (the document stencil), or on a Visio "standalone" Stencil file (a file with an extension of .VSS). The power of a Master Shape is twofold. Firstly, when symbols are dragged from Stencils to Diagram pages, the resultant SmartShape symbol is an instance of the Master. This means that it inherits much of what it is from the Master and is therefore much, much more efficient than a symbol that was uniquely created and copied again and again on the diagram page. Secondly, a Visio Stencil file is its own file. Therefore, it can be transported and shared with any Visio user. This means that the Master symbols you create and place on a unique stencil are available not only to the current diagram but to any diagram on your desktop, and furthermore to any user of Visio who has a copy of your Stencil file.

How, then, do you create a Master Shape in Visio? The process is actually deceptively simple. To create a Master Shape, simply drag any SmartShape symbol from a diagram page to a Stencil that has been opened as read-write. Under Visio 5.0, you must explicitly open the Stencil file to be read-write. Under Visio 2000, if the Stencil has been opened read-only, you will be prompted to let Visio change the status to read-write. Then simply drop the SmartShape symbol onto the Stencil—you have created a Master Shape.

Actually, we must learn more before we can fully exploit the power of Master Shapes. One of the concepts I want to make clear is the concept of Grouping. Remember grouping from Chapter 3, "Modifying Visio SmartShape Symbols and Groups of Symbols"? Imagine you have three symbols you want to drag over to a Stencil and create as a single Master. Not a problem. Select all three and drag them over to the Stencil and drop them. Master Created! But wait—when you attempt to drag the Master off the Stencil and drop it back into the diagram, you find you only have one symbol. You had expected the three symbols to be available to you. What happened?

When you drag several symbols to a Stencil and make a Master, they are held on the stencil as separate unique SmartShape symbols. When you drag this Master off the stencil and drop back into the diagram, Visio groups the symbols on drop. You must explicitly select Shape, Grouping, Ungroup to get your three symbols back again. I strongly recommend that you group the symbols *before* you create the Master. Visio will not need to create a new Group every time you attempt to instance the Master. This is far more efficient and will create much better diagrams.

Let's walk through the procedures for creating a new Master on a New Stencil.

1. Select File, Stencils, New Stencil from the menus. A new Stencil window is opened. It will be "unnamed" and contain the name Stencil1, Stencil2, and so on on its title bar.

2. Select the symbol you want to be your Master Shape. Here, my recommendation is to use Ctrl+drag to drag it over to the Stencil. This creates a copy of the SmartShape symbol as a Master. Had you simply dragged it over, it would have moved it to the stencil and deleted it from the diagram. This is the difference between copying and moving (using a very old DOS metaphor).

3. Activate the Stencil window and select File, Save As from the menus. Select the Save As Type list for .VSS (Stencil) and then click OK.

That's all there is to it. You can now distribute your custom SmartShape symbol(s) to any Visio user that needs to utilize the symbol in their diagram. Notice that the new Master in the Stencil has a less-than-desirable name of "Master.0". Don't worry, you can change this. Now, let's look at the options for dealing with a Master on a Stencil. Right-click the new Master that you just created. Notice that the context menu has the following options: Cut, Copy, Paste, Paste Shortcut, Delete, Select All, Duplicate, Create Shortcut, New Master, Master Properties, Edit Master, Edit Icon, Help.

Quite a few of these are highly self-explanatory; however, I want to concentrate on four of the options:

- Master Properties
- Edit Master
- Edit Icon
- Help

I'll detail them below as they apply to Visio 2000. For Visio 5.0, these are very similar, although you might find a small difference in where these items are placed in the User Interface.

Master Properties

When you right-click and select Master Properties, the Master Properties dialog box appears. This dialog box is broken into two discrete sections: Properties and Behavior. Let's start with the Properties section.

There are four items here, as seen in Figure 4.1: Name, Prompt, Icon Size, and Align Master Name.

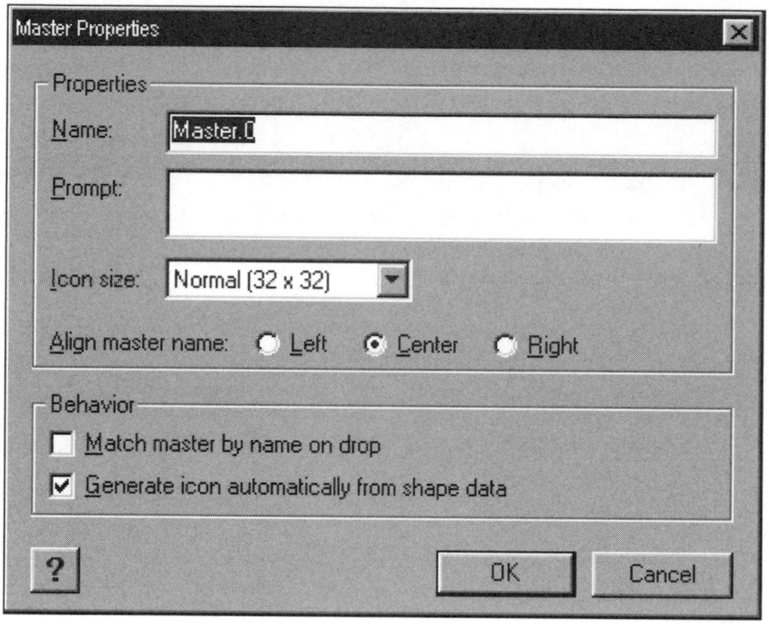

FIGURE 4.1

Master Properties dialog box.

The Name is a text box control. Here you can enter a new name for this master. (This is how you get rid of the Master.0 mess.) The name you provide persists. Instances that are generated from it will then have instance designations appended. For example, if you changed the Name from Master.0 to InletValve, the first instance of this master in a drawing would be InletValve; the next instance would be InletValve.[n], where [n] is the unique identifier number for the instance in the drawing.

The Prompt is a text box control as well. In this text entry field, you can place a line of descriptive text that appears on the status line at the bottom of the Visio window. This prompt is an assistance to the user of your Master. The text should tell the user what the symbol does and why it is to be used in the diagram. It should NOT restate the obvious. For example, in the Valve we are dealing with, the prompt should read "Control valve for high temperature inline fuel flow application," rather than "Drag and drop a valve symbol into the diagram." If the user can not understand that he is dragging and dropping the symbol while he is actually performing the act, perhaps he should switch to a different graphics application, one with a less intuitive interface. (I won't name any names here!)

The Icon Size is a drop-down list box control. You have four choices for the size of the icon as it appears in the Stencil window: Normal [32×32], Tall [32×64], Wide [64×32], and Double

[64×64]. Although Visio was created in Seattle, the Mecca of coffee drinks and lattés, you still cannot get a "double-tall" icon (sorry…bad bit of Seattle humor).

The Align Master Name is a set of Radio Button controls. Here you can choose how you wish the Name of the Master to appear under the Icon for the Master: left justified, centered, or right justified.

The next section is the Behavior section. This section contains only two controls, both check box controls: the Match Master by Name on Drop and the Generate Icon Automatically from Shape Data.

The Match Master by name on drop requires just a little explanation. Imagine that you have two standalone stencils open. Stencil "A" contains a master called Valve that is shaped like a triangle and is set to a red fill color. Stencil "B" contains a master called Valve which is shaped like a rectangle and is set to a blue fill color. The diagram currently contains no instances of either Valve.

When you drop the red triangle Valve from Stencil "A," a copy of that Master is placed in the current diagram's local Stencil. The diagram now knows about the valve. What happens when you drop the blue rectangle Valve from Stencil "B"? Correct! You get the blue rectangle Master. Because Visio realized that there were two symbols with the same name, Visio intervened on your behalf and gave the first Master the Name Valve and the second the Master Name Valve.[n]. If, however, the Master for the red triangle Valve on Stencil "A" had the Match Master by Name on Drop selected, after it was dropped, it would look for any other master with that same name and use *only* the Red Triangle as its definition.

Generate Icon Automatically from Shape Data controls whether every time you make changes to the Master SmartShape symbol, Visio regenerates a new icon that approximates the look of the actual symbol. If this is checked, Automatic generation takes place; if not, any customization you might make to the icon using Visio's Icon editor will remain intact.

Edit Master

Selecting Edit Master opens up a new window in Visio where you can make changes to any aspect of the master you have selected. It is just like the diagram window. Through it, you also have full access to the ShapeSheet for that Master shape and any subordinate SmartShape symbols should the symbol be a group symbol. When you make changes and close the window, one of two things will happen. A dialog box will appear asking you if you wish to save the changes to this Master. However, if the master is a local master, a dialog box will appear asking you if you want to save the changes to this Master *and* all of its instances, if you have any instances of this Master in the currently open diagram.

Edit Icon

The Visio Icon editor is a typical Icon editor. You can design your own icon for a Master Shape here. The size of the icon is determined by the Icon Size setting in the Master Properties dialog box. By default in Visio 2000, the background for the icon is the same as the Stencil itself (or transparent). By default under Visio 5.0, the Icon Background color is yellow for 1D symbols and gray for 2D symbols. Under any version of Visio, you are free to alter this to suit your needs.

Help

I mentioned quite a while ago that Visio contains many help mechanisms to ensure that the user of a Visio solution could obtain the assistance required to make working with Visio and your Visio solution very easy and intuitive. As you can see, every SmartShape symbol and especially those being used as Masters can have Help associated with them. In order to access this help, all the user must do is right-click any SmartShape symbol or Master Shape and select the Help option from the context menu.

How then do you associate the Help with the symbol itself? For a SmartShape symbol in a diagram, select the symbol. Then select Format, Special from the menu. For a Master, first Select Edit Master from the context menu for the Master. When you are in the Master editing window, select the SmartShape symbol and then select Format, Special from the menu. In the resulting dialog box, you will see a text entry box for Help. In this text box, you must enter the properly formatted context for the associated help file. The format is as follows:

Under Visio 5.0, enter the Help File name, which will have a .HLP extension, followed by the pound sign or hash mark (#) and the context number. Under Visio 2000, enter the Help filename, which will have a .CHM extension, followed by the pound sign or hash mark (#), followed by the context number. Your Help compiler will, due to your labors during the Help file development, generate the context numbers for each topic. Remember that whereas Visio 5.0 and preceding versions use traditional Windows Help file format, Visio 2000 uses the new Windows HTML style Help file format. Do note, however, that the older .HLP format files still work under Visio 2000.

Here are two examples of properly formatted Help file entries:

Visio 5.0	Shape.HLP#18370
Visio 2000	Vis_SOCS.CHM#23469

It is understood that you have placed your custom Help file in either Visio's Help directory or in a directory appended to Visio's search path for Help files. To do this, do the following:

Under both Visio 2000 and Visio 5.0, select Tools, Options from the menu. In the Options dialog box, select the File Paths tab. Append to the existing Help File paths a semicolon (;) and the path to your own Help file directory. Click OK.

Stencils

Visio Stencils are one of the things that make Visio so unique. The concept of stencils came from old engineering architecture and data processing school assignments. When drawing diagrams, students used to work with green Berol Ellipse templates and Flowchart templates. These templates or "stencils" were a tracing guide for the needed symbols. Each stencil contained numerous symbol outlines, all related in a common subject or theme. Visio forwarded this concept and created Visio Stencils of SmartShape symbols. The Stencils are green as a tribute to those old stencils. Visio Stencils are an organizational structure for SmartShape symbols. SmartShape symbols for a particular solution are grouped together on a Stencil and are accessible when the end user begins a diagram based on a particular diagram type.

We have already seen how Masters can be added to Stencils, how new Stencils can be created and saved, and how, under Visio 2000, Visio will open a Stencil in read-write mode that was previously opened only in read-only mode.

Stencils may, under both Visio 5.0 and 2000, be docked or floating. Under Visio 2000, Stencils may be docked to any of the four edges of a diagram: top, bottom, left, or right.

Stencils may display Icons and Names, Icons only, or Names only for all of the Masters on the Stencil. To affect this change, right-click the title bar for the Stencil and select the appropriate item from the context menu.

Instancing Master Shapes

For those of you who are familiar with object-oriented programming, this should be a very easy concept to grasp. Each one of these instances looks back to the Local Master for information about what makes them function: their geometry, their custom formulas and properties, and their formatting and behavior. Instancing Masters is *far* more efficient than creating duplicates of "raw" SmartShape symbols on a page.

Important Concept Number Eight

When you drag a Master from a standalone Stencil into a diagram and drop it on the drawing page, you actually first create a copy of that Master in the diagram's local Stencil (or document Stencil). This is very important, as we shall see in a moment. First, this means that after the symbol is instanced in the diagram, the Stencil on

continues

which it initially resided is no longer necessary. This makes the diagram even that much more portable. Each copy that is dropped onto the drawing page is an Instance of the Local Master.

To digress a wee bit: A client of Visio's came to me with a SmartShape symbol that had been made into a Master and resided on a Stencil. The client was complaining because when the symbol was instanced, Visio seemed to come to an absolute halt and would not respond for an inordinately long time. I was asked to perform an analysis of this symbol to ascertain just what was making the performance so poor.

I began dissecting the symbol. It represented a piece of electronic test equipment with hundreds of knobs and switches. What I found formed the basis for numerous lectures and papers I subsequently wrote.

Firstly the developer created a circle (for a knob). He then created a small rectangle to act as the pointer on the face of the knob. He grouped these two together to act as one knob. He then Ctrl+dragged a copy of the knob to make a duplicate of the "raw" group knob. Remember, because he grouped the circle and the rectangle, he has three ShapeSheets for one group. He then grouped the two group shapes together to make a pair of knobs as a single symbol. Now he has seven ShapeSheets and seven not-so-SmartShape symbols in the one group; three for each inner-group and one for the outer group shell. He then Ctrl+dragged out a duplicate of THIS group of seven and made another two-knob cluster. He then grouped THIS pair of clusters to make a four-knob cluster. He now has 15 symbols nested four levels deep. He repeated this process of duplicating and grouping until he could see 40 knobs. He actually now had 159 shapes nested 8 levels deep. He then copied the entire piece of equipment to a Stencil and began instancing the collection of more than 80 shapes all dragged to the stencil, which meant that Visio had to group the collection with each drop and ferret down the now nine levels to recalculate every PinX and PinY for the drop.

Until he created the "master" from the collection of symbols, he was purely working with unique symbols. No inheritance was being implemented at all. Between the severe nesting and the complete lack of inheritance, the performance, was, of course, abysmal. I ripped the entire assembly apart and created a single knob by using a Boolean Combine operation between the circle and the rectangle. This gave me one ShapeSheet with two Geometry sections. I then made a Master of the knob and instanced that knob 40 times. 40 ShapeSheets, 40 SmartShape symbols. Inheritance ensured that most of the information about the knob was being seen only once and then referenced. I made a master of the total piece of equipment after grouping the equipment as one SmartShape symbol. When I instanced the new equipment symbol, it popped up immediately and could be moved easily when it needed to be relocated. When I needed to make a change to the equipment, I needed to make the change only in the Local Stencil's Master and all of the equipment items took on the change.

The moral here? Do not nest groups deeply; do not copy raw symbols. Use masters. Group once before collecting things to make the final Master for complex symbology. Your performance will be light years ahead of improper mucking about with hundreds of raw shapes. This is very important for the developer to understand. It will mean the difference between a great solution and an extremely poor one.

Inheritance Versus Local Formatting

As I just pointed out in detail, when you drag a Master from a Stencil into a diagram, Visio first makes a copy of that Master in the diagram's Local Stencil and then instances it on the drawing page. The next time you perform the same operation, Visio looks at the Local Stencil first and asks, "Do I have a copy of this here?" If it finds a copy in its Local Stencil, Visio simply uses that definition to instance another of the symbols at the appropriate location.

Why is this important? Let me illustrate via another brief tale. Suppose that you had just used Visio to complete the drawings for your new corporate headquarters. Now suppose as the Fire Warden reviews the plans for egress and access regulation confirmation, he discovers that all of the fire doors in the building are currently 34 inches wide, contrary to regulations that clearly state they must be 42 inches wide. Furthermore, the doors must be marked in red and have a special symbol associated with them to annotate them on the drawings as a fire door. If you did not have a master for the Fire Door, you would have to go to each and every door and manually change the door opening width, the color, and add the special tag, a daunting and tedious process at best. However, because you are indeed using Visio, you can open the Local Stencil, open the Master for the fire door, change its opening width from 34 to 42 inches, change its fill to red, and add the wee symbol to annotate it. You need do this only once and then close the Master. Instantly, every fire door in the building is updated. This saves many, many hours of work!

Think back and remember the Shape Transform section of the ShapeSheet. There are the PinX and PinY cells as well as many more. There are numerous other cells in many other sections as well. When you instance a SmartShape symbol into a diagram, the only cells that are NOT inherited from the Local Master are the PinX and PinY cell formulas and values. This makes the symbol very efficient.

How can you tell what is inherited and what is not? Select a symbol for any Visio Stencil. Instance that symbol. Select Window, Show Document Stencil (Visio 2000) or Window, Show Master Shapes (Visio 5.0). Notice how the Master you just instanced is now in the diagram's Local Stencil. Making sure that the symbol you just instanced is selected, open the ShapeSheet for that symbol. With the ShapeSheet window active, select View, Sections from the menu. In the dialog box, click the All button. Click OK. Note that in the ShapeSheet, any cell with its formula or value shown in blue is a Local override, whereas any formula or value that is shown in black is Inherited. Activate the diagram window. Make some change to the size, orientation, rotation, or formatting of the symbol. See in the ShapeSheet window how the cell changes from black to blue. This assists you the developer in locating Local Overrides in any given SmartShape symbol.

When a local override is registered in a ShapeSheet cell, that cell no longer inherits from the Local Master. When a change is made to the Local Master, that change is normally proliferated down through every instance of that Master. However, a Local Override blocks this inheritance.

So this is just grand! Because you might have made a local override by changing the formatting or size, you have just eliminated the possibility to gain the inheritance for that cell for the future if the local Master changes. How, then, can you regain the inheritance? Pay close attention, folks; this is not covered in the documentation. Here's the trick:

Click into the offending cell. Wipe out the entire formula that resides in the cell and replace it with a single equal sign (=). Visio looks at what resides in that cell. Visio says it is not legal to have absolutely no formula in this cell; therefore, because YOU didn't tell me what to put in here, I'll go to the last known valid source for that information and put that into the cell. Visio then looks back at the Local Master, takes the value for that cell from the Master, and fills in the cell in the Instance, thereby regaining the inheritance for the instance. Pretty neat stuff!

Templates in Visio

When you work in Microsoft Word or Excel, you often begin a new document or spreadsheet based on a specific template file. That template provides you with the working environment you need to create the particular document or spreadsheet for the task you have chosen. Similarly, when you begin a new Visio diagram, you often base your new diagram on a particular diagram type: organizational chart, flowchart, business process diagram, or network design. This is done by choosing a particular template in Visio. Visio understands that you do not want to alter the original template but, rather, that you want to create a new diagram based upon the parameters and environment that the particular template provides.

A template is actually a very easy thing to create. A template consists of a drawing, any associated Stencils of Visio SmartShape symbols, and the specific layout of all of the graphic elements that enhance the understanding of the particular diagram type you wish to produce.

Important Concept Number Nine

In order for you to create a Template in Visio, everything in your environment must be named. That is, the basic drawing file and the stencils must all be named files.

When we begin to discuss automation, you will discover that you can attach code to these templates so when a new document is created based on this Template, certain code is executed. Furthermore, each time the document is opened in the future, code may be executed as well.

Here are the steps to creating your own template file:

1. Create a new drawing, either based on no given drawing type, or based on a template that is most beneficial for your solution.

2. Create any custom SmartShape symbols that you need for your solution.

3. Add these new custom SmartShape symbols to an external stencil, or a series of external Stencils.

4. Save this Stencil or these Stencils each under their own name.

5. Save the drawing file under its own name.

6. Now Select File, Save As from the menus. In the dialog box, set the Save As Type listing to Template (.VST) and name the template. Click Save.

Now to test your work, close every window within Visio. Select File, New, Choose Drawing Type from the menus. In the dialog box, click the Browse Templates button. Navigate to where you stored your Template file. Select it and click Open. Did the environment come back exactly as you saved it? Note the position, size, and relationship of all windows in your environment. See how this makes it easier to create solutions based on your requirements?

If your solution would be enhanced by providing information already on the drawing page such as a title block and prototypical information, ensure that it is also part of the basic drawing.

Now that you are comfortable building your own Stencils of SmartShape symbols and creating an environment from which to work, we need to get back to work and learn more about enhancing SmartShape symbol's behavior. In the next chapter, "Enhancing SmartShape Symbol Behavior," you will learn about ShapeSheet-based events. You will look at each cell in the Events section in detail. You will learn about creating your own custom additions to a SmartShape symbol's right-click or context menu by creating an Actions section to that symbol's ShapeSheet.

You will also learn about the page in Visio and how it has its own ShapeSheet, as well as how to exploit that page's ShapeSheet to make your own symbols more intelligent. You will explore Visio's concept of layers and learn how Visio can help you utilize them as organizational and query-related tools.

Enhancing SmartShape Symbol Behavior

IN THIS CHAPTER

ShapeSheet-Based Events

All Visio SmartShape symbols are objects. Those of you who are programmers already know an object has three things that distinguish it as such: properties, methods, and events. The cells of a SmartShape symbol's ShapeSheet equate to the properties. The user directs many of the methods, and the Events section of a ShapeSheet controls the most basic of the available events.

Drag out a rectangle SmartShape symbol onto a page and open its ShapeSheet. If you must, ensure that all sections are visible by selecting View, Sections. Click All and then OK. Now scroll down in the ShapeSheet until you find the Events section of the ShapeSheet. Notice that there are five supported events. They are

- EventDblClick
- EventXFMod
- EventDrop
- TheText
- TheData

Keep in mind that Event cells are evaluated only when the event occurs, not upon formula entry. I'll detail each of these cells in the following sections.

EventDblClick

Any formula that resides in the EventDblClick cell is evaluated whenever the SmartShape symbol is double-clicked. By default, a formula that states =OPENTEXTWIN() resides in the EventDblClick cell. This Visio function opens the text-editing mode for the SmartShape symbol. This is the default behavior a user expects for any basic SmartShape symbol. You can modify this cell to contain any function or Automation call you desire.

EventXFMod

Any formula that resides in the EventXFMod cell is evaluated whenever the SmartShape symbol is altered in any manner in one of the following modes:

- Change in height
- Change in width
- Change in aspect ratio
- Change in orientation (placement angle)
- Change in placement position in X or Y on the page
- Change in flip status across the X Axis
- Change in flip status across the Y Axis

By default, the formula in this cell reads <No Formula>; that is, the cell is totally blank. You can modify this cell to contain any function or Automation call you prefer.

EventDrop

Any formula that resides in the EventDrop cell is evaluated whenever the SmartShape symbol is instanced either by a drop from a Visio external Stencil, from a Local Stencil (Document Stencil), or by Ctrl+dragging a duplicate onto the page. By default, the formula in this cell reads <No Formula>; that is, the cell is totally blank. You can modify this cell to contain any function or Automation call you would like.

TheText

Any formula that resides in the TheText cell is evaluated whenever the SmartShape symbol's text is modified in any manner. If text is added, deleted, or modified, this cell will be evaluated. By default, the formula in this Cell reads <No Formula>; that is, the cell is totally blank. You can modify this cell to contain any function or Automation call you want.

There is a behavior particular to this event that confuses developers. Keep in mind that the text that resides on any SmartShape symbol is a continuous stream. The properties of the text block's width, height, margins, and orientation place formatting characters into the text stream to facilitate line wrapping and line breaking. When the height or width of a SmartShape symbol is altered, by default, this alters the height or width of the text block. This forces a recalculation of the text stream to facilitate new line wrap and break points. This, then, triggers the evaluation of TheText just as if the text had been altered during editing. The developer is led to assume the cell had been erroneously evaluated as if it were an EventXFMod evaluation when, in fact, it is a totally separate event.

TheData

As of Visio 2000, the TheData cell is still reserved for future use; therefore, any formula placed into this cell will not be evaluated.

An Events Lab Exercise

Here's a lab exercise for you to try that utilizes the Events section to cycle the Fill Foreground color through the first 24 possible colors. To create this SmartShape symbol, drag out a rectangle. Any size will do. Open the ShapeSheet for the rectangle and add a User-defined section to the ShapeSheet. Now scroll down to the Events section of the ShapeSheet (by now I should no longer have to tell you about viewing all sections, should I?). In the Events section, find the EventDblClick cell—the cell controlling the SmartShape symbol's Double Click behavior. Enter the following formula:

```
EventDblClick: "=SETF("FillForegnd", FillForegnd+1)"
```

Scroll back up the ShapeSheet and enter the following formula in the value cell of the first row of the User-defined section of the ShapeSheet:

```
User defined...: "=IF(FillForegnd>23,SETF("FillForegnd",0),0)"
```

Scroll down through the ShapeSheet until you can see the Fill Format section and the FillForegnd cell. Return to the diagram window and begin double-clicking the SmartShape symbol. Notice how the color for the symbol is changing. The value in the FillForegnd cell is continuously incrementing with each double-click of the SmartShape symbol. When the value in the FillForegnd cell goes above 23, note it is reset back to zero. Let's analyze the two formulas we created and see how they work.

We'll take the EventDblClick cell first. The formula was

```
"=SETF("FillForegnd", FillForegnd+1)"
```

In other words, this states, "Set the value of the cell whose quoted name is FillForegnd to the value currently in the FillForegnd cell plus the integer one." In more concise terms, it says, "With each double-click of the SmartShape symbol, increment the value that resides in the FillForegnd cell."

The User-defined cell holds the formula that was

```
"=IF(FillForegnd>23,SETF("FillForegnd",0),0)"
```

In plain English, this states, "If the value that resides in the FillForegnd cell ever gets above 23, set the value of the cell whose quoted name is FillForegnd to a value of zero; otherwise, do nothing at all."

Each and every time the SmartShape symbol is double-clicked, both of these cells are evaluated. The value of the FillForegnd cell is incremented and then checked against the IF() criteria and reset to zero if it gets above the acceptable limitation.

From this example, you can begin to see the power of Visio's recalculation engine and how with a well-crafted formula or two you can make SmartShape symbols that respond to actions taken by the user at the User Interface level.

The Actions Section of the ShapeSheet

The Actions section of the ShapeSheet is not included by default. This section must be added explicitly by opening the ShapeSheet and selecting Insert, Sections; checking the check box for Actions; and then clicking OK. The Actions section will then be added to the ShapeSheet above the Geometry section. The Actions section gives the user additional items on the context (right-click) menu for the selected SmartShape symbol. The developer, in programming the

Actions row, has the ability to direct the placement of the item(s) either to the top or bottom of the context menu as well as control what action will be taken when the context menu item is selected by the user.

The Actions section consists of one or more rows (rows may be added by planting your cursor in an existing Actions row and selecting Insert, Row or Insert Row After from the menu). Each Action row consists of five cells. They are

- Action
- Menu
- Prompt
- Checked
- Disabled

I'll detail these cells one at a time:

Action

The Action cell holds any valid formula or function that defines the action to be taken upon the user selecting the associated menu item from the context menu.

Menu

The Menu cell holds the actual text string that is the Menu item visible to the user when the context menu is selected for the selected SmartShape symbol. The menu items are sequentially listed in accordance with the row order in the Actions section, with the following enhancements:

- If the first character of the Menu item is an underscore (_), a divider bar will be placed ABOVE the menu item in the context menu.
- If the first character of the Menu item is a percent character (%), the menu item will be displayed at the bottom of the context menu.
- If an ampersand (&) is placed immediately prior to any letter in the Menu Item string, that letter will act as an accelerator (hot key) to activate that menu item.

These three extensions may be used in conjunction with each other on any one or more Menu items to place the Menu item(s) where you desire, add separator bars over them, and add accelerator keys to them.

For example, here are five Menu items and how they would appear in a context menu:

Re&set
_Go Left

Go Right

%Go Up

%Go Down

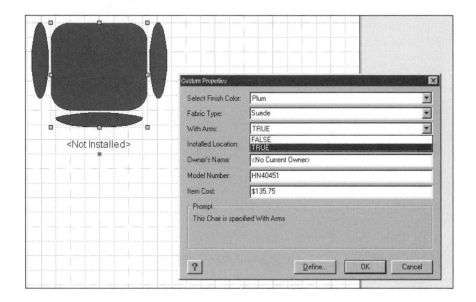

Prompt

The Prompt cell holds a text string that displays as a prompt in Visio's Status Line when the user places his mouse cursor over the selected context Actions menu item prior to clicking it. This prompt is an assistance to the user to guide them in the functionality and usage of this particular Action.

Checked

The Checked cell holds a Boolean FALSE or TRUE value that displays a check mark as the first character in the menu item for the Actions row in the Context menu.

Disabled

The Disabled cell holds a Boolean FALSE or TRUE value that disables (grays out and makes unavailable) the menu item for the Actions row in the Context menu.

Let's put this knowledge to work for us. In this lab exercise, we want to create a Visio rectangle SmartShape symbol with a Context Menu item that forces the rectangle to be a square when the Context Menu Item is selected. The "squaring" of the rectangle symbol should be based upon whichever is greater, the height or the width.

Drag out a rectangle and open the ShapeSheet for the selected rectangle SmartShape symbol. Insert a User-defined section and name the new User-defined row User.FindMax. Insert an Actions section.

In the User-defined User.FindMax row, place the following formula in the Value cell:

```
"=IF(Width>Height,2,IF(Height>Width,1,0))"
```

In the Prompt cell, place the following formula:

```
="Determine which is greater, Height, Width or is it a Square"
```

In the Actions section, in the first row, type the following formula in the Action cell:

```
"=IF(User.FindMax<>0,IF(User.FindMax=1,SETF("Width",Height),
➥SETF("Height",Width)),0)"
```

In the Menu cell, place this formula:

```
="S&QUARE THE RECTANGLE"
```

In the Prompt cell, insert the following formula:

```
="Make the Rectangle a Square based on the greater proportion."
```

Place the following formula in the Checked cell:

```
"=IF(User.FindMax=0,TRUE,FALSE)"
```

In the Disabled cell, enter this formula:

```
=IF(User.FindMax=0,TRUE,FALSE)
```

Now let's test the SmartShape symbol. Ctrl+drag out a copy of the symbol. Tug on the sizing handles, both in height and width. Notice you have complete control over the sizing of the symbol. Right-click the symbol. The Context Menu displays the menu item SQUARE THE RECTANGLE. The "Q" in SQUARE is underlined. Either press the Q key or click the menu item. The symbol should change either its height or width to create a square of the maximum of either the height or width. Right-click the symbol. The Context Menu displays the Menu Item, but this time the menu item is disabled and checked. (It's grayed out and contains a check mark as the first character.) Resize the square to make it a rectangle again. Right-click the symbol. The context menu displays the menu item in an enabled mode again.

Here's what happened: The User-defined cell contains a formula that reads

```
"=IF(Width>Height,2,IF(Height>Width,1,0))"
```

Stated in plain English, "If the value in the width cell is greater than the value in the height cell, store a value of 2 in this User.FindMax Cell; otherwise, if the value in the height cell is greater than the value in the width cell, store a value of 1 in this User.FindMax Cell. If height and width are exactly equal, store a value of zero in this User.FindMax Cell."

The formula checks which dimension is greater, height or width. It returns two if width is greater, one if height is greater, and zero if it is exactly a square.

Now the Action cell of the first row of the Actions section contains a formula that reads

```
"=IF(User.FindMax<>0,IF(User.FindMax=1,SETF("Width",Height),
➥SETF("Height",Width)),0)"
```

Put more simply, "If the Value in the User.FindMax Cell is not equal to zero, (not a square), and if the value in the User.FindMax is equal to one (height is greater than width), set the value of the cell whose quoted name is width to a value that is identical to the value stored in the height cell. Otherwise, set the value of the cell whose quoted name is height to a value that is identical to the value stored in the width cell; otherwise, do nothing at all."

This formula first checks to see if the height and width are exactly equal. If they are, it does nothing at all. If they are not, it then finds the greater of the two, height or width, and sets the value of the smaller to the value of the larger.

The Action Section's first row's Menu cell contains the formula

```
="S&QUARE THE RECTANGLE"
```

Notice that the Menu item itself has the hot key "Q" underlined. If the user simply presses "Q", the formula in the Action Cell is evaluated. Similarly, if the menu item is clicked with the mouse, the formula in the Action Cell is evaluated.

The Action section's first row's Checked cell contains the formula that reads

```
"=IF(User.FindMax=0,TRUE,FALSE)"
```

In other words, "If the value stored in the User.FindMax cell is equal to zero (a square), place a check mark as the first character in the Menu string. Otherwise, do not place a check mark as the first character in the Menu string."

The Action section's first row's Disabled cell contains the formula that reads

```
"=IF(User.FindMax=0,TRUE,FALSE)"
```

Stated in plain English, "If the value stored in the User.FindMax cell is equal to zero (a square), gray out and disable the Menu string; otherwise, do not gray out and disable the Menu string."

Here's another example. You will find on the companion CD-ROM a Visio drawing file of a chair SmartShape symbol. Open this file and right-click the chair. Notice the Context Menu has a menu item that states "Modify/Set Chair Parameters." When you select the menu item, a dialog appears that will allow you to toggle the visability of the chair's arms.

How is this done? Remember how the Geometry section of a given ShapeSheet contains a cell known as the NoShow cell? Under Visio 5.0, this is labeled as the B cell. Under Visio 2000, this is labeled the NoShow cell. When this cell is set to TRUE, that geometry section simply does not display. The chair is a single SmartShape symbol comprised of four separate Geometry sections; one for the chair's seat, one for the chair's back, and one for each of the chair's two arms. A User-defined section has been added to the ShapeSheet. This first User-defined row, User.Arms, simply contains a value of either FALSE or TRUE. The Actions section contains one row. The Action has the following formula:

```
"=SETF("User.Arms", NOT(User.Arms))"
```

Stated plainly, "set the value of the cell whose quoted name is User.Arms to a value that is the opposite the value currently stored in that cell; that is, if it is set to TRUE, make it FALSE, if it is FALSE, make it TRUE."

Each of the "arm" Geometry section's NoShow cells hold a formula that is an intercell reference. It reads

```
"=User.Arms"
```

The two Arm Geometry sections take their visibility conditions from the User-defined cell, and the value of the User-defined cell is toggled by the Action cell in the Actions section.

The menu in the Actions section was able to switch from saying "Hide Arms" to "Show Arms" and back again, depending on the status of the visibility of the arms. How was this accomplished?

The Menu cell in the Actions section holds the following formula:

```
"=IF(User.Arms=FALSE, "Hide Arms", "Show Arms")"
```

In plain English, "If the value in the User.Arms cell is FALSE, display the Menu Item "Hide Arms."; otherwise, display the menu item 'Show Arms'."

It is truly no more difficult than that. What you have just seen demonstrated is what Visio refers to as a Multi-Shape. A Multi-Shape is a Visio SmartShape symbol that can change its configuration to look like any number of differing symbols depending upon the current condition of the symbol. A classic example of this type of symbol is the Flowchart Shapes symbol found on the Basic Flowchart Shapes Stencil. When the SmartShape symbol is initially instanced, it appears as a Process symbol. When the user right-clicks and selects the context menu, four options appear: Process, Decision, Document, and Data. The currently selected option has the check mark.

If you dissect the Flowchart Shapes SmartShape symbol, you will see that it contains four Geometry Sections. It also contains an Actions section. In the Actions section, selecting any one of the Actions: Process, Decision, Document, or Data, simply sets the value of the Scratch.A1 cell to a given integer corresponding to the proper symbol requirements (1=Process, 2=Decision, 3=Document, and 4=Data). Each appropriate Geometry section's NoShow cell contains a formula that reads

```
"=NOT(Scratch.A1=[n])" where [n] is the proper integer for the required symbol.
```

The NOT() function is a Boolean function; that is, it can only return TRUE or FALSE. Remember that the NoShow cell is a Boolean TRUE or FALSE cell as well. NOT() looks at the argument in the formula, decides whether it is correct, and returns the opposite. If it returns FALSE, the NoShow cell will show that particular Geometry section; otherwise, it will not (returning TRUE).

As you gain a comfort level in working with Multi-Shape SmartShape symbol development, you will be able to build highly efficient symbols that will allow you to place on a Stencil one symbol that takes the place of many symbols. Think about the efficiency. As you drop the Master into this diagram, you add only one SmartShape symbol Master to the Local Stencil. As you continue to instance many of this same Master, you are still inheriting from the same Master. You are not only eliminating the number of Masters required to implement your solution but, by using instances, keeping your diagram small in file size, efficient, and very, very fast.

The Visio Page's ShapeSheet

Just as any SmartShape symbol in Visio has a ShapeSheet, so too does the page itself have its own ShapeSheet. Remember that all of these things (SmartShape symbols, pages, documents, and so on) are objects, and the ShapeSheet is effectively the interface to the object's properties, methods, and events.

Whereas the SmartShape symbol has a Shape Transform section in its ShapeSheet, the Page's ShapeSheet contains a Page Properties section. This section controls numerous aspects of the page's visual and performance characteristics. Under Visio 5.0, this Section contains eight cells. They are

- PageWidth
- PageHeight
- PageScale
- DrawingScale

- ShadowOffsetX
- ShadowOffsetY
- DrawingSizeType
- DrawingScaleType

Visio 2000 contains one additional cell. It is

- InhibitSnap

I will detail these cells in the paragraphs to come.

PageWidth

This cell contains the unit-ed number that controls the printed width of the page. As with any unit-ed cell, if you enter a "raw" number (a number without a unit attached), Visio will assume that you are referring to inches and append that for you.

PageHeight

This cell contains the unit-ed number that controls the printed height of the page.

PageScale

This cell contains the unit-ed number that represents the value of the page unit in the current drawing scale. The drawing scale for the page is the ratio of the page unit to the drawing unit shown in the DrawingScale cell.

DrawingScale

This cell contains the unit-ed number that represents the value of the drawing unit in the current drawing scale. The drawing scale for the page is the ratio of the page unit shown in the PageScale cell to the drawing unit.

ShadowOffsetX

This cell contains the unit-ed number that represents the distance in page units that a shape's drop shadow is offset horizontally from the shape.

ShadowOffsetY

This cell contains the unit-ed number that represents the distance in page units that a shape's drop shadow is offset vertically from the shape.

DrawingSizeType

This cell contains the integer value that determines the drawing size. The DrawingSizeType cell has the following eight valid values:

0	Same as printer
1	Fit page to drawing contents
2	Standard
3	Custom page size
4	Custom scaled drawing size
5	Metric (ISO)
6	ANSI engineering
7	ANSI architectural

DrawingScaleType

This cell contains the integer value that determines the drawing scale. The DrawingScaleType cell has the following six valid values:

0	NoScale
1	Architectural Scale
2	Civil Engineering Scale
3	Custom Scale
4	Metric
5	Mechanical Engineering Scale

The combination of the DrawingScaleType, DrawingSizeType, DrawingScale, PageScale, PageWidth, and PageHeight determine the size, scale, and units displayed for the page in the current Visio diagram.

InhibitSnap

This cell contains the Boolean FALSE or TRUE value that determines whether the shapes on a foreground page snap to other objects on the page and shapes on the background page. Set the value of this cell to TRUE to inhibit all snapping on the page, except for snapping to the ruler and grid, and set it to FALSE to enable snapping. This cell is available to Visio 2000 only.

A Title Block Exercise

Before we continue to the other two important page-oriented sections of the page's ShapeSheet, let's take a moment to run through a lab exercise designed to test your knowledge of the sections you already know and stretch your logical thinking just a wee bit further. We want to design a Visio SmartShape symbol that performs in the following manner:

- It resides on a Local Stencil as a Master.
- It can be dropped anywhere on the page and it will relocate itself properly.
- When it is dropped onto the page of the current document, it will always be one inch tall in printed size.
- When it is dropped onto the page of the current document, it will always have a one inch margin from the top of the diagram in printed size.
- When it is dropped onto the page of the current document, it will always have a one inch margin from both the left and right sides of the diagram in printed size.
- It cannot be flipped in either X or Y axis.
- It cannot be rotated from its original horizontal orientation.
- When it is dropped, it will immediately prompt you to enter your name and then place you into Text Entry mode for the SmartShape symbol just dropped.

Sound like a daunting task? Not really. The completed SmartShape symbol is on your companion CD-ROM. Let's take it a step at a time.

First, let's try instancing the Master to see if it performs as "advertised." Select File, Page Setup from the menu, select the Page Size tab, and set the page size to any size you desire (bonus points are given for using real logical page sizes). Select the Drawing Scale tab and set to any desired drawing scale (same bonus points apply here). Click OK. Now drag and drop the Who Am I Master from the Local Stencil onto the drawing page. Drop it anywhere at all. The Symbol relocated itself properly, a dialog box popped up reminding you to enter your name and sign in, and then you were immediately placed in Text Entry mode. When you click out of the symbol, the symbol conforms to the required specifications. Open up the ShapeSheet for the Who Am I shape instance. Look at the cells in the symbol's Shape Transform section.

The Width cell contains the following formula:

```
"=GUARD(ThePage!PageWidth-((ThePage!DrawingScale/ThePage!PageScale)*2 in.))"
```

In plain English, "Read the value of the page's ShapeSheet and obtain the page width from the PageWidth cell. Take the value read from the page's DrawingScale cell and divide it by the value read from the page's PageScale cell to obtain a scaling factor (this will be one in an unscaled drawing). Then multiply that unit-less number by two inches to obtain a unit-ed number to subtract from the total page width." We guard this cell's formula so it cannot be altered by the user from the user interface. This formula allows the width of the SmartShape symbol to always be two inches less in printed size than the total width of the page, giving us the one inch margin on each side that we will require.

The Height cell contains the following formula:

```
"=GUARD(1 in.*(ThePage!DrawingScale/ThePage!PageScale))"
```

In plain English, take the unit-ed number one inch and multiply it by the unit-less number obtained by taking the value read from the Page's DrawingScale cell and dividing it by the value read from the Page's PageScale cell to obtain a scaling factor (this will be one in an unscaled drawing). The resulting unit-ed number will ensure that the height of the SmartShape symbol is always one inch high in printed size.

The Angle, FlipX, and FlipY cells are all guarded at their default values. This ensures that the symbol cannot be flipped or rotated.

The LocPinX cell has been guarded at "=0 in," which simply places the local pin on the far left side. The LocPinY cell has been guarded at a value of height, which places the local pin at the top. Therefore, the local pin is in the upper-left corner of the symbol. This makes it easier to calculate the required placement position for the symbol utilizing the PinX and PinY cells.

The PinX cell has a formula that states

```
"=GUARD((ThePage!DrawingScale/ThePage!PageScale)*1 in.)"
```

Another way of saying it would be: "Find the scale factor for the page and multiply that scale factor times one inch to set the position in X in printed size for the symbol." Because the symbol's local PinX is at the left side, this is an easy number to obtain.

The PinY cell has a formula that states

```
"=GUARD(ThePage!PageHeight-((ThePage!DrawingScale/ThePage!PageScale)*1 in.))"
```

To phrase it another way, "Find the total height of the page, and subtract one inch times the scaling factor to position the symbol one printed inch below the top of the page."

Do you see how utilizing formulas from the page itself can assist in sizing and placing the SmartShape symbol? Remember that the page can always be referred to in ShapeSheet formulas in inter-shape references as either "ThePage" (a Visio keyword) or Sheet.0 because the page itself is the "base" sheet for all of the SmartShape symbols that are dropped upon it.

But, I'm sure you are asking, how did we get that nifty dialog box to appear and how did we automatically enter text editing mode? Remember the Events section? Here is the formula we placed in the EventDrop cell that ensures this will be evaluated every time the symbol is instanced:

```
"=RUNADDON("MsgBox ""Enter your name and sign in please...""")+OPENTEXTWIN()"
```

There are actually two functions placed here. Notice the plus symbol between the two functions. This acts as the separator between the functions we want to evaluate and establishes the order of evaluation.

The first function is a RUNADDON() function. In it, we simply placed a standard Visual Basic Message Box function to display the quoted message string. Note the double sets of quotes required to enclose the actual message string. This is because the single argument to the RUNADDON() function is a string. In order for the interpreter to differentiate between the function as a string and its specific argument as a sub-string, we need the double-double quotes. The second function was simply a call to the Visio OPENTEXTWIN() function. It then places the user directly in Text Editing mode for the selected symbol.

The next ShapeSheet section of importance to the page is the Ruler and Grid Section. The Ruler and Grid section of a page's ShapeSheet consists of ten cells. These cells control all aspects of the grid as it is seen on the page in Visio's User Interface. The cells are

- XGridDensity
- XGridOrigin
- XGridSpacing
- XRulerDensity
- XRulerOrigin
- YGridDensity
- YGridOrigin
- YGridSpacing
- YRulerDensity
- YRulerOrigin

I'll detail these cells in the following paragraphs.

XgridDensity

This cell contains the integer value that specifies the type of horizontal grid to use. The valid integer values are

0	Fixed
2	Coarse
4	Normal (default)
8	Fine

If an invalid value is entered, Visio specifies the same type as 4.

XGridOrigin

This cell contains the unit-ed number that represents the horizontal coordinate of the grid origin.

XGridSpacing

This cell contains the unit-ed number that represents the distance between horizontal lines in a fixed grid (XGridDensity = 0).

XRulerDensity

This cell contains the integer value that specifies the horizontal subdivisions on the ruler for the page. The valid integer values are

8	Coarse
16	Normal
32	Fine

Note that if an invalid value or no value is entered, Visio specifies the same subdivisions as 16.

XRulerOrigin

This cell contains the unit-ed number that represents the zero point on the x-axis ruler for the page.

YGridDensity

This cell contains the integer value that specifies the type of vertical grid to use. The valid integer values are

0	Fixed
2	Coarse
4	Normal (default)
8	Fine

Note if an invalid value is entered, Visio specifies the same type as 4.

YGridOrigin

This cell contains the unit-ed number that represents the vertical coordinate of the grid origin.

YGridSpacing

This cell contains the unit-ed number that represents the distance between vertical lines in a fixed grid (YGridDensity= 0).

YRulerDensity

This cell contains the integer value that specifies the vertical subdivisions on the ruler for the page. The valid integer values are

8	Coarse
16	Normal
32	Fine

Note that if an invalid value or no value is entered, Visio specifies the same subdivisions as 16.

YRulerOrigin

This cell contains the unit-ed number that represents the zero point on the y-axis ruler for the page.

The last ShapeSheet section of importance to the page is the Page Layout section. The Page Layout section of a Page's ShapeSheet consists of twenty-four cells. These cells control all aspects of how shapes arrange themselves by default (based on their own Shape Layout section of their own ShapeSheet) on the page in Visio's User Interface. The cells are

- PlaceStyle
- PlaceDepth
- PlowCode
- ResizePage
- DynamicsOff
- EnableGrid
- CtrlAsInput
- LineAdjustFrom
- LineAdjustTo
- BlockSizeX
- BlockSizeY
- AvenueSizeX
- AvenueSizeY
- RouteStyle
- PageLineJumpDirX
- PageLineJumpDirY
- LineToNodeX
- LineToNodeY
- LineToLineX
- LineToLineY

- LineJumpFactorX
- LineJumpFactorY
- LineJumpCode
- LineJumpStyle

I'll detail each of these cells in the next several paragraphs.

PlaceStyle

This cell contains the integer value that specifies how shapes are placed on the page when you are automatically laying them out. The valid integer values are

0	Default; radial for page and shape
1	Top to bottom
2	Left to right
3	Radial
4	Bottom to top
5	Right to left
6	Circular

PlaceDepth

This cell contains the integer value that specifies the method by which the drawing is analyzed before creating the layout and determines the type of layout. The valid integer values are

0	Page default
1	Medium
2	Deep
3	Shallow

PlowCode

This cell contains the integer value that specifies whether placeable shapes move away when you drop one placeable shape near another on the drawing page. The valid integer values are

0	Don't move shapes
1	Move shapes

ResizePage

This cell contains the Boolean FALSE or TRUE value that specifies whether to enlarge the page to enclose the drawing after automatically laying out shapes using the Lay Out Shapes command. Set the value of this cell to TRUE to enlarge the page or FALSE not to enlarge it.

DynamicsOff

This cell contains the Boolean FALSE or TRUE value that specifies whether placeable shapes move and connectors reroute around other shapes and connectors on the drawing page. To disable dynamics, set the value of this cell to TRUE. To enable dynamics, set the value of this cell to FALSE.

Note that the dynamics can be disabled to increase a solution's performance. As an example, if a solution adds placeable shapes to a drawing and it is not desirable to have Visio reroute connectors and reposition shapes each time a shape is added, dynamics can be disabled. After the solution adds the shapes, dynamics can be re-enabled.

EnableGrid

This cell contains the Boolean FALSE or TRUE value that specifies whether Visio lays out shapes based on an internal, invisible page grid when using the Lay Out Shapes command. Set the value of this cell to TRUE to use this internal page grid, or FALSE not to use the internal page grid.

Note: When this feature is enabled, Visio aligns each placeable shape's center point with the center of a block on the internal page grid.

CtrlAsInput

This cell contains the Boolean FALSE or TRUE value that specifies which shape is the parent when using shapes by control handles. The default value for this cell is FALSE. By default, the shape that contains the control handle is the parent. Set the value of this cell to TRUE to set the shape to which the control handle is connected as the parent. This cell sets the behavior for all the shapes on the drawing page.

LineAdjustFrom

This cell contains the integer value that specifies which dynamic connectors Visio spaces apart if they route on top of each other. The valid integer values are

0	Unrelated lines
1	All lines
2	No lines
3	Routing style default

LineAdjustTo

This cell contains the integer value that determines which dynamic connectors line up on top of one another. The valid integer values are

0	Routing style default
1	Lines that are close to each other
2	No lines
3	Related lines

BlockSizeX

This cell contains the unit-ed number that determines the horizontal block size, the area in which each of your shapes must fit on the drawing page when you automatically lay out shapes using the Lay Out Shapes dialog box.

BlockSizeY

This cell contains the unit-ed number that determines the vertical block size, the area in which each of your shapes must fit on the drawing page when you automatically lay out shapes using the Lay Out Shapes dialog box.

AvenueSizeX

This cell contains the unit-ed number that determines the amount of horizontal space between shapes on the drawing page when you automatically lay out shapes.

Note: The dynamic grid also uses avenue size.

AvenueSizeY

This cell contains the unit-ed number that determines the amount of vertical space between shapes on the drawing page when you automatically lay out shapes.

Notice that the dynamic grid also uses avenue size.

RouteStyle

This cell contains the integer value that determines the routing style and direction for all connectors on the drawing page that don't have a local routing style. The valid integer values are

Routing Style	Direction
0 Default; Right angle	none
1 Right angle	none
2 Straight	none
3 Organization chart	top-to-bottom
4 Organization chart	left-to-right

5	Flowchart	top-to-bottom
6	Flowchart	left-to-right
7	Tree	top-to-bottom
8	Tree	left-to-right
9	Network	none
10	Organization chart	bottom-to-top
11	Organization chart	right-to-left
12	Flowchart	bottom-to-top
13	Flowchart	right-to-left
14	Tree	bottom-to-top
15	Tree	right-to-left
16	Center-to-center	none
17	Simple	top-to-bottom
18	Simple	left-to-right
19	Simple	bottom-to-top
20	Simple	right-to-left
21	Simple horizontal-vertical	none
22	Simple vertical-horizontal	none

This setting affects only those connectors whose Line Routing style is set as the Page Default.

PageLineJumpDirX

This cell contains the integer value that specifies the direction of line jumps on horizontal dynamic connectors on the drawing page for which you haven't applied a local jump direction. The valid integer values are

0	Default; left or the page's setting for shapes
1	Up
2	Down

PageLineJumpDirY

This cell contains the integer value that specifies the direction of line jumps on vertical dynamic connectors on the drawing page for which you haven't applied a local jump direction. The valid integer values are

0	Default; left or the page's setting for shapes
1	Left
2	Right

LineToNodeX

This cell contains the unit-ed number that determines the horizontal clearance between all connectors and shapes on the drawing page.

LineToNodeY

This cell contains the unit-ed number that determines the vertical clearance between all connectors and shapes on the drawing page.

LineToLineX

This cell contains the unit-ed number that determines the horizontal clearance between all connectors on the drawing page.

LineToLineY

This cell contains the unit-ed number that determines the vertical clearance between all connectors on the drawing page.

LineJumpFactorX

This cell contains the unit-ed number that determines the size of line jumps on horizontal dynamic connectors on the page, relative to the value of the LineToLineX cell.

LineJumpFactorY

This cell contains the unit-ed number that determines the size of line jumps on vertical dynamic connectors on the page, relative to the value of the LineToLineY cell.

LineJumpCode

This cell contains the integer value that determines the connectors to which you want to add jumps. The valid integer values are

0	None
1	Horizontal Lines
2	Vertical Lines
3	Last Routed Line
4	Last displayed line (top shape in the z-order)
5	First displayed line (shape at the bottom of the z-order)

LineJumpStyle

This cell contains the integer value that determines the line jump style for all connectors on the drawing page that don't have a local line jump style. The valid integer values are

0	Arc
1	Arc
2	Gap
3	Square
4	Two Sides
5	Three Sides
6	Four Sides
7	Five Sides
8	Six Sides
9	Seven Sides

As with any other ShapeSheet, the Page's ShapeSheet can have sections added to it by selecting Insert, Sections. You will note, however, that you may only add User-defined, Custom Properties, Hyper-link, Actions, Scratch, and Layers sections to a page's ShapeSheet. By adding any one or a number of these sections to a page's ShapeSheet, you, as the developer, can provide the user with a rich feature set that is easily accessible. You can store page "global" information that every one of the SmartShape symbols on the page may access to set their parameters, just as we did with the page size and scale information.

Visio Documents and Layers

If any of you come from a Computer Assisted Design and Drafting (CADD) background, the concept of layers will be quite familiar to you. For the rest of you who might not know about layers, here's a brief history.

In the beginning, there was drafting. This was accomplished on single sheets of paper (well, actually papyrus or parchment, but that's a different story altogether). Drawings were painstakingly copied from one sheet of paper to another to create copies. This went on for centuries (quite literally). Then some disgruntled and free-thinking draftsperson got the bright idea that if the sheets of paper were transparent enough, you could stack them, one on top of another, and see through to the information on the sheet below without having to redraw it. A brilliant beginning, but the sheets kept shifting. So another bright lad came up with the concept of punching holes into the tops of each sheet and lining them all up on a "pin-bar" in order to keep them perfectly aligned. (He must have been dreaming about school three-ring binders.)

This was all well and good until some daft supervisor expected the lad to actually print out this stack of sheets. The first time the lad attempted to stuff all of the sheets through a blue-line printer (I know…I've jumped quite literally centuries ahead here past ammonia tube blueprinting), the sheets all slipped and the entire print was illegible. This would never do. Hence, the light table was invented. This was a huge frame with light tubes under glass with a very heavy lid above it, replete with the now famous pin-bar. The draftsperson would then place all of the sheets inside along with the sheet of blueline paper, close the lid, turn on the light, and wait three or four millenium for the light to actually burn its way through this mess to make the image. It worked, but far too slow to be truly practical.

Computer drafting (CADD) came along and the concept of "pin-bar" drafting was brought up again. This time, however, because there were no physical sheets of paper to get in the way, the concept could be successfully implemented. Each "sheet" of paper in the computer was a "layer" in the stack of sheets. If you were to draw the walls of a building on one layer, you could see those walls when you needed to place the electrical fixtures on another layer.

CADD traditionally has held onto the concept that any single symbol may reside on any single layer and either be visible or not depending on the status of that layer (think of the sheet being pulled out of the stack of sheets as the manual equivalent of turning the layer's visibility off). This is a one-to-one correspondence. One symbol gets one, and only one, layer.

Visio, however, has revolutionized this concept by introducing the concept of one-to-many layers. One symbol may be associated with any one or any number of layers, or with no particular layer at all. This gives the draftsperson, designer, manager, and any person who needs it, access to the document or diagram—a huge new freedom, as well as a powerful new query tool. A query tool, you say? Indeed! Here's how this works…

Let's suppose that you work for Bright-and-Shiny Office Furnishings Manufacturing. You manufacture a brilliant line of office furniture: desks, chairs, file cabinets, and the like. In fact, the desks that you manufacture are available in numerous woods and finishes: oak, maple, cherry, teak, satin finish, polished finish…you get the idea here. Now imagine that a very large client like Mendolson's Wax Company has selected you along with four other vendors to supply all of the office furnishings in their new corporate headquarters. They have created a brilliant Visio diagram of their headquarters, showing the location of each and every piece of furniture in the entire office building. Now you need to figure out how much you need to bill Mendolson's for the maple, satin finish, 2 meter by 1.6 meter executive desks.

Here's where Visio absolutely shines. Using Visio, the person who created the diagram assigned the maple, satin finish, 2 meter by 1.6 meter executive desks to the following layers:

- Office furnishings
- Bright-and-Shiny Office Furnishings Manufacturing
- Desks

- Wood
- Maple
- Satin finish
- 2 meter by 1.6 meter
- Executive

Now among all the myriad desks in the corporate headquarters, you can use Visio's Layer tools and Visio's Property Reporting Wizard to generate a query that effectively asks for the following:

Show me all of Bright-and-Shiny Office Furnishings Manufacturing's maple, satin finish, 2 meter by 1.6 meter executive desks in the corporate headquarters diagram by turning off all of the layers except the office furnishings, the desks, the wood, the maple, the satin finish, the 2 meter by 1.6 meter, and the executive layers. When this is done, use the Property Reporting Wizard and generate a full report on only that which is visible. This totally eliminates any desks or other furnishings supplied by any other vendor as well as those desks that might be teak or have a different finish.

The lesson here? Visio's layers are a hierarchical structuring tool with great flexibility and power. If used properly, the effective use of layers can save significant amounts of time in organizing, filtering, displaying, and printing only the information you need.

Think in terms of an organizational diagram. Perhaps out of the entire organization, you wish to see and print only those employees in the Quality Assurance department who have been with the firm less than two years. Layers can make this task much easier.

With all of this said, how do you set up layers in a Visio diagram? Select View, Layer Properties from the menu. A dialog box will appear. The pane that takes up the vast majority of the dialog box will display all of the layers currently within the diagram. You will note there are nine columns in this pane. The columns are

- Name
- #
- Visible
- Print
- Active
- Lock
- Snap
- Glue
- Color

I'll detail each of these in the next few paragraphs.

Name

Name, quite obviously, is the name of the layer. This can be up to 32 characters in length and can contain spaces and punctuation as desired.

# #

This is a query tool in and of itself. This is the Number column. When the header for this column is clicked, Visio places an integer in the column for each named entry that indicated the number of symbols currently assigned to this named layer.

Visible

This controls whether the named layer is visible; that is, whether you actually see the symbols assigned to this layer in your diagram.

Print

This controls whether this named layer will print; that is, whether the symbols assigned to this layer will print as part of your decision to print the diagram when you select File, Print.

Active

This controls the use of the layer as the active or default layer. By default in Visio, when you place symbols into a diagram, they are not assigned to any layer at all. However, if a named layer is selected as active, any new symbol added to the diagram will automatically be assigned to that layer (as well as any layer previously designated as associated with that symbol).

Lock

This controls whether a layer is locked. That is, whether symbols assigned to the named layer may be accessed or altered in any manner. If the layer is locked, the symbols can be seen by the user, but not accessed or manipulated.

Snap

This controls whether symbols may snap to any geometry as part of a symbol assigned to this named layer.

Glue

This controls whether symbols may glue to any valid geometry as part of a symbol assigned to this named layer.

Color

This controls the line color for any symbol placed on this named layer if the symbol has not otherwise been assigned a color other than color zero when created. If a symbol has its own color designation, this setting is moot. If a symbol has no specific color designation, and is assigned to a named layer, the color assignment for that layer will control the line color for that symbol. If a symbol has no specific color designation, and is assigned to several named layers with differing color designations, Visio does not attempt to mitigate the colors or "color-blend"; it simply shows the symbol as color zero (black) until the color conflict is resolved.

The Layer Color drop-down list is used to associate a color with the currently highlighted row in the listing of named layers. If the Color column is checked, this color will be applied (subject to the conditions above). If the Color is unchecked, the assignment remains but the application is withheld.

The New button allows the creation of a new layer within this dialog box. A sub-dialog box will appear and prompt the user to enter the name for a new layer.

The Remove and Rename buttons should be self-explanatory. The wee check box called Remove Unreferenced Layers is a feature that traditional CADD users will truly appreciate. If this check box is checked and the user clicks either Apply or OK, Visio will scan the entire diagram looking for the valid assignment of every named layer. If a layer is found to have no symbols associated with it, Visio will then remove the layer from the dialog box and purge it from the diagram. This differs from the tedious, slow, repetitive, painful process required under traditional CADD. (I won't detail here...you truly don't want to know.)

We have thus far discussed layers as they apply to the user interface, but how is all of this manifested in a Visio ShapeSheet?

Important Concept Number Nine

Visio Layer information is stored in the page's ShapeSheet. Indexing is stored in the SmartShape symbol's ShapeSheet. Let's illustrate this concept. Begin a new Visio diagram. Drag out two rectangles of any size. Select View, Layer Properties from the menu. In the dialog box, click the New button. In the sub-dialog box, enter the name "Alpha." Click OK to exit the sub-dialog. Repeat this process two more times, creating the layers "Beta" and "Omega." Click OK to exit the Layers dialog box.

Open the ShapeSheet for the page. Remember, you must ensure that no symbols are selected to access the page's ShapeSheet. If you are not viewing all sections of the ShapeSheet, ensure that the ShapeSheet window is active, select View, Sections from the menu, and click All and then OK. Scroll down in the Page's ShapeSheet and find the Layers section of the ShapeSheet. Notice that there is a row for each layer that you just created. There are columns for each of the Visible, Print, Active, Lock, Snap, Glue, and Color items. The name of the row, in addition to the row number, are shown as the first (row number) and second (layer name) items in the row. The Layers index is actually a zero-based index. Therefore, row number one is index zero, row number two is index one, and so on. All the other columns are effectively Boolean entries (zero is off and one is on), with the exception of the Color column, which displays a 0 to 255 based integer for the color associated with that particular layer. The cell names within the Layers section of the ShapeSheet are referenced as

- Layers.Active
- Layers.Color
- Layers.Glue
- Layers.Lock
- Layers.Print
- Layers.Snap
- Layers.Visible

See the previous descriptions of the Layer properties for the valid data entries and ranges.

Close the page's ShapeSheet. Select one of the rectangle SmartShape symbols you created a moment ago. With the symbol selected, select Format, Layer from the menu. In the dialog box, click the Alpha layer name, and then hold Ctrl and click the Omega layer name. Click OK to close the dialog box. Now with the rectangle SmartShape symbol still selected, open its ShapeSheet. If you are not viewing all sections of the ShapeSheet, ensure that the ShapeSheet window is active, select View, Sections from the menu, and click All and then OK. Scroll down in the SmartShape symbol's ShapeSheet and find the Layer Membership section of the ShapeSheet. Notice that the entry in the single cell of the single row says

```
="0;2"
```

The name that can be referenced for this cell is the LayerMember cell. Note that the entry is a deliminated list of the index numbers for the entries in the Layers section of the page's ShapeSheet. Keep in mind that this is a zero-based index. This is why when you selected the Alpha layer and the Omega layer to assign to this SmartShape symbol, you had selected the first and third entry. Therefore, the formula reads "0" for entry one (Alpha), and "2" for entry three (Omega). Later, when you begin to develop Automation solutions that must access information about the layer assignments for a particular SmartShape symbol, you will need to look up the indexes in the symbol's ShapeSheet and then look at the page's ShapeSheet for the status and actual name of the layer itself.

In this chapter, we have looked at events associated with SmartShape symbols accessible through their ShapeSheets and how to add context menu items via the Actions section of the ShapeSheet. We have also looked at the page itself in Visio, all of the cells that control properties associated with the page, and certain symbols that reside on the page. Additionally, we looked at how the proper use of layers can greatly enhance your Visio solutions.

In the next chapter, we will study associating data with Visio SmartShape symbols. We will look at Visio's original methodologies for storing data, the newer and more powerful custom properties, and hyperlinks. I'll also walk you through using Visio's Database Wizard to connect Visio SmartShape symbols to an external ODBC-compliant data source.

Associating Data with Visio SmartShape Symbols

IN THIS CHAPTER

Long, long ago, in a galaxy far, far away—Oh, wait—that's another story...

In the beginning, Visio created SmartShape symbols. With those SmartShape symbols, Visio created a mechanism for storing external data. This method, the SmartShape symbol's Data1, Data2, and Data3 fields storage area, still exists under Visio 2000 exactly as it did under Visio 1.0. You may or may not have ever encountered these three storage areas in Visio SmartShape symbols. To access them, select any SmartShape symbol on the page of any Visio diagram. Select Format, Special from the menus. At the bottom of the dialog box, you will see three text box controls. These boxes allow you to enter any type of information you wish. This can be numeric, purely textual, or, through programmatic input, even a binary stream. Each of these three fields can hold up to 64KB of data. (Actually, the 64KB limit was removed from Data1, 2, and 3 under Visio 2000. However, I wouldn't recommend placing much more than that in the stream. Still, you could do it if you really wanted to.)

When I look at Automation mechanisms for accessing SmartShape symbol's information, I will discuss obtaining the data in these cells as Shape.Data1, Shape.Data2, and Shape.Data3. However, for now, you as a developer should know that the information in these three fields is available by placing the formulas `Data1()`, `Data2()`, or `Data3()` into any cell as a reference.

The positive side of having the Data1, Data2, and Data3 fields available is that they are so easily accessible. Unfortunately, the negative side of having the Data1, Data2, and Data3 fields available is also that they are so easily accessible. Seriously though, because the names for these fields are fixed and accessible to any developer, it is possible that any developer's Automation application could write to one or more of these three fields and obliterate the data that your Automation application placed there. I'm not telling you not to use these three fields; simply that if you are going to use them, be very sure of the data that you are accessing. If it is your own data, great! Manipulate and access away! But, if it is not your data, leave it alone, or at least store the data somewhere until you are through mucking about with the access to the fields, and then put it back again! It's a wee bit like kindergarten: Just remember to play nice with the other kids.

The Custom Properties Section of the ShapeSheet

Because of the inherent issues with the Data1, Data2, and Data3 fields that I discussed above, under Visio 3.0, Visio created Custom Properties. This was a brilliant step forward in the capability to store data in association with SmartShape symbols. There is a wizard under Visio 5.0 that enables you to add Custom Properties to a ShapeSheet. Under Visio 2000, it is even easier. What I am going to do next is address how, as a developer, you add Custom Properties through the ShapeSheet. When I have finished, I will then show you the method newly available to you under 2000 from within the User Interface. You then can decide for yourself how you want to add the Custom Property cells and how you want your users to access the data stored there.

Let's start by dragging out a rectangle and placing it on the page. Turn your creativity loose and imagine that the rectangle symbol is a plan view of a desktop. There are many different bits of information that might be very important to store in association with that desktop—the manufacturer, the model number, the price, the material, the finish, who the desk is assigned to, and in what office it is located. It doesn't make sense to devise a scheme for delimiting all of this information and storing it in the Data1, Data2, or Data3 fields, so I will create a Custom Properties dialog box to make entering and accessing this information easier.

Open the ShapeSheet for the Rectangle. If you are not viewing all of the sections, be sure that the ShapeSheet window is active and select Insert, Sections from the menus. Check the Custom Properties check box control and click OK to close the dialog box.

The Custom Properties section can contain as many rows as you need to store the different bits of information. Like a database, each row equates to a field in a table. Just like a database table definition can contain as many fields as is necessary, the Custom Properties section can contain as many rows as are necessary. To add a row, click into a current Custom Property row and select Insert, Row or Insert, Row After from the menus.

A Custom Properties row is comprised of nine cells:

- Name
- Label
- Prompt
- Type
- Format
- Value
- SortKey
- Invisible
- Ask

I'll detail each of these cells in the next several paragraphs.

Name

The Name cell in a Custom Property row is the red text cell that by default is named Prop.Row_1. To rename this cell to a name that makes more sense, is of more value, and is unique to your application so other developers will not tread upon it as they could with Data1, Data2, and Data3, click into the cell and type in a new name for the cell. You are allowed up to 32 characters for the name. Only letters, numbers, dashes, and underscores can be used; no spaces. Those are the rules.

Label

The Label is the short, terse, concise, brief (am I making my point here?) item of text that will appear to the left of the Custom Property item when it is displayed in the Custom Properties dialog box. You may use any text and punctuation here. You are limited to 32 characters.

Prompt

The Prompt is the text that appears in the box at the bottom of the Custom Properties dialog box when the particular Custom Property item is selected in the list above. You can be a bit more verbose here. The text that you place here can include spaces and punctuation. It should reflect what you are wanting from the user of the SmartShape symbol and the dialog box. Keep in mind that there are several types of data entry available to the user via this interface: A user can enter text, numbers, currency values, dates, times, and other data into a text box control. A user can also select items from a fixed list, just like a list box control. A user can select items or enter data into a variable list. This is the same as a combo box control. Your prompt should assist the user in dealing with this requirement:

> *For a Text Field:* "Enter [blah, blah, bla]…"
> *For a Fixed List:* "Select [blah, blah, bla]…"
> *For a Variable List:* Select [blah, blah, bla] or enter [blah, blah, bla]…"

Type

Under both Visio 5.0 and Visio 2000, the data types available have been expanded from the original Text, Number, Fixed List, Variable List and Boolean to the following list of integer values:

0	String
1	FixedList. Displays the list items in a drop-down list box in the Custom Properties dialog box. Specify the list items in the Format cell. Users can select only one item from the list.
2	Number. Includes date, time, duration, and currency values as well as scalars, dimensions, and angles. Specify a format picture in the Format cell.
3	Boolean. Displays FALSE and TRUE as items users can select from a drop-down list box in the Custom Properties dialog box.
4	VariableList. Displays the list items in a drop-down combo box in the Custom Properties dialog box. Specify the list items in the Format cell. Users can select a list item or enter a new item that is added to the current list in the Format cell.
5	Date or Time. Displays days, months, and years, or seconds, minutes, and hours, or a combined date and time value. Specify a format picture in the Format cell.

| 6 | Duration. Displays elapsed time. Specify a format picture in the Format cell. |
| 7 | Currency. Uses the system's current Regional Settings. Specify a format picture in the Format cell. |

Format

When the information being entered into the Text Box control is of data type 2 (Numeric) or 0 (String) and it needs to have its display formatted, place a valid Format Picture here. The valid format pictures are

String and numeric values#	Digit placeholder. Displays either a digit or nothing. Leading and trailing zeroes are not displayed. If more digits than placeholders are to the left of the decimal, all digits are displayed. If more digits than placeholders are to the right of the decimal, the fraction is rounded to the number of placeholders. For a dimension, if the placeholder is the leftmost digit, subunits that are 0 are not displayed. For example, `FORMAT(0ft. 11.25in.,"#.##u")` displays 11.25 inches.
0	Digit placeholder (zero). Displays either a digit or nothing. Leading and trailing zeroes are displayed. If more digits than placeholders are to the left of the decimal, all digits are displayed. If more digits than placeholders are to the right of the decimal, the fraction is rounded to the number of placeholders. For a dimension, subunits that are 0 are displayed. For example, `FORMAT(2ft. 11.33in.,"0.## u")` displays 2 feet, 11.33 inches.
.	Decimal placeholder. Determines how many digits are displayed to the left and right of the decimal position. In a multipart unit, the decimal is used in the smallest (rightmost) subunit. Displays the decimal character defined for the system's Regional Settings. For example, `FORMAT(250 cm.,"0.000 u")` displays 250.000 centimeters.
,	Thousands separator. If surrounded by digit placeholders (# or 0), the separator separates thousands from hundreds within a number that has four or more digits to the left of the decimal. Displays the thousands separator defined for the system's regional settings.
E- E+ e- e+	Scientific format. If the format contains at least one digit placeholder to the right of these symbols, the number is displayed in scientific format. Inserts the E or e between the number and its exponent. For E+ or e+, displays the + sign before positive exponents and the - sign before negative exponents. For E- or e-, displays the - sign only when the exponent is negative. For example, `FORMAT(12345.67,"###.#e+#")` results in 123.5e+2.

u or U	Short label placeholder. Inserts abbreviated unit labels after each sub-unit. For example: in., ft., deg. The u placeholder inserts lowercase labels and U inserts uppercase labels. Inserts the same number of spaces before the label as before the placeholder. For example, FORMAT(12 ciceros 13 didots,"#u") displays 13c1.
uu or UU	Long label placeholder. Inserts unit labels after each subunit. For example: inches, feet, degrees. The u placeholder inserts lowercase labels and U inserts uppercase labels. Inserts the same number of spaces before the label as before the placeholder. For example, FORMAT(12.43in.,"# #/4 UU") displays 12 2/4 inches.
uuu or UUU	Universal label placeholder. Inserts the universal (internal to Visio) form of unit labels after each subunit. The u placeholder inserts lower-case labels and U inserts uppercase labels. Inserts the same number of spaces before the label as before the placeholder.
/	Fraction placeholder. Displays expression as a whole number with fraction if a leading digit placeholder is present. Otherwise, displays only the whole number in the numerator. If a number follows the digit placeholder in the denominator, rounds the fraction to the nearest fraction whose numerator is 1 and simplifies it. If a number is specified in the denominator without the digit placeholder, rounds to the nearest fraction but does not simplify it. For example, FORMAT(12.43,"# #/4") displays 12 2/4.
space	Displays a space character in the formatted output. To display another character, use the \ (backslash) character.

Currency Values

$	Currency symbol. Displays the currency symbol defined in the system's regional settings.
u or U	Short label placeholder. Inserts the standard symbol for local currency or the three-character currency constant for nonlocal currencies. For example, $99.00, 42.70 FRF. The u placeholder inserts lowercase or mixed-case labels and U inserts uppercase labels.
uu or UU	Long label placeholder. Inserts long currency labels after each subunit. For example: United States dollar, French franc. The u placeholder inserts lowercase or mixed-case labels and U inserts uppercase labels.
uuu or UUU	Universal label placeholder. Inserts the universal three-character currency constant for all currencies after each subunit. For example, 99.00 USD, 42.70 FRF. The u placeholder inserts lowercase labels and U inserts uppercase labels. Inserts the same number of spaces before the label as before the placeholder.

Associating Data with Visio SmartShape Symbols

CHAPTER 6 169

6

ASSOCIATING DATA
WITH VISIO
SMARTSHAPE
SYMBOLS

Text

\	Display the next character as is. To display the backslash character, type \\. See also "text."
"text" or 'text'	Displays the text enclosed in quotes as is. See also \ (backslash).
@	Text placeholder. Replaces a string if the value of expression is a string. For example, FORMAT("Hello", "'You entered ('@')'") results in "You entered (Hello)".
@+	Uppercase text placeholder. For string values, substitutes the input with uppercase. For example, FORMAT("Hello", "@ @+ @-") results in "Hello HELLO hello)".
@-	Text placeholder. For string values, substitutes the input with lower-case. For example, FORMAT("Hello", "@ @+ @-") results in "Hello HELLO hello)".

Date Values

c or C	Date or time placeholder. Displays date and time values using a short (c) or long (C) date format and the general time format. Visio versions 4.0 and lower ignore this placeholder. For example: FORMAT(DATE-TIME("6/25/97 12:05"),"C") displays Wednesday, June 25, 1997 12:05:00 PM. FORMAT(DATETIME("Jun. 25, 1997"),"c") displays 6/25/97.
/	Date separator. If the expression is a date, separates the date components. Displays the date separator defined for the system's regional settings.
[ ]	Elapsed date placeholder. Used with the d, dd, w, and ww placeholders to display duration units. For example, [d] is elapsed days, [ww] is elapsed weeks.
d	Day placeholder. Displays the day as a number (1-31) without a leading zero.
dd	Day placeholder. Displays the day as a number (01-31) with a leading zero.
ddd or w	Short day of week placeholder. Displays the day as an abbreviation (Sun-Sat).
dddd or ww	Long day of week placeholder. Displays the day as a full name (Sunday-Saturday).
ddddd	Short date placeholder. Displays a date in the short form defined for the system's regional settings.
dddddd	Long date placeholder. Displays a date in the long form defined for the system's regional settings.

M	Month placeholder. Displays the month as a number (1-12) without a leading zero. See also m (minute placeholder).
MM	Month placeholder. Displays the month as a number (01-12) with a leading zero. See also mm (minute placeholder).
MMM	Month placeholder. Displays the month in abbreviated form (Jan-Dec).
MMMM	Month placeholder. Displays the full name of the month (January-December).
yy	Year placeholder. Displays the year as a two-digit number (00-99).
yyyy	Year placeholder. Displays the year as a four-digit number (1900-2078).

Time values

:	Time separator. Displays the time defined for the system's regional settings.
[ ]	Elapsed time placeholder. Used with the h, hh, m, mm, s, and ss placeholders to display duration units. For example, [h] is elapsed hours, [ss] is elapsed seconds.
h	Hour placeholder. Displays the hour without a leading zero in 12-hour form (0-12).
hh	Hour placeholder. Displays the hour with a leading zero in 12-hour form (00-12).
H	Hour placeholder. Displays the hour without a leading zero in 24-hour form (0-24).
HH	Hour placeholder. Displays the hour with a leading zero in 24-hour form (00-24).
m	Minute placeholder. Displays the minutes without a leading zero (0-59).
mm	Minute placeholder. Displays the minutes with a leading zero (00-59).
s	Seconds placeholder. Displays the seconds without a leading zero (0-59).
ss	Seconds placeholder. Displays the seconds with a leading zero (00-59).
t	AM/PM abbreviation. Displays the abbreviation defined for the system's regional settings.
tt	AM/PM designator. Displays the full designator defined for the system's regional settings.
T	General time format.

When the information being entered into the Custom Properties dialog box is designed for either data type 1 (Fixed List) or data type 4 (Variable List), the list itself must be a single string that is delimited by the proper delimiter (semicolon (;) in America). An example of a valid format for a fixed list containing sports types for a sports field multishape would be

```
="Football;Baseball;Basketball;Hockey;Jai-Alai;Tennis;Squash;Racquetball;
Handball"
```

Value

A default value may be "primed" into the Custom Properties dialog box by placing a valid entry into the Value cell of the Custom Properties row. Additionally, when the user makes a selection or enters data from within the Custom Properties dialog box, the value is stored in this cell.

SortKey

This cell holds a string value that represents the order in which items are to be displayed in the Custom Properties dialog box. Developers by nature tend to think of this as numeric and beginning with one, increasing incrementally for each row. However, the SortKey cell specifies a key by which items in the Custom Properties dialog box are listed. The sort is locale-specific, descending, and not case-sensitive. The sort key is a string, which Visio automatically encloses in quotation marks.

Invisible

The Invisible cell is a Boolean FALSE or TRUE (zero (0) or non-zero (-1)) value that specifies whether the subject Custom Properties row will be displayed in the Custom Properties dialog box. The valid range of integers are

0 FALSE	Visible
1 TRUE	Invisible

Ask

The Ask cell is a Boolean FALSE or TRUE (zero (0) or non-zero (-1)) value that specifies whether or not the subject Custom Properties row will be displayed in the Custom Properties dialog box when the SmartShape symbol containing that Custom Property row is first instanced. Subsequent to its instantiation, its access is controlled strictly by the Invisible cell's setting. Even during instantiation, the Invisible cell will always take precedence. The valid range of integers are

0 FALSE	Don't Ask
1 TRUE	Ask

Getting back to our table symbol—be sure that your Table SmartShape symbol has seven rows. Manipulate the cells in the rows to ensure that your information matches the following:

```
Row Number One
Name = Prop.Manufacturer
Label = "Manufacturer's Name"
Prompt = "Select the approved Manufacturer from the list."
Type = 1 (Fixed List)
Format = "MetalCase;Han;KroftWorks;Billabong"
Value = "MetalCase"
SortKey = "1"
Invisible = "0"
Ask = "1"
Row Number Two
Name = Prop.ModelNumber
Label = "Manufacturer's Model Number"
Prompt = "Enter the proper model number for this desk."
Type = 0 (String)
Format = <blank>
Value = <blank>
SortKey = "2"
Invisible = "0"
Ask = "1"
Row Number Three
Name = Prop.Price
Label = "Item Cost"
Prompt = "Enter the price for this desk."
Type = 7 (Currency)
Format = <blank>
Value = 0.00
SortKey = "3"
Invisible = "0"
Ask = "1"
Row Number Four
Name = Prop.Material
Label = "Base Wood for the Desk"
Prompt = "Select the base wood for the desk from the list."
Type = 1 (Fixed List)
Format = "Oak;Cherry;Teak;Ash;Maple;Mahogany"
Value = "Teak"
SortKey = "4"
Invisible = "0"
Ask = "1"
Row Number Five
Name = Prop.Finish
Label = "Desk Finish Type"
```

Associating Data with Visio SmartShape Symbols

CHAPTER 6

173

6

ASSOCIATING DATA
WITH VISIO
SMARTSHAPE
SYMBOLS

```
Prompt = "Select the Desk Finish from the list."
Type = 1 (Fixed List)
Format = "Satin;High Gloss;Painted"
Value = "Satin"
SortKey = "1"
Invisible = "0"
Ask = "1"
Row Number Six
Name = Prop.Assignment
Label = "Desk Occupant"
Prompt = "Enter the person's name assigned to this desk."
Type = 0 (String)
Format = <blank>
Value = <blank>
SortKey = "6"
Invisible = "0"
Ask = "1"
Row Number Seven
Name = Prop.Office
Label = "Location"
Prompt = "Enter the office location for this desk."
Type = 0 (String)
Format = <blank>
Value = <blank>
SortKey = "7"
Invisible = "0"
Ask = "1"
```

After this is done, add an Actions section to your ShapeSheet. In the Action cell, place the following formula:

```
=DOCMD(1312)
```

`DOCMD()` is a function to execute a Visio Command Constant and 1312 is the Visio Command Constant to call up the Custom Properties dialog box. In the Menu cell, place the following formula:

```
="Edit Desk Properties"
```

Close the ShapeSheet window. Ctrl+drag out a copy of the desk SmartShape symbol. Note that immediately upon instancing, the Custom Properties dialog box is launched. Fill in all required information and click OK. Now right-click the desk symbol. Select Edit Desk Properties from the Context menu. Note how the Custom Properties dialog box reappears with the selection of this menu item. Edit as necessary and click OK.

Developer be forewarned! Although there is no limit on the number of Custom Properties that can be added to a given SmartShape symbol via its ShapeSheet, there *is* a limit on the number of Custom Properties that can be displayed onscreen at any one time. With a 640×40 resolution, this limit is about 19. With a 1024×768 resolution, the limit is about 24. If you must display a very large number of Custom Properties, I would suggest Visio 2000's new Properties window. Or, if your users still must use Visio 5.0 or earlier, create your own tabbed dialog box using C++, VB, or VBA and populate the dialog box under Automation with information drawn from the Custom Properties Rows in the ShapeSheet. Next, send it back upon the dialog box's CommandButton_Click event for the command button used for the OK button in the dialog box.

This is the "hard-core" developer's method of adding Custom Properties to a SmartShape symbol and later accessing those Custom Properties. Be aware that your Users can always access the Custom Properties for any SmartShape symbol that contains them by right-clicking the symbol and selecting Shape, Custom Properties from the Context Menu. Under Visio 5.0 and earlier versions, if a user attempted to access the Custom Properties of a SmartShape symbol that did not contain any them, Visio would simply pop up an error dialog box informing the user that the selected shape did not contain any Custom Properties.

Under Visio 2000, another method of dealing with Custom Properties has been added. In Visio 2000, select View, Windows, Custom Properties from the menus. Select your desk SmartShape symbol. Note that the Custom Properties are immediately available to you. Under Visio 2000, try selecting Shape, Custom Properties from the SmartShape symbol's Context menu for a symbol that does not already have Custom Properties. Notice how you are now asked if you wish to add Custom Properties to the symbol—much nicer. A new dialog box appears allowing you to enter all of the same information you previously had to enter via the ShapeSheet. Right-clicking the new Properties window for a SmartShape symbol, even if it has no current Custom Properties defined, will bring up a Context menu item to define Custom Properties that will launch this same new dialog box.

The Hyperlinks Section of the ShapeSheet

Visio has, through successive product upgrades, increased the ability to hyperlink from any object in a Visio diagram to any logical link in the user's local machine, the network, or the intranet/Internet. Under Visio 2000, the process is as simple as selecting Insert, Hyperlinks from the menus. If a shape or a page was selected prior to this action, when the process is complete, a new Hyperlinks section will be added to the ShapeSheet for either the selected SmartShape symbol or the page, depending on the context.

A Hyperlinks section consists of eight cells:

- Name
- Description
- Address

Associating Data with Visio SmartShape Symbols

CHAPTER 6

175

6

ASSOCIATING DATA
WITH VISIO
SMARTSHAPE
SYMBOLS

- SubAddress
- ExtraInfo
- Frame
- NewWindow
- Default

I'll detail each of these cells in the next sections.

Name

The Name cell is the storage facility for a unique name for the Hyperlink row. By default, this will be named Hyperlink.Row_1, Hyperlink.Row_2, and so on. Just as with User-defined cells and Connections cells, this row can be renamed by the developer to suit the application development need.

Description

This cell holds a text string that represents descriptive text for the subject hyperlink. This cell may be used to retain comments about the hyperlink. It is also the text string that is displayed when the user pauses her mouse pointer over the SmartShape symbol containing the hyperlink.

Address

This cell holds a text string that specifies a URL address, DOS file name, or UNC to which to jump. You can specify Address as a relative path based on the base path defined for the document in the Options dialog box. If the document has no base path, Visio navigates based on the document path. If the document hasn't been saved, the hyperlink is undefined.

SubAddress

This cell holds a text string that specifies a location to which to link within the target document. For example, if the Address cell is MyDrawing.VSD, the SubAddress cell can specify a page name such as Page-3. If the Address cell is the Microsoft Excel file WeeDrams.xls, the value of this cell can be a worksheet or range within a worksheet, such as "Malt Distilleries" or "Sheet1!A1:D10." If the Address cell is http://www.visio.com/vdn/, the value of this cell can be a named anchor such as "solutions" within the document.

ExtraInfo

This cell holds the string value that represents a string that passes information to be used in resolving a URL, such as the coordinates of an image map. For example, in the ExtraInfo cell, x=41&y=7 specifies the coordinates of an image map.

Frame

This cell holds the string value that represents the name of a frame to target when Visio is open as an ActiveX document in an ActiveX container, such as Microsoft Internet Explorer 3.0 or later. The default is an empty string.

NewWindow

This cell holds the Boolean FALSE or TRUE (zero (0) or non-zero (-1)) value that determines whether to open the hyperlink in a new window. If TRUE, Visio opens the linked page, document, or Web site in a new window. The default is FALSE.

Default

This cell holds the Boolean FALSE or TRUE value that determines the default hyperlink for a shape or page. Set the value of this cell to TRUE to set a hyperlink as the default.

Linking Visio SmartShapes Symbols to Databases—The Visio Database Wizard

I'm sure you have heard it many times—Visio is more than just static pictures or clip art. Visio allows real-world data to be represented in an easy-to-use graphical manner. One mechanism that makes this more than a marketing ploy is Visio's introduction of the Database Wizard. The Database Wizard was introduced under Visio 4.0 and has improved with each iteration. I will walk through the process of creating a sample Microsoft Access database, creating an ODBC Datasource, and linking a Visio shape to a particular record in the required database. Additionally I will describe in detail the cells in the Visio ShapeSheet environment that are added or modified after the Wizard has run and discuss the capabilities that you acquire with your newly data-enabled Visio SmartShapes symbol.

I will create a custom Visio SmartShapes symbol to be used in a corporate organizational chart. Rather than start from scratch, I will "adaptively reuse" one of Visio's own organizational charting symbols and modify it to suit our needs. First, I will create an Access database. Next, I will set up an ODBC Datasource using the Access database I just created. Then I will go into Visio, modify our custom SmartShapes symbol, and run the Database Wizard. When the Wizard is finished, I will have a data-enabled SmartShapes symbol to use in our organizational chart.

I am presuming here that you are working with Microsoft Access 97. If you are using Office 2000, the dialog box might look slightly different. Go ahead and launch Access. As soon as it's initialized, you will see a dialog box that looks like Figure 6.1.

Associating Data with Visio SmartShape Symbols

CHAPTER 6

177

6

ASSOCIATING DATA
WITH VISIO
SMARTSHAPE
SYMBOLS

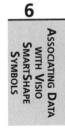

FIGURE 6.1
Microsoft Access database dialog box.

You are being asked to either open an existing database, run Access's Database Wizard, or create a new blank database. I will create my own database, so select the top option as shown above, and then click OK. Next, you will see Figure 6.2.

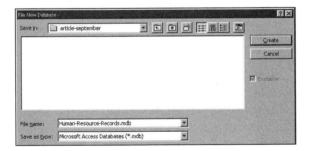

FIGURE 6.2
File New database dialog box.

This navigable dialog box allows you to select the directory where you want to place the new database and the name that you choose to give it. I will call mine "Human-Resource-Records." Select the directory where you want your database to reside, type in the name as I have done in Figure 6.2 above, and then click the Create button. You will next see the Database system objects window as shown in Figure 6.3.

Now that I have the shell of our database created, I must actually design the structure of the table that will be used to hold the data I need to reference in our SmartShapes symbols. To do this, be sure the Tables tab is selected and then click on the New button. A dialog box will appear asking you to select the mode in which you want to create your table (see Figure 6.4).

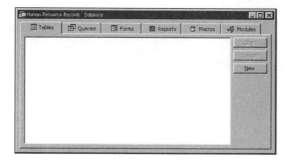

FIGURE 6.3

Access database system objects window.

FIGURE 6.4

New Table dialog box.

Select the Design view and click OK. You will now enter the Table Design window. Enter the information as shown in Figure 6.5.

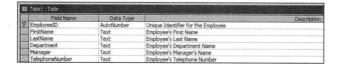

FIGURE 6.5

Access data table.

Make sure that you set the first field, "EmployeeID," as the key field by clicking on the small "key" icon above the window. Note the data type for each field. It is not necessary to add the descriptions for each field, but it certainly helps in making changes later...especially for those of you who use cryptic field names! When you have completed the entries, click the "X" in the upper-right corner of the window to close it. A dialog box (see Figure 6.6) will appear asking you if you want to save your changes.

Associating Data with Visio SmartShape Symbols 179

CHAPTER 6

6

ASSOCIATING DATA
WITH VISIO
SMARTSHAPE
SYMBOLS

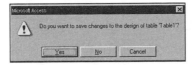

FIGURE 6.6
The Confirm Save Table dialog box.

Click Yes. A dialog box will then pop up asking you to name the table. Name it Employee and click OK (see Figure 6.7).

FIGURE 6.7
Named Employee Table dialog box.

Your Database System Objects window should now look like Figure 6.8.

FIGURE 6.8
Access database system objects dialog box with table.

Before I finish with Access, I should probably enter some sample data to fill the records in the newly created table. With the Tables tab active and the Employee table name highlighted, click Open. This will bring you into the data entry window for the Employee table. Add the four record entries as shown in Figure 6.9.

When complete, close the data entry window and then exit Access. Step one is complete. Now that you have created the database, you must let your system know that it exists and will be available for use through Open DataBase Connectivity (DDBC). This is accomplished relatively easily through the 32-bit ODBC Data Source Administrator. From the Start menu on your desktop, go to Control Panel. Here you will find an icon for the 32-bit ODBC Data Source Administrator. Double-click it to launch the application. When it is launched, you will see a window similar to the one shown in Figure 6.10.

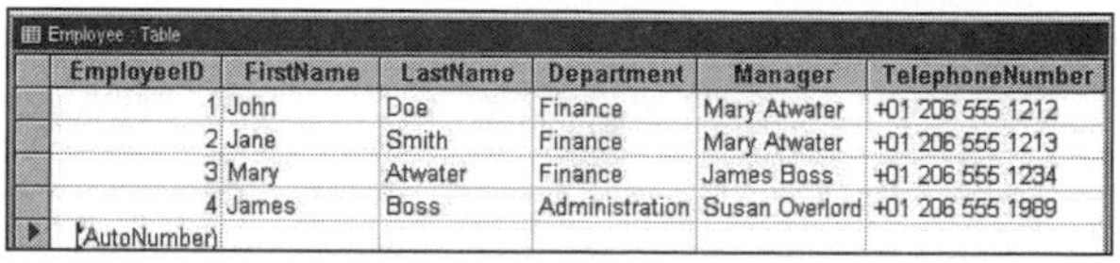

EmployeeID	FirstName	LastName	Department	Manager	TelephoneNumber
1	John	Doe	Finance	Mary Atwater	+01 206 555 1212
2	Jane	Smith	Finance	Mary Atwater	+01 206 555 1213
3	Mary	Atwater	Finance	James Boss	+01 206 555 1234
4	James	Boss	Administration	Susan Overlord	+01 206 555 1989
(AutoNumber)					

FIGURE 6.9

Employee table records.

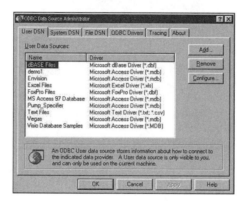

FIGURE 6.10

The 32-bit ODBC Data Source Administrator dialog box.

The User Data Sources listing may differ, but the rest will be as you see it here. I must create a new User Data Source. With the User DSN tab selected, click the Add button. The Create New Data Source dialog box will appear as shown in Figure 6.11.

Because I just completed creating an Access database, I will select the Microsoft Access Driver from the list of available drivers. With the Access Driver selected, click Finish. When you are returned to the Administrator, fill in the name of the data source as "My Employees" and then click on the Select button in the Database frame. You will now see the Select Database dialog box as shown in Figure 6.12.

Associating Data with Visio SmartShape Symbols

CHAPTER 6

181

6

ASSOCIATING DATA
WITH VISIO
SMARTSHAPE
SYMBOLS

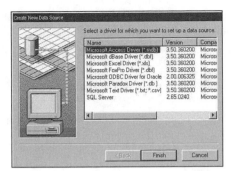

FIGURE 6.11
Create New Data Source dialog box.

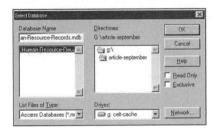

FIGURE 6.12
Select Database dialog box.

Select the Access database you just finished creating. The path to your own copy of this may differ from the one that I have shown, but the process is identical. When you have selected our Human-Resource-Records.MDB database, click OK. The 32-bit ODBC Data Source Administrator should now look very much like the one shown in Figure 6.13.

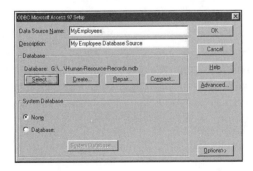

FIGURE 6.13
Data Source dialog box.

After you have completed these tasks and your window looks similar to the one shown above, click OK. You will be returned to the main 32-bit ODBC Administrator window. It should look very similar to the one shown in Figure 6.14, with your new Data Source listed.

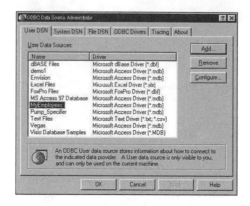

FIGURE 6.14

32-bit ODBC administrator with new data source.

Very good! That's all there is to creating a new data source. With the database in order and the data source established, I can now turn our attention to Visio and the customization of the organizational chart shape.

Go ahead and launch Visio 5.0 or Visio 2000, any edition, Standard, Technical, Professional, or Enterprise. Begin a new drawing based on the Business Diagram Organization Chart.VST template. You can do this by selecting File, New, Organization Chart, Organization Chart from the menu. Drag a position shape from the Stencil and drop it anywhere on the page. Now right-click the Stencil and close it. The Stencil will no longer be required here. Next, select Window, Show Document Stencil from the menu. The local stencil for the drawing will be opened. Find the master for the Position shape and delete it by selecting it in the stencil and right-clicking and selecting delete. A message box will appear, warning you that this will sever the connection between the master and the instance in the drawing. This is perfectly fine because you want to customize your own shape and simply reuse it as it was originally created for the basis of our work. Click OK to confirm your choice. Now close the local Stencil window. Next select Window, Show ShapeSheet from the menu. Your drawing should look similar to the Figure 6.15.

Notice the Custom Properties Section of the ShapeSheet window. There are already several Custom Properties supplied with this Position shape. Department, Telephone, HideBox,

Associating Data with Visio SmartShape Symbols 183

CHAPTER 6

6

ASSOCIATING DATA
WITH VISIO
SMARTSHAPE
SYMBOLS

ShowDivider, and ConnOffset are already set up for our use. You need to add the following additional Custom Properties: FirstName, LastName, Manager, and EmployeeID. You will need to add the additional rows by selecting Insert, Row from the menu for each row you need. When the rows have been added, fill in the cells in the rows as shown above. Modify the SortKey order as shown above and make your ShapeSheet look as much like Figure 6.15 as possible. When this is complete, close the ShapeSheet window. You are now ready to run Visio's Database Wizard to finish the data linking for this shape.

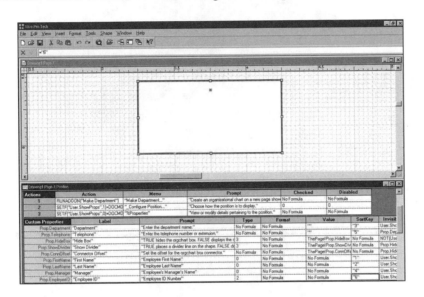

FIGURE 6.15

Customize position SmartShape symbol in Visio.

Select Tools, Macro, Macros, Visio Extras, Database Wizard as shown in Figure 6.16.

This will begin the execution of Visio's Database Wizard. The first screen you will see is the opening or "splash" screen as shown in Figure 6.17.

This is designed to familiarize you with the functionality of the Wizard. Click Next to continue. You will be taken to the Choose Task screen as shown in Figure 6.18.

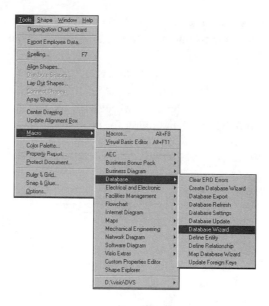

FIGURE 6.16

The menu to start the Database Wizard.

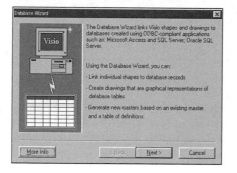

FIGURE 6.17

The Database Wizard opening screen.

Here, you can link a shape to a database record (which is exactly what you want to do), create a linked drawing, or generate new masters. Make sure the first radio button is selected as shown in Figure 6.18 and click Next. You will be taken to the Choose Shape screen as shown in Figure 6.19.

Associating Data with Visio SmartShape Symbols

CHAPTER 6

185

6

ASSOCIATING DATA
WITH VISIO
SMARTSHAPE
SYMBOLS

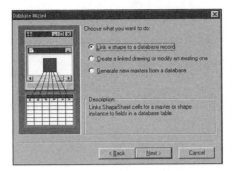

FIGURE 6.18
The Database Wizard screen used to choose the task.

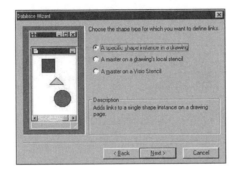

FIGURE 6.19
The Database Wizard screen used to choose the desired shape.

Here, you can choose a specific shape(s) in the drawing (which is what you want to do), a master on a local stencil, or a master on a standalone stencil. Because you want to link our own custom shape, choose the first option. Be sure the first radio button is selected and click Next. The next page will appear as shown in Figure 6.20.

Notice that the Database Wizard has already found the current drawing, the current page, and the shapes on the page. You should select the Position shape from the list because this Position shape is the one I will link to the database. Select the Position shape from the list and then click Next. You will be taken to the Choose Data Source screen as shown in Figure 6.21.

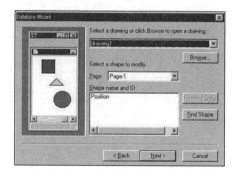

FIGURE 6.20

The Database Wizard screen used to choose drawing page and shape.

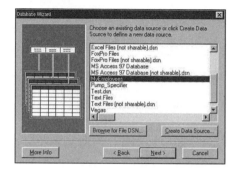

FIGURE 6.21

Database Wizard screen used to choose data source.

Notice in the list of data sources, our "MyEmployees" data source is listed. If you have not previously created a data source, the Visio Database Wizard allows you to create one now via the Create Data Source button. Because you have done your homework properly, you simply need to ensure that the "MyEmployees" data source is selected and click Next. This will take you to the Choose Table screen as shown in Figure 6.22.

Note that the Human-Resource-Records database is already filled in and the Employee Table is selected. You have the capability to link to tables, views (queries), system tables, and aliases. With the Employees Table selected, click Next. You will be taken to a screen that enables you to choose the number of keys you would like, as shown in Figure 6.23.

The database that you created has one table, and that one table has one key field. Therefore, you want to ensure that the Database Wizard is looking for one primary key. Note, however, that the Wizard can use as many as five fields in a highly complex key structure if necessary. Ensure that the "1" is selected in the Number of Fields drop-down list and click Next. You will be taken to the Choose Primary Key Field screen as shown in Figure 6.24.

Associating Data with Visio SmartShape Symbols 187

CHAPTER 6

6

ASSOCIATING DATA
WITH VISIO
SMARTSHAPE
SYMBOLS

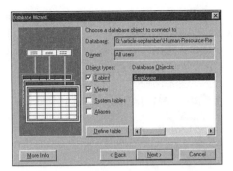

FIGURE 6.22
Database Wizard screen for choosing a table.

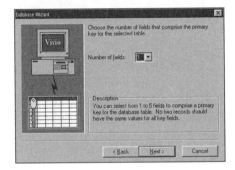

FIGURE 6.23
Database Wizard screen used to choose the number of keys.

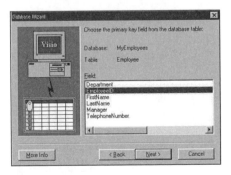

FIGURE 6.24
Database Wizard screen used to select the primary key.

Note that the primary key I created when I created the Access database is already selected. It is the EmployeeID field. Note also that all of the fields in the table definition are listed here. Ensure that the EmployeeID field is selected and click Next. You will be taken to the Choose Default Key screen as shown in Figure 6.25.

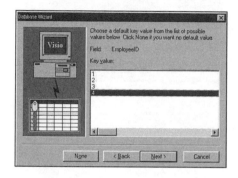

FIGURE 6.25

The Database Wizard screen used to choose the default record.

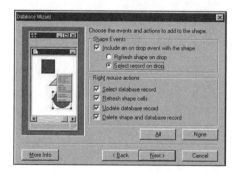

FIGURE 6.26

Database Wizard screen to choose events.

All the Employee ID numbers for all the current records in the database are listed here. You have the option of either using one of these as the default record or having no default record selected. To select no default record, click None. In this case, you will use the boss, record number/employee number 4 as our default. Select 4 in the key values list and click Next. You will be taken to a screen that allows you to choose events, as shown in Figure 6.26.

Here I select the features I want to be enabled after the Database Wizard has completed and I begin using my data-enabled shape. Under the Shape Events, I have a choice of either refreshing the shape from its default record on drop, or selecting a record on drop. Because I want to

Associating Data with Visio SmartShape Symbols

CHAPTER 6

189

6

ASSOCIATING DATA
WITH VISIO
SMARTSHAPE
SYMBOLS

select an employee's record each time I drop a shape, I'll click the radio button labeled Select Record on Drop. The next check box list controls the right mouse actions. Here I choose what actions should be made available to this shape: Select a Database Record, Refresh Shape Cells, Update Database Record, and Delete Shape and Database Record. For the purposes of this tutorial, I will select all of the available options. Ensure that all four are checked and then click Next. This will take you to the Choose ShapeSheet cell to link the key field screen as shown in Figure 6.27.

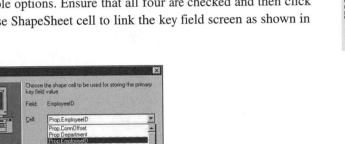

FIGURE 6.27
The Database Wizard screen to choose cell.

Here I choose the shape's ShapeSheet cell to link to the Database's key field. If I have a cell that has the same name as the key field, the Database Wizard will find and use that cell as shown above. If not, a new cell will be suggested and made available to be used for that purpose. Ensure that the Prop.EmployeeID cell is selected and then click Next. This will take you to the Match Fields and Cells screen as shown in Figure 6.28.

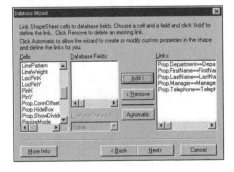

FIGURE 6.28
Database Wizard screen to match fields and cells.

This screen allows us to map cells in the shape's ShapeSheet environment to the fields in the database record. There are two columns: cells and database fields. Click a cell name, click a corresponding database field, and then click Add. For example, to add the Telephone field, click and highlight the Prop.Telephone item in the cells list, click and highlight the Telephone field from the Database Fields list, and then click Add. Repeat this for each item in the Database Fields listing. Now click Next. This will take you to a screen that lets you review your choices, as shown in Figure 6.29.

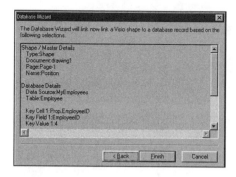

FIGURE 6.29
Database Wizard screen for reviewing choices.

This screen presents you with a scrollable listing of all the choices you have made in the Visio Database Wizard. If, for any reason, you made an error in selection or judgment, you can use the Back button to go back and correct the particular item. If, however, your choices are all correct and the items look appropriate, click Finish to complete the run of the Wizard. Your new Visio SmartShapes symbol is almost complete.

I also want to display some of the database information as text on the face of the shape. To do this, double-click the Position shape. Press Delete to remove any default text on the shape. Now choose Insert, Field from the menu. The Visio Text Field dialog box will appear as shown in Figure 6.30.

FIGURE 6.30
Insert text field menu.

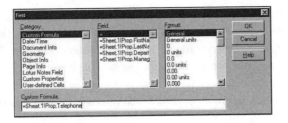

FIGURE 6.31

Text fields dialog box.

Select Custom Formula in the Category List. Now enter the formula
=Sheet.1!Prop.FirstName in the Custom Formula line at the bottom of the dialog box. Click
OK. The Record Information for the First Name in the selected record will appear as text on
the shape. Repeat this process for each of the additional items that you want on the shape: Last
Name, Department, Manager, and Telephone.

Congratulations! Your new data-enabled SmartShape is complete, linked with the Visio
Database Wizard, and ready to use.

Before you make a master out of this SmartShape and use it as part of your solution, it would
be wise to see just what the Visio Database Wizard did to your shape. Select the shape and
choose Window, Show ShapeSheet from the menu. The ShapeSheet window will open. The
newly created and modified ShapeSheet cells should look as shown in Figure 6.32.

4	RUNADDON("Database Select Rec	"Select database record"	"Select a record from the database table."	0		0	
5	RUNADDON("Database Refresh Sh	"Refresh shape properties"	"Refresh linked shape cells using values from the	0		0	
6	RUNADDON("Database Update Rec	"Update database record"	"Update linked record in database table with shape	0		0	
7	RUNADDON("Database Delete Sha	"Delete shape and record"	"Delete the selected shape and the associated reco	0		0	

Custom Properties	Label	Prompt	Type	Format	Value	SortKey
Prop.Department	"Department"	"Enter the department name."	No Formula	No Formula	"Administration"	"3"
Prop.Telephone	"Telephone"	"Enter the telephone number or extension."	No Formula	No Formula	"+01 206 555 1989"	"5"
Prop.HideBox	"Hide Box"	"TRUE hides the orgchart box. FALSE displays the o	3	No Formula	ThePage!Prop.HideBox	No Formula
Prop.ShowDivider	"Show Divider"	"TRUE places a divider line on the shape. FALSE do	3	No Formula	ThePage!Prop.ShowDiv	No Formula
Prop.ConnOffset	"Connector Offset"	"Set the offset for the orgchart box connector."	No Formula	No Formula	ThePage!Prop.ConnOffs	No Formula
Prop.FirstName	"First Name"	"Employee First Name"	0	No Formula	"James"	"1"
Prop.LastName	"Last Name"	"Employee Last Name"	0	No Formula	"Boss"	"2"
Prop.Manager	"Manager"	"Employee's Manager's Name"	0	No Formula	"Susan Overlord"	"4"
Prop.EmployeeID	"Employee ID"	"Employee ID Number"	2	No Formula	"4"	"5"

User-defined Cells	Value	Prompt				
User.MinOffset	0.125 in.	No Formula				
User.ShowProps	0	No Formula				
User.ODBCDataSource	"MyEmployees"	"The ODBC data source to which the shape is linked				
User.ODBCQualifier	""	"Qualifier cell. This cell contains the name of t				
User.ODBCTable	"Employee"	"The database table to which the shape is linked."				
User.ODBCKeyField1	"EmployeeID"	"Key field link. This cell stores the name of a c				
User.ODBCKeyCell1	"Prop.EmployeeID"	"Key cell. This cell contains the name of a custo				
User.ODBCKeyMirror1	"4"	"Key field mirror cell. This cell contains the mo				
User.ODBCLink1	"Prop.Department==Department==0"	"A link field. Specifies which cell in the shape				
User.ODBCMirror1	"Administration"	"A mirror field. Stores the most recently retriev				
User.ODBCLink2	"Prop.FirstName==FirstName==0"	"A link field. Specifies which cell in the shape				
User.ODBCMirror2	"James"	"A mirror field. Stores the most recently retriev				
User.ODBCLink3	"Prop.LastName==LastName==0"	"A link field. Specifies which cell in the shape				
User.ODBCMirror3	"Boss"	"A mirror field. Stores the most recently retriev				
User.ODBCLink4	"Prop.Manager==Manager==0"	"A link field. Specifies which cell in the shape				
User.ODBCMirror4	"Susan Overlord"	"A mirror field. Stores the most recently retriev				
User.ODBCLink5	"Prop.Telephone==TelephoneNumbe	"A link field. Specifies which cell in the shape				
User.ODBCMirror5	"+01 206 555 1989"	"A mirror field. Stores the most recently retriev				

FIGURE 6.32

New ShapeSheet cells.

Note that a large number of User-defined cells have been added, as well as a series of Action cells. Each of the Action cells equates to the running of a particular function that you chose in the Database Wizard. Notice there are four action items: Select Database Record, Refresh Shape Properties, Update Database Record, and Delete Shape and Record. These directly correspond to the items you chose using the Choose Events screen. Each of these include a =RUNADDON() function with the proper arguments to run the required functionality.

The User Defined cells are actually quite self-explanatory after you begin looking at them. Note that there are cells like User.ODBCDataSource, which holds the name of the ODBC Datasource you created, User.ODBCTable, which holds the name of the table that you are referencing. Notice the User.ODBCKeyField1 holding the "EmployeeID" key field name and how that is mapped to the User.ODBCKeyCell1 holding the "Prop.EmployeeID" name and the User.ODBCKeyMirror1 holding the "4" value that is the currently selected EmployeeID Record value. This same schema is used for each of the remaining linked fields. Note that here is a link and mirror for each. The link establishes the mapping and the mirror holds the value. Where the link refers to the Custom Properties Prop.XXX item, the value from the mirror is passed to that cell as well.

Figure 6.33 shows the Visio drawing with a new local master for our Position shape and a simple diagram created from this new local master.

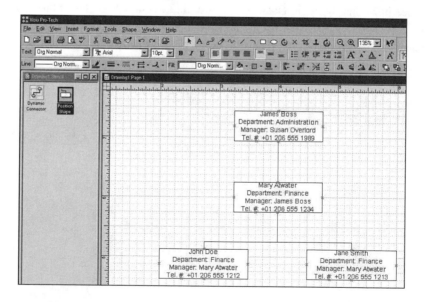

FIGURE 6.33

Drawing and new local master.

Finally, Figure 6.34 below shows the right-click menus created by the wizard for manipulating the shape and the corresponding database records.

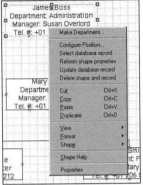

FIGURE 6.34

New right-click menus.

There you have it, folks: the Visio Database Wizard. I've shown you how to create an Access database, an ODBC data source, a custom Visio SmartShapes symbol, how to run the Visio Database Wizard, and what happens when the Wizard runs. With this information, you should be able to create your own custom data-enabled Visio SmartShapes symbols—the key to making your solutions valuable, intelligent, and powerful!

This has been a fairly data-intensive chapter. I've looked at Visio's original methodology for storing data: the Data1, Data2, and Data3 fields. I've looked in-depth at Custom Properties and have explored just the surface of what can be accomplished by tapping into the power of Custom Properties. I've analyzed how hyperlinks are stored in a Visio ShapeSheet. Finally, I stepped through Visio's Database Wizard to learn how to connect an ODBC-compliant data source to any Visio SmartShape symbol.

In the next chapter, I will take a slightly different course. I will cover some very specialized Visio SmartShape symbol behaviors, as well as 1D symbols. I will discuss how 1D symbols are classified and how glue is established in Visio symbols. I will also cover the GlueInfo section of a ShapeSheet and discuss dynamic connectors as well as Autorouting.

Specialized Visio SmartShape Symbol Behavior

IN THIS CHAPTER

One of the traditional hallmarks of Visio is the ease of creation of connected diagrams: those diagrams that use SmartShape symbols connected by lines. These lines represent the flow and direction of the connections between the symbols and assist the user of the diagram in understanding the intent of the diagram. Some examples of connected diagrams are flowcharts, organizational charts, business process diagrams, process and identification (P&ID) diagrams, workflow diagrams, and basic software design and development diagrams.

All of the above diagram types make use of "lines" that are 1D SmartShape symbols as connectors. However there are also many, many other types of 1D symbols. In fact, any Visio SmartShape symbol can be either a 1D or a ;2D symbols2D symbol. It is not how the symbol looks that distinguishes it as a 1D or a 2D symbol; rather, it is how the symbol behaves. Remember also that under Visio 5.0 and earlier, 1D symbols glue to 2D symbols. 2D symbols do not glue to 1D symbols. Under Visio 2000 we can, in fact, establish glue between 2D symbols.

Let's try an experiment. Drag out a rectangle. Make the rectangle SmartShape symbol exactly two inches wide by one inch tall. Now Ctrl+drag out a copy of that rectangle SmartShape symbol and place it a small distance below the first. On the upper or first rectangle, add text to the symbol that says "2D." On the lower or second rectangle, add text to the symbol which says "1D."

Select only the lower or "1D" Rectangle SmartShape symbol. With the symbol selected, select Format, Behavior from the menus. In the Behavior dialog box, select the Behavior Tab. Look at the Interaction Style area of the dialog box. You will notice that there are two options selectable here as radio buttons: line (1D) and box (2D). By default, when the rectangle SmartShape symbol was created, because it had both Height and width, it was created as a 2D symbol using the box interaction style. Click the line (1D) Interaction style radio button and then click OK to exit the dialog box. Now that you are back in the drawing window environment, alternately click and select the 2D and 1D symbols. Notice that the 2D symbol has sizing handles at all four corners and at all four midpoints of its bounding box. The 1D symbol has different sizing handles at the apparent midpoints of each side of the bounding box. Notice also that the sizing handle at the left of the symbol has a small X and that the sizing handle at the right has a small +. Note that the sizing handles at the top and bottom are similar to those on 2D symbols. There are no sizing handles at the four corners on the 1D symbol.

Select the 2D symbol again. If you want to rotate the symbol, you must select the Rotation tool from the Toolbar. When selected, this tool allows you to "grab" any one corner of the Rectangle SmartShape symbol and rotate the symbol about its pin, the small dot that is seen at the center of the symbol (designated by the location of the LocPinX and LocPinY in the ShapeSheet for the symbol). Reselect the pointer tool. Now select the 1D symbol. To rotate this symbol, simply grab either the X (begin point) or the + (end point) of the symbol and reposition it as you like. Note that this not only rotates the symbol but also can resize the symbol's width. Select the Rotation tool. As you can see the begin and end points become round green handles and that the SmartShape symbol can be manipulated in a manner similar to a 2D symbol rotating about its pin.

The key here is the interaction style. A 2D symbol interacts with the user by being controlled by the parameters of the bounding box. A 1D symbol interacts with the user by being controlled by an imaginary "line" between the begin and end points of the symbol.

Now that you understand the differences between a 1D and a 2D symbol as they apply to the user from the user interface, we should examine just what happened when we selected Format, Behavior, and transformed the 2D symbol into a 1D symbol. Select the 2D Rectangle symbol. Open its ShapeSheet. Select the 1D Rectangle symbol. Open its ShapeSheet.

You should immediately note that the 1D SmartShape symbol's ShapeSheet has a new section added: a 1D Endpoints section. This section contains four cells: BeginX, BeginY, EndX, and EndY. They should be quite self-explanatory. They are the X ordinate and Y abscissa of the begin point (the X) and the end point (the +) of the 1D symbol. Notice also how four of the formulas in the Shape Transform section have been changed dramatically. The Width, Angle, PinX, and PinY cells have new and rather complex formulas in them.

Important Concept Number Ten

When you change a SmartShape symbol's interaction from 2D to 1D, any formulas in the Width, Angle, PinX and PinY cells will be destroyed and replaced with these new default formulas. You may then alter them at will.

Let's look at each of the formulas in these four cells. We'll begin with the Width cell. The new formula reads

```
"=SQRT((EndX-BeginX)^2+(EndY-BeginY)^2)"
```

In the Angle cell, the new formula reads

```
"=ATAN2(EndY-BeginY,EndX-BeginX)"
```

In the PinX cell, the new formula reads

```
"=(BeginX+EndX)/2"
```

And in the PinY cell, the new formula reads

```
"=(BeginY+EndY)/2"
```

Take a look at Figure 7.1.

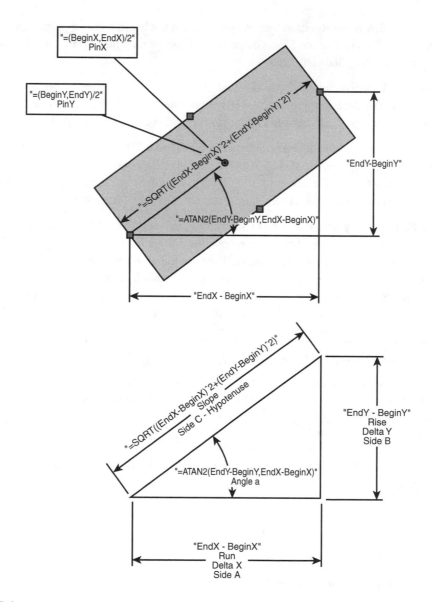

FIGURE 7.1

Trigonometry of a 1D SmartShape symbol.

Notice that the width of the symbol (that is, if not rotated, the horizontal distance between the begin point and the end point) is defined by the Pythagorean theorem. Remember the Pythagorean theorem from your trigonometry class? The length of the hypotenuse is equal to the square root of the run squared plus the rise squared, the old $A^2+B^2=C^2$. In our case, the rise is equal to the change in Y from begin to end, and the run is equal to the change in X from begin to end. Therefore, the width is equal to the square root of the sum of the change in Y squared and the change in X squared.

In a right triangle, the angle can be derived from the arctangent of rise over run, so in our case, the arctangent of the change in Y divided by the change in X. The pin of the shape is designated, of course, by the pairing of the PinX and the PinY. The formulas for these are relatively simple. The PinX is half the change in X, and the pin is half the change in Y.

These are the default formulas Visio places in the cells. Again, after the transformation has taken place from 2D to 1D, you are free to alter these formulas in any manner you like to create the custom behavior you seek for your SmartShape symbol.

Important Concept Number Eleven

When Visio transforms a 2D SmartShape symbol into a 1D SmartShape symbol, it does so left to right. In other words, the begin point will always be placed at what was width times zero (=Width*0) in X and height times one half (=Height*0.5) in Y, and the endpoint will always be placed at what was width times one (=Width*1) in X and height times one half (=Height*0.5) in Y. Therefore, when you create a SmartShape symbol you plan to transform from 2D to 1D, do so with this left-to-right orientation in mind.

Classes of 1D SmartShapes Symbols

In terms of Visio's view of 1D symbols, there are essentially two classes of 1D SmartShape symbols: height-based and right-side-up. As we progress, we are going to build one of each of these classes of 1D SmartShape symbols as well as discuss their performance and how they are both used and interacted with.

Let's take the height-based 1D SmartShape symbols first. A height-based 1D SmartShape symbol is referred to as such not only because the user interacts with the endpoints as they would with any other 1D symbol, but also because the sizing of the symbol is totally controlled by the height of the symbol rather than the width. This eliminated the rather strange "stretching" that would otherwise occur when the endpoints are located either nearer to or farther apart from each other. Examples of this class of 1D symbology are electronic components such as diodes or resistors on wires, valve symbols, and any schematic symbol used as part of a connected diagram.

Open the diode drawing from the companion CD-ROM. Each time you want to work with, test, or reverse-engineer any of these symbols, remember to drag out a copy of the symbol and work with the copy. Look first at the diode symbol. When you select it, notice that you see the begin-point ("X") and end-point (+) symbols; however, you do not see the height symbols. Instead, you see two control handles on the diode symbol. Float your cursor over first one and then the other control handle. The Control handle at the left controls the position of the diode along the length of the wire. The other control handle controls the size of the diode symbol itself. It does not matter where you move the endpoints of the wire; the diode keeps its proper proportion. Next, take a look at the resistor symbol. The control handle controls the size of the resistor component along the wire as well as the height does. This gives the user lots of flexibility for symbol-sizing when utilizing the resistor symbol. Finally, look at the gate symbol. Because it is width-controlled, it is distorted when the endpoints are moved. Notice the double-click behavior. The gate opens and closes with each double-click. By now, you should begin to get a feel for how these SmartShape symbol implementations work. Remember the Controls section, the Events section, the Shape Transform section, the Geometry section, the User-Defined section, and the Protection section. You will be looking at all these sections as you analyze the symbols in a moment.

Let's create our own diode symbol. Draw a triangle with its apex to the left and its base vertically placed to the right, just as you see it in the diode drawing. Set the fill foreground color to black. Draw the single vertical line at the left side of the triangle. Draw a line from the apex of the triangle to the left to act as the left wire. Finally draw a line from the midpoint of the triangle's base to the right to act as the right wire. Your symbol should now consist of one triangle and three lines. Everything should be solid black. Select the triangle. Now hold down Shift and select (in this order): the vertical line, the left wire line, and the right wire line. Select Shape, Operations, Combine from the menus. The order in which we selected these is important! Remember, we stated earlier that the new SmartShape symbol created from the destruction of the former selected symbols takes on its properties from the first symbol selected. Furthermore, the order in which they were selected determines the order of the new Geometry sections in the new Combined symbol. Next, with the new symbol selected, select Format, Behavior from the menus. Change the interaction style to 1D and click OK to exit the dialog box. Now open the ShapeSheet for the new diode SmartShape symbol.

There should be four Geometry sections in your ShapeSheet. The first is the triangle, the second should be the vertical line, the third should be the left wire, and finally the fourth should be the right wire. All of the X Cells in the Geometry section are referring to some fractional amount of width. This is why when the endpoints are moved and the shape is changed in width, the shape proportionally distorts. What we need to do is change the references in the X cells to be based on a percentage of height instead. In the triangle that I created, I made the height of the triangle equal to the distance across its base. This made the triangle fit within a "square" area. Because of this, it is very easy to make the formula changes that referred to width now refer to height. In my symbol, I placed two control handles to do the work for us. I'm going to list the applicable sections of the ShapeSheet and at the end of each section describe the new formulas (see Table 7.1).

TABLE 7.1   SHAPESHEET : SHEET.5 Start Section : 1D ENDPOINTS

Cell	Value	Formula
BeginX	3.0000 in.	3 inches
BeginY	6.2500 in.	6.25 inches
EndX	5.5000 in.	5.5 inches
EndY	6.2500 in.	6.25 inches
End Section : 1D ENDPOINTS (CELLS TOTAL : 4)		

The Endpoints section simply lists the placement of the endpoints as the SmartShape symbol sits on the page at design time.

As you can see in Table 7.2, when we converted the symbol from 2D to 1D, the custom formulas were added to the Shape Transform section of the ShapeSheet.

TABLE 7.2   Start Section : SHAPE TRANSFORM

Cell	Value	Formula
Width	2.5000 in.	`SQRT((EndX-BeginX)^2+(EndY-BeginY)^2)`
Height	0.5000 in.	`GUARD(Controls.Y2)`
Angle	0.0000 deg.	`ATAN2(EndY-BeginY,EndX-BeginX)`
PinX	4.2500 in.	`(BeginX+EndX)/2`
PinY	6.2500 in.	`(BeginY+EndY)/2`
LocPinX	1.2500 in.	`Width*0.5`
LocPinY	0.2500 in.	`Height*0.5`
FlipX	FALSE	`FALSE`
FlipY	FALSE	`FALSE`
ResizeMode	0	`0`
End Section : SHAPE TRANSFORM (CELLS TOTAL : 10)		

In the User-defined cells (see Table 7.3), I set up certain perameters that I force the controls to follow. The first two rows prohibit the diode from sliding off the wire. This is done by restricting the travel of the control handle. The formulas state that if the control handle ever gets less that the zero width point plus a small amount, we simply force the control handle back there. The same is true if the control handle ever progresses too far to the right. The second two rows perform similar actions by never letting the diode symbol get larger in height than the total width of the symbol, nor let it get smaller than an arbitrary eighth of an inch.

TABLE 7.3 Start Section : USER DEFINED CELLS

Cell	Value	Formula
User.MinLeftTravel	0.0000	IF(Controls.X1<0.125 inches,SETF("Controls.X1", 0.125 inches),0)
User.MinLeftTravel.Prompt	Set the maximum leftward distance - the diode can travel on the wire	Set the maximum leftward distance the diode can travel on the wire
User.MaxRightTravel	0.0000	IF(Controls.X1>Width-(Height+0.125 inches),SETF("Controls.X1", Width-(Height+0.125 inches)),0)
User.MaxRightTravel.Prompt	Set the maximum rightward distance the diode can travel on the wire	Set the maximum rightward distance the diode can travel on the wire
User.MaxTopTravel	0.0000	IF(Controls.Y2>Width-(Height+0.25 inches),SETF("Controls.Y2", Width-(Height+0.25 inches)),0)
User.MaxTopTravel.Prompt	Set the largest allowable size for the symbol	Set the largest allowable size for the symbol
User.MaxBottomT	0.0000	IF(Controls.Y2<0.125 inches,SETF("Controls.Y2", 0.125 inches),0)

Cell	Value	Formula
User.MaxBottomT.Prompt	Set the smallest allowable height for the symbol	`Set the smallest allowable height for the symbol`
End Section : USER DEFINED CELLS (CELLS TOTAL : 8)		

The movement along the wire control (see Table 7.4) has been restricted in Y movement because the Ybehavior is locked (1).

TABLE 7.4   Start Section : CONTROLS

Cell	Value	Formula
Controls.X1	1.0000 in.	`Width/2+-0.25 inches`
Controls.Y1	0.2500 in.	`Height*0.5`
Controls.XDyn	1.0000 in.	`Controls.X1`
Controls.YDyn	0.2500 in.	`Controls.Y1`
Controls.XCon	3	`3`
Controls.YCon	1	`1`
Controls.CanGlue	FALSE	`FALSE`
Controls.Prompt	Adjust the position of the diode along the wire	`Adjust the position of the diode along the wire`
Controls.X2	1.5000 in.	`GUARD(Controls.X1+Height)`
Controls.Y2	0.5000 in.	`Height*1`
Controls.XDyn[2]	1.5000 in.	`Controls.X2`
Controls.YDyn[2]	0.5000 in.	`Controls.Y2`
Controls.XCon[2]	3	`3`
Controls.YCon[2]	0	`0`
Controls.CanGlue[2]	FALSE	`FALSE`
Controls.Prompt[2]	Adjust the size of the diode	`Adjust the size of the diode`
End Section : CONTROLS (CELLS TOTAL : 16)		

In the first (triangle's) Geometry section (see Table 7.5), we take the apex of the triangle and make it totally controlled by the first control handle. Notice that because the triangle's size was a square, we could make the next X cell read `Controls.X1 + Height`, which still gave us exactly the same proportion as if we were referring to the change in X from Apex to base of the Triangle. We set this for the X ordinate of both ends of the triangle's base.

TABLE 7.5 Start Section : GEOMETRY

Cell	Value	Formula
Geometry1.NoFill(Component)	FALSE	FALSE
Geometry1.NoLine(Component)	FALSE	FALSE
Geometry1.NoShow(Component)	FALSE	FALSE
Geometry1.NoSnap(Component)	FALSE	FALSE
Geometry1.X1(MoveTo)	1.0000 in.	Controls.X1
Geometry1.Y1(MoveTo)	0.2500 in.	Height*0.5
Geometry1.X2(LineTo)	1.5000 in.	Controls.X1+Height
Geometry1.Y2(LineTo)	0.0000 in.	0 inches
Geometry1.X3(LineTo)	1.5000 in.	Controls.X1+Height
Geometry1.Y3(LineTo)	0.5000 in.	Height
Geometry1.X4(LineTo)	1.0000 in.	Geometry1.X1
Geometry1.Y4(LineTo)	0.2500 in.	Height*0.5

In Geometry section two (the vertical line, Table 7.6), we simply referred the X values directly to the first control handle.

TABLE 7.6 Start Section : GEOMETRY

Cell	Value	Formula
Geometry2.NoFill(Component)	TRUE	TRUE
Geometry2.NoLine(Component)	FALSE	FALSE
Geometry2.NoShow(Component)	FALSE	FALSE
Geometry2.NoSnap(Component)	FALSE	FALSE
Geometry2.X1(MoveTo)	1.0000 in.	Controls.X1
Geometry2.Y1(MoveTo)	0.5000 in.	Height*1
Geometry2.X2(LineTo)	1.0000 in.	Controls.X1
Geometry2.Y2(LineTo)	0.0000 in.	Height*0

The right end of the line in the third geometry section (the left wire, Table 7.7) is likewise controlled in X directly by the control handle.

TABLE 7.7   Start Section : GEOMETRY

Cell	Value	Formula
Geometry3.NoFill(Component)	TRUE	TRUE
Geometry3.NoLine(Component)	FALSE	FALSE
Geometry3.NoShow(Component)	FALSE	FALSE
Geometry3.NoSnap(Component)	FALSE	FALSE
Geometry3.X1(MoveTo)	0.0000 in.	0 inches
Geometry3.Y1(MoveTo)	0.2500 in.	Height*0.5
Geometry3.X2(LineTo)	1.0000 in.	Controls.X1
Geometry3.Y2(LineTo)	0.2500 in.	Height*0.5

Finally, the left end of the line in the fourth geometry section (the right wire, see Table 7.8) is likewise controlled in X directly by the control handle plus the height.

TABLE 7.8   Start Section : GEOMETRY

Cell	Value	Formula
Geometry4.NoFill(Component)	TRUE	TRUE
Geometry4.NoLine(Component)	FALSE	FALSE
Geometry4.NoShow(Component)	FALSE	FALSE
Geometry4.NoSnap(Component)	FALSE	FALSE
Geometry4.X1(MoveTo)	1.5000 in.	Controls.X1+Height
Geometry4.Y1(MoveTo)	0.2500 in.	Height*0.5
Geometry4.X2(LineTo)	2.5000 in.	Width
Geometry4.Y2(LineTo)	0.2500 in.	Height*0.5

The only change in the Protection section is to lock the height of the symbol from the user interface. In a 1D shape, this simply "turns off" the height handles. We do not need them because the height of our symbol is being controlled by the second control handle (see Table 7.9).

TABLE 7.9 Start Section : PROTECTION

Cell	Value	Formula
LockWidth	0	0
LockHeight	1	1
LockAspect	0	0
LockMoveX	0	0
LockMoveY	0	0
LockRotate	0	0
LockBegin	0	0
LockEnd	0	0
LockDelete	0	0
LockSelect	0	0
LockFormat	0	0
LockTextEdit	0	0
LockVtxEdit	0	0
LockCrop	0	0
LockGroup	0	0
LockCalcWH	0	0
End Section : PROTECTION (CELLS TOTAL : 16)		

Notice in the Miscellaneous section (see Table 7.10), we have turned off the Alignment box. This makes the symbol clean without any distracting bounding box to take away from the "wire" orientation of our symbol.

TABLE 7.10 Start Section : MISCELLANEOUS

Cell	Value	Formula
NoObjHandles	FALSE	FALSE
NoCtlHandles	FALSE	FALSE
NoAlignBox	TRUE	TRUE
NonPrinting	FALSE	FALSE
HideText	FALSE	FALSE
UpdateAlignBox	FALSE	FALSE
DynFeedback	0	0

Cell	Value	Formula
NoLiveDynamics	FALSE	FALSE
ObjType	4	4
IsDropSource	FALSE	FALSE
Comment	No Formula	No Formula
End Section : MISCELLANEOUS (CELLS TOTAL : 11)		

That's all there is to creating height-based 1D SmartShape symbols. Next we will look at the second class of 1D symbols, the so-called "right-side-up" or multilegged connector type of 1D SmartShape symbol.

The next class of 1D symbols are those that Visio has traditionally referred to as "always-right-side-up." By that they mean that no matter how the endpoints are positioned, thc "legs" of the segmented conncctor symbol always maintain a purely vertical and horizontal position. For our purposes, I will refer to this class of symbols as angled connector symbols.

Angled connector symbols consist of a series of horizontal and vertical legs that extend from the begin to the end point. Let's begin the process of creating our own 1D Angled Connector symbol. In the process, we will change the default Shape Transform section formulas so the end points will define the opposite corners of the symbol. Also, the bounding box (should we choose to have it visible) will always be locked at a purely horizontal and vertical orientation (an angle of 0 degrees).

Begin by drawing a 2D symbol. Using the Line tool, draw a line straight up, straight over, and finally straight up again. Now convert the 2D symbol to a 1D symbol by selecting Format, Behavior and clicking the 1D interaction style, and then clicking OK to clear the dialog box. On a copy of your symbol, test the behavior a bit. Move the end points around. Does the symbol behave as a Connector symbol should? No, it doesn't. Delete the copy and return to the original new 1D symbol.

Switch to the rotation tool. Rotate the entire symbol up somewhere between 30 and 45 degrees. The exact angle is not critical; what we need is the midpoint of the right side to be somewhat higher that the midpoint of the left side. Great! Now open the ShapeSheet for the new 1D SmartShape symbol. Note how, just as before, the 1D end points section was added and how many formulas in the Shape Transform section were altered to contain the new trigonometric-based formulas to describe the default behavior.

Set the angle cell in the Shape Transform section to the following formula:

```
"=GUARD(0 deg.)"
```

Test your symbol on a copy. As you can see, the width and height are all wrong. The endpoints have been "knocked off" the end points of the symbol itself. Delete the duplicate. Again, remember your general geometry and trigonometry. The width of the symbol should be the difference between the end X and the begin X. The height should be the difference between the end Y and the begin Y. Let's make these changes as well. Set the width cell's formula to

```
"=GUARD(ABS(EndX-BeginX))"
```

We use the absolute value formula because we want to always obtain a scalar number, which is the positive difference between the beginning and ending points. If we obtained a negative number, the width could be negative, and therefore any text on the symbol could, and would in this case, simply implode. Not a pretty sight! Set the height cell's formula to

```
"=GUARD(ABS(EndY-BeginY))"
```

Test your duplicate's performance now. Close. It seems to perform whenever it is in at least two orientations. When the symbol is oriented in the upper-right or the lower left quadrant of the Cartesian coordinate system, the symbol behaves properly. However, when in the upper-left or the lower-right, the end points fall off the symbol again. These latter two orientations are the same as flipping the symbol in either X or Y. We need to compensate for this aberrant behavior by negating the "flip action." Delete your duplicate. Place the following formula in the FlipX cell:

```
"=GUARD(EndX<BeginX)"
```

Whenever the begin point is less than the end point in X, this formula evaluates to TRUE and flips the symbol. Whenever the endpoint in X is not less than the end point in X, this evaluates to FALSE and the flip is negated.

Place the following formula in the FlipY cell:

```
"=GUARD(EndY<BeginY)"
```

When the begin point is less than the end point in Y, this formula evaluates to TRUE and flips the symbol. Whenever the endpoint in Y is not less than the end point in Y, this evaluates to FALSE and the flip is negated.

This ensures that we get proper behavior in all four quadrants. Test your symbol on a duplicate. It seems to perform brilliantly!

Now on to a bit of cosmetics. Delete your duplicate. In the Protection section, set the value of the LockHeight cell to one. This will, as you remember from before, turn off the height sizing handles in a 1D symbol. Next, go to the Miscellaneous section and set the value of the NoAlignBox cell to TRUE. This turns off the alignment (bounding) box and gives our symbol that true Connector look and feel. Finally, add a Controls section to your symbol's ShapeSheet.

Lock the Xbehavior by setting it to a value of one, position the handle by setting its X Cell to =Width*0.5, and its Y Cell to =Height*0.5. Now find rows two and three in the Geometry section. The Y cell's formula is set to =Height*0.5. Change these two formulas to reference the control handle's Y cell by changing the formula to read =Controls.Y1. You can set the Tip cell in the Control handle to whatever suits you, perhaps "Adjust the horizontal member's position." Close the ShapeSheet and drag out a duplicate. Congratulations! You now have a properly performing Connector symbol. Test it a while. Make sure that it works in all possible rotations, angles, sizes, and orientations.

In terms of a quick review, note that when you transform a 2D symbol to a 1D symbol, a new 1D end points section is added. Cells in the Shape Transform section obtain new complex trigonometric formulas. To create height-based 1D symbols, we alter the behavior of the Geometry so it all refers to a percentage of height rather than any dependency on width. To create the so-called "always-right-side-up" or "angled connector" symbols, we make wholesale changes to the new default trigonometric formulas by guarding the angle to zero degrees, guarding the width to the absolute value of the end in X minus the begin in X, guarding the height to the absolute value of the end in Y minus the begin in Y, guarding the FlipX to EndX less than BeginX, and guarding the FlipY to EndY less than BeginY. These changes ensure proper vertical and horizontal orientation and behavior. Cosmetically, we lock the height in the Protection section, and turn off the bounding box in the Miscellaneous section.

Types of Glue in Visio

Under Visio 5.0, 1D symbols glued to 2D symbols. 2D symbols do not glue to anything at all. Controls on 2D symbols could glue to other 2D symbols or 1D symbols if they were neither locked in X nor Y. Under Visio 2000, 2D symbols can now in fact glue to other 2D symbols. There are, however, restrictions, limitations, and conditions, just as in the fine print on the used car warranty. You will need to be very aware of how this works.

I'll return to the Visio 2000 glue mechanics in a moment. First, I'd like to set the stage for all this by explaining glue behavior under Visio 5.0. What you learn about Visio 5.0 glue behavior will carry forward to Visio 2000. We will then add Visio 2000's new capabilities to that.

Under Visio 5.0, there are essentially two types of Glue: Point-to-Point (regular) and Dynamic. Let's try a wee demonstration. Begin by dragging out two basic rectangles. Place them apart and side by side. Label the left rectangle "A," and the right rectangle "B." Next, drag out a connector shape from the toolbar. Label it "C." Select Tools, Snap and Glue . Ensure that all of the potential glue items are checked and then click OK to exit the dialog box. Drag one end of the connector, C, to the right midpoint side of the left rectangle, A. It will glue to that point. This is designated by the small red square at the connector's end point. Deselect everything. Notice a small blue "X" is now located at the glue point. This is a new connection point. Repeat the gluing process with the other end of the connector C and the left midpoint side of the right rectangle, B. The connector C is now glued to the left rectangle A and the right rectangle B. Move rectangle A around. See how the connector C stays connected. Move rectangle B around. Again, connector C stays connected. However, if B ends up on the left and A ends up on the right, C is crossing over the both of them or routing around them awkwardly and the diagram looks less than professional.

Move A back to the left and B back to the right. Now move the connector C below the two rectangles. The glue is now broken, and connector C is moving independently. The 1D symbol (the connector) glued to the 2D symbols (the rectangles), not the other way around. When the connector is moved, it can break the glue just as it established it. The 1D is in control of the gluing process. Hold down Ctrl and move the left endpoint of the connector C over the middle of rectangle A. The outline of the rectangle changes to a double line. Release the line—the red square is larger. This designates dynamic glue. Repeat the process with connector C and rectangle B. Again note the indication of dynamic glue. As you reposition Rectangles A and B, note how the connector C finds the most direct route between the rectangles. The connector C is glued to the entire symbols A and B, rather then the individual connection points on the symbols. This is the hallmark of Dynamic glue; the glue is between the 1D connector's endpoint and the entire 2D symbol rather than in point-to-point, where the 1D symbol's endpoint is glued to a POINT on the 2D symbol.

Under Visio 2000, glue takes on an entirely new and expanded functionality. But—and here's the fine print—you must be in developer mode for this to work.

Important Concept Number Twelve

For the new Visio 2000 enhanced gluing to work, you *must* have established working in Developer mode by selecting Tools, Options. Next select the Advanced tab, check the Run in Developer mode check box, and then click OK to exit the dialog box.

To place a Connection point on any symbol, select the Connection Point tool (the tool with the blue "X" from the toolbar), hold down Ctrl, and click the selected symbol where you wish to establish the new connection point.

Let's try another experiment. Drag out two rectangle symbols, place them side by side, label the left rectangle A, and the right rectangle B. Select the Connection Point tool from the toolbar. Select rectangle A. Hold down Ctrl and click on the right edge of rectangle A. A green triangle, black line, and blue X appeared. Repeat this by selecting rectangle B and then clicking on the left edge of rectangle B with the Connection Point tool while holding down Ctrl. When

Specialized Visio SmartShape Symbol Behavior

CHAPTER 7

211

7

SPECIALIZED VISIO
SMARTSHAPE
SYMBOL BEHAVIOR

you have deselected all, you should now see two small blue X's on the two rectangles. But what were those bizarre green triangles inside the rectangles while you were using the Connection Point tool? Those are the new directional glue indicators.

Remember when you used to play with wee wooden trains on wooden tracks? Do you remember the train carriages had inward and outward ends so the carriages could be connected? This is the same thing. In order for 2D to 2D glue to be created, we need an inward and an outward connection.

Select the Connection Point tool. Now select rectangle A. Click the blue connection point. As you can see, the directional indicator appears. Right-click the connection point. A context menu that allows you to determine the type of connection (inward, outward, or inward and outward) appears. Select Outward. As you probably noticed, the small blue X turned to a small blue dot (.). Repeat the process with rectangle B, ensuring that its connection type is inward. Select the pointer tool. Select rectangle B (with the inward connection point). Move it so its small blue X lines up with rectangle A's small blue dot. Glue is NOT established. Move it away again. Now select rectangle A (with the outward connection point) and move it so that its small blue dot lines up with the small blue X on rectangle B. Note how glue IS established. Rectangle A is glued to rectangle B, not the other way around. Glue is still a one way connection. The Outward connection glues to the inward connection.

Move A away from B. Select the Connection Point tool again. Click on the connection point on A. Grab the green triangle and change the direction of the connection pointer from directly out to the right to angling somewhat upward. Repeat the process with rectangle B, angling its inward connection somewhat downward. Select the pointer tool again and re-glue A to B. What did you notice? Correct! Rectangle A changed its orientation to accommodate the new alignment directions between the outward connection on A and the inward connection on B.

As you can see, Visio 2000's new enhanced glue brings about a wealth of possibilities for connected diagrams. You as the developer should train yourself to exploit the functionality here and begin creating even more intelligent connected diagrams and solutions.

So what happens when a 1D symbol is glued to a 2D symbol? Let's take a look into the ShapeSheet for each and see what transformations take place. Begin a new drawing and drag out a single line and a single rectangle. Create a single default connection point anywhere on the perimeter of the rectangle. Open the ShapeSheet for both symbols. Note immediately that when you established the new connection point on the rectangle, its ShapeSheet gained a new Connection Points section. If you need to, look back to our previous discussion (in Chapter 2, "An Introduction to ShapeSheet Programming") of the Connection Points section in the ShapeSheet.

Go ahead and glue the right end of the line to the newly established connection point on the rectangle. Now look at the EndX and EndY cells in the 1D end points section of the line's ShapeSheet. Both cells contain the following formula:

```
"=PAR(PNT(Sheet.2!Connections.X1,Sheet.2!Connections.Y1))"
```

In this case the sheet name is Sheet.2; your actual sheet number may differ. The formula is actually nested. It is the Point formula, `PNT()`, wrapped in the Parent formula `PAR()`. This establishes the point expressed in the parent symbol's coordinate system. In this case, it says that the End X and End Y of the line (the 1D symbol) are now determined by the parent coordinate system for the connection point on the rectangle symbol. This `PAR(PNT())` notation is used because a connection point is, by nature, expressed in the symbols' local coordinate system, and we must map it out to the page where the end point of the line must be established. In this manner, we can determine to what the line is glued; in this case, it's the rectangle.

The Glue Info Section of the ShapeSheet

Every symbol, whether it has been glued to something or had something glued to it, contains a Glue Info section. If this is not visible, ensure that the ShapeSheet window is active and then select View, Sections. Click the All button and then click OK to exit the dialog box. Scroll down in the ShapeSheet and find the Glue Info section. The Glue Info section is comprised of four cells. They are

> BegTrigger
> EndTrigger
> GlueType
> WalkPreference

I'll detail these for you next.

BegTrigger

The BegTrigger cell contains a trigger formula generated by Visio that determines whether to move the begin point of a 1D shape to maintain its connection to another shape. When a 1D shape is glued to another shape using dynamic glue, Visio generates a formula that refers to the EventXFMod cell of the other shape. When that shape is changed, Visio recalculates any formula that refers to its EventXFMod cell, including the formula in the BegTrigger cell. Other ShapeSheet formulas for the 1D shape refer to the BegTrigger cell and move the begin point of the 1D shape or alter the shape as needed.

EndTrigger

The EndTrigger cell contains a trigger formula generated by Visio that determines whether to move the end point of a 1D shape to maintain its connection to another shape. When a 1D shape is glued to another shape using dynamic glue, Visio generates a formula that refers to the EventXFMod cell of the other shape. When that shape is changed, Visio recalculates any formula that refers to its EventXFMod cell, including the formula in the EndTrigger cell. Other ShapeSheet formulas of the 1D shape refer to the EndTrigger cell and move the end point of the 1D shape or alter the shape as needed.

GlueType

This cell contains an integer value that determines whether a 1D shape uses static (point-to-point) or dynamic (shape-to-shape) glue when it is glued to another shape. The valid range of integers are

0	Uses Static Glue
1	Unassigned
2	Unassigned
3	Uses Dynamic Glue. Visio writes default formulas in the BegTrigger and EndTrigger cells.

WalkPreference

This cell contains an integer value that determines whether an endpoint of a 1D shape moves to a horizontal or vertical connection point on the shape it is glued to with dynamic glue when the shape is moved to an ambiguous position. The valid range of integers are

0	Both endpoints of the 1D shape move to horizontal connection points (side-to-side connections).
1	The begin point of the 1D shape moves to a vertical connection point, and the end point moves to a horizontal connection point (top-to-side or bottom-to-side connections).
2	The begin point of the 1D shape moves to a horizontal connection point, and the end point moves to a vertical connection point (side-to-top or side-to-bottom connections).
3	Both endpoints of the 1D shape move to vertical connection points (top-to-bottom connections).

Dynamics Connectors and Autorouting

With the introduction of Visio 5.0, Visio replaced the old style of connectors with the new dynamic connectors. You have seen how dynamic glue with dynamic connectors can create much more readable diagrams. Additionally the dynamic connectors can be set so when a new symbol is dropped on top of a dynamic connector, it will move and reroute itself to avoid the collision. Where dynamic connectors cross each other, a jump is established.

Drop a dynamic connector into a Visio diagram. Notice the control handles on each leg. These control handles reposition the legs to suit the user's needs. Now hold down Shift as you drag a control handle. Three new legs are added to accommodate routing. Note that each leg now has its own control handle. Hold Ctrl down while dragging a control handle. As you can see, the endpoints of the leg segment remain fixed while the handle acts as a vertex and moves the line as if it were two line segments. Each new line segment gets its own new control handles. This new behavior is unique to dynamic connectors. Keep in mind that each time you perform any of these actions you are continuously adding new rows to the Geometry section of the SmartShape symbol in question.

Be aware that cells in both the Miscellaneous section (such as the object type) and cells in the new Shape Layout section under Visio 2000 control the behavior of not only the dynamic connector shapes, but also any SmartShape symbol you as the developer choose to imbue with this autorouting behavior. For a refresher in the Shape Layout section, look back earlier in the book to Chapters 2, "Introduction to ShapeSheet Programming" and 3, "Modifying Visio SmartShape Symbols and Groups of Symbols."

In this chapter, we've had a thorough look at 1D symbology: what constitutes a 1D symbol, how to transform a 2D symbol into a 1D symbol, and how to interact with 1D symbols. We've looked at the two general classes of 1D symbols: height-based and connectors. And we've gained a much better understanding of glue in all of its many forms under both Visio 5.0 and Visio 2000.

In the next chapter, I will explore the depths of Text behavior and Visio SmartShape symbols. I'll look at how text is positioned and rotated. You will discover how the text block differs from the symbol itself explore text fields. Then I'll move on to looking at styles in Visio. We'll see how styles affect text, line, and fill properties of symbols, and learn how we can prevent symbols from being overridden by the application of a style.

Text Behavior and Style Theory in Visio SmartShape Symbols

IN THIS CHAPTER

As you are well aware, the user can enter text directly onto the symbol for every Visio SmartShape symbol. This is true unless that capability has been explicitly altered or removed for a particular purpose. However, text behavior in SmartShape symbols involves much, much more than the mere capability of displaying text.

Entering Text in a SmartShape Symbol

Begin a new diagram in Visio based on a blank document. Select the Text tool from the toolbar (the tool that looks like the capital letter A). You will notice your cursor changes to a plus sign (+) with a small page attached. This is your visual cue you are using the Text tool. Now click, hold, and drag out an area in which to enter text. Next, enter the phrase "Visio SmartShape symbols" and then click off of the text area. Switch back to the pointer tool.

What have you accomplished? Does it appear that you have placed a string of text on the page itself? If you assumed that this was the case, you might wish to reconsider. Using the pointer tool, select the text. Next select Format, Line. In the dialog box, select pattern one in the Pattern list and click OK to exit. Next select Format, Fill from the menus. In the dialog box, in the Pattern list, select pattern one and click OK to exit. If you are using Visio 5.0, you should see a white rectangle with a black line at its perimeter. If you are using Visio 2000, you will still see the text alone. Open the ShapeSheet for the text symbol. Notice the Fill Format section and the Line Format section. The changes you have made to the SmartShape symbol's formatting appear here.

Let's try it from the other direction. Drag out a rectangle. On the rectangle, type "This is a line of text." Next select Format, Line from the menus. In the dialog box, select pattern 0 in the Pattern list and click OK to exit. Next select Format, Fill from the menus. In the dialog box, select pattern 0 in the Pattern list and click OK to exit. Note that the rectangle and the text symbol appear identical. Text is an inherent part of a SmartShape symbol. Under Visio 5.0, the difference is that all of the visibility elements of the Geometry section have been effectively disabled. Under Visio 2000, the Geometry section has simply been removed completely.

Delete the two text item symbols. Drag out a new rectangle. Enter some text onto its face. Now select the Text Rotation tool from the toolbar. (This is the tool that looks like a capital letter A inside a circular arrow.) Now carefully move your mouse pointer over the center bottom edge of the symbol. The cursor changes to a solid line hollow rectangle with a dashed line hollow rectangle behind it. This allows you to move the text block independently of the SmartShape symbol's geometry. Move your mouse pointer to any of the four corners. The cursor changes to a double circular arrow. This allows you to rotate the text block independently of the SmartShape symbol's geometry. Move your cursor over the top, bottom, left, or right sizing handle. Your cursor changes to either a double-headed vertical or a double-headed horizontal arrow. This allows you to resize the text block independently of the SmartShape symbol's geometry. Move your cursor directly over the text itself. The cursor changes to a solid line hollow rectangle with a dashed line hollow rectangle behind it. This allows you to move the text block independently of the SmartShape symbol's geometry. Go ahead and make a few of these size, position, and rotational changes. Now go back and select the pointer tool. Move the SmartShape symbol around and resize it. Select the rotation tool and rotate the SmartShape symbol. The relationship between the text block and the SmartShape symbol is maintained even through the SmartShape symbol's transformations. If the text was rotated around to the left and was at the bottom of the symbol, no matter how you rotated the symbol and moved it about, it would still be in this position relative to the symbol itself.

Important Concept Number Thirteen

As a developer, you should keep in mind that the Text block's geometry has a parent and that the parent is the symbol itself. All transformations of the text block are relative to the symbol. As soon as you began manipulating the text block, a new section was added to the ShapeSheet for this symbol; a Text Transform section. By default, the text block is the same size and position as the SmartShape symbol's bounding box. However, as you have already seen, this relationship can be altered at will.

Let's take a look at the Text Transform section. The Text Transform has seven cells. These seven cells control the size, rotation, and placement of the text block relative to the SmartShape symbol itself. The seven cells are

- TxtWidth
- TxtHeight
- TxtAngle
- TxtPinX
- TxtPinY
- TxtLocPinX
- TxtLocPinY

I'll detail these in the next few paragraphs.

TxtWidth

This cell contains the united pair that is the width of the text block. The relationship of the number and units is exactly the same as any with other unit-ed–number, as are the restrictions and defaults. The default for this cell is always a percentage of the parent SmartShape symbol's width and is expressed relative to the symbol itself.

TxtHeight

This cell contains the unit-ed pair that is the height of the text block. The relationship of the number and units is exactly the same as with any other unit-ed–number, as are the restrictions and defaults. The default for this cell is always a percentage of the parent SmartShape symbol's height and is expressed relative to the symbol itself.

TxtAngle

This cell contains the unit-ed pair that is the angle of the text block relative to the SmartShape symbol itself. The relationship of the number and units is exactly the same as with any other unit-ed–number, as are the restrictions and defaults. The default for this cell is always an angle in degrees relative to the coordinate system of the SmartShape symbol and is expressed relative to the symbol itself.

TxtPinX

This cell contains the unit-ed pair that is the X ordinate of the position of the text block. The relationship of the number and units is exactly the same as with any other unit-ed–number, as are the restrictions and defaults. The default for this cell is always a percentage of the parent SmartShape symbol's width and is expressed relative to the symbol itself.

TxtPinY

This cell contains the unit-ed pair that is the Y abscissa of the position of the text block. The relationship of the number and units is exactly the same as with any other unit-ed–number, as are the restrictions and defaults. The default for this cell is always a percentage of the parent SmartShape symbol's height and is expressed relative to the symbol itself.

TxtLocPinX

This cell contains the unit-ed pair that is the X ordinate of the position of the text block's local pin. The relationship of the number and units is exactly the same as with any other unit-ed–number, as are the restrictions and defaults. The default for this cell is always a percentage of the text block's width and is expressed relative to the text block.

TxtLocPinY

This cell contains the unit-ed pair that is the Y abscissa of the position of the text block's local pin. The relationship of the number and units is exactly the same as with any other unit-ed–number, as are the restrictions and defaults. The default for this cell is always a percentage of the text block's height and is expressed relative to the text block.

In terms of text position, we classify the behavior in three general categories: Centered Text, Offset Text, and Text with Control Handles.

Centered text is, in fact, the default behavior for text blocks in a Visio SmartShape symbol. This behavior means the TxtLocPinX and TxtLocPinY are at `TxtWidth*0.5` and `TxtHeight*0.5` respectively, and the TxtWidth and TxtHeight are at `Width*0.5` and `Height*0.5` respectively. Generally the Text Block's width is identical to the SmartShape symbol's width, much as the height and angle match the symbol's height and angle. The usage for this text block behavior is where text should be centered on a SmartShape symbol. Imagine a plan view of a policeman's patrol car. The car number should be atop the passenger compartment of the vehicle. The SmartShape symbol would be designed so the width of the text block was the distance from left to right in the passenger compartment, and the text block height was the distance from the top of the windshield to the back of the rear seat.

Offset text is text placed in a highly specific location on the SmartShape symbol. The text block's height and width as well as angle are often customized to accommodate this required location. One example of this type of behavior is if a valve number needs to lie parallel to and along the side of the graphic of the valve no matter how it is positioned.

Visio end users seem to have great difficulty discovering and mastering the Text Rotation tool. Accordingly, it is often necessary to make use of a control handle on a SmartShape symbol to allow the user to relocate the text wherever the functional or aesthetic requirements dictate. Text with control handles accommodate this requirement. The text block's TxtPinX and TxtPinY are guarded to a formula that explicitly references a control handle associated with the SmartShape symbol. Because the X and Y location of the control handle as well as the TxtPinX and TxtPinY are all expressed in the same coordinate system (that of the local coordinate system of the SmartShape symbol itself), the referencing is quite easy.

Let's practice this last behavior. Drag out a new rectangle onto the page. Open the ShapeSheet for the Rectangle and add a Text Transform section to the ShapeSheet. In the TxtPinX cell, place the following formula:

```
"=Controls.X1"
```

In the TxtPinY cell, place the following formula:

```
"=Controls.Y1"
```

In the control handle's Tip cell, place the following formula:

```
="Relocate the Smart Rectangle's Text"
```

Close the ShapeSheet and test your work on the duplicate of the original symbol. Enter some text onto the SmartShape symbol. Select the pointer tool and let your cursor rest over the symbol's control handle. See the tip pop up? Drag the text about to its new location.

If the SmartShape symbol is moved, the newly relocated text follows along properly. Notice how easy it is for the user to relocate the text.

In terms of Text Rotation, we classify the behavior in three general categories: Rotating with the Symbol, Always Level, and Gravity Text.

Rotating with the symbol is, in fact, the default behavior style for SmartShape symbols. The TxtAngle cell directly utilizes a user-determined number of degrees. When a SmartShape symbol is rotated, it will maintain that number of degrees relative to the symbol itself. An example of this sort of behavior is a traffic sign symbol. If the direction of travel is from top to bottom of the diagram, the text is oriented in the direction of travel.

Always Level behavior is a wee bit more complex. In Always Level behavior, the text is always horizontal to the base of the page, regardless of how the symbol is rotated. Diagrams that are always read from a single direction would make great use of this behavior style. At first glance, one would assume that this would be a very easy behavior to program. Simply set the formula in the TxtAngle cell to read

```
"=-Angle"
```

This works very well until the SmartShape symbol is flipped in *either* the X or Y axis. If flipped in both the X and Y axis, the aberrant behavior seems to clear up. Let's explore why this is the case.

Drag out a rectangle. Enter some text onto the face of the symbol. Open the symbol's ShapeSheet. In the TxtAngle cell, enter

```
"=-Angle"
```

Rotate the symbol 20 to 40 degrees. The text seems to stay perfectly level, does it not? Grand! Flip the symbol in either X or Y. Not only did the text no longer remain level, but, in fact, it doubled in its rotational offset from the symbol. Flip the symbol across the opposite axis. Everything is correct again.

Now that we know how the symbol misbehaves, we can write a formula to correct this behavior. In the TxtAngle cell, enter the following formula:

```
"=IF(BITXOR(FlipX, FlipY),Angle, -Angle)"
```

Translated into simple English, "If the symbol itself is ever either flipped in X OR in Y but not both, set the value in the TxtAngle Cell equal to Angle; otherwise, if both or neither flips have occurred, set the value in the TxtAngle cell to minus the Angle (-Angle)". This formula properly counter-rotates the text in any occurrence of the symbol.

The final rotational behavior is Gravity Text. This behavior says that if a symbol is rotated, the text will always be either readable from the right or below, the two ordinal methods of reading a diagram in general practice. As the symbol is rotated, the text rotates along with it. When it passes through 90 degrees, it automatically flips over and is still readable until the symbol passes through 270 degrees, whereupon it flips back again, making it readable once again. This behavior tends to be utilized in roadside directional indicators.

The formula that is placed in the TxtAngle cell is

```
"=GRAVITY(Angle)"
```

In terms of Text Resizing, we classify the behavior in two general categories: Resizing the Symbol Resizes the Text, Resizing or Modifying the Text Resizes the Symbol.

Imagine the local school crossing in your city. The sign reads "SCHOOL ZONE, 15 M.P.H." If the sign gets larger, the lettering on the sign gets larger as well. This is the design constraint behind the behavior Resizing the Symbol Resizes the Text. In order to accomplish this behavior, let's replicate this signage. Drag out a rectangle and resize it so it is exactly two inches wide by three inches high. With the new rectangle SmartShape symbol selected, enter the following text onto the face of the rectangle:

```
"SCHOOL" <carriage return>
"ZONE" <carriage return>
"15" <carriage return>
"M.P.H."
```

Highlight the words "SCHOOL" and "ZONE" and select a font size of 30 points from the toolbar. Do the same for the word "M.P.H." Highlight the number "15" and select a font size of 60 points from the toolbar.

Open the ShapeSheet for the new sign SmartShape symbol. Scroll down to the Character section of the ShapeSheet. In the Characters section, there will now be several rows (entries). You should see rows with the size cells listed as "30," "12," "60," "12," and finally "30" again. Quite obviously these equate to the font size changes we just made to the symbol. Remember: Our sign symbol was originally designed at a size of two inches wide by three inches high.

In the row currently posting a Size value of 30, place the following formula in the Size cell:

```
"=(Height/3 in.) * 30 pt."
```

In the row currently posting a Size value of 12, place the following formula in the Size cell:

```
"=(Height/3 in.) * 12 pt."
```

In the row currently posting a Size value of 60, place the following formula in the Size cell:

```
"=(Height/3 in.) * 60 pt."
```

In the row currently posting a Size value of 12, place the following formula in the Size cell:

```
"=(Height/3 in.) * 12 pt."
```

In the row currently posting a Size value of 30, place the following formula in the Size cell:

```
"=(Height/3 in.) * 30 pt."
```

This formula takes the ratio of the current height of the symbol to the designed size of the symbol (in this case three inches) and multiplies that ratio times the designated character size to determine the new and current character (font) size. We also want to ensure that the symbol's width grows along with the height. To accomplish this, scroll up to the Protection section and set the value of the LockAspect cell to one. Close the ShapeSheet. Drag out a duplicate of the new signage SmartShape symbol and test your work on the duplicate.

In cartoons, the character's thoughts and words are always captured in a "balloon." When the words are entered there, the thoughts and words are always contained within the confines of the balloon. In other words, as more text is added, the size of the symbol grows or shrinks to accommodate the text.

Here are two formulas that elicit this behavior; one for the width and one for the height of a SmartShape symbol. Obviously, these would be placed in the width and height cells respectively.

For width:

```
"=GUARD(TEXTWIDTH(TheText))"
```

For height:

```
"=GUARD(TEXTHEIGHT(TheText, Width))"
```

Before we launch into using these formulas, let's take a wee bit of time to determine what these formulas actually do. I need you to imagine for a moment that you are Johannas Gutenburg. You have just set the type for all of the text to be printed in a printing frame (see Figure 8.1). There are some concepts that you must keep in mind. All of the text to be typeset must fit into the frame. The total width of the frame includes the width of the text's copy as well as the left and right margins. The total length of the frame is determined by the total width along with the top and bottom margins. The narrower the frame, the longer the frame.

Take a look at the cartoon balloon symbol from the companion CD-ROM. Play with it a bit. Notice how it properly resizes whenever the text is altered. The formula I have placed in the height cell is

```
"=GUARD(MAX(0.5 in.,TEXTHEIGHT(TheText,Width)))"
```

This ensures that the symbol will never collapse to less than one half inch in width, even if no text is present on the symbol. The formula I have placed in the width cell is

```
=GUARD(MAX(0.5 in.,TEXTWIDTH(TheText)))
```

This ensures the symbol will never collapse to less than one half inch in eight, even if no text is present on the symbol.

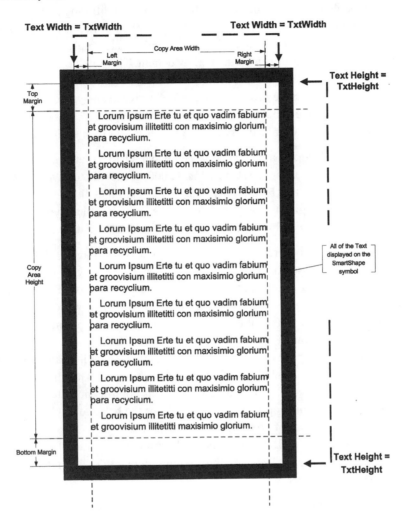

FIGURE 8.1
Typesetting frame.

Multiple Text Blocks

Under Visio 5.0 and earlier, the rule was always "one SmartShape symbol, lne text block." Period. End of story. Groups did not contain their own text block. If you desired multiple text blocks within a symbol, you created a group shape and then had the ability to sub-select the sub-symbol and enter text into that sub-symbol's text block. The advantage of this scheme was that you could, through the use of multiple text blocks, position differing items of text in exacting positions within or outside of the confines of the symbol's geometry. The disadvantage of this scheme was that when a person selected a group symbol and simply began typing, the topmost sub-symbol in the z-order accepted the text by default. This often caused confusion about when sub-selection should take place and where the text input would fall. Often the designer would be compelled to go into the Protection section of a given sub-symbol and, in the LockTextEdit cell, remove the capability of the symbol to accept text. This, of course, triggered bizarre warnings to the user of the symbol, which was less than desirable.

Under Visio 2000, the behavior that you experienced under Visio 5.0 and previous versions is still in force, with one major exception. Under Visio 2000, groups themselves contain their own text blocks. The group's text block is, by default, the text block that receives the text input when the user selects and begins typing. There are, however, two settings you should make yourself aware of under Visio 2000. They are both found in the Format, Behavior dialog box.

To get a look at them, try this exercise. Drag out a rectangle. Ctrl+drag out three more rectangles. Arrange them into a loosely rectangular pattern. Label the rectangles "A" through "D" by entering the appropriate letter as text on the symbol. Now select all four of the rectangle symbols and select Shape, Grouping, Group from the menus. With the group selected, simply type the letter "E." Notice how the text went to the group rather than the front-most in z-order symbol in the group. Now, with the group selected, select Format, Behavior. Look in the Group Behavior area of the Behavior tab of the dialog box. Two drop-down lists are provided to alter the text behavior of the group symbol. The first is the Selection list. This list has three possible options: Group Only, Group First, and Members First. This controls how items in the group are and can be selected. Try all three options and get a feel for the behavior style. Keep in mind that this is the behavior the user of your symbol will experience. Keep it as intuitive as possible. The second list is the Group Data list. This list determines the order of display for text or sub-symbols as part of the group. There are three options here: Hide, Behind Member Shapes, and In Front of Member Shapes.

Hide means that the group's text or geometry, except for connection points and control handles, is hidden.

Behind Member Shapes dictates that the group's components go to the very back of the z-order stack.

In Front of Member Shapes means that the group's components go to the very front of the z-order stack.

Text Fields

When you are working on a document in Microsoft Word, you may often want to add an area at the bottom of the page that prints the current page number and total number of pages in that document; for example, "Page 1 of 47 Pages." In order to do this, go to the footer, type in the word "Page," click the Page Number button, type in the word "of," click the Number of Pages button, and then finally type the word "Pages." Each time you clicked one of those buttons, you were actually adding a text field to the footer. A text field is an automatic entry, a calculated entry, or an entry of information about the page, document, or creator.

Visio has this same capability. As a SmartShape symbol developer, you should learn to take maximum advantage of this capability. Using text fields, you can display information about a symbol's geometry, its dimensions, or its custom properties. In fact, anything contained in the symbol's ShapeSheet and data fields can be displayed, as well as any custom formula you devise.

I could write an entire chapter detailing every possibile text field; however, I am sure that you can figure out what each one of these permutations do. What I will detail for you is how to access this capability and what happens after you use it.

To add a Text Field to a SmartShape symbol, enter the text editing mode. You can try this out now by dragging out a rectangle and then double-clicking the rectangle symbol. After you have entered the text editing mode and your cursor is a vertical bar, blinking away, awaiting your bidding, select Insert, Field from the menus.

The Field dialog box is activated and you are presented with three columns from which to choose: Category, Field, and Format. Again, I'll not detail every option here. However, for demonstration purposes, select the Custom Formula item in the first column, Category. In the editing line below, enter the following:

```
"=Width * Height"
```

In the last column, Format, select the "0.00 units" item. Click OK to accept your choices and close the dialog box.

Notice that as you subsequently resize the symbol, Visio continuously updates the value that appeared there. This custom formula, of course, calculated the area of the rectangle based on the custom entered formula height × width. Now open the ShapeSheet for the selected rectangle symbol. Again, if all sections are not visible, make them so by selecting View, Sections, clicking All, and clicking OK to close and confirm. Scroll down until you find the text fields section of the ShapeSheet. You will see any custom formulas that you have created here for Text fields. Under Visio 5.0 and previous versions, the field information would not appear in the text fields section of the ShapeSheet if you selected a standard field from the three lists. However, under Visio 2000, every text field created will be displayed as part of this section.

Style Theory

At the risk of being redundant, I shall use Microsoft Word again to illustrate the concept of styles. When you highlight a paragraph of information in your Word document and select Heading 1 from the drop-down listing on the Formatting toolbar, you are applying a paragraph style to that selected paragraph. The paragraph style controls the typeface (the font), the point size, whether it is bold, italic, underline, strikethrough, super- or subscript, black or another color, and more. The paragraph style controls alignment such as left, center, or right justification. It controls the spacing before and after the paragraph and whether the paragraph is enclosed in a box. I am sure that there are many, many more aspects of a paragraph's appearance that style can control, but this should give you a general idea.

Visio makes use of the concept of styles as well. In Visio, styles are generalized into three areas: Text, Line, and Fill. A style in Visio can include one, several, or all of these three style areas.

Styles are comprised of formatting options. Formatting options control how a SmartShape symbol's text, paragraph, line, and fill attributes look.

> **Important Concept Number Fourteen**
>
> The application of a style overrides any local application of formatting unless the cell in the ShapeSheet of that particular SmartShape symbol has been guarded and the LockFormat cell set to one.

Be aware that, just as in Microsoft Word, styles inherit from the parent style they were based upon. If a parent style is deleted, the child style moves one step further up the inheritance ladder to inherit from that deleted parent's parent. There are only four styles that cannot be deleted. These are the four base styles: "Normal," "None," "Text Only," and "No Style."

When a symbol with a style applied to it is instanced in another diagram, it carries that style definition along with it. If that named style does not exist in the target diagram, it is added to the diagram and the style is accessible from the style listings.

Styles are unique by name and scoped to the document. If there are two documents that both have styles named Rugger that differ dramatically from each other, they will not affect each other. The local version of a style always a'plies t all lo al symb ls.

For example, imagine diagram A's Rugger style has blue dashed lines and diagram B's Rugger style has green solid lines. If you instance a symbol with diagram A's Rugger style from diagram A into diagram B, the definition of Rugger style as it is appears in diagram B will prevail. The definition of diagram A's Rugger will be ignored.

There are two methods for creating a style. The first method is to select Format, Define Styles from the menu. This will activate the Define Styles dialog box. In the Style combo box, enter the name of the style you wish to define. In the Based On combo box, select the style your new style should be based upon. Check the appropriate sub-style members for inclusion in your named style: Text, Line, and Fill. Finally, select the Text, Line, and Fill buttons and drill down, applying all formatting that should be applied to the style in question. Finally, click OK to confirm your selections and exit. The style will be listed in the Style drop-down lists in the Format Shape toolbar.

The second method is to select a SmartShape symbol that already has the desired local formatting options applied to it. With this symbol selected, choose Format, Define Styles. After you have entered the Define Styles dialog box, change the entry in the Style combo-box to <New Style> and then type in your own unique style name. Click Add and then click OK to confirm your selections and exit. The style will be listed in the Style drop-down lists in the Format Shape toolbar. The style will be defined based on all the local formatting options "primed" into the dialog box from the Selected SmartShape symbol.

In the next three sections, I will briefly list each of the possible local formatting options that comprise the definable text, line, and fill options. For details about each and every option, I encourage you to apply these formatting options to a SmartShape symbol and see the effects.

8

Text Styles

Font	Spacing Before
Font	Spacing After
Size	Spacing Line
Color	Text Block
Underline	Vertical Alignment
Case	Top Margin
Position	Left Margin
Language	Bottom Margin
Bold	Right Margin
Italic	Text Background Visibility
Strikethrough	Text Background Color
Character Scale	Tabs
Character Spacing	Tab Stop Position
Paragraph	Alignment
Horizontal Alignment	Bullets
Indentation Left	Bullet Type
Indentation Right	Custom Bullet Type
Indentation First	

Line Styles	*Fill Styles*
Line	Fill
Pattern	Color
Weight	Pattern
Color	Pattern Color
Cap	Shadow
Line Ends	
Begin	
End	
Begin Size	
End Size	
Corner Rounding	
Amount	
Custom Amount	

Protecting Visio SmartShapes Symbols Formatting

Earlier I told you that the application of a style overrides any local formatting applied to a Visio SmartShape symbol. The consequence of this is the overwriting of any value, formula, or custom formula that might be in the cell targeted by the application of that style. I want to remind you that the LockFormat cell in the Protection section will prohibit the application of a style to a SmartShape symbol just as explicitly placing a GUARD() function around any value, formula, or custom formula in that cell will protect that one cell from being overwritten.

Thus far we have seen how Visio handles text on a SmartShape symbol and how we can customize the behavior to make text work as a tool for our solutions. We have also delved into the concept of styles and looked at their creation, application, and management.

In the next chapter, we will look at creating and using scaled diagrams in Visio. We will discuss the basics of scaling and how this affects the behavior of symbols in the diagrams. We will find out where the scale information is stored and learn the special formulas to access and use this information in scaled drawings. You will learn to unlock the mystery of the "range-of-eight," as well as find out how to develop symbols that always scale as well as and symbols that never scale.

Creating and Using Scaled Drawings in Visio

IN THIS CHAPTER

For those of you who come from a Computer Assisted Drafting and Design (CADD) background, this chapter on scaling should be, for the most part, a bit of fluff. However, for the rest of the world, scaling is something that brings about much consternation, if not outright confusion. Why do we have scaled drawings and diagrams in the first place? Due to my architectural background, I will use a built-environment illustration here. If you wanted to represent, say Holyrood Palace in Edinburg or the Sears Tower in Chicago, could you draw that floor plate on an A4 or an 8 1/2"×11" sheet of paper? Certainly not at the same size as they are in the real world. You would not even be able to represent the opening of the front door of either building, much less the building as a whole.

Visualize a measuring stick. It may be a meter stick, or a 12-inch ruler; it doesn't matter. Both are broken down into incrementally smaller and smaller divisions. Each one of these divisions, just like the ruler divisions in Visio, represents a scalar or linear distance between two points. Let's take the example of the 12-inch ruler. From the mark where the number 0 is printed to the mark where the number 12 is printed is recognized as a foot in the United States. Each major division (number) is recognized as an "inch." There are 12 incremental inches to the foot. However, if each of these major divisions represented a foot rather than an inch, the ruler would represent the distance of 12 feet. The *scale* would be 1 inch equals 12 inches, or 1 inch equals a foot, or 1/12 (one to twelve). If we drew on our sheet of paper with this new scale, as we drew out a line along the length of the ruler, we could be drawing out a line up to, say, 8-1/2' or 11'. Now we could at least draw the building's entry. The greater the ratio between the real world and the divisions as they would be understood in the ruler, the more of the building we could fit onto the sheet of paper, until finally at a sufficiently appropriate scale, we could display the entire floor plate with room around it to make notations.

Visio can also change the scaled ruler designations as they exist in relationship to the real world to create scaled drawings and diagrams. The scale of a drawing is the relationship between the paper or printed coordinates and the world coordinates. Visio uses the terms Page units and Page scale for the paper coordinates and Drawing units and Drawing scale for the world coordinates. The scale ratio is the ratio of Page units to Drawing units.

Here are some examples of scales:

- 1/8" = 1'-0" (architectural scale)
- Page units = 1/8", Drawing units = 1'-0"
- Scale ratio = 1:96
- 1cm = 1M (metric scale)
- Page units = 1 cm, Drawing units = 1M
- Scale ratio = 1:100
- 1" = 0.1" (custom scale)

- Page units = 1", Drawing units = 0.1"
- Scale ratio = 10:1

Scaled drawings are set up in Visio via selecting File, Page Setup. In the Page Setup dialog box, the Drawing Scale tab allows the user to set the scale ratio between Page units and Drawing units as well as between Page scale and Drawing scale. The Page Size tab allows the user to set the printed page size. The Drawing Scale tab displays the real-world area represented by the sheet of paper at this page size and scale factor.

Where the Scale Information Is Held

All the information that determines this scale ratio and page size is stored in the Page's ShapeSheet. Make sure that nothing is selected on the current page of your open Visio diagram. Now select Window, Show ShapeSheet. The very first section at the top of the Page's ShapeSheet is the Page Properties section. This section consists of nine cells. The particular cells that we are interested in are the PageWidth, PageHeight, PageScale, and DrawingScale cells. PageWidth and PageHeight are, as you would expect, unit-ed cells. PageScale and DrawingScale hold either integer or real number values.

A given ShapeSheet contains several cells that are dependent and operate only within the confines of either Page units or Drawing units. I will list these or describe the dependencies for you in the following sections.

Page Units

The following cells are dependant upon Page units:

> Paragraph Indents and spacing
> Text Margins
> Font Size
> Line Weight
> Page Shadow Offset
> Page Scale

In point of fact, any cell that has direct reference to what is printed is dependent upon Page units.

Drawing Units

The following cells are dependant upon Drawing units:

> Width
> Height
> Geometry Section cells
> Corner rounding

In point of fact, any cell that has direct reference to what is represented in the real world is dependent upon Drawing units.

Scaling and Anti-Scaling Ratios and Formulas

The Scale ratio is the following formula:

```
"=ThePage!PageScale/ThePage!DrawingScale"
```

Another formula we will be discussing in a moment is the Anti-scale ratio, which is the following formula:

```
"=ThePage!DrawingScale/ThePage!PageScale"
```

Enough with the theory already! Let's put this into practice. We are going to try another experiment. Close any open documents you might have in Visio. Now create two new blank documents. Select Window, Tile. You should have both Drawing 1:Page-1 and Drawing 2:Page-1 shown on the child windows in Visio. Make Drawing 2 active. Select File, Page Setup from the menus. In the Page Setup dialog box, select the Drawing Scale tab. In Visio 2000, click the Custom Scale radio button. In Visio 5.0, look at the two boxes at the top of the Drawing Scale frame. For the left text box, enter 1 and the units you are using (generally either inches or centimeters). For the right text box, enter 4 and the units you are using (generally either inches or centimeters). Click OK to confirm your selections and exit the dialog box.

Look at the rulers for both drawings. Notice that in drawing two the rulers are at a much finer increment. The same 8 1/2"×11" or A4 sheet of paper is capable of holding four times the information in the second drawing versus the first drawing. This is because the scale factor is now 1:4. Activate Drawing 1. We will quickly make a rectangle with text that scales just as we did in the previous chapter.

Drag out a rectangle SmartShape symbol and make it three inches wide by two inches high. On the face of the rectangle, enter the following text:

```
"Symbol with text that scales."
```

Open the ShapeSheet for the new rectangle symbol. Scroll down to the Character section of the ShapeSheet. In the Size cell, place the following formula:

```
"=(Height/2in.)*30 pt."
```

Remember that this was the mechanism for having text scale with the new size of the symbol. Ctrl+drag out a new copy of this symbol. Using one of the corner sizing handles, make the rectangle larger. Notice how the font size increased accordingly.

Now reselect the original symbol. Ctrl+drag out a copy of the symbol and drop it onto the Drawing 2 diagram. Notice the rectangle got smaller by a factor of four, just as it should have.

Drawing 2 is at a scale factor of 1:4. The rectangle is still three inches wide by two inches high, but its printed size is now 3/4" wide by 1/2" high. But what about the text, you say? What happened to the text on the symbol? The text did not scale with the symbol and is still exactly the same designated 30 points in size. Why is this so?

Remember, we learned that some things are always in Drawing units and other things are always in Page units. The Shape Transform cells and the Geometry Cells are in Drawing units and the Character cells are in Page units. This is why the shape re-scaled and the text did not (properly so, according to its own rules). If we want the text to scale along with the Geometry, we must alter the formula for the text.

In Drawing 2, delete the rectangle symbol. In Drawing 1, delete the duplicate, select the original rectangle SmartShape symbol, and open its ShapeSheet. Scroll down to the Characters section and in the Size cell enter the following formula:

```
"=((Height/2 in.)*30 pt.)*(ThePage!PageScale/ThePage!DrawingScale)"
```

Close the ShapeSheet for the original rectangle SmartShape symbol and select Window, Tile. Ctrl+drag out a new copy of this symbol. Using one of the corner sizing handles, increase the size of the rectangle. As you can see, the font size increased properly.

Now reselect the original symbol. Ctrl+drag out a copy of the symbol and drop it onto the Drawing 2 diagram. The rectangle got smaller by a factor of four, just as it should have. Drawing 2 is at a scale factor of 1:4. The rectangle is still three inches wide by two inches high, but its printed size is now 3/4" wide by 1/2" high. But what about the text, you say? What happened to the text on the symbol? It now sizes appropriately along with the symbol itself. Multiplying the entire original formula by the Scale Ratio formula brought about proper and consistent behavior in the rectangle SmartShape symbol and its text.

The Mystical "Range-Of-Eight"

Delete the symbol from Drawing 2. With Drawing 2 active, select File, Page Setup from the menus and change the scale from 1:4 to 1:30. Exit the dialog box. Now Ctrl+drag out a copy of the original rectangle SmartShape symbol from Drawing 1 into Drawing 2. Look at what transpired this time. Did all of your hard programming work just go up in smoke? Is Visio fatally flawed? Has global warming caused a shift in the way scaling works? No…none of the above.

If the scale of a master symbol or SmartShape symbol differs from the drawing scale, the symbol's scale changes to match the drawing scale. However, if the two scales differ by too much, Visio enables an internal bit of functionality triggered by what is referred to as "the range-of-eight." If the scale ratios differ by more than a factor of eight, the symbol is "anti-scaled." The symbol appears in the target diagram at the same *printed* size as in the source diagram. This keeps the symbol from becoming either drastically miniscule or from obscuring the drawing page. This does, however, limit the range of diagram scales within which the symbol can properly function.

Important Concept Number Fourteen
This "range-of-eight" affects *only* the height and width cells.

Imagine a drawing of a grand piano, created in a diagram with a scale of 1/8"=1'-0". This carefully crafted piano SmartShape symbol is then stored on a stencil. Your crack development team ships this stencil to your clients. One of them opens the stencil and attempts to drop the piano into a standard unscaled A4 sheet of paper. Remember that the piano is almost 2.4 meters long and nearly 2 meters wide. If instanced on the un-scaled sheet of A4 paper, it would drastically obscure the entire page and cause massive confusion on the part of the user. Anti-scaling and the range-of-eight assist the user by disallowing the unusual scaling to take place in the first place. An interesting side effect of this behavior is that it allows scaled symbols to be used as "clip art" in business diagrams. A user could conceivably use the piano symbol to illustrate piano sales figures for the upcoming quarter.

Visio SmartShapes Symbols That Always Scale

How then, do we create a SmartShape symbol that *always* scales? There are several things that you could do to work around the range-of-eight to ensure that symbols always scale. Firstly, and most expediently, you could simply guard the height and width formulas because the range-of-eight affects only those cells. However, if you do opt for this route, be aware that the user will not be able to change the symbol in either height or width in her diagram.

It might be better to design the symbols in a scale that is least likely to trigger the "range-of-eight" anti-scaling. Design the symbol in a scale that falls in the center of the two most likely extremes.

If SR equals Scale Range, your symbol should be designed to ensure that

$SR_{small} > SR_{master} > SR_{large}$

For the exact center of scale range:

$SR_{master} = SQRT(SR_{small} * SR_{large})$

For example, in Visio's Space Planning templates, Visio uses the following scales:

1/2" = 1'-0" (1:24) for small areas

1/4" = 1'-0" (1:48) for large areas

For site work, a scale might even be larger, perhaps 1:120.

It is possible to redefine the range-of-eight. Under Visio 5.0 and earlier versions, you must open the Visio.INI file and add an entry in the [application] section that reads:

```
INIShowAll = 1
```

Then save the .INI file. Open and run Visio, exit it, and then open the Visio.INI file for editing again. Scroll down to the [*document*] section and set the AutoScaleConversionRatio from its current value of eight to your desired factor. The range-of-eight could now become the range-of-fifty should you so desire.

Under Visio 2000, this is a bit more complex yet. In your running instance of Visio 2000, select Tools, Options. In the Options dialog box, go to the Advanced tab. Ensure that the Put All Settings in Windows Registry check box is checked and click OK to confirm your selection and exit the dialog box. Now close down your instance of Visio 2000. Next click on the Start button under Windows 95, 98, 2000, or NT 4.X. Select Run. In the Open list box, enter the following:

```
"regedit"
```

Click the OK button. This will launch the Windows Registry editor.

CAUTION

It is very easy to thrash your installation of Windows if you begin mucking about with your Registry settings without knowing what they do. Proceed with caution.

In the Registry Editor, click the plus sign (+) next to the word HKEY_CURRENT_USER to expand this entry. Look down the list for the word Software. Click the plus sign next to it to expand this entry. Click the plus sign (+) next to the word Visio to expand it. Find the word Visio 2000 and click the plus sign next to it to expand this entry. Click the word Document to list the entries for the Document settings. Look for the entry that says AutoScaleConversionRatio. Notice that it has a value of 8. Right-click this item and select Modify from the context menu. In the text box, enter your required value and click OK to confirm. Select Registry, Exit from the menus to exit the Registry Editor.

Before you decide to muck about with the range-of-eight, keep in mind that many of the symbols that you and your users work with have been created with the understanding that the range-of-eight is intact. If you make changes to this setting, every user of your solution will have to make the same change and this could definitively affect the performance of symbols supplied by both Visio and other SmartShape symbol designers.

Visio SmartShapes Symbols that Never Scale

You may need to create symbols that always appear at the same printed size regardless of the scale of the diagram that they are instanced into. In order to accommodate this behavior, you can use any one of several different design tricks.

Firstly, you could design the symbol in a diagram where the user would almost never encounter the design scale. For example, you could design the symbol in a diagram with the scale set to 1:100,000. When the symbol was instanced into a diagram of a normal scale, the range-of-eight would take effect and the symbol would always be anti-scaled.

Another methodology would be to always use custom formulas in the width, height, and initial control handle position cells by multiplying their formulas by the anti-scaling formula:

```
"=ThePage!DrawingScale/ThePage!PageScale"
```

Remember to make the formulas accessible so your users can adjust the size of the symbol as necessary.

Now we have taken a look at how we can both create and work with Scaled diagrams. We have seen how Visio handles scales, where the information about scaling is held in a Visio ShapeSheet, and learned about scaling and anti-scaling ratios and formulas as well as the mysterious range-of-eight. We have seen how to create shapes that always scale as well as shapes that never scale. Don't be afraid of scaled drawings. As I stated earlier, those of you from CADD backgrounds are already quite comfortable with the concepts. For those of you not immersed in CADD and scaled diagramming concepts, take heart: You may never need to create a scaled diagram, but on the off-chance that you or your users will need this capability, isn't it nice to know that you are now an expert?

Next we will look at a few limitations of Visio's ShapeSheet programming environment: constraints and constructs, if you will. We will briefly discuss where you can go for a single source location for information about every ShapeSheet cell and function. Finally, I will clue you in a bit why everything you have learned thus far is so important when, beginning in Chapter 12, "Visio VBA Automation Basics," we begin programming Visio through an Automation Interface and utilizing VBA. We will put our ShapeSheet knowledge to the test!

ShapeSheet Mastery

IN THIS CHAPTER

As with all great software applications, Visio continues to mature and address the features and functions that developers and users most often request. However, with each version of Visio, you need to be aware of a few limitations as a developer. Knowing these limitations can prevent problems from occurring. I'll address some of the ShapeSheet cell limitations under Visio 5.0 and earlier first. Next, I will look alternately at the new Visio 2000 ShapeSheet cells and see what has been improved as well as what limitations still exist.

ShapeSheet cells have always been the key to ShapeSheet development, and as such, most of the limitations I will discuss relate to these cells. Under Visio 5.0, all formulas in ShapeSheet cells are stored as strings. These strings have a maximum string length of 252 characters. Under automation, you can actually force a much longer string into a ShapeSheet cell, but if a developer or user ever clicks on that cell and then clicks the check mark on the editing line to simply accept the information contained in that cell, it will be truncated to a maximum of 252 characters. In Visio 5.0 and prior versions, it was strongly recommended that you make liberal use of user-defined and scratch cells to build portions of formulas and then combine them into more complex formulas with shorter string lengths. Here's an example:

```
User.A = "=Height/3in."
User.B = "=ThePage!DrawingScale/ThePage!PageScale"
Characters.Size = "=(User.A*User.B)*30 pt."
```

This takes 71 characters in the Characters.Size cell and makes them 267 characters. Granted, the 71 characters are nowhere near the 252 character limitation; however, the idea is still valid. Under Visio 2000, this 252-character limitation has been removed and, within reason, you can generate formulas as long as are necessary to complete the requirements you might have.

Under Visio 5.0, all editing of a formula or value needs to take place in the editing line at the top of the workspace. As a developer, to alter an existing formula, you must click on a ShapeSheet cell and then click up into the editing line. In Visio 2000, you can now edit directly within any given ShapeSheet cell. Simply click into the cell and then move your cursor wherever you need to edit the information at hand.

Under Visio 5.0, ShapeSheet cells are in a length determined by Visio itself. You, as the developer, have no means to change the cell width as you did in Microsoft Excel. Under Visio 2000, you simply need to place your cursor atop the vertical dividing line between two cells, and click and drag the cell to the left to its new desired width. This will greatly assist you in working with formulas in ShapeSheet cells.

In order to access the Insert Function dialog box under Visio 5.0, you need to have your cursor planted in the editing line. You then select Insert, Function from the menu. The Insert Function dialog box is then activated. Complete help for each function is available within this dialog box as well as the ability to paste the function (with arguments, should you desire) into the current cell being edited. Under Visio 2000, this functionality is directly accessible while your cursor is active within the ShapeSheet cell.

Under both Visio 5.0 and Visio 2000, if you use the standard Windows methodology for copying and pasting, you can copy information contained within a given ShapeSheet cell to another ShapeSheet cell. However, the wholesale copying of cells, rows, or sections is still not implemented.

In Visio 5.0, the scope of references is limited to between cells in the same ShapeSheet, between cells of any ShapeSheet on a current page using friendly names, provided they are at the same scoping level, and between cells of any ShapeSheet on a current page using sheet-dot references if they are at differing scoping levels. In Visio 2000, the scope of references has been extended with cross-container references to between any pages within the same document as well.

Under Visio 5.0, if a cell contains a Boolean FALSE or TRUE, or contains a fixed and limited selection of options, although it would be very nice to have a drop-down list or combo-box list for that cell, the developer or user is still required to manually enter the information into the ShapeSheet cell. Under Visio 2000, this is still the case. Developers need things to work on for the next release, don't they? It's called job security.

In Visio 5.0 and prior releases, if you need help in any given ShapeSheet cell, you select Help, Visio Help, Developer Reference, ShapeSheet Reference to get to the contents and listings for the individual ShapeSheet cells. In Visio 2000, you simply need to plant your cursor into any given ShapeSheet cell and press F1 to obtain context-sensitive help for that particular cell.

In case you Visio developers and users are not aware, you can print to the printer, to any named file, any number of ShapeSheets. Select the desired Visio SmartShape symbols you need listings of and then select Tools, Macros, Visio Extras, Print ShapeSheet from the menus. This will really help when developing complex SmartShape symbols and replicating some of their behavior.

A Visio SmartShapes Symbol ShapeSheet Cell Compendium (on the CD-ROM)

The appendixes of this book are going to become your very best friend... Not that you developers and users don't have mates and significant others; it's simply that what you will find in the appendixes is a complete listing of every Visio ShapeSheet cell. This compendium will be broken down by first object type, such as the page's ShapeSheet, a SmartShape symbol's ShapeSheet, and a foreign object's ShapeSheet. It is then broken down further by available sections and further still by all possible cells within that particular section. Additionally, I want to encourage each of you to take advantage of the new fully context-sensitive help functionality within Visio 2000 as it refers to ShapeSheet cells.

A Visio SmartShapes Symbol ShapeSheet Function Compendium

In the appendixes on the companion CD, you will find a complete compendium of every available Visio ShapeSheet function as well. The applicable version number will be listed where necessary. All of the required and optional arguments will be listed, as will all of their valid values and return values. Additionally, I want to encourage each of you to take advantage of the help functionality within Visio 2000 as it refers to ShapeSheet formulas.

Why All of This Is So Important—Preview of Things To Come

If you are reading this right now, I am assuming that you have made it through Chapters 1 through 9. You are to be congratulated! Most developers, as I have stated before, are used to diving right in with C, C++, VB, or VBA and slamming together code to make their automation applications function. But let me restate that automation interfaces are inherently worth very little if they are not backed by a quality object model that exposes the objects and their properties, methods, and events.

It is fundamental when working with these objects that you understand how things are done in the ShapeSheet environment. Keep focusing on the concept that the ShapeSheet is in fact the exposure of all the properties of any given SmartShape symbol or even the page itself. When you create automation applications, you are, in effect, pulling values and formulas out of ShapeSheet cells and pushing formulas back into them. In this manner, you have complete control over what happens to any given SmartShape symbol.

Once you become comfortable with the ShapeSheet paradigm, you will find that automation application programming for the Visio environment will be quite easy. From manipulating SmartShape symbols and pages, you can move on to manipulating the documents themselves. In fact, any part of the Visio User Interface (UI) can be completely controlled within your application. Additionally, you can pull information from other applications and use that information to drive changes in Visio, as well as making Visio manipulate other applications and their data.

Remember that Microsoft has altered the view of the software universe. Applications are no longer massive, monolithic, isolated, linearly coded entities unto themselves. Today's applications are in effect, all objects. These objects speak to one another through the synaptic connections of automation interfaces. This synaptic connection between application objects and their constituent subordinate objects creates the new "digital nervous system." This synaptic communication means that the user no longer sees the world through application-centric eyes.

He now experiences the world through data-centric senses. Because of this new vision, the sharing of information is easier, faster, homogeneous, and robust, as well as secure.

Think of Visio as the graphics visualization object within your digital nervous system. Over the next 16 chapters, we will learn how to make Visio respond to automation application programming as well as communicate with other applications through VBA as the synaptic neuron threads. Oh, by the way, we're going to have fun learning and implementing this as well!

Visio ActiveX Development

IN THIS PART

ActiveX Basics

IN THIS CHAPTER

So far, this book has concentrated on Visio's ShapeSheet environment and the power of the SmartShape symbols that you can create with it. As you read the next 15 chapters, keep in mind this phrase: "Shapes first, and then code." This means you should accomplish as much as you can in the ShapeSheet programming environment (which is considerable). Then, and only then, should you begin to extend these capabilities with the incredible power of Automation programming to expand your solutions into enterprisewide solutions.

To begin our journey into Automation programming, let's review a bit about ActiveX Automation, which was formerly known as OLE Automation. This chapter looks at what it is and what it can do and covers some VBA fundamentals. This review will ensure that we start off on the same footing.

Servers, References, and Automation Models

What is ActiveX Automation? *ActiveX Automation* is a method for one application to incorporate the functionality of another application by referring to, and therefore utilizing, its objects. ActiveX encompasses many services defined under the OLE 2.0 specification, such as linking and embedding objects, in-place editing, and many others. The foundation of this technology is COM, and ActiveX Automation is based on COM (Component Object Modeling). COM defines the interfaces for the objects the application exposes. The interface structure that COM defines enables COM objects to make their services available to other applications.

What then do you need to have in order to do ActiveX Automation? To provide ActiveX Automation in its most (excuse the pun) basic format, you need two things: an Automation controller and an Automation server. The application that controls the Automation is sometimes called the ActiveX controller or client or container application. You develop this application in a programming language that supports ActiveX Automation, such as Visual Basic, VBA, C, or C++. This book focuses on VBA; however, you can use this same methodology with Visual Basic, C, and C++ equally well. The application to be automated is sometimes called an ActiveX server or source application. This application exposes its objects for the controller to use. The objects have properties and methods that the controller can use to manipulate the objects as well as events that can be raised by the object. As you might guess, Visio is the ActiveX server that this book focuses on. However, this book also looks at the exposed objects of Microsoft Office 2000: Word, Excel, Access, PowerPoint, and Outlook.

Some applications, such as Visio or Excel, can act as both ActiveX controllers and ActiveX servers by embedding VBA. You can use Visio or Excel to control another ActiveX server's objects, or you can control Visio or Excel's objects from another ActiveX controller.

Visio's Implementation of VBA

Visio 2000 Standard Edition, Technical Edition, Professional Edition, and Enterprise Edition all include as core technology a fully licensed implementation of Microsoft Visual Basic, Applications Edition revision 6.0. This addition brings to Visio a fully integrated programming environment that will facilitate custom applications running within Visio's Application Memory Space. As a result, applications written using Visio's licensing of VBA will run at a rate of up to 10 times faster than those written in standalone implementations of Microsoft Visual Basic 6.0 and will offer complete language and function parity with VB 6.0.

The Visio implementation of the VBA integrated development environment (IDE) is fully consistent with the VBA IDE implementation shipping with Microsoft Office 2000 (Microsoft Excel 2000, Word 2000, PowerPoint 2000, Microsoft Access 2000, and Microsoft Outlook 2000). The menu system, development environment, and macro launch are identical to the VBA menu in Office 2000. Additionally, the Visio 2000 family allows macros written in VBA to be launched via an event registered in VBA or a Visio SmartShapes shape sheet or via a shortcut menu item on either a Visio SmartShapes symbol or a Visio drawing page.

The Visio VBA IDE starts from a single menu item (Tools, Macro, Visual Basic Editor or Alt+F11) and, when active, presents you, the developer, with a Project Explorer window as well as a Properties window and a Watch window. This Visio VBA IDE, though in its own window, is fully running in Visio's memory as an "In-Process" application. The Visio VBA IDE supports multiple projects being opened simultaneously.

The Project Explorer, similar to the standard Windows Explorer under Windows 95, 98, and 2000, displays a hierarchical tree view of the Visio VBA project. This tree begins with the current drawing (Drawing 1, for example) and continues down to Visio Objects and, below that, ThisDocument. The object ThisDocument hosts, by default, a whole new range of properties and methods (which are discussed later in the chapter). You can add additional modules, class modules, and user forms to the project through the Insert menu.

The Properties window in Visio VBA is similar to the Properties window found in Visual Basic. The window displays the available properties for the selected object and enables you to set new values for these properties. These properties may be listed by category or alphabetically.

When you add a user form to a project, Forms and, below that, User Form1 are added to the Project Explorer tree. Furthermore, two new windows are added to the Visio VBA IDE for the form. The first window contains the design mode of the form. The second window contains the toolbox and its associated palette of controls. You can add third-party controls by selecting Additional Controls from the Tools menu. Adding OLE Automation controls to a VBA project in this manner provides even greater interoperability between applications through object-centric encapsulated control usage.

Because the toolbox supports multiple pages, you can organize controls into logical pages. These pages may be imported and exported between projects, which facilitates the use of a common suite of tools between VBA projects.

Typical drag-and-drop functionality common in the designing of VB forms is fully implemented in Visio's VBA as well. A suite of new formatting, viewing, and tab-ordering tools is also fully supported.

When the user double-clicks on any control within the user form, the control's code window is launched. As with any VB control and code, a user can access the full listing of supported events code within the code window by selecting the event from the drop-down list at the top of the code window. All usual Copy, Cut, and Paste commands are fully implemented. By right-clicking the toolbar, you can activate an Edit toolbar. This floating toolbar includes such features as Indent, Outdent, Comment, Uncomment, Toggle Breakpoint, Toggle Bookmark, and many more.

The Visio VBA implementation also fully supports the IntelliSense feature set. Included within this set is AutoList for Properties and Methods. This feature is activated when the user types an object name followed by a dot, as in *appVisio*. As soon as you type the period key, a drop-down list of available objects, methods, or properties of that object is displayed. You can, by beginning to type in the required name, automatically scroll to that object's position within the list. Alternately, you can use the list's thumb and find the object in question. When the desired object is in view, a double-click on the object writes its name to the code line, thereby eliminating a potential typographic error. For any VBA keyword, object property, or method requiring arguments, the IntelliSense feature set includes automatic Tooltips for complete syntax as well as Parameter Information drop-down lists.

The full running and debugging feature set has been implemented, including VCR-style Run, Pause, and End buttons, the capability to set and clear watches and breakpoints, as well as step into and over functionality. Included also is a full Object Browser, which allows you to scan any object and look at the available methods and properties of that object.

In addition to the events `TheText`, `EventDblClick`, `EventXFMod`, and `EventDrop` available directly within the Visio SmartShapes ShapeSheet feature, the Visio 2000 family now supports the following events in the document itself:

Event	Description
BeforeDocumentClose	Triggered prior to closing a Visio document
BeforeDocumentSave	Triggered prior to saving a Visio document
BeforeDocumentSaveAs	Triggered prior to saving a Visio document under a new unique name

Event	Description
BeforeMasterDelete	Triggered prior to deleting a Master from a Stencil or Local Stencil
BeforePageDelete	Triggered prior to deleting a Visio document page
BeforeSelectionDelete	Triggered prior to deleting a selection on a Visio document page
BeforeShapeTextEdit	Triggered prior to a shape's text being changed
BeforeStyleDelete	Triggered prior to deleting a style from the active document
ConvertToGroupCanceled	Triggered when the user cancels the request to convert selected shapes to a group
DesignModeEntered	Triggered when the user changes the Visio run focus to Design mode
DocumentChanged	Triggered when a Visio document has changed
DocumentCloseCanceled	Triggered when the user cancels a request to close a document
DocumentCreated	Triggered when a new Visio document is created based on a template with an event programmed
DocumentOpened	Triggered when a Visio document containing programming is opened
DocumentSaved	Triggered when a Visio document is saved
DocumentSavedAs	Triggered when a Visio document is saved under a new name
MasterAdded	Triggered when a new Master is added to a Stencil or Local Stencil
MasterChanged	Triggered when a Master is changed
MasterDeleteCanceled	Triggered when the user cancels a request to delete a Master shape
PageAdded	Triggered when a page is added to a Visio document
PageChanged	Triggered when a page is changed in a Visio document
PageDeleteCanceled	Triggered when the user cancels a request to delete a page
QueryCancelConvertToGroup	Triggered when the Automation application validates whether the ConvertToGroupCanceled event has been triggered
QueryCancelDocumentClose	Triggered when the Automation application validates whether the DocumentCloseCanceled event has been triggered

Event	Description
QueryCancelMasterDelete	Triggered when the Automation application validates whether the `MasterDeleteCanceled` has been triggered
QueryCancelPageDelete	Triggered when the Automation application validates whether the `PageDeleteCanceled` event has been triggered
QueryCancelSelectionDelete	Triggered when the Automation application validates whether the `SelectionDeleteCanceled` event has been triggered
QueryCancelStyleDelete	Triggered when the Automation application validates whether the `StyleDeleteCanceled` event has been triggered
QueryCancelUngroup	Triggered when the Automation application validates whether the `UngroupCanceled` event has been triggered
RunModeEntered	Triggered when the user changes the Visio run focus to Run mode
SelectionDeleteCanceled	Triggered when the user cancels a request to delete a selection of shapes
ShapeAdded	Triggered when a shape is added to a Visio document
ShapeExitedTextEdit	Triggered when a shape's text editing is complete in a Visio document
ShapeParentChanged	Triggered when a SmartShape symbol's parent shape is changed
StyleAdded	Triggered when a style is added to a Visio document
StyleChanged	Triggered when a style is changed in a Visio document
StyleDeleteCanceled	Triggered when the user cancels a request to delete a style
UngroupCanceled	Triggered when the Ungroup command is canceled for the selected shapes in a Visio document

You may choose to write event handlers for one or more of these supported events; by doing so, you can achieve a much finer control over the processing of a Visio document. For example, you can decide to write an event handler that, when assigned to the `BeforeSelectionDelete` event, ensures that the corresponding record in an associated database is also deleted. This event handler will ensure a level of integrity between the Visio document's view of the data and the database's view of the data.

Utilizing the `BeforePageDelete` event may allow you to trap an end user's attempt to delete a valid page in the Visio drawing and, if the action is valid, remove all links to that page. As a result, the Visio document's integrity as well as the proper links from shapes on the remaining pages in the document are maintained. Writing an event handler for the ShapeModified event can allow for intervention to ensure that the change made conforms to a given set of criteria based in corporate rules, such as text font maintenance or standardized width of charting objects.

Over 85 new Automation objects, methods, properties and events have been added to Visio 2000 with VBA 6.0 since the release of Visio 5.0. In previous versions of Visio, when utilizing Visual Basic to locate a shape on a page in a document within Visio, you would be required to declare all local variables explicitly as objects and set their values based on an explicit traverse of the Visio Object Model. The following code example illustrates this point:

```
Private Sub Command1_Click ()
        Dim appVisio As Object
        Dim docsObj As Object
        Dim docObj As Object
        Dim pagsObj As Object
        Dim pagObj As Object
        Dim shpsObj As Object
        Dim shpObj As Object
        Dim szShpTxt  As String
        Set appVisio = GetObject(, "visio.application")
        Set docsObj = appVisio.Documents
        Set docObj = docsObj.Item(1)
        Set pagsObj = docObj.Pages
        Set pagObj = pagsObj.Item(1)
        Set shpsObj = pagObj.Shapes
        Set shpObj = shpsObj.Item(1)
        szShpTxt = shpObj.Text
End Sub
```

By utilizing the new Type Library under VBA in the Visio 2000 family, a programmer can directly declare the local variables as the object class in question and access them in a far more direct manner, as shown in the following code example:

```
Private Sub Command1_Click ()
        Dim docObj As Visio.Document
        Dim pagObj As Visio.Page
        Dim shpsObj As Visio.Shapes
        Dim shpObj As Visio.Shape
        Dim szShpTxt As String
        Set docObj = Documents.Item(1)
        Set pagObj = docObj.Pages.Item(1)
        Set shpsObj = pagObj.Shapes
        Set shpObj = shpsObj.Item(1)
        szShpTxt = shpObj.Text
End Sub
```

The same thing can be done even more succinctly:

```
Private Sub Command1_Click ()
        Dim szShpTxt As String
        SzShpTxt = Visio.ActivePage.Shapes(1).Text
EndSub
```

Clearly, the Type Library saves a lot of time and effort writing code.

From a programmer's perspective, the Visio products with VBA provide a rich and seamless development environment with a full feature set. This feature set and Visio's Type Library bring development to a far greater scope of Visio users who want to develop custom solutions working within the Visio environment. Visio with VBA has greatly expanded access to powerful programming in an object-oriented, cutting-edge application.

Both independent beta testing and internal Visio testing have indicated that, in general, a tenfold increase in performance in VBA versus Visual Basic is realized across the interface due to running in process and with dual interfaces on OLE servers. This results in an average performance increase of between 4 and 10 times in actual program performance. Tests have also shown performance parity between VBA applications in process and C++ applications crossing process boundaries.

Visio's easily available document events and simple event sink implementation using the VBA With Events keyword make programming far easier and quicker. Less code needs to be written, and with more events exposed, a tighter granularity can be programmed into controlling interaction with the Visio environment.

The inclusion of the Type Library in Visio allows VBA IntelliSense to assist you in selecting and implementing Visio Interface methods and constants. The Type Library also allows browsing of the Visio Object Model in the Object Browser window. This same Type Library enables you to use Visio object names in the VBA code environment.

Visio was the first company other than Microsoft to release a product with VBA. Visio is using the identical VBA 6.0 that Microsoft is delivering in Office 2000, so the macro scheme will be familiar to Office 2000 users.

VBA ships as an integral component of the entire Visio 2000 product family. The development environment is easy to access, as are the event structures that VBA and the Visio object model have exposed. VBA code is integrated within the Visio drawing, which allows easier distribution of Visio solutions using VBA.

Because VBA runs in the same process space as Visio, Visio application interfaces are built into the VBA instance. In addition, all the power of VBA (ActiveX, OLE Automation Controls, DAO, and so on) can be used.

The VBA IDE

As I stated earlier, the VBA IDE in Visio 5.0 is identical to that within Microsoft Office 97. Visio 5.0 is utilizing VBA 5.0, as does Office 97. The VBA IDE in Visio 2000 is identical to that within Microsoft Office 2000. Visio 2000 is utilizing VBA 6.0, as does Office 2000. The beauty of this parity is that once you have learned the IDE in any one application, you are fully up-to-speed in any other application. The only learning curve you must traverse is the particular object model for the application you want to control with your Automation Controller application. All of the services provided in VBA that you have used while developing Microsoft Office applications are fully implemented in Visio's VBA IDE.

I'll presume that you are comfortable with the VBA IDE and will not detail each and every feature in it. Should you want more information about VBA and programming within the VBA IDE, I direct you to a rather brilliant book by two friends and colleagues of mine, Ken Getz and Mike Gilbert. The book is entitled *VBA Developer's Handbook* (Sybex 1997). It weighs in at as much, if not more than, this book, so by sheer heft alone you are increasing your programming strength.

References and Options

Unlike objects you create using the ActiveX controls in Visual Basic or C++, objects that you access through ActiveX Automation remain with the object's server. They are not incorporated as part of your application. They are made available by reference, as shown in Figure 11.1.

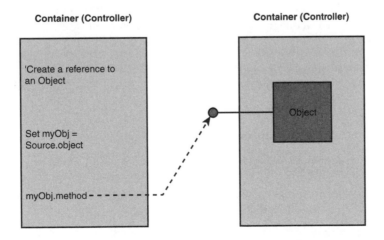

FIGURE 11.1

The object container creates and holds a reference to the object. Access to the properties and methods of the object is available through the interface provided by the object. The object always resides with its source.

Everything you do with a server's object you do by way of a reference to that object. You assign that reference to an object variable in your application. You manipulate the objects remotely from your application by setting properties and invoking methods through the object variable. When a method is triggered, this raises an event, an event that your application can capture and act upon.

An object reference is similar to a pointer in classic programming in that it is valid at runtime, but it is not something that you can store between executions. Furthermore, having a reference does not guarantee that you still have the object. For example, you can get a reference to a SmartShape symbol on a page in Visio, but if the user deletes the symbol, you have a reference that it is not referring to anything valid or useful (a "zombie"). An attempt to make a call to any property or method would cause an Automation error and could conceivably bring down your application. (Of course, your applications are all so well-crafted and make such extensive use of error trapping that this would never happen. Right?)

The Object Browser

In the Visio VBA IDE, pressing the F2 key initiates and displays the Object Browser. When the Object Browser is first activated, it displays all of the objects that it knows about. Note in the upper-left-hand corner of the browser, the list box displays All Libraries. Use the button to open the list and select Visio to limit the Object Browser to looking at only Visio objects.

The Classes list will present a listing of all the top-level objects. The Members of Application Object list will show the properties, methods, and events, as well as constants for this object level and subobjects below this object level. The Details pane at the bottom lists all of the details for this object. The iconography can be difficult to figure out, so each icon is identified in the following list.

Icon	*Identification*
	Property
	Default property
	Method
	Default method
	Event

Icon	Identification
⊞	Constant
⚒	Module
🖼	Class
🗂	User-defined type
●	Global
📚	Library
🎲	Project
🗔	Built-in keywords and types
🗄	Enums

So why do you care about how to access and browse the Object Browser? By including a reference to any given application's type library, you immediately gain access to the exposure of all of its objects as well as their properties, methods, and events. If you understand the hierarchy as well as the purpose of each object, programming with these objects should be much, much easier.

The Visio Object Model

With every copy of Visio 5.0 and Visio 2000, you will, if you choose to perform a complete install, find in the \Visio\DVS directory, a copy of the Visio drawing file Object Model.VSD. In addition to being a helpful visual reference to the entire object hierarchy within Visio, the Object Model additionally serves as a complete hyperlink system to obtain help on any object within Visio. Simply select the object you want to learn more about, right-click the object, and select Object Help from the context menu. The Visio Help system will then display the help reference for that particular object. From there, you can find a listing and subsequent help on any property, method, or event for that object. Using the Object Model will significantly shorten your development cycle, as well as lower your blood pressure, make your hair grow back in, and garner immediate praise from every middle-manager monitoring your development project's progress!

That concludes this brief overview of ActiveX Automation. In the next chapter, you will create your first VBA Automation application. You will learn more about properties, methods, and references as they apply to Visio VBA programming and discover the benefits of early binding versus late binding of object variables. I will discuss when, where, and how to run your application and focus on the RUNADDON() and CALLTHIS() functions within Visio. You will also take a brief look at the files shipped with Visio that are VB specific and learn how to interpret the return from the command string when an Automation application is launched in Visio.

Visio VBA Automation Basics

IN THIS CHAPTER

Let's get things started by dissecting a simple Visio Automation application. The purpose of this automation code is to retrieve the name of a selected SmartShape symbol in the current page of the current Visio diagram.

This code is found in a Visio diagram called GetShape.VSD. This is found on the companion CD for this book. In order to run this application, select the truck on the page, and then select Tools, Macros, ModuleGetShape, GetShape from the menus. When the application is launched, it executes the single line of code within the subroutine called GetShape():

```
frmGetShape.Show
```

Notice how the form's name is frmGetShape. This form object has a method. That method is the Show method. The Show method initializes the form, activates it, and makes it visible to the user. The full subroutine looks like the following code:

```
Public Sub GetShape()
      frmGetShape.Show
End Sub
```

The form that is displayed has two controls on it: a CommandButton and a TextBox. The CommandButton's name is CommandButton1 and the TextBox is named txtShapeName. The Caption property of the CommandButton1 control is set to the value Get Shape Name. When the user clicks on the CommandButton1 control, the procedure behind that control is a subroutine called CommandButton1_Click () and is shown in Listing 12.1.

LISTING 12.1 The CommandButton1_Click Subroutine

```
Private Sub CommandButton1_Click()
        'Retrieve the Name of the first shape in the first page of the
        'first drawing in Visio
        Dim docsObj As Visio.Documents       'Documents collection
        Dim docObj As Visio.Document         'Document object
        Dim pagsObj As Visio.Pages           'Pages collection
        Dim pagObj As Visio.Page             'Page object
        Dim shpsObj As Visio.Shapes          'Shapes collection
        Dim shpObj As Visio.Shape            'Shape object
        Dim shpNameStr As String
        Set docsObj = Visio.Documents
        Set docObj = docsObj.Item(1)
        Set pagsObj = docObj.Pages
        Set pagObj = pagsObj.Item(1)
        Set shpsObj = pagObj.Shapes
        Set shpObj = shpsObj.Item(1)
        shpNameStr = shpObj.Name
        txtShapeName.Text = shpNameStr
End Sub
```

Visio VBA Automation Basics

CHAPTER 12

259

12

VISIO VBA
AUTOMATION
BASICS

The first seven lines within the subroutine are the declarations. The important thing to notice here is how I have explicitly declared every object variable I am using and furthermore explicitly declared its object type. There is an order to this declaration: First there is a reference to the Documents collection, followed by a reference to the document within that Documents collection. Next is a reference to the Pages collection, followed by a reference to the page within the Pages collection. Then comes a reference to the Shapes collection, followed by a reference to the shape within the Shapes collection. Finally, a text value is established as a property of the shape. Here is the structure of these declarations.

```
Dim docsObj As Visio.Documents    'Documents collection
Dim docObj As Visio.Document      'Document object
Dim pagsObj As Visio.Pages        'Pages collection
Dim pagObj As Visio.Page          'Page object
Dim shpsObj As Visio.Shapes       'Shapes collection
Dim shpObj As Visio.Shape         'Shape object
Dim shpNameStr As String
```

To put objects in perspective, remember back, way back, to the very beginning of Basic as a language. The very first practical version of Visual Basic for the personal computer was GWBasic, otherwise known as "Gee-Whiz-Basic." GWBasic programs looked somewhat similar to the following code:

```
10 Mary = "Hello"
20 Fred = 3.1415926
30 Sally = Mary
40 Fred = " World!"
50 Mary = Sally + Fred
60 Print Mary
```

Do you remember typing in all those line numbers? Notice how Mary was a string, Fred was a real number and then a string, and Sally was a string. GWBasic programmers could play fast and loose with the data types of the variables they used, and they could use a new variable name whenever it suited them (which was a tad less professional, but what the heck!).

Astoundingly enough, these rules (if you dare to call them that) still apply unless you are talking about objects. When you reference objects, you must explicitly declare and type your variables prior to using them. Failure to do so will raise a runtime error, and the application will fail.

The next eight lines of the program step through the object hierarchy. Note that when you get references to objects VBA demands that you explicitly use the SET keyword:

```
Set docsObj = Visio.Documents
```

This line uses the Documents property of the Visio application object to get a reference to the Documents collection object. That reference is stored in a variable, which was previously declared and typed, named docsObj.

```
Set docObj = docsObj.Item(1)
```

This line uses the `Item` property of the `Documents` collection object to get a reference to the `Document` object. The `docObj` variable, which was previously declared and typed, stores this reference. Notice that the `Item` property requires you to name the item or enumerate the item you want to look for, in this case the first item.

```
Set pagsObj = docObj.Pages
```

This line uses the `Pages` property of the `Document` object to get a reference to the `Pages` collection object. That reference is stored in a variable, previously declared and typed, named `pagsObj`.

```
Set pagObj = pagsObj.Item(1)
```

This line uses the `Item` property of the `Pages` collection object to get a reference to the `Page` object. That reference is stored in a variable, previously declared and typed, named `pagObj`. The `(1)`, which specifies the first item, is necessary because the `Item` property requires you to name the item or enumerate the item you want to look for.

```
Set shpsObj = pagObj.Shapes
```

This line uses the `Shapes` property of the `Page` object to get a reference to the `Shapes` collection object. That reference is stored in a variable, previously declared and typed, named `shpsObj`.

```
Set shpObj = shpsObj.Item(1)
```

This line uses the `Item` property of the `Shapes` collection object to get a reference to the `Shape` object. That reference is stored in a variable, previously declared and typed, named `shpObj`. As in the previous lines, you must name the item or enumerate the item you want to look for, in this case the first item, to use the `Item` property.

```
shpNameStr = shpObj.Name
```

This line uses the `Name` property of the `Shape` object to retrieve a string value, which is the name of the SmartShape symbol represented by the `Shape` object. Notice that this line does not use the keyword `SET` because the value that is being retrieved is not an object, but rather a string. I store that reference in the `shpNameStr` variable, which was previously declared and typed.

```
txtShapeName.Text = shpNameStr
```

This line uses the `Text` property of the `TextBox` object to pass the value stored in the `shpNameStr` variable into the `TextBox` control on the form as a string. When executed, the entire subroutine retrieves the name from the SmartShape symbol and displays it in the `TextBox` control on the form, and then the subroutine ends.

To browse the entire code we have just dissected, open the VBA IDE. If you haven't already figured out how to open the VBA IDE, there are two methods for doing so:

- Select Tools, Macros, Visual Basic Editor from the menus.
- Press Alt+F11 (this is the Microsoft insider's methodology).

When you have the VBA IDE open, double-click the `ModuleGetShape` module, and then double-click the `frmGetShape` form, and then double-click on the CommandButton control. Now you should be able to browse the code.

This example, though far less than the most efficient way of performing this task, illustrates several points:

- The code navigates down the Visio Object Model starting with `<Global>` object.
- The code retrieves the SmartShape symbol's `Name` property and displays its value on a form.
- The code uses Microsoft-compliant standard naming conventions for object variables.

Be cautious in creating the names for your object variables. Notice that the only difference between a collection and a member of that collection is the small *s* in the middle of the name. If you are as poor a typist as I am, you might find yourself spending a significant amount of time debugging only to find that a wee typo is the problem instead of a code logic flaw.

Here is the same code we just ran as `CommandButton1_Click()` in a far more optimized version:

```
Private Sub CommandButton1_Click ()
        Dim shpObj As Visio.Shape
        Set shpObj = Visio.ActivePage.Shapes.Item(1)
        txtShapeName.Text = shpObj.Name
End Sub
```

To be as terse as humanly possible, here is the less-than-recommended, but still fully usable, version of this routine:

```
Private Sub CommandButton1_Click ()
        txtShapeName.Text = Visio.ActivePage.Shapes(1).Name
End Sub
```

In a short while, I will explain why the brevity of this code leads to problems that you might avoid by being just a bit more verbose.

Properties, Methods, and References

Once you get a reference to the object you want to query or manipulate, you might want to find out about other properties of that object. For example, in addition to the Name property, the Shape object has a Text property that returns, as a string, the text on the SmartShape symbol and a Type property that returns an identifier for the type of Visio SmartShape symbol, such as a group, a guide, or other type of symbol. Most properties that do not return objects return strings or integers.

You can set properties as well, as long as they are not read-only. In the Visio environment, properties can be read-only, read-write, or in a few rare cases, write-only (custom menus and toolbars are examples of these).

Remember that any time a property returns an object, it must be declared and must be accessed with the VB keyword SET, as in the following example:

```
Dim objVar As Visio.ObjType
Set objVar = object.objProperty
```

Any time a property returns something other than an object, for example a string, integer, or double, it should be declared and must not be accessed with the VB keyword SET:

```
Dim strVar As String
strVar = object.strProperty
```

To set the property of an object, use the VB declarative format, as in the following example:

```
object.strProperty = "string"
```

The following format also works:

```
object.intProperty = 1
```

Any time an object's method creates an object, it must be declared and must be accessed with the VB keyword SET, as in the following example:

```
Dim objVar As Visio.ObjType
Set objVar = object.Method
```

Any time an object's method creates something other than an object, for example, a string, integer, or double, use the VB declarative format:

```
Object.Method
```

Or alternately

```
XxxxVar = Object.Method
```

Some properties and methods contain mandatory, optional, or mandatory and optional arguments to the property or method.

This property is returning an object:

```
Set objVar = object.Property(arguments)
```

This property is returning something other than an object:

```
StrVar = object.strProperty(arguments)
```

This method is creating an object:

```
Set objVar = object.Method(arguments)
```

This method is creating something other than an object:

```
object.Method(arguments)
```

Or alternately

```
XxxxVar = Object.Method(arguments)
```

Methods were not used in the example that dealt with the name of the symbol on the page, but as you can see from the preceding examples, their syntax is similar to the property syntax.

As you have seen, both properties and methods can take arguments. For example, a `Shape` object's `Cells` property takes the name of the ShapeSheet cell to return. A `Document Collection` object's `Add` method takes the name of the template on which to base the new document.

In many of the examples in this book, I will, in an attempt to teach and illustrate, declare an object variable and then set it for every object as the application traverses the Object Model. As I showed previously, this process is not necessary; you can concatenate Visio object references, properties, and methods just as you can with any other Visual Basic objects.

There are, however, some trade-offs, and simple references can be, at times, better. If you use any of the intermediate objects in your application—for example, if you are going to be working with more than one `Shape` object from the `Shapes Collection` object—it makes sense to assign the intermediate objects to object variables so that you have them available for other uses. Assigning variables to intermediate objects ultimately takes less overhead than repeatedly calling a compound statement.

A compound statement can also be harder to debug. Each expression is evaluated and its return value plugged into the statement before the next expression can be evaluated. If one fails, you will get an Automation error at the erroneous statement line, but it may not be obvious where in that line the failure occurred.

Early Versus Late Binding of Object Variables

If a given object is defined to be a specific type at design-time, such as with the following statement, it is bound to that data type at design-time:

```
Dim docObj As Visio.Document
```

This is referred to as *early binding*. Design-time checks, such as testing assignment statements, can ensure the correct data type is being used. This strategy creates more efficient runtime code.

If late binding is used, the type of the object must be determined at runtime, and assigning the wrong type of data to the object can cause a runtime error. The following statement is an example of late binding:

```
Dim docObj As Object
```

When, Where, and How to Run Your Automation Program

Using VBA code as part of your solution makes the distribution of your application easy because the VBA code is held within the document itself. However, updating the code is difficult. In this section, I will discuss the CALLTHIS() function and how this new functionality can both enhance your solutions and, even more importantly, make them more portable.

Remember that the VBA code in your diagram is accessible to the user. However, you can protect the code from viewing by selecting Properties from the Tools menu from within VBA. Next, select the Protection tab and select Lock Project for Viewing, and then enter a password and confirm it. Finally, save your project and close it. The next time the project is opened, the project is locked, and a password must be entered to view or edit the project.

There are several different methodologies for executing your application:

- Your application can run each and every time Visio is launched.
- Your application can run by the user selecting the application from the Macros or Add-ons menu from under the Tools menu, as well as from the Macro or Add-on dialog box.
- Your application can run each time the user opens the diagram or creates a new diagram based on the template you design.
- Your application can run when a listing for your application is chosen from a context menu when the user right-clicks on a particular SmartShape symbol or on the page itself.

To run your application when Visio is launched, place the Visual Basic, C, or C++ executable into the Visio\Startup directory. This directory is not automatically created for you when you install Visio; you must create it yourself. Any executable file that resides in this directory will be launched whenever Visio is launched. With VBA applications, either place the code or reference it in the DocumentOpened event of the ThisDocument module.

To run your application from the Add-ons menu or the Macros menu, place the Visual Basic, C, or C++ executable into the Visio\Solutions directory or a directory registered in the Solutions file paths from the Options dialog box.

To run your application each time the user opens the diagram or creates a new diagram based on the template you design, place the code or reference it in the DocumentOpened event or the DocumentCreated event of the ThisDocument module.

To run your application from the context menu, create an entry in the Actions section of the applicable ShapeSheet and place either a RUNADDON() or CALLTHIS() function in the Action cell. If the application is a Visual Basic, C, or C++ executable, place it into \Visio\Solutions directory or a directory registered in the Solutions File Paths from the Options dialog box.

The RUNADDON() Function

The RUNADDON() function passes an add-on or code to be executed to the VBA project of the document containing the argument.

Syntax

In the following syntax, *string* is an ASCII string that VBA recognizes, such as the name of a macro, a procedure with arguments, a command that the VBA Immediate window can execute, or the name of an add-on:

```
RUNADDON("string")
```

If the project cannot execute *string*, Visio runs the add-on named string. If Visio cannot find an add-on named string, Visio does nothing and reports no error.

Note: In earlier versions of Visio, this function appears as _RUNADDON. Visio versions 4.0 and later accept either style.

Examples

This example calls the VBA procedure named summation and passes three arguments:

```
RUNADDON("summation 1 2 3")
```

This example prints *"xyz"* in the VBA Immediate window:

```
RUNADDON("debug.print ""xyz""")
```

This example saves the document containing the function:

```
RUNADDON("ThisDocument.Save")
```

This example launches the CALENDAR.EXE add-on:

```
RUNADDON("calendar.exe")
```

The RUNADDONWARGS() Function

The RUNADDONWARGS() function runs filenames and passes the command line arguments to the program as a string. Use the RUNADDONWARGS() function to bind a program, such as an add-on, to an Actions cell.

Syntax

When using the following syntax, keep in mind that the arguments should be 50 characters or fewer:

```
RUNADDONWARGS("filename","arguments")
```

In earlier versions of Visio, this function appears as _RUNADDONWARGS. Visio versions 4.0 and later accept either style.

Example

The following example launches the add-on GRAPHMKR.EXE and passes it the argument /GraphMaker=Stack:

```
RUNADDONWARGS("GRAPHMKR.EXE","/GraphMaker=Stack")
```

In earlier versions of Visio, the RUNADDON() function merely looked up the named function, the string argument to the function, in the add-on list and executed it. With the introduction of VBA, the RUNADDON() function was modified to do extra duty. The string argument to RUNADDON() is now overloaded. By this I mean that the VBA project of a cell's document first looks at the string and tries to parse it. If the VBA project recognizes the string as valid VBA code, it will execute the code. This capability allows you to effectively write VBA code in your ShapeSheet and execute it by wrapping a RUNADDON() function around it. It also explains how public subroutines of a VBA project can be called with RUNADDON() even though these subroutines do not exist in the Add-ons list. As mentioned before, if the string is not recognized as VBA code, the RUNADDON() function looks for *string* in the Add-ons list and executes that add-on if it finds one.

Keep this overloading in mind when we discuss creating custom menus and toolbars in later chapters. You can apply this same technique in that context as well. The file RunAddon.VSD included on the companion CD has some grand examples of using the RUNADDON() function.

The CALLTHIS() Function

The CALLTHIS() function calls a procedure in a VBA project. The CALLTHIS() function differs from the RUNADDON() function in that a document's project need not reference another project in order to call into that project.

Syntax

In the following syntax, *procedure* is the name of the procedure to call; a string is required. A string is optional for *project,* which is the project that contains the procedure. The arguments, indicated by *arg*, can be of any type, including number, string, date, and currency values, passed as parameters to the procedure.

```
CALLTHIS("procedure",["project"],[arg1,arg2,...])
```

In the VBA project, *procedure* is defined as follows:

```
procedure( shpObj As Visio.shape [arg1 As type, arg2 As type...])
```

In this definition, *shpObj* is a reference to the Shape object that contains the CALLTHIS formula being evaluated, and *arg1* and *arg2* are the arguments specified in that formula.

Notice that *shpObj* is very much like the "this" argument passed to a C++ member procedure, hence the name CALLTHIS. In effect, a cell that contains a formula with CALLTHIS is saying, "Call this procedure and pass it a reference to my shape."

If a project is specified, Visio scans all open documents for the one containing that project and calls a procedure in that project. If the project is omitted or null (""), the procedure is assumed to be in the VBA project of the document that contains the CALLTHIS formula being evaluated.

Numbers in the arguments are passed in external units. For example, if you pass the value of the Height cell from a 3-cm-tall shape, 3 is passed. To pass different units with a number, use the FORMATEX function or explicitly coerce units by adding a null number-unit pair, for example, 0 ft + Height.

> **NOTE**
>
> The second comma in the CALLTHIS() function is optional. It corresponds to the number of additional parameters added to your procedure. If you do not use any additional parameters, except shpObj as Visio.Shape, do not add the second comma; use CALLTHIS("",) instead. If you add two additional parameters, for example, use CALLTHIS("",,,).

The CALLTHIS() function always evaluates to 0, and the call to the named procedure occurs during idle time after the recalculation process finishes. The procedure can return a value, but Visio ignores it. The procedure can simulate returning a value that Visio can recognize by setting the formula or result of another cell in the document, but not the cell that called the procedure unless you want to overwrite the CALLTHIS formula.

Examples

The following example calls the procedure named p located in a module and passes the value of Height in centimeters, such as 7.62 cm:

```
CALLTHIS("p",,FORMATEX(Height,"#.00 u",,"cm"))
```

The following example calls the procedure named q located in a module and passes the cell's height in centimeters and Sheet.2's width in internal units:

```
CALLTHIS("q",,0 cm.+Height,Sheet.2!Width)
```

Use the following procedure in the ThisDocument class module:

```
Sub A(shpObj As Visio.Shape)
     MsgBox "Click OK."
End Sub
Sub B(shpObj As Visio.Shape, strA As String)
    MsgBox strA
End Sub
Sub C(shpObj As Visio.Shape, strA As String, strB As String)
     MsgBox strA & strB
End Sub
```

Use any of the following syntax in a shape's EventDblClick cell with the previous procedures:

```
CALLTHIS("ThisDocument.A",)
```

```
CALLTHIS("ThisDocument.B",,"Click")
```

```
CALLTHIS("ThisDocument.C",,"Click", " OK.")
```

Another reason that the CALLTHIS() function is so important is the issue of code portability. I stated earlier that VBA code resides within the diagram. A drawback to this is that updating code becomes very difficult. If a new revision of your solution is present, the documents created using older versions will never see the changes. However, if the code lives in a Visio stencil and is called from that stencil each time it needs to be executed, the stencil always contains the latest version of the code. When you need to update your code, simply ship a new stencil, and the document referencing that code will run the newest version of the solution.

More on the CALLTHIS() Function

As an adjunct to this discussion, I am including the following paper written by Mike Fredrick, one of Visio's first and foremost engine developers. In this paper, Mike discusses even more intricacies of the CALLTHIS() function usage.

Visio 5.0 (and Visio 2000) provides a new ShapeSheet function named CALLTHIS(). Its syntax is as follows:

```
CallThis(ProcName, [ProjName], {Argi})
```

In this syntax, ProcName is a string and is required. ProjName is a string that can be omitted or null. Argi (1≤i≤n, n≥0) can be of any type and is optional.

CALLTHIS() is a second-generation variation of what was done to the RUNADDON() function in Visio 4.5. In Visio 4.5, we enhanced RunAddon(SomeString) so it will first check whether VBA accepts SomeString as code it can execute. Only if VBA rejects SomeString will Visio invoke an add-on named SomeString.

VBA accepts quite a large set of strings, essentially anything a user could enter into the Immediate window. Here are some examples:

```
=RUNADDON("MacroName")

=RUNADDON("ProcName 1, 2, ""This shape's height is "&Height&"""")

=RUNADDON("FormName.Show")

=RUNADDON("ProjectName.ModuleName.Proc")

=RUNADDON("app.alertresponse=1: activewin.selection.ungroup:
app.alertresponse=0")
```

The last example is particularly interesting if it is contained in a master's OnDrop cell. A new instance of the master will ungroup itself with no intervening user alert. A variation of this ploy is suggested later.

An evaluation of =CALLTHIS("p", ["ProjName"], { ai }) in a cell of sheet S in document D will cause Visio to call a VBA procedure. The call will be of the following form, where ipS is a Shape or Style object representing sheet S and the vai are discussed later:

```
p(ipS, va1, va2, . . . , van)
```

CALLTHIS() is thus a mechanism whereby a cell can be made to call a custom member method of its shape. If the project's name is omitted or null, p will be invoked in the VBA project of document D. Otherwise, all open documents will be scanned for one whose project's name is ProjName, and p will be invoked in that project. Thus custom members of a shape needn't be in the shape's document.

CALLTHIS() is like RUNADDON() in the sense that it will always evaluate to 0 and will be performed during idle time after the recalculation process has finished. Procedure p can return a value, but Visio will ignore it.

(Note: The sheet engine presently isn't reentrant enough to allow synchronous invocation of external code. Procedure p can simulate returning a value by setting the formula or result of some cell, but not the cell that caused p's invocation, unless losing the CALLTHIS() operand is okay. A possible future enhancement would allow changing a cell's value but not its formula.)

Using CallThis() to Call Code in Other Documents' Projects

The following was one of the RUNADDON() examples cited previously:

```
=RUNADDON("ProjectName.ModuleName.Proc")
```

Suppose this formula is in a cell in document D whose project name isn't Projectname. If Document D's project references a project named ProjectName (possibly the project of a Visio document, possibly not), then VBA can execute "ModuleName.Proc" in that project. Otherwise, VBA can't execute it.

References from Visio documents have their pluses and minuses. CALLTHIS() is different from RUNADDON() in that no reference is required to cause the invocation of a procedure in another document's project. Suppose a cell in document D has the following formula:

```
=CALLTHIS("p", "ProjectName")
```

If there is a document open at the time the cell evaluates whose project name is ProjectName, an attempt will be made to invoke procedure p in that project. If multiple open documents have projects named ProjectName, Visio determines which one is called.

Argument Passing

Using CALLTHIS(), you can call a VBA procedure that takes no arguments, one argument, or several arguments. An evaluation of =CALLTHIS("p", ["ProjName"], a1, a2, . . . , an) where n≥0 will cause Visio to make the following procedure call:

```
p(ipS, va1, va2, . . . , van)
```

Each ai is a ShapeSheet token. Each vai is a variant. The mapping from token to variant is as follows: If ai refers to a cell whose value is a Currency, vai will be of type VT_CY. The value passed is an 8-byte, 15.4 fixed-point number. The value passed is unitless and therefore useless unless assumptions are made. VBA sees a currency.

If ai refers to a cell whose value is a DateTime, vai will be of type VT_DATE. The value passed is an 8-byte, floating-point, and so on. VBA sees a date.

If ai is a quoted string or a cell whose value is a quoted string, vai will be of type VT_BSTR. The value passed is a SysAlloc'd BSTR. VBA sees a string.

If ai is or can be converted to a number, vai will be of type VT_R8. The value passed is an 8-byte, floating-point number. VBA sees a double. If no units are specified, vai will be of type VT_EMPTY. VBA sees an empty variant.

CALLTHIS() will often bind successfully to a procedure whose arguments don't exactly match in type the arguments Visio passes to it. This is because IDispatch::Invoke will coerce passed arguments to expected types. A successful bind will occur, for example, if a double is passed to a procedure that takes an integer.

Consider the following code:

```
=CALLTHIS("p",, Height)
```

Suppose `Height` (as reported in the sheet window) is 3 centimeters. Visio could choose to pass the value expressed in external units (3) or internal units (3×2.54==7.62). Visio passes external units.

The caller can cause Visio to pass an argument in specified units by prefixing the argument with `"0<unit>+"`. To pass `Height` in inches, use the following:

```
=CALLTHIS("p",, 0 in. + Height)
```

Binding a CALLTHIS Operand to a Particular Procedure in a Particular Project

When `CALLTHIS()` evaluates, Visio first binds to a project to call into and then binds to a particular procedure in that project and then calls the procedure. The procedure will execute if the arguments Visio passes it are coercible to arguments the procedure actually takes.

Any of these steps may fail; there may be no such project or no such procedure, or the passed arguments may not match actual arguments. If a step fails, `CALLTHIS()` will behave like `RUNADDON()`: it will do nothing. (Visio 5.0 exposes a new `App.TraceFlags` property. Amongst other things, this property can be made to record to the VBA Immediate window calls and attempted calls into VBA. Thus the developer shall be able to determine whether `CALLTHIS()` has succeeded.)

If `"p"` is the name of the procedure to be called, and if the target project has exactly only one standard module procedure named `"p"`, `=CALLTHIS("p")` will do the trick. Use example `"module1.p"` if the project has more than one standard module procedure named `"p"`.

If `"p"` is a member of `ThisDocument`, `"ThisDocument.p"` must be passed to `CALLTHIS()`. `CALLTHIS()` cannot bind to project items that can have multiple instances. You cannot call a method of an instance of a class module or UserForm using `CALLTHIS()`.

Generic No-Argument Call

Suppose you want to call this procedure:

```
Public Sub p(this As Visio.Shape)
        Debug.Print "p got called with this=" + this.Name
End Sub
```

Use the following if p is in a standard module of the formula's document's project (the local project):

```
=CALLTHIS("p")
```

Use this syntax if more than one standard module in the local project has a procedure named p:

```
=CALLTHIS("module1.p")
```

Use this syntax if p is in the ThisDocument object of the local project:

```
=CALLTHIS("thisdocument.p")
```

Use this syntax if p is in a standard module of a nonlocal (but open) project named targProj:

```
=CALLTHIS("p","targProj")
```

Passing a Date

Suppose you want to call this procedure:

```
Public Sub p(this As Visio.Shape, d As Date)
        Debug.Print "p got called with date="; d
End Sub
```

If there is a User.Date cell whose formula is =NOW(), evaluating

```
=CALLTHIS("p",,User.Date)
```

will result in

```
p got called with date=3/12/97 6:17:44 PM
```

Passing Strings

Suppose you want to call this procedure:

```
Public Sub p(this As Visio.Shape, s As String)
        Debug.Print s
End Sub
```

The following examples presume p is in a standard module of the local project:

```
=CALLTHIS("p",,"abc")                                   => abc
```

```
=CALLTHIS("p",,FORMATEX(Height,"#.00 u",,"cm"))        => 7.62 cm.
```

If there is a custom property Bozo with value ="Type 3 flying saucer.", the code would look like the following:

```
=CALLTHIS("p",,Prop.Bozo)                               => Type 3 flying saucer.
```

Monitoring Cell Changes

Suppose you want to call this procedure:

```
Public Sub p(this As Visio.Shape, cellName As String)
        Debug.Print this.Cells(cellName).Name + " just changed"
End Sub
```

You can monitor cell changes by setting user or scratch cells, as demonstrated in this code:

```
=DEPENDSON(Height)+CALLTHIS("p",,"Height")          => Height just changed
```

Passing Numbers

Suppose you want to call this procedure:

```
Public Sub p(this As Visio.Shape, h As Double, w As Integer)
        Debug.Print h
        Debug.Print w
End Sub
```

Here is the ShapeSheet function version of the code above:

```
=CALLTHIS("p",,1.66,2.75)                          => 1.66, 3
```

The following is legal but sort of silly, given that you can get height and width from "this":

```
=CALLTHIS("p",,Height,Width)
```

But the following might not be so silly. It will print the height and width of another shape in external units. Suppose Sheet.2's height is 4.25 centimeters, and its width is 3.25 inches.

```
=CALLTHIS("p",,Sheet.2!Height,Sheet.2!Width)       => 4.25, 3
```

You can dictate that both values will be passed as centimeters by changing the formula to the following:

```
=CALLTHIS("p",,0 cm.+Height,0 cm.+Width)           => 4.25, 8
```

Or you can have a User.Units cell with a value of =0 cm., 0 in., etc. and use this code:

```
=CALLTHIS("p",,User.Units+Height,User.Units+Width)
```

The preceding formula has dependencies to the Height and Width cells. If they change, the formula will reevaluate. In some cases, you may not want a dependency (subscription) from an argument referring to a cell to that cell. Suppose you want to pass height but only depend on width:

```
=CALLTHIS("p",,0 cm.+"Height",0 cm.+Width)
```

This code will get called when the width changes. It will not get called if just the height changes. The `0 cm.+"Height"` tells Visio to pass a number, and it will construe `"Height"` as a cell reference in such a context. But there is no dependency from the formula to the `Height` cell.

Code Behind a Master

The example in this section uses `CALLTHIS()` to put code behind a master. It shows how a master can be made to push code from its project into the project of a document into which the master has just been instanced. This example is only meant to be illustrative. This scheme may not suffice for production-quality solutions, and particular details shown here are specific for this example.

Follow these steps:

1. Make a stencil file with a project named `srcProj`. The project is going to make use of VBA's Object Model, so it must be made to reference the Microsoft Visual Basic for Applications Extensibility type library.

2. Add some masters to the stencil. Set the `EventDrop` cell of each master's top-level sheet to

   `=CALLTHIS("push","srcProj")`

   Note that this example is lazy. It requires the top-level sheet of each master to have a scratch section.

3. Add `module1` to the stencil's project.

4. Add the `Push` procedure to the module, followed by the source. The idea is that `Push` will get called when the stencil's masters are instanced.

When `Push` is called and passed a reference to the new sheet, `Push` will do the following:

- Obtain access to the new sheet's project.

- Determine whether the project has a module named `PushedMod` and make one if there isn't one.

- Determine whether `PushedMod` has a procedure named `PushedProc` and make one if there isn't one. In this example, `PushedProc` just changes the color of the shape passed to it.

- Set cells in the new sheet to call `PushedProc`. In this example, `Scratch.A1` is set to

  `=DEPENDSON(Height)+CALLTHIS("PushedCode")`

The net effect is that instances of the stencil's masters will change color when their height changes. Listing 12.2 is the routine that pushes code into the new instance's document.

LISTING 12.2   Push Code into New Instance's Document

```
Public Sub push(this As Visio.Shape)
     On Error GoTo shucks
     Debug.Print "push called for: "; this.Name
```

```
        ' Push proc PushedProc to module PushedMod of
        ' project of this if no such proc already.
        ' 1. Get project of this
        Dim targProj As VBIDE.VBProject
        Set targProj = this.Document.VBProject
        ' 2. Get module PushedMod. Make one if one not there.
        Debug.Print "   got project"
        Dim targComp As VBIDE.VBComponent
        On Error Resume Next
        Set targComp = targProj.VBComponents("PushedMod")
        If 0 <> Err Then
                On Error GoTo shucks
                Set targComp = targProj.VBComponents.Add(vbext_ct_StdModule)
                targComp.Name = "PushedMod"
                Debug.Print "   pushed module"
        End If
        ' 3. Get proc PushedProc. Make one if not one already.
        Debug.Print "   got module"
        Dim code As VBIDE.CodeModule, i As Long
        Set code = targComp.CodeModule
        On Error Resume Next
        i = code.ProcBodyLine("PushedCode", vbext_pk_Proc)
        If 0 <> Err Then
                On Error GoTo shucks
                code.AddFromString ("Public Sub PushedCode(this As
                ➥Visio.Shape)")
                i = code.ProcBodyLine("PushedCode", vbext_pk_Proc)
                code.InsertLines i + 1, "  Dim fc As Visio.Cell"
                code.InsertLines i + 2, "  Set fc = this.Cells(""FillForegnd"")"
                code.InsertLines i + 3, "    Dim i As Integer"
                code.InsertLines i + 4, _
                "    i = (fc.ResultInt(visNumber, visRound) + 1) Mod 24"
                code.InsertLines i + 5, "    fc.ResultFromInt(visNumber) = i"
                code.InsertLines i + 6, "End Sub"
                Debug.Print "   pushed procedure"
        End If
        ' 4. Put formula into scratch cell of this that will cause PushedCode to
        '    get called if height of this changes.
        this.Cells("Scratch.A1").Formula = _
        "=DEPENDSON(Height)+CALLTHIS(""PushedCode"")"
        Debug.Print "   pushed formula"
        Exit Sub
shucks:
        Debug.Print "Oh, darn."
        Exit Sub
End Sub
```

VB-Specific Files in Visio

If you are building your solution based upon an external Automation controller, such as Visual Basic, rather then Visio's internal VBA, you need to know about of two files designed to assist you. These files are VISCONST.BAS and VISREG.BAS.

VISCONST.BAS is a Visual Basic file that contains the Visio constant values for each of the returns from functions as well as arguments to functions. Many, if not most, of the arguments to Visio properties and methods seem, to the programmer, to be rather arbitrary numeric values. As an example, the `Type` property of a Window object returns the integer 1, 2, 3, or 4 to indicate the window type. VISCONST.BAS contains defined constants for these values: `visDrawing`, `visStencil`, `visSheet`, and `visIcon`. Using these constants will make your code easier to read and maintain. Listing 12.3 is an example of using these constants in code:

LISTING 12.3 Window Type Reporting

```
Public Sub WinTypeSussOut()
    Dim objVisApp As Visio.Application
    Dim objWinCurrent As Visio.Window
    Dim intWinType As Integer
    Dim szWinTypeString As String
    Set objVisApp = Visio.Application
    Set objWinCurrent = objVisApp.ActiveWindow
    intWinType = objWinCurrent.Type
    Select Case intWinType
        Case visDrawing
            szWinTypeString = "Visio Drawing Page"
        Case visStencil
            szWinTypeString = "Visio Stencil"
        Case visSheet
            szWinTypeString = "Visio ShapeSheet"
        Case visIcon
            szWinTypeString = "Visio Icon Editor"
        Case Else
            szWinTypeString = "Window Unidentified to Visio"
    End Select
    MsgBox "The Current Window type is a " & szWinTypeString, vbInformation,
    ➥ "Window Type"
End Sub
```

In this example, the Visio constants for each window type have been mapped to a string that describes the window type in simple English. The return from the `Type` property of the `ActiveWindow` object is an integer. However, the constants defined for `visDrawing`, `visStencil`, `visSheet`, and `visIcon` are defined as integers as well. The `Select Case` statement looks for the integer bound to the `intWinType` variable and checks it against the Visio constants. When the appropriate constant is matched, the string is assigned and used as part of a message displayed in the `MsgBox` function.

Here's a brief fragment from the VISCONST.BAS file:

```
' Type codes returned by window.type.
Global Const visWinOther% =                          0
Global Const visDrawing% =                           1  _
        '       ' Use subtype to get particular kind
Global Const visStencil% =                           2
Global Const visSheet% =                             3
Global Const visIcon% =                              4
Global Const visAnchorBarBuiltIn% =                  6  _
        '       ' Use ID to get particular kind
Global Const visDockedStencilBuiltIn% = 7
Global Const visDrawingAddon% =  8 ' Add-on window with drawing window behavior
Global Const visStencilAddon% =  9 ' Add-on window with stencil window behavior
Global Const visAnchorBarAddon% =  10 ' Add-on window with anchor bar behavior
Global Const visDockedStencilAddon% = 11 ' Add-on window with docked stencil
behavior
```

You may not need the entire VISCONST.BAS file in your project. You can copy just the constants that you need from the file into your application. Many of the constants defined in VISCONST.BAS are used with the `CellsSRC` property of the `Shape` object. Many others define menu and toolbar contexts and other values that are only used with UI objects. You may not need these in your application. However, if you use a constant that is not defined, you may get an Automation error, or you may get indeterminate results.

Remember that Visio utilizing Visual Basic 4.0, 5.0, 6.0 and VBA 5.0 and 6.0 can make use of Visio's Type Library and therefore can eliminate the need to explicitly include all or part of the VISCONST.BAS file. Remember also that you may run into issues with the Type Library when you are using events because the Type Library does not support some of the constants as defined in VISCONST.BAS.

Earlier I showed you that you can obtain a reference to Visio, the application, via one of two Visual Basic function calls: `GetObject` or `CreateObject`. Remember that a call to `GetObject` always expects the application in question to be running. If it is not, you will get an Automation error, and your application will crash. When you make a call to `CreateObject`, that call always creates a new instance of that `Application` object; that is, it always launches a new instance of the application, regardless of whether an instance is running. The reference is always to the new instance, not to any previously running instance. You can readily see that using `GetObject` and `CreateObject` is fraught with the possibilities for errors.

Visio has come to the rescue by providing you with a function in the file VISREG.BAS that will take care of determining whether Visio is running and returning a reference to the proper instance of Visio. The function is vaoGetObject(), and it returns a reference to the current running instance of Visio if Visio is already up and running, launches Visio and returns a reference to the new running instance of Visio if Visio was not already up and running, or returns visError if it is not possible to launch Visio due to Visio not having been installed or some files required for running being deleted. The return from vaoGetObject() always binds to a global object explicitly named g_appVisio.

Here is an example of using vaoGetObject() in code:

```
Public Sub FindPage ()
        Dim pagsObj As Visio.Pages
        Dim pagObj AS Visio.Page
        If vaoGetObject () <> visOK Then
                MsgBox "Visio is not properly installed on this machine!"
        Else
                Set pagsObj = g_appVisio.ActiveDocument.Pages
                Set pagObj = pagsObj.Item(1)
        End If
End Sub
```

Interpreting the Command String

When an add-in (written in C, C++, VB, or other external Automation controller) is executed, a command string is sent to identify Visio as the environment that launched the application. The command string contains values that you can use to retrieve objects. This is in addition to any arguments you may have passed to your application. To access this return, use the Visual Basic function Command$() and then use Mid$() or StrComp() to parse the string.

Here is an example of a return string generated on a launch:

```
"/visio=<instanceHandle>/doc=<docIndex>/page=<pagIndex>/shape=<nameID>"
```

This example is the string sent when an application is run when a formula is evaluated in a SmartShape symbol's ShapeSheet cell. The code section /visio=<instanceHandle> indicates the application was run from Visio and not some inappropriate environment; instancehandle is the Windows handle of the Visio instance, which you typically will not use. The indexes of the document and page within their respective collections are indicated by /doc=<docIndex> and /page=<pagIndex>. You can use these values to obtain references to the corresponding objects. The code /shape=nameID is the NameID property of the SmartShape symbol whose formula was evaluated. You can use this value to obtain a reference to the corresponding Shape object.

You now have been initiated into Automation programming within Visio. In the next chapter, you will learn how to drill into Visio deeper by getting an instance of Visio, creating a new Visio document, opening a Visio stencil, getting a reference to a master SmartShape symbol on a Visio stencil, dropping a master SmartShape symbol onto a Visio drawing page, and adding text to the new SmartShape symbol instance on the page. You will also learn how to access the individual cells within a given Visio SmartShape symbol, compare formulas with results, and learn how to set the formula in a cell.

Generating Visio Drawings with ActiveX Automation

IN THIS CHAPTER

The last chapter discussed getting an instance of Visio and how you were free to use either `GetObject()` or `CreateObject()` to obtain the reference. Additionally, I discussed how `vaoGetObject()` could assist you in obtaining the proper reference to the instance of Visio that you want to work with. The following examples demonstrate each of these three methodologies.

This code uses `GetObject()`:

```
Public Sub LookForExistingVisio ()
      Dim appVisio As Visio.Application
      Set appVisio = GetObject ( , "visio.application")
End Sub
```

Notice that the first argument to the `GetObject()` function is left blank and the second argument is the quoted keyword string `"visio.application"`.

This code uses `CreateObject()`:

```
Public Sub LaunchNewVisio ()
      Dim appVisio As Visio.Application
      Set appVisio = CreateObject ("visio.application")
End Sub
```

Notice that the quoted keyword string `"visio.application"` is the only argument to the `CreateObject()` function.

This code uses `vaoGetObject()`:

```
Public Sub UseTheRightVisio ()
      Dim appVisio As Visio.Application
      If vaoGetObject() <> visOK Then
            MsgBox "Visio can not be launched"
            Exit Sub
      Else
            Set appVisio = g_appVisio
      End If
End Sub
```

In this case, `g_appVisio` was redundantly bound to `appVisio` for the sake of consistency. There is no real need to create this redundant binding; you can use `g_appVisio` directly.

Keep in mind that if you are using VBA from within Visio as your Automation controller, you do not need to obtain a reference to the Visio application. Because you are already running within Visio, Visio is by nature already active, and you have your reference implicitly. If you are attempting to communicate with Visio via some other application's VBA (for example, Excel) you will still need to use one of the previous methodologies.

Creating a Visio Document

Now that you have your reference to the `Application` object (whether explicitly or implicitly), the next step down the Object Model hierarchy is a reference to the `Documents` collection object and then to the document. Keep in mind that if you use `CreateObject()` to create a new instance of Visio, the documents collection in a new Visio instance will contain zero members. You will then need to use the `Add` method of the `Documents` collection object to create the Visio drawing.

If Visio is running, the `Count` property of the `Documents` collection object will return the number of open documents in the running instance of Visio. Remember that because the Automation call is creating an object reference, you must explicitly use the `SET` keyword when binding the return to the reference. Here is an example of getting a reference to the first (and presuming only) open document in the running instance of Visio:

```
Public Sub FindFirstDoc()
        Dim appVisio As Visio.Application
        Dim docsObj As Visio.Documents
        Dim inCount As Integer
        Dim docObj As Visio.Document
        Set appVisio = GetObject("Visio.Application")
        Set docsObj = appVisio.Documents
        inCount = docsObj.Count
        Set docObj = docsObj.Item(inCount)
End Sub
```

If you are writing your application using Visio's VBA, you have a much shorter method available to you. Remember that you are by nature currently in a running instance of Visio, and a document is currently open. Therefore the reference is as follows:

```
Public Sub FindActiveDoc()
        Dim docObj As Visio.Document
        Set docObj = Visio.ActiveDocument
End Sub
```

As I just stated, if you have a new instance of Visio, you currently have zero members in your documents collection. In order to create a new document, you will need to access the `Add` method of the `Documents` collection object. There are two slightly differing syntaxes for using this method. The first utilizes the access to a given template file from within Visio; the second creates a totally blank document based on no template at all.

To create a new document based on an existing template from within Visio, use this syntax:

```
Public Sub MakeNewDocLikeFlowchart ()
        Dim docsObj As Visio.Documents
```

```
        Dim docObj As Visio.Document
        Set docsObj = Visio.Documents
        Set docObj = docsObj.Add("Basic Flowchart.VST")
End Sub
```

If you look at the directory structure under your installation of Visio, you will see a Solutions directory. Within that Solutions directory you will find several directories for the various solutions that ship with Visio. Within each of those directories you will find files with an extension .VST. These are Visio template files. I discussed template files in Chapter 4, "SmartShape Symbol Reuse." You will need to include the name of a currently available .VST file as a quoted string to create a new document based upon this named template.

To base the creation of a new document on no template at all and create a new totally blank Visio document, use this syntax:

```
Public Sub MakeNewDocTotallyEmpty ()
        Dim docsObj As Visio.Documents
        Dim docObj As Visio.Document
        Set docsObj = Visio.Documents
        Set docObj = docsObj.Add("")
End Sub
```

Notice that the quoted string, which would otherwise be the template name, is included as a blank string (a double-quote followed immediately by another double-quote).

To have your solution run on older 16-bit versions of Visio, your application must use Visio's older 8,3 DOS-style file-naming conventions for standard stencils and templates. Visio, in these dual 16- and 32-bit versions, maps the short to long names internally. You can override these mappings or define your own additional mappings by adding to the Visio.INI file. You will need to create (if it is not already present) a new [CustomFNMapping] section in the Visio.INI file, and then add your entries below this section heading. Here is an example:

```
[CustomFNMapping]
MYNAME.VST=My Very Own custom Long Filename.vst
```

Opening a Visio Stencil

You now have a new document based upon a specific template, and that template opened up both a new drawing page and one or more Stencils. The next thing you need to do is explicitly get a reference to the Stencil object so that you can work with the Masters on the Stencil. The documents collection has an Item property. The Item property can reference items within the Documents collection object either by integer (the sequence of the item within the collection) or explicitly by name. I will use the latter of these two methodologies to obtain a reference to a Stencil. Study the following example:

```
Public Sub ReferenceFlowchartStencil ()
        Dim docsObj As Visio.Documents
        Dim docObj As Visio.Document
        Dim stnObj As Visio.Document
        Set docsObj = Visio.Documents
        Set docObj = docsObj.Add("Basic Flowchart.VST")
        Set stnObj = docsObj.Item("Basic Flowchart Shapes.vss")
        Msgbox stnObj.Name
End Sub
```

Notice how this code declares two document objects: one for the drawing itself and one for the Stencil. Remember that every drawing has its own Stencil and every Stencil has its own drawing page. Both drawings and Stencils are documents and as such are members of the Documents collection object.

When you open a new drawing based upon a particular template, quite often one or more Stencils will be opened as well as the new drawing page. Now the documents collection contains multiple members. When you use ActiveX Automation to drop a Master from a Stencil into a document, you will be working with two Document objects: one for the Stencil (the source, if you will) and one for the new drawing (the target).

I make this point only to draw attention to the fact that you need to make very sure which Stencil you want to reference because the Document object has a Masters Collection property, which means that both an open Stencil and the drawing have a Masters collection. However, in a brand new document, the Masters collection of the drawing has zero members, whereas the Masters collection of the Stencil has one or more members. Do not attempt to access members of the drawing's Masters collection in a new blank drawing, or you will encounter an Automation error.

Getting a Reference to a Master on a Stencil

After you have the reference to the Stencil object, you will need to obtain a reference to the Masters collection of that Stencil. To do this, you use the Masters property of the Stencil Document object. You must do this step before you can reference any individual Master SmartShape symbol on the Stencil. Study the code framework in Listing 13.1.

LISTING 13.1 Finding a Master on a Stencil

```
Public Sub ReferenceFlowchartMaster()
    Dim docsObj As Visio.Documents
    Dim docObj As Visio.Document
    Dim stnObj As Visio.Document
    Dim mastsObj As Visio.Masters
    Dim mastObj As Visio.Master
```

continues

LISTING 13.1 Continued

```
    Set docsObj = Visio.Documents
    Set docObj = docsObj.Add("Basic Flowchart.VST")
    Set stnObj = docsObj.Item("Basic Flowchart Shapes.vss")
    Set mastsObj = stnObj.Masters
    Set mastObj = mastsObj.Item("Process")
    MsgBox mastObj.Name
End Sub
```

Building on the previous code framework, this code declares a Masters object, mastsObj, and a Master object, mastObj. After obtaining the reference to the Stencil object, I use the Masters property of the Stencil object to get the reference to the Masters collection. With the Masters collection in hand, I then use the Item property of the Masters collection object, calling out the specific Master I want by name as a quoted string. This returns a reference to the specific Master we need to access.

Keep in mind the the following two lines are identical:

```
Set mastObj = mastsObj.Item("Process")
```

```
Set mastObj = mastsObj ("Process")
```

Because Item is the default property of the Masters collection object (just as it is for many collection objects), you can omit the direct listing of the word *Item*. To my mind, this practice is dangerous and sloppy and can come back to haunt you if you are not very careful.

Also keep in mind that because you are the designer of your own solution, you know the name of the template you want to base your new drawing on, you know the name of the Stencil(s) you need to reference, and you also know the name(s) of the Master(s) you want to use. For this reason, you can hard-code these string names into your code. In a robust, world-class solution, you should be error-checking to ensure that the template file, the Stencil file(s), and the Master(s) on the given Stencil(s) exist and are available for use.

Dropping a Master on a Page

Now that you have a reference to the Master you want to use, you need just one more thing before you can drop that Master into your document. You need a reference to the page itself. The Pages collection object is a property of the Document object (remember you want the page of the drawing, not the Stencil). The Page object is referenced through the Item property of the Pages collection object, as shown in Listing 13.2.

LISTING 13.2 Getting a Page Reference

```
Public Sub ReferenceThePage()
    Dim docsObj As Visio.Documents
```

```
    Dim docObj As Visio.Document
    Dim stnObj As Visio.Document
    Dim mastsObj As Visio.Masters
    Dim mastObj As Visio.Master
    Dim pagsObj As Visio.Pages
    Dim pagObj As Visio.Page
    Set docsObj = Visio.Documents
    Set docObj = docsObj.Add("Basic Flowchart.VST")
    Set stnObj = docsObj.Item("Basic Flowchart Shapes.vss")
    Set mastsObj = stnObj.Masters
    Set mastObj = mastsObj.Item("Process")
    Set pagsObj = docObj.Pages
    Set pagObj = pagsObj.Item(1)
    MsgBox pagObj.Name
End Sub
```

Note how I obtained the reference to the Pages collection object through the Pages property of the Document object. Note how I also obtained a reference to the Page object via the Item property of the Pages collection object, specifying the first page in the pages collection. This practice is fairly safe because a new Visio diagram contains at least one and in this case, only one, page.

With this arsenal of references to work with, we can now drop the Master SmartShape symbol onto the referenced page. We accomplish this by accessing the Drop method of the Page object. Remember that the Drop method is a method of the page, not of the Master. The Drop method takes three arguments:

- The reference to the Master to be dropped.

- The X ordinate of the coordinate pair specifying where the Master is to be dropped. This is a double and is unitless; inches are always the understood unit.

- The Y abscissa of the coordinate pair specifying where the Master is to be dropped. This is a double and is unitless; inches are always the understood unit.

Here is a typical code fragment for a Drop method:

```
Set shpObj = pagObj.Drop(mastObj, 4.25, 5.5)
```

Notice that because the Drop method creates a new Shape object, it explicitly uses a SET keyword. Notice also that the return from the Drop method is bound to a reference to the new Shape object, shpObj, as the new SmartShape symbol just added to the page.

Study the code fragment in Listing 13.3. As stated, I used the Drop method of the Page object and specified the Master object to drop at an X and Y value of 4.25 and 5.5, which happen to be the coordinates for the center of an 8 1/2"×11" sheet of paper, the default page size for this template.

13

GENERATING VISIO
DRAWINGS WITH
ACTIVEX
AUTOMATION

LISTING 13.3   Dropping a SmartShape Symbol on a Page

```
Public Sub DropTheShape()
    Dim docsObj As Visio.Documents
    Dim docObj As Visio.Document
    Dim stnObj As Visio.Document
    Dim mastsObj As Visio.Masters
    Dim mastObj As Visio.Master
    Dim pagsObj As Visio.Pages
    Dim pagObj As Visio.Page
    Dim shpObj As Visio.Shape
    Set docsObj = Visio.Documents
    Set docObj = docsObj.Add("Basic Flowchart.VST")
    Set stnObj = docsObj.Item("Basic Flowchart Shapes.vss")
    Set mastsObj = stnObj.Masters
    Set mastObj = mastsObj.Item("Process")
    Set pagsObj = docObj.Pages
    Set pagObj = pagsObj.Item(1)
    Set shpObj = pagObj.Drop(mastObj, 4.25, 5.5)
End Sub
```

Remember that you can use properties of the page itself to determine the available area and determine the proper location to perform the drop. I'll show you later in this chapter how you can access this capability.

Adding Text to a Visio SmartShapes Symbol

The text that is normally typed onto a SmartShape symbol is a property of the Shape object. The text is a string and not an object, therefore no explicit SET statement is required to bind the return from the Text property call to the variable holding the value. You will need to use LineFeed Chr$(10) symbol in a string to break the string. An alternative is to use the Visual Basic vbCrLf constant. If you want to include double-quote marks in your text string, you will need to either use Chr$(34)

```
shpObj.Text = Chr$(34) & "Hello?" & Chr$(34)
```

or triple the double quotes

```
shpObj.Text = """Hello?"""
```

The Text property of the Shape object can contain up to 64KB worth of characters. This limit should give you more than enough space to add whatever text is appropriate to the SmartShape symbol.

Listing 13.4 is the complete code for creating a new Visio diagram based on the flowchart template, dropping a process Master SmartShape symbol in the center of the page, and then adding three lines of text to the SmartShape symbol.

LISTING 13.4 A Visio "Hello World" Application

```
Public Sub MakeHelloWorld()
    Dim docsObj As Visio.Documents
    Dim docObj As Visio.Document
    Dim stnObj As Visio.Document
    Dim mastsObj As Visio.Masters
    Dim mastObj As Visio.Master
    Dim pagsObj As Visio.Pages
    Dim pagObj As Visio.Page
    Dim shpObj As Visio.Shape
    Dim szText As String
    Set docsObj = Visio.Documents
    Set docObj = docsObj.Add("Basic Flowchart.VST")
    Set stnObj = docsObj.Item("Basic Flowchart Shapes.vss")
    Set mastsObj = stnObj.Masters
    Set mastObj = mastsObj.Item("Process")
    Set pagsObj = docObj.Pages
    Set pagObj = pagsObj.Item(1)
    Set shpObj = pagObj.Drop(mastObj, 4.25, 5.5)
    szText = "Process Number 1: " & vbCrLf
    szText = szText & "Read the Manual... THEN " & vbCrLf
    szText = szText & "Make your " & Chr$(34) & "Hello World" _
    & Chr$(34) & " Application."
    shpObj.Text = szText
End Sub
```

13

GENERATING VISIO DRAWINGS WITH ACTIVEX AUTOMATION

Listing 13.5 is the optimized VBA rendition of the application in Listing 13.4.

LISTING 13.5 A More Concise "Hello World"

```
Public Sub MakeTightHelloWorld()
    Dim docsObj As Visio.Documents
    Dim docObj As Visio.Document
    Dim stnObj As Visio.Document
    Dim pagObj As Visio.Page
    Dim mastObj As Visio.Master
    Dim shpObj As Visio.Shape
    Dim szText As String
    Set docsObj = Visio.Documents
    Set docObj = docsObj.Add("Basic Flowchart.vst")
    Set stnObj = docsObj.Item("Basic Flowchart Shapes.vss")
    Set mastObj = stnObj.Masters.Item("Process")
    Set pagObj = docObj.Pages.Item(1)
    Set shpObj = pagObj.Drop(mastObj, 4.25, 5.5)
    szText = "Process Number 1: " & vbCrLf
```

continues

LISTING 13.5   Continued

```
    szText = szText & "Read the Manual... THEN " & vbCrLf
    szText = szText & "Make your " & Chr$(34) & "Hello World" _
    & Chr$(34) & " Application."
    shpObj.Text = szText
End Sub
```

Getting Formulas of Visio SmartShapes Symbols and Pages

If you will remember, I told you that you would need a clear understanding of the ShapeSheet to exploit the power of an Automation controller application. This section is where we begin to put this statement into practice. When you have a reference to a SmartShape symbol in a Visio diagram, you can obtain any available type of information about any aspect of that symbol by accessing the `Cells` property and then the `Formula` property of that particular cell.

To obtain the cell you are interested in, you need to get a reference to the `Cell` object. To get this reference, use the `Cells` property of the `Shape` object and explicitly call out the quoted string for the name of the desired cell, as in the following example:

```
Set celObjWidth = shpObj.Cells("Width")
```

Remember that some cell names are not necessarily as they are labeled in the ShapeSheet. For example, the cell that controls the visibility of a given `Geometry` section is not the `Geometry1.B` cell, it is the `Geometry1.NoShow` cell.

When you have a reference to a given cell, you can then obtain the formula that resides in the cell by accessing the `Formula` property of the `Cell` object. This code snippet gets a cell reference and then gets the formula within that cell:

```
Public Sub GrabWidthFormula()
    Dim shpObj As Visio.Shape
    Dim celObj As Visio.Cell
    Dim szCellFormula As String
    Set shpObj = Visio.ActivePage.Shapes.Item(1)
    Set celObj = shpObj.Cells("Width")
    szCellFormula = celObj.Formula
    MsgBox szCellFormula
End Sub
```

Getting a reference to a cell in a page's ShapeSheet is a little different from getting the similar information from a SmartShape symbol's ShapeSheet. The syntax is as follows:

```
Dim pagObj As Visio.Page
Dim pagShpObj As Visio.Shape
```

```
Dim celObj As Visio.Cell
Set pagObj = Visio.ActivePage
Set pagShpObj = pagObj.PageSheet
Set celObj = pagShpObj.Cells("PageWidth")
```

Remember that in addition to getting the formula for a given ShapeSheet cell, you can set the formula for a cell. The process is very similar (see Listing 13.6).

LISTING 13.6   Parametric Sizing via VBA Code

```
Public Sub PoundNewSizeIn()
    Dim shpObj As Visio.Shape
    Dim celObj As Visio.Cell
    Dim szCellFormula As String
    Set shpObj = Visio.ActivePage.Shapes.Item(1)
    szCellFormula = InputBox("Enter New Width", "Width")
    Set celObj = shpObj.Cells("Width")
    celObj.Formula = szCellFormula
    szCellFormula = InputBox("Enter New Height", "Height")
    Set celObj = shpObj.Cells("Height")
    celObj.Formula = szCellFormula
End Sub
```

The code in Listing 13.6 uses the standard VB/VBA `InputBox()` function to obtain user input. It then passes that input to the `Formula` property of the subject cell and modifies the physical geometry of the SmartShape symbol based on the input parameters.

Let's modify the application we wrote earlier to make the following changes:

1. Use the page's size to determine the center for the drop of the Master SmartShape symbol.

2. Set the formula for the width and height of the SmartShape symbol to accommodate the text that has been placed on the face of the symbol (see Listing 13.7).

LISTING 13.7   More Elegant "Hello World"

```
Public Sub FancyDropFlowchartSymbol()
    Dim docsObj As Visio.Documents
    Dim docObj As Visio.Document
    Dim stnObj As Visio.Document
    Dim pagObj As Visio.Page
    Dim pagShpObj As Visio.Shape
    Dim celObjPagHeight As Visio.Cell
    Dim celObjPagWidth As Visio.Cell
    Dim mastObj As Visio.Master
    Dim shpObj As Visio.Shape
```

13

GENERATING VISIO
DRAWINGS WITH
ACTIVEX
AUTOMATION

continues

LISTING 13.7 Continued

```
    Dim celObjWidth As Visio.Cell
    Dim celObjHeight As Visio.Cell
    Dim szText As String
    Set docsObj = Visio.Documents
    Set docObj = docsObj.Add("Basic Flowchart.vst")
    Set stnObj = docsObj.Item("Basic Flowchart Shapes.vss")
    Set mastObj = stnObj.Masters.Item("Process")
    Set pagObj = docObj.Pages.Item(1)
    Set pagShpObj = pagObj.PageSheet
    Set celObjPagHeight = pagShpObj.Cells("PageHeight")
    Set celObjPagWidth = pagShpObj.Cells("PageWidth")
    Set shpObj = pagObj.Drop(mastObj, celObjPagWidth.Result("in.") / 2, _
    celObjPagHeight.Result("in.") / 2)
    szText = "Process Number 1: " & vbCrLf
    szText = szText & "Read the Manual... THEN " & vbCrLf
    szText = szText & "Make your " & Chr$(34) & "Hello World" _
    & Chr$(34) & " Application."
    shpObj.Text = szText
    Set celObjWidth = shpObj.Cells("Width")
    Set celObjHeight = shpObj.Cells("Height")
    celObjWidth.Formula = "=GUARD(TEXTWIDTH(TheText))"
    celObjHeight.Formula = "=GUARD(TEXTHEIGHT(TheText, Width))"
End Sub
```

Note here how I obtained the page's height and width and divided each by two and then passed them as parameters or arguments to the Drop method. I obtained the values stored in the cells using the Result property. (I will discuss this property in greater detail in the following section.) Note also how I used the ShapeSheet formulas for resizing the height and width of the SmartShape symbol based on the text that is in the symbol. As you can see, understanding how information is stored and retrieved from a ShapeSheet cell is the key that unlocks the power of ActiveX Automation applications as they apply to Visio.

Formulas Versus Results

As you have just seen, accessing the Formula property of a Cell object causes the return of the information stored in the SmartShape symbol's ShapeSheet cell in the form of the formula as a string. Remember when we first began looking at ShapeSheet cells in Chapter 2, "An Introduction to ShapeSheet Programming." We discussed back then that there were two different methods of viewing a ShapeSheet cell: viewing formulas or viewing values. ActiveX Automation has a direct corollary. There are two distinct retrieval properties of a Cell object: the Formula property (which equates to the Formula view in a ShapeSheet) and the Result property (which equates to the Value view in a ShapeSheet). The `Result` property has four variants: `Result`, `ResultInt` (a long integer), `ResultIU` (result in internal units), and `ResultStr` (result as a string only).

As shown previously, accessing the `Formula` property returns a string and is called with the following syntax:

```
szFormulaString = celObj.Formula
```

The `Result` property returns a double as a unitless number and is called with the following syntax:

```
rnResult = celObj.Result("in.")
```

Notice that the argument to the `Result` property must be a valid unit type such as `"in."` for inches, `"mm"` for millimeters, and so on. Using a void string as the argument (`""`) returns internal units. You may also use any of Visio's constants for unit types:

VisAngleUnits	visElapsedMin	visMin
visCentimeters	visElapsedSec	visNautMiles
visCiceros	visElapsedWeek	visNoCast
visCurrency	visFeet	visNumber
visDate	visFeetAndInches	visPageUnits
visDegreeMinSec	visInches	visPicas
visDegrees	visInchFrac	visPoints
visDidots	visKilometers	visRadians
visDrawingUnits	visMeters	visSec
visDurationUnits	visMileFrac	visTypeUnits
visElapsedDay	visMiles	visYards
visElapsedHour	visMillimeters	

Keep in mind that the value stored in a given SmartShape symbol's ShapeSheet cell can be in any unit, and you can retrieve it in any other unit with Visio performing the conversion calculation for you. For example, the value in a ShapeSheet user-defined cell might be stored in inches, and you may opt to have it retrieved in centimeters. Visio will take the value in inches, convert that value to centimeters, and return to you the double as a unitless number representing that value in centimeters.

`ResultInt` always returns a long integer and has a syntax as follows:

```
intResult = celObj.ResultInt("in.", 0)
```

ResultIU always returns a double in Visio's internal units (inches) and has a syntax as follows:

```
rnResult = celObj.ResultIU("in.")
```

ResultStr always returns a string representation of the conversion of the unitless number and has a syntax as follows:

```
szResult = celObj.ResultStr("in.")
```

Remember that Visio's internal units are inches for linear dimensions and radians for angular measurements.

Setting a Visio Cell's Formula

As I have illustrated previously, to set a Cell object's Formula property, you use the standard Visual Basic assignment syntax. Here is an example of setting the Formula property of a Geometry1.X6 cell presuming that a Geometry1.X6 cell exists:

```
Dim shpObj As Visio.Shape
Dim celObj As Visio.Cell
Set shpObj = Visio.ActivePage.Shapes.Item(1)
Set celObj = shpObj.Cells("Geometry1.X6")
celObj.Formula = "=Geometry1.X1"
```

This example sets an intercell formula into the X6 cell to make it reference the X1 cell. The equals sign at the beginning of the formula is optional just as it is when working directly within the ShapeSheet environment.

You can also set the Result property to replace a formula with its result by using the following syntax:

```
CelObjResult(visNumber) = celObj.Result(visNumber)
```

What this code does is retrieve the value in a ShapeSheet cell and return the number by passing it back into the cell and overwriting the formula with the number. This effectively makes the cell a constant rather than a calculated cell. You can also set ResultInt and ResultIU in this way; however, ResultStr is a read-only property.

If you are working with a cell whose formula is guarded and you want to set its formula to a different formula, presume that the Width cell of a SmartShape symbol's ShapeSheet has a formula residing in it that reads: "=GUARD(Height*0.25)". Your application makes the following calls:

```
Dim shpObj As Visio.Shape
Dim celObj As Visio.Cell
Set shpObj = Visio.ActivePage.Shapes.Item(1)
Set celObj = shpObj.Cells("Width")
celObj.Formula = "=Height*1.625"
```

Your application ran properly, no error was raised, and the application terminated properly. However, the cell's formula is still `"=GUARD(Height*0.25)"`, not `"=Height*1.625"` as you desired. This is because the cell was guarded. In order to override the guard and force your new formula into the formula of the subject cell, you will need to use the `FormulaForce` property. There is a direct equivalent of the `Formula` property in a `FormulaForce` property as is true with most `Result` properties.

Formula *Property*	*Equivalent* FormulaForce *Property*
celObj.Formula	celObj.FormulaForce
celObj.Result	celObj.ResultForce
celObj.ResultInt	celObj.ResultIntForce
celObj.ResultIU	celObj.ResultIUForce

In the case of our preceding example, the proper methodology would be as follows:

```
Dim shpObj As Visio.Shape
Dim celObj As Visio.Cell
Set shpObj = Visio.ActivePage.Shapes.Item(1)
Set celObj = shpObj.Cells("Width")
celObj.FormulaForce = "=Height*1.625"
```

You have seen thus far how to create a new instance of Visio, begin a new drawing, get a reference to a drawing and a Stencil, get a reference to a Master, get a reference to a Drawing page, instance the Master onto the page, add text to the SmartShape symbol just instanced, and retrieve or modify any SmartShape symbol's ShapeSheet cell utilizing the `Formula` and `Result` properties of the `Cell` object. Pretty powerful stuff!

In the next chapter, we will discuss connecting SmartShape symbols, gluing SmartShape symbols under ActiveX Automation, and positioning or repositioning SmartShape symbols on a page of a Visio diagram.

13

GENERATING VISIO
DRAWINGS WITH
ACTIVEX
AUTOMATION

Connecting and Positioning Visio SmartShape Symbols under Automation

IN THIS CHAPTER

Many different diagram types in Visio involve connected diagrams. That is, they require individual SmartShape symbols be connected via lines, connectors, or other symbols. In the past chapter, we have seen how we can add symbols to a page. We need to look at how symbols can be connected under ActiveX Automation. Here you will work with the `Cell` object and the `Cell` object's `Formula` and `Result` properties, and also learn about two new methods of a Cell object: the `GlueTo` method and the `GlueToPos` method.

Connecting SmartShapes Symbols

Presume that you have a Connector SmartShape symbol; we will call this symbol A. Presume also that you have an Organizational Chart Position SmartShape symbol; we will call this symbol B. Under Automation, we want to glue the endpoint of A to a location on B. This process involves the following steps:

1. We need to get references to each of the A and B symbols. You already understand how to do this.

2. We need to get a reference to the glueable part of A, that is, its endpoint, by getting a reference to A's EndX or EndY cell.

3. We need to get a reference to either a location on B or to a connection point on B by getting a reference to the Connections.X1 cell, for example.

4. We need to use the `GlueTo` or `GlueToPos` method of the `Cell` object in A to glue it to B.

Using the `GlueTo` method of A's `Cell` object indicates that you want to glue directly to a particular element on B, a connection point, for example, represented by the specific connections `Cell` object on B. Using the `GlueToPos` method of A's `Cell` object indicates that you want to glue to a location relative to B's bounding box expressed in terms of B's coordinate system.

Getting the Cell to Glue

After getting references to the SmartShape symbols in question, the first thing we need to do is get a reference to A's glueable entity. This entity can be a control handle, a begin point, an end point, or the edge of a SmartShape symbol. You need to obtain a reference to either the X ordinate or the Y abscissa of the coordinate pair that makes up the entity to hold the proper reference.

The code for getting a reference to a control handle on an Organizational Chart Position SmartShape symbol looks like the following:

```
Dim shpObj As Visio.Shape
Dim celObj As Visio.Cell
Set shpObj = Visio.ActivePage.Shapes.Item("Position")
Set celObj = shpObj.Cells("Controls.X1")
```

The code for getting a reference to an end point on a Visio Dynamic Connector SmartShape symbol looks like the following:

```
Dim shpObj As Visio.Shape
Dim celObj As Visio.Cell
Set shpObj = Visio.ActivePage.Shapes.Item("Dynamic Connector")
Set celObj = shpObj.Cells("EndX")
```

The code for getting a reference to an edge of the geometry on an Organizational Chart Position SmartShape symbol (gluing to a guide) looks like the following:

```
Dim shpObj As Visio.Shape
Dim celObj As Visio.Cell
Set shpObj = Visio.ActivePage.Shapes.Item("Position")
Set celObj = shpObj.Cells("AlignLeft")
```

Gluing to the Other Shape

The next step is to get a reference to either the explicit entity you want to glue to, as in the case of a connection point, or to the position we want to glue to, as in the case of the location with respect to the target SmartShape symbol. When you have the reference you need, you can then use the `GlueTo` or `GlueToPos` method of the Gluing SmartShape symbol to glue to the other SmartShape symbol.

Listing 14.1 is an example of gluing a control handle on the Position SmartShape symbol to a connection point on a Manager SmartShape symbol. This example uses a Manager and Position SmartShape symbol that I created from two rectangles. You can find the sample drawing for this on the CD-ROM that accompanies this book. Be aware that the symbols from the Organizational Chart Solution have very specialized visibility behavior based on the solution itself, and this behavior can interfere with the visibility of the connection line.

14

LISTING 14.1   Gluing Shapes

```
Public Sub GluePositionToManager()
        Dim shpObjManager As Visio.Shape
        Dim shpObjPosition As Visio.Shape
        Dim celObjCtrl As Visio.Cell
        Dim intRetVal As Integer
        Set shpObjManager = Visio.ActivePage.Shapes.Item("Manager")
        Set shpObjPosition = Visio.ActivePage.Shapes.Item("Position")
        Set celObjCtrl = shpObjPosition.Cells("Controls.X1")
        intRetVal = MsgBox("Ready to Glue?", vbYesNo + vbQuestion, "Glue Demo")
        If intRetVal = vbYes Then
                celObjCtrl.GlueTo shpObjManager.Cells("Connections.Bottom")
                MsgBox "Finished Gluing"
```

continues

LISTING 14.1 Continued

```
        Else
                MsgBox "Canceling the Glue Operation"
        End If
End Sub
```

Notice the syntax of the `GlueTo` method:

```
celObjCtrl.GlueTo shpObjManager.Cells("Connections.Bottom")
```

In this syntax, `celObjCtrl` is the `Cell` object for the control handle `Controls.X1` cell on the Position SmartShape symbol. The `Shape` object for the Manager SmartShape symbol is indicated by `shpObjManager`. `Cells` is the `Cells` property of the `shpObjManager` SmartShape symbol. `"Connections.Bottom"` is the named connections row in the ShapeSheet of the Manager SmartShape symbol and is placed as a quoted string.

Listing 14.2 is an example of getting a Visio Dynamic Connector SmartShape symbol we'll call C to glue to a point halfway up the right side of a Rectangle SmartShape symbol we'll call A and halfway up the left-hand side of a Rectangle SmartShape symbol we'll call B. This example illustrates the `GlueToPos` method. Keep in mind that whenever you use the `GlueToPos` method you will always create a connection point, even if one already exists at that location.

LISTING 14.2 Gluing a Connector to Two Shapes

```
Public Sub GlueCToBothAandB()
        Dim shpObjA As Visio.Shape
        Dim shpObjB As Visio.Shape
        Dim shpObjC As Visio.Shape
        Dim celObjBeginX As Visio.Cell
        Dim celObjEndX As Visio.Cell
        Dim intRetVal As Integer
        Set shpObjA = Visio.ActivePage.Shapes.Item("A")
        Set shpObjB = Visio.ActivePage.Shapes.Item("B")
        Set shpObjC = Visio.ActivePage.Shapes.Item("C")
        Set celObjBeginX = shpObjC.Cells("BeginX")
        Set celObjEndX = shpObjC.Cells("EndX")
        intRetVal = MsgBox("Ready to Glue?", vbYesNo + vbQuestion, "Glue Demo")
        If intRetVal = vbYes Then
                celObjBeginX.GlueToPos shpObjA, 1#, 0.5
                celObjEndX.GlueToPos shpObjB, 0#, 0.5
                MsgBox "Finished Gluing"
        Else
                MsgBox "Canceling the Glue Operation"
        End If
End Sub
```

Notice the syntax of the `GlueToPos` method:

```
celObjBeginX.GlueToPos shpObjA, 1.0, 0.5
```

In this syntax, `celObjBeginX` is the `Cell` object for the `BeginX` cell on the C SmartShape symbol. `GlueToPos` is the `GlueToPos` method of the `celObjBeginX` `Cell` object. The `Shape` object for the A SmartShape symbol is indicated by `shpObjA`. the X value as a percentage of the total width of SmartShape symbol A's bounding box is `1.0` (in this case 1.0 equals the full width or the far right side). `0.5` is the Y value as a percentage of the total height of SmartShape symbol A's bounding box (in this case 0.5 equals half the height of the symbol).

To tie all of this together, let's look at an application that drops both Dynamic Connector SmartShape symbols and a series of simple Rectangle SmartShape symbols onto a Visio drawing page and then connects them. Additionally, the application (see Listing 14.3) names the various Rectangle symbols, places text upon them, and places text on the Dynamic Connector symbols indicating routing.

LISTING 14.3   A Directed Diagram

```
Public Sub MakeADirectedDiagramme()
        Dim docObj As Visio.Document
        Dim mastsObj As Visio.Masters
        Dim mastObjConnector As Visio.Master
        Dim mastObjBox As Visio.Master
        Dim pagObj As Visio.Page
        Dim pagShpObj As Visio.Shape
        Dim celObjPagWidth As Visio.Cell
        Dim celObjPagHeight As Visio.Cell
        Dim shpObjConn As Visio.Shape
        Dim celObjBeginX As Visio.Cell
        Dim celObjEndX As Visio.Cell
        Dim shpObjBoxItem1 As Visio.Shape
        Dim shpObjBoxItem2 As Visio.Shape
        Dim szFaceString As String
        Set docObj = Visio.ActiveDocument
        Set mastsObj = docObj.Masters
        Set mastObjConnector = mastsObj.Item("Dynamic Connector")
        Set mastObjBox = mastsObj.Item("Box")
        Set pagObj = docObj.Pages.Item(1)
        Set pagShpObj = pagObj.PageSheet
        Set celObjPagWidth = pagShpObj.Cells("PageWidth")
        Set celObjPagHeight = pagShpObj.Cells("PageHeight")
        Set shpObjBoxItem1 = pagObj.Drop(mastObjBox, celObjPagWidth.Result
(visNumber) / 2, celObjPagHeight.Result(visNumber) / 2)
        shpObjBoxItem1.Name = "1"
        shpObjBoxItem1.Text = "Center"
```

14

continues

LISTING 14.3 Continued

```
Set shpObjBoxItem1 = pagObj.Drop(mastObjBox, celObjPagWidth.Result(visNumber)
 / 4, (celObjPagHeight.Result(visNumber) / 4) * 3)
        shpObjBoxItem1.Name = "2"
        shpObjBoxItem1.Text = "Top-Left"
Set shpObjBoxItem1 = pagObj.Drop(mastObjBox, (celObjPagWidth.Result(visNumber)
 / 4) * 3, (celObjPagHeight.Result(visNumber) / 4) * 3)
        shpObjBoxItem1.Name = "3"
        shpObjBoxItem1.Text = "Top-Right"
Set shpObjBoxItem1 = pagObj.Drop(mastObjBox, (celObjPagWidth.Result(visNumber)
 / 4) * 3, celObjPagHeight.Result(visNumber) / 4)
        shpObjBoxItem1.Name = "4"
        shpObjBoxItem1.Text = "Bottom-Right"
Set shpObjBoxItem1 = pagObj.Drop(mastObjBox, celObjPagWidth.Result(visNumber)
 / 4, celObjPagHeight.Result(visNumber) / 4)
        shpObjBoxItem1.Name = "5"
        shpObjBoxItem1.Text = "Bottom-Left"
Set shpObjConn = pagObj.Drop(mastObjConnector, celObjPagWidth.Result(visNumber)
 / 2, celObjPagHeight.Result(visNumber) / 2)
        Set celObjBeginX = shpObjConn.Cells("BeginX")
        Set celObjEndX = shpObjConn.Cells("EndX")
        Set shpObjBoxItem1 = Visio.ActivePage.Shapes.Item("2")
        Set shpObjBoxItem2 = Visio.ActivePage.Shapes.Item("1")
        celObjBeginX.GlueTo shpObjBoxItem1.Cells("Connections.Right")
        celObjEndX.GlueTo shpObjBoxItem2.Cells("Connections.Top")
        szFaceString = "From: " & shpObjBoxItem1.Text & vbCrLf
        szFaceString = szFaceString & "To: " & shpObjBoxItem2.Text
        shpObjConn.Text = szFaceString
Set shpObjConn = pagObj.Drop(mastObjConnector, celObjPagWidth.Result(visNumber)
 / 2, celObjPagHeight.Result(visNumber) / 2)
        Set celObjBeginX = shpObjConn.Cells("BeginX")
        Set celObjEndX = shpObjConn.Cells("EndX")
        Set shpObjBoxItem1 = Visio.ActivePage.Shapes.Item("1")
        Set shpObjBoxItem2 = Visio.ActivePage.Shapes.Item("3")
        celObjBeginX.GlueTo shpObjBoxItem1.Cells("Connections.Right")
        celObjEndX.GlueTo shpObjBoxItem2.Cells("Connections.Left")
        szFaceString = "From: " & shpObjBoxItem1.Text & vbCrLf
        szFaceString = szFaceString & "To: " & shpObjBoxItem2.Text
        shpObjConn.Text = szFaceString
Set shpObjConn = pagObj.Drop(mastObjConnector, celObjPagWidth.Result(visNumber)
 / 2, celObjPagHeight.Result(visNumber) / 2)
        Set celObjBeginX = shpObjConn.Cells("BeginX")
        Set celObjEndX = shpObjConn.Cells("EndX")
        Set shpObjBoxItem1 = Visio.ActivePage.Shapes.Item("3")
        Set shpObjBoxItem2 = Visio.ActivePage.Shapes.Item("4")
```

```
        celObjBeginX.GlueTo shpObjBoxItem1.Cells("Connections.Bottom")
        celObjEndX.GlueTo shpObjBoxItem2.Cells("Connections.Top")
        szFaceString = "From: " & shpObjBoxItem1.Text & vbCrLf
        szFaceString = szFaceString & "To: " & shpObjBoxItem2.Text
        shpObjConn.Text = szFaceString
Set shpObjConn = pagObj.Drop(mastObjConnector, celObjPagWidth.Result(visNumber)
 / 2, celObjPagHeight.Result(visNumber) / 2)
        Set celObjBeginX = shpObjConn.Cells("BeginX")
        Set celObjEndX = shpObjConn.Cells("EndX")
        Set shpObjBoxItem1 = Visio.ActivePage.Shapes.Item("4")
        Set shpObjBoxItem2 = Visio.ActivePage.Shapes.Item("1")
        celObjBeginX.GlueTo shpObjBoxItem1.Cells("Connections.Left")
        celObjEndX.GlueTo shpObjBoxItem2.Cells("Connections.Bottom")
        szFaceString = "From: " & shpObjBoxItem1.Text & vbCrLf
        szFaceString = szFaceString & "To: " & shpObjBoxItem2.Text
        shpObjConn.Text = szFaceString
Set shpObjConn = pagObj.Drop(mastObjConnector, celObjPagWidth.Result(visNumber)
 / 2, celObjPagHeight.Result(visNumber) / 2)
        Set celObjBeginX = shpObjConn.Cells("BeginX")
        Set celObjEndX = shpObjConn.Cells("EndX")
        Set shpObjBoxItem1 = Visio.ActivePage.Shapes.Item("1")
        Set shpObjBoxItem2 = Visio.ActivePage.Shapes.Item("5")
        celObjBeginX.GlueTo shpObjBoxItem1.Cells("Connections.Left")
        celObjEndX.GlueTo shpObjBoxItem2.Cells("Connections.Right")
        szFaceString = "From: " & shpObjBoxItem1.Text & vbCrLf
        szFaceString = szFaceString & "To: " & shpObjBoxItem2.Text
        shpObjConn.Text = szFaceString
Set shpObjConn = pagObj.Drop(mastObjConnector, _
 celObjPagWidth.Result(visNumber) / 2, celObjPagHeight.Result(visNumber) / 2)
        Set celObjBeginX = shpObjConn.Cells("BeginX")
        Set celObjEndX = shpObjConn.Cells("EndX")
        Set shpObjBoxItem1 = Visio.ActivePage.Shapes.Item("5")
        Set shpObjBoxItem2 = Visio.ActivePage.Shapes.Item("2")
        celObjBeginX.GlueTo shpObjBoxItem1.Cells("Connections.Top")
        celObjEndX.GlueTo shpObjBoxItem2.Cells("Connections.Bottom")
        szFaceString = "From: " & shpObjBoxItem1.Text & vbCrLf
        szFaceString = szFaceString & "To: " & shpObjBoxItem2.Text
        shpObjConn.Text = szFaceString
        szFaceString = "Modern Organisational Routing"
        MsgBox szFaceString, vbOKOnly + vbInformation, "Optimizing Work Flow"
End Sub
```

I'll not bore you with a line-by-line, blow-by-blow analysis of every step in this application. However, let's take an in-depth look at a couple of critical chunks of the code:

```
Set shpObjBoxItem1 = pagObj.Drop(mastObjBox, _
 (celObjPagWidth.Result(visNumber) / 4) * 3, _
 (celObjPagHeight.Result(visNumber) / 4) * 3)
shpObjBoxItem1.Name = "3"
shpObjBoxItem1.Text = "Top-Right"
```

Notice here how the `Drop` method of the page is used to drop a box master at a position that is three quarters of the way across the page and three quarters of the way up the page. The code then assigns a unique name to the new SmartShape symbol for this box and places text on its face. This is done for all five boxes in the diagram.

```
Set shpObjConn = pagObj.Drop(mastObjConnector, _
 celObjPagWidth.Result(visNumber) / 2, _
 celObjPagHeight.Result(visNumber) / 2)
Set celObjBeginX = shpObjConn.Cells("BeginX")
Set celObjEndX = shpObjConn.Cells("EndX")
Set shpObjBoxItem1 = Visio.ActivePage.Shapes.Item("1")
Set shpObjBoxItem2 = Visio.ActivePage.Shapes.Item("3")
celObjBeginX.GlueTo shpObjBoxItem1.Cells("Connections.Right")
celObjEndX.GlueTo shpObjBoxItem2.Cells("Connections.Left")
szFaceString = "From: " & shpObjBoxItem1.Text & vbCrLf
szFaceString = szFaceString & "To: " & shpObjBoxItem2.Text
shpObjConn.Text = szFaceString
```

This section of code uses the `Drop` method of the page to drop a Dynamic Connector SmartShape symbol at a position in the center of the page. It then obtains references to two of the Box SmartShape symbols of interest as well as the `BeginX` and `EndX` cells of the Dynamic Connector symbol. It connects the `BeginX` cell to the properly named connection point on the first, or "from," Box symbol and the `EndX` cell to the properly named connection point on the second, or "to", Box symbol. It then pulls the text from both the "from" and "to" Box symbols and uses it to build the text for the Dynamic Connector symbol to indicate work flow direction. This symbol is in addition to the designed Begin and End symbols for the connector itself.

Positioning or Repositioning SmartShape Symbols on a Page

As you have seen from Listing 14.3, positioning SmartShape symbols on a diagram page can be a challenge. How you attack this challenge is generally determined by the type of diagram that you are trying to produce. You have seen thus far that you can position symbols through a direct reference to an explicit X and Y value or by a percentage of the height and width of the page itself. Additional methods include relative offsets from symbols already on the page or layout algorithms established for the given diagram type.

Numerous references have been written with an incredible number of different theories about how auto-layout should be accomplished. The purpose of this book is not to teach auto-layout. I will leave that to the experts in that field. What is important here is that you understand that by using ActiveX Automation, accessing the `Drop` method of the page for initial placement, and later by accessing the `PinX` and `PinY` `Cell` objects and setting a new `Formula` property for the `Cell` object, you can locate and relocate any SmartShape symbol anywhere you need to on the page. Additionally, you can refer to the `Page` and `Shape` properties for layout under Visio 2000, as we have discussed previously, for assistance in placement.

You have now seen how connected diagrams are built. You have seen how glue is established under ActiveX Automation and how cells can be manipulated to locate SmartShape symbols wherever you need them. In the next chapter, you will learn how to open a Visio diagram in an already running instance of Visio and how to print a diagram, save a diagram, and close a diagram. You will learn how to end a Visio session as well as clean up after yourself both programmatically and in terms of creating efficient diagrams.

Opening, Printing, Saving, Closing, and Ending Visio Documents

IN THIS CHAPTER

Opening Visio Documents

Earlier we looked at how to begin a new Visio diagram either based on a specific template or based on a totally blank document. There will, however, be times that your Automation application will want to open and access a Visio diagram that has already been created and stored either on the user's local hard drive or some other location accessible to the user's network. Opening a Visio diagram via Automation is a straightforward process. Look at the following code:

```
Public Sub OpenTheExistingDrawing()
    Dim docsObj As Visio.Documents
    Dim docObj As Visio.Document
    Set docsObj = Visio.Documents
    Set docObj = docsObj.Open("d:\Book-Macmillan\Routing CH14.VSD")
End Sub
```

After obtaining a reference to the Documents collection object, you invoke the Open method of the Documents collection object, passing it the fully qualified path and filename as a quoted string. Note that the return from this method creates a reference to the newly opened Document object, and therefore must be called with the keyword SET.

A very similar but even more specific version of the Open method is the OpenEx() method. The OpenEx() method has the following syntax:

```
Set docObj = docsObj.OpenEx(<"fully qualified path and file name">, <flag>)
```

In this syntax, docObj is the reference to the newly opened Document object; docsObj is the reference to the Documents collection object. OpenEx is the method of the Documents collection object to open the requested document. The string containing the fully qualified path and filename for the desired document to be opened is indicated by <"fully qualified path and file name">.

The <flag> qualifier indicates how the file is to be opened. It is an integer value, and the valid choices are a combination of one or more of the following:

1 = visOpenCopy	If visOpenCopy is specified, Visio opens a copy of the requested document.
2 = visOpenRO	If visOpenRO is specified, Visio opens the requested document in read-only mode.
4 = OpenDocked	If visOpenDocked is specified, the file is shown in a docked rather than an MDI window, provided that the file is a stencil file and there is an active drawing window in which to put the docked stencil window.

8 = visOpenDontList	If visOpenDontList is specified, the name of the opened file doesn't appear in the list of recently opened documents on the File menu.
&H10 = visOpenMinimized	If visOpenMinimized is specified, the file is opened minimized; it is not active. This flag is not supported in versions of the Visio application prior to 5.0b.

The user of the application often needs to be able to choose which Visio diagram to open before the application continues with processing. To address this need, you could use VBA's dialog features to create an ersatz File dialog box and select the proper drive, directory, and filename. You could also invoke the Windows common dialog box features via Windows API calls and additional function definitions. However, the following is a much, much easier method:

```
Public Sub OpenViaDialogue()
    Dim docObj As Visio.Document
    Visio.Application.DoCmd (visCmdFileOpen)
    Set docObj = Visio.ActiveDocument
End Sub
```

In this example, you obtain a reference to the Visio Application object and invoke the DoCmd method of the Application object, passing it the Visio constant for the FileOpen dialog command. This triggers the Visio mechanism for the Open dialog box already programmed within Visio. After the required file has been opened, it has the immediate focus, and you then invoke the ActiveDocument property of the Visio Application object to obtain a reference to the desired file.

When invoking Visio's Open dialog box, you have full access to the drive, directory, and file selection mechanisms. Additionally, you receive access to the "Files of Type" filter, the "File Preview Graphics," and the "Description" from the File properties. You also have the choice of opening the requested file as original, copy, or read-only, which are at least a portion of, and most probably the most often used, options from the OpenEx method.

Printing Visio Documents

Generally you will want to let the user of Visio print on demand, that is, select File, Print whenever the user is ready to print the diagram she is working on. However, if you want to programmatically print, you have two options. The first is to use the Print method of the Page object or the Print method of the Document object. The Print method returns a null that must be captured, so the structure of the Print method must be as follows:

```
Dim varDummy As Variant
varDummy = pagObj.[Print]
```

or

```
Dim varDummy As Variant
varDummy = docObj.[Print]
```

The second option is similar to what I described previously when I showed you the DoCmd method for opening a file. You can invoke the DoCmd method for printing a file as follows:

```
Public Sub PrintViaDialogue()
    Dim docObj As Visio.Document
    Set docObj = Visio.ActiveDocument
    Visio.Application.DoCmd (visCmdFilePrint)
End Sub
```

If the user chooses this method of printing make sure to set On Error Goto somewhere in the code so it can catch the error that is thrown if the user presses the Cancel button.

Using this methodology gives you full access to all of Visio's print services and subdialog options, such as selecting the printer to use page orientation. However, if you need fully "hands-off" sequential opening, printing, and closing of multiple documents, you may need to use the Print method of either the Page or Document object.

Saving Visio Documents

Your Automation application can also save a document or save a document under a new name through the Save and SaveAs methods of the Document object.

The syntax for the SaveAs method is as follows:

```
docObj.SaveAs "D:\Book-Macmillan\Routing CH14.VSD"
```

SaveAs requires only that you pass the name as a fully qualified, quoted path and filename. SaveAs will then save the document referenced to the subject Document object under that name.

The syntax for the Save method is as follows:

```
docObj.Save
```

Warning! Invoke the Save method only if the file has been saved at least once before and therefore has a valid fully qualified path and filename. If you invoke the Save method on a new file that has never been saved before, you will raise an error, and your application will crash.

```
Const ERR_NODOCNAME = &H86DB089A

Public Sub SaveDoc()
On Error Resume Next
    Dim doc As Visio.Document
    Set doc = ThisDocument
```

```
'    Attempt a Save first.
'
doc.Save

'    If the error code returned is ERR_NODOCNAME then go ahead and
'    perform a SaveAs on the file.
'
If (Err.Number = ERR_NODOCNAME) Then
    doc.SaveAs "c:\temp\EdsonBook14SaveAs.vsd"
End If
End Sub
```

Just as in prior examples, you can use Visio's services to perform either the Save or SaveAs method using DoCmd. The syntax for the Save method is as follows:

```
Public Sub SaveViaDialogue()
    Dim docObj As Visio.Document
    Set docObj = Visio.ActiveDocument
    Visio.Application.DoCmd (visCmdFileSave)
End Sub
```

Here is the syntax for SaveAs:

```
Public Sub SaveAsViaDialogue()
    Dim docObj As Visio.Document
    Set docObj = Visio.ActiveDocument
    Visio.Application.DoCmd (visCmdFileSaveAs)
End Sub
```

Remember that these methods do call dialogs and will require user interaction. If you need these services without intervention, you should rely on the SaveAs method of the Document object.

Remember that it is always safe to use the SaveAs method even if you pass the method the existing name of the document obtained from the FullName property of the Document object. The Document object has, in fact, a name, a path, and a FullName property. Using these properties, you can obtain the proper fully qualified path and filename to pass to the SaveAs method.

Closing Visio Documents

The Document Object has a Close method with this syntax:

```
docObj.Close
```

However, if you are running your application from VBA within Visio, you need to ensure that you are not closing the document that contains the code you are executing. This may seem obvious; however, a bit of planning will save you hours of grief when you deal with misbehaving applications.

If you have a document orchestrating the automated opening, printing, and closing of other documents within the given session of Visio, the Close method of the Document object is a perfect method of closing out the documents after you are through working with them. Remember that the Close method does exactly that: it immediately closes the document. No changes are saved; the document is simply closed. However, a BeforeDocumentClose event is raised when you close a document. You can write your own procedure to inspect the document for changes through the Saved property of the Document object. The Saved property returns -1 if the document has no unsaved changes or a zero to indicate unsaved changes exist.

Ending a Visio Session

Closing Visio itself is also a very straightforward process. The syntax is as follows:

```
appVisio.Quit
Set appVisio = Nothing
```

Notice that this is a two-step process, and it presumes that you are invoking it from outside of Visio, either from some other application's VBA or from an external Automation controller such as VB, C, or C++. Like the Close method, the Quit method of the Application object does exactly that: it quits Visio without saving any unsaved changes to anything in the environment, documents, stencils, or settings.

Notice also the Set appVisio = Nothing statement. Nothing is a VB/VBA keyword that frees the memory allocation for the object in question. Visio is a very good Windows citizen in that it cleans up after itself quite nicely. Other applications out there leave more and more memory locked up with each use. To free system resources, it is always good programming style to explicitly set object variables to Nothing when you want them to go out of scope.

This chapter has covered the general Visio Document Utilities: opening, printing, saving, and closing. You have learned how to open existing Visio diagrams, how to print them, how to save them, and how to close them when you are done with them. In the next chapter, you will learn how to manipulate a SmartShape symbol's ShapeSheet even further by adding data to the ShapeSheet. You will learn how to add new sections to a ShapeSheet as well as how to add new rows within a new or existing section of a ShapeSheet. Once you have the new sections and rows, you can then manipulate and modify the formulas in any cell within that subject row. Through this method, you can modify the behavior of any Visio SmartShape symbol or even create your own SmartShape symbol on the fly.

Adding Data to Visio SmartShape Symbols Under Automation

IN THIS CHAPTER

You have already learned how to retrieve and set information in Visio SmartShape symbol's ShapeSheet cells via the `Formula` and `Result` properties of a `Cell` object. However, there may be times when the information that you want to manipulate does not exist yet. Perhaps your application wants to add a specialized context-menu (right-click) item to a specific SmartShape symbol. Perhaps you need to programmatically populate a given SmartShape symbol with custom properties to track information about the particular symbol. Perhaps you even want to create your own SmartShape symbols on-the-fly.

All of this is possible via Automation. Through Automation you have the ability to add valid sections to a ShapeSheet, and you have the ability to add valid rows to any given section of a subject ShapeSheet. In this chapter, you'll discover how to do just that.

Adding Sections to SmartShapes Symbols' ShapeSheets

To add a section to a SmartShape symbol's ShapeSheet, you use the `AddSection` method of the `Shape` object. The syntax is as follows:

```
shpObj.AddSection <section constant>
```

In this syntax, `shpObj` is the valid reference to the `Shape` object. `AddSection` is the `Add Section` method of the `Shape` object; `<section constant>` is the Visio constant for the valid and available sections in a ShapeSheet that a user can legally add.

The section constants are in the following list:

`visSectionFirstComponent`	Geometry1 section
`visSectionFirstComponent +1`	Geometry2 section
`visSectionFirstComponent +n`	Geometry[n] section
`visSectionAction`	Actions section
`visSectionCharacter`	Characters section
`visSectionConnectionPts`	Connection Points section
`visSectionControls`	Controls section
`visSectionHyperlink`	Hyperlink section
`visSectionLayer`	Layers section
`visSectionParagraph`	Paragraph section
`visSectionProp`	Custom Properties section
`visSectionScratch`	Scratch section
`visSectionTab`	Tabs section
`visSectionTextField`	Text Fields section
`visSectionUser`	User-defined section

Adding a section to a ShapeSheet through the ShapeSheet and Menu interface by selecting Insert, Sections gives you the first row in the section automatically. In contrast, the AddSection method simply adds the section framework. You must explicitly then add the desired row or rows using the AddRow, AddRows, or AddNamedRow method of the Shape object. After you add a row, you have complete access to any cell within that row. You do not need to add the individual cells yourself. A word of caution here: If you attempt to add a new section using the AddSection method and the section already exists, an error will be raised, and your application will crash unless you add the appropriate error trapping (which, of course, I am sure that you always do. Right?).

Adding Rows to SmartShapes Symbols' ShapeSheets

To add a row to a section using the AddRow method of the Shape object, call the AddRow method using the following syntax:

```
shpObj.AddRow <section constant> <row number> <row Tag constant>
```

In this syntax, shpObj is the valid reference to the Shape object. AddRow is the AddRow method of the Shape object, and <section constant> is the Visio constant for the valid and available sections in a ShapeSheet that a user can legally add. The constants were listed earlier in the chapter.

The integer row number where the new row is to be placed is indicated by <row number>; <row Tag constant> is the Visio constant for the valid and available row types in a ShapeSheet that a user can legally add. The constants are as follows:

visTagArcTo	ArcTo row
visTagCnnctNamed	Named Connection Point row
visTagCnnctPt	Connection row
visTagComponent	Component property in a Geometry row
visTagCtlPt	Control Point row
visTagCtlPtTip	Control Point Tip row
visTagEllipse	Ellipse row
visTagEllipticalArcTo	Elliptical ArcTo row
visTagInfiniteLine	Infinite Line row
visTagLineTo	LineTo row
visTagMoveTo	MoveTo row
visTagNURBSTo	NURBSTo row
visTagPolylineTo	PolylineTo row

visTagSplineBeg	Spline Begin row
visTagSplineSpan	Spline Span row
visTagTab0	Tab row with 0 tab stops
visTagTab10	Tab row with 10 tab stops
visTagTab2	Tab row with 2 tab stops
visTagTab60	Tab row with 60 tab stops

To add more than one row to a section using the AddRows method of the Shape object, call the AddRows method using the following syntax:

```
shpObj.AddRows <section constant> <row number> <row Tag constant> <row count>
```

In this syntax, shpObj is the valid reference to the Shape object. AddRows is the AddRows method of the Shape object; <section constant> is the Visio constant for the valid and available sections in a ShapeSheet that a user can legally add. The constants were listed earlier in the chapter.

The integer row number where the new row is to be placed is indicated by <row number>; <row Tag constant> is the Visio constant for the valid and available row types in a ShapeSheet that a user can legally add. The constants were listed earlier in the chapter. Lastly, <row count> is the integer number of rows to be added.

To add a row to a section using the AddNamedRow method of the Shape object, call the AddNamedRow method using the following syntax:

```
shpObj.AddNamedRow <section constant> <row name> <row Tag constant>
```

In this syntax, shpObj is the valid reference to the Shape object. AddNamedRow is the AddNamedRow method of the Shape object; <section constant> is the Visio constant for the valid and available sections in a ShapeSheet that a user can legally add. The constants were listed earlier in the chapter.

The quoted string specifying the name of the row to be added is indicated by <row name>; <row Tag constant> is the Visio constant for the valid and available row types in a ShapeSheet that a user can legally add. The constants were listed earlier in the chapter.

An added advantage of using the AddRow, AddRows, and AddNamedRow methods is that if the section specified by <section constant> does not exist, the method will first create the section and then create the row(s). If the section already exists, the method will create just the row(s). You can, however, validate the existence of a given section by calling the SectionExists property of the Shape object, passing it the section constant for the section in question. SectionExists returns 0 (FALSE) if the section does not exist and 1 (TRUE) if it does.

The Automated-Stop-Sign-Generation Application

The code in Listing 16.1 uses the `DrawRectangle` method of the `Page` object to place a simple Rectangle SmartShape symbol at the center of the page. The goal of this application is to modify this simple Rectangle symbol through Automation such that it becomes a red octagon with the white lettering "STOP" on it.

Additionally, the application will have a custom property entry for the intersection number where the sign is to be placed and a right-click (context menu) action to bring up the Custom Properties dialog box. The application will modify the rectangle by adding all of the required sections and rows to perform the translation from rectangle to octagon and the formatting changes. It will then call the Custom Properties dialog box to allow the user to add the proper data to the Stop Sign SmartShape symbol. Read through the code. I have liberally sprinkled comments to explain the functionality as the application proceeds.

LISTING 16.1 Modifying a Shape to Transform It from a Simple Rectangle to a Complex Stop Sign

```
Public Sub MakeAStopSign()
        ' general declarations for the page, _
                'shape and cell as well as the return from
        ' the AddRows() Function
    Dim pagObj As Visio.Page
    Dim shpObj As Visio.Shape
    Dim celObj As Visio.Cell
    Dim intRowPos As Integer
        ' get the active page
    Set pagObj = Visio.ActivePage
        ' draw a rectangle on the page by calling the DrawRectangle method of
'the Page Object the 4 arguments are the upper-left X, upper-left Y, lower-
'right X and lower-right Y locations for the diagonally opposite corners of the
'rectangle. They are expressed as real numbers where inches is implicit as
'the required units.
    Set shpObj = pagObj.DrawRectangle(3.25, 6.5, 5.25, 4.5)
        ' throw up a message box to pause the application _
        'and let the user see that
        ' a rectangle was actually created. In a real _
        'running application, this would
' be omitted.
    MsgBox "This is the basic Rectangle. Click OK to continue...",
    ➥vbInformation + vbOKOnly, "Demonstration"
```

continues

LISTING 16.1   Continued

```
    ' call the AddRows method to add rows to the existing Geometry section
intRowPos = shpObj.AddRows(visSectionFirstComponent, 6, visTagLineTo, 4)
    ' now get a reference to the X cell of the subject row...
Set celObj = shpObj.Cells("Geometry1.X1")
    ' and set the new formula for that row
    ' repeat the procedure for all 9 rows, both X and Y cells
celObj.Formula = "=Width*0.25"
Set celObj = shpObj.Cells("Geometry1.Y1")
celObj.Formula = "=Height*0"
Set celObj = shpObj.Cells("Geometry1.X2")
celObj.Formula = "=Width*0.75"
Set celObj = shpObj.Cells("Geometry1.Y2")
celObj.Formula = "=Height*0"
Set celObj = shpObj.Cells("Geometry1.X3")
celObj.Formula = "=Width*1"
Set celObj = shpObj.Cells("Geometry1.Y3")
celObj.Formula = "=Height*0.25"
Set celObj = shpObj.Cells("Geometry1.X4")
celObj.Formula = "=Width*1"
Set celObj = shpObj.Cells("Geometry1.Y4")
celObj.Formula = "=Height*0.75"
Set celObj = shpObj.Cells("Geometry1.X5")
celObj.Formula = "=Width*0.75"
Set celObj = shpObj.Cells("Geometry1.Y5")
celObj.Formula = "=Height*1"
Set celObj = shpObj.Cells("Geometry1.X6")
celObj.Formula = "=Width*0.25"
Set celObj = shpObj.Cells("Geometry1.Y6")
celObj.Formula = "=Height*1"
Set celObj = shpObj.Cells("Geometry1.X7")
celObj.Formula = "=Width*0"
Set celObj = shpObj.Cells("Geometry1.Y7")
celObj.Formula = "=Height*0.75"
Set celObj = shpObj.Cells("Geometry1.X8")
celObj.Formula = "=Width*0"
Set celObj = shpObj.Cells("Geometry1.Y8")
celObj.Formula = "=Height*0.25"
Set celObj = shpObj.Cells("Geometry1.X9")
celObj.Formula = "=Geometry1.X1"
Set celObj = shpObj.Cells("Geometry1.Y9")
celObj.Formula = "=Geometry1.Y1"
    ' the shape is now an octagon
    '
    ' get a reference to the existing Fill Foreground cell
```

Adding Data to Visio SmartShape Symbols Under Automation

CHAPTER 16

319

16

ADDING DATA TO
SMARTSHAPE
SYMBOLS UNDER
AUTOMATION

```
Set celObj = shpObj.Cells("FillForegnd")
    ' turn the Shape Red by setting the value to 2
celObj.Formula = "=2"
    ' put text on the shape for the word STOP
shpObj.Text = "STOP"
    ' get a reference to the Character Size Cell
Set celObj = shpObj.Cells("Char.Size")
    ' make it 48 point in size
celObj.Formula = "=48 pt."
    ' get a reference to the Character Color Cell
Set celObj = shpObj.Cells("Char.Color")
    ' make it White by setting the value to 1
celObj.Formula = "=1"
    ' get a reference to the Character Style Cell
Set celObj = shpObj.Cells("Char.Style")
    ' make it Bold by setting the value to 1
celObj.Formula = "=1"
    ' get a reference to the Character Case Cell
Set celObj = shpObj.Cells("Char.Case")
    ' make it Upper Case by setting the value to 1
celObj.Formula = "=1"
    ' add a new Custom Properties Section and a new first row
    ' named Intersection
shpObj.AddNamedRow visSectionProp, "Intersection", 0
    ' get a reference to the Label Cell
Set celObj = shpObj.Cells("Prop.Intersection.Label")
    ' make its label Named Intersection
    ' note that you must use double-double quotes around the actual
    ' text string
celObj.Formula = "=""Named Intersection"""
    ' get a reference to the Prompt Cell
Set celObj = shpObj.Cells("Prop.Intersection.Prompt")
    ' make its prompt Enter the Placement Intersection Number Grid
celObj.Formula = "=""Enter the Placement Intersection Number Grid"""
    ' get a reference to the Type Cell
Set celObj = shpObj.Cells("Prop.Intersection.Type")
    ' set its Type to 0 for String
celObj.Formula = "=0"
    ' get a reference to the Format Cell
Set celObj = shpObj.Cells("Prop.Intersection.Format")
    ' leave it blank or No Formula
celObj.Formula = "="
    ' get a reference to the Value Cell
Set celObj = shpObj.Cells("Prop.Intersection.Value")
    ' leave it blank or No Formula
```

continues

LISTING 16.1 Continued

```
    celObj.Formula = "="
        ' get a reference to the SortKey Cell
    Set celObj = shpObj.Cells("Prop.Intersection.SortKey")
' set its value to 1 for the first entry
    celObj.Formula = "=1"
        ' get a reference to the Invisible Cell
    Set celObj = shpObj.Cells("Prop.Intersection.Invisible")
        ' set its value to FALSE or Yes, it should be visible
    celObj.Formula = "=FALSE"
        ' add a new Actions section to the Shape using the AddRow
        ' method of the Shape
    shpObj.AddRow visSectionAction, 1, 0
        ' get a reference to the Action Cell
    Set celObj = shpObj.Cells("Actions.Action")
        ' place the formula for showing the Custom Properties dialog box
    celObj.Formula = "=DoCmd(1312)"
        ' get a reference to the Menu Cell
    Set celObj = shpObj.Cells("Actions.Menu")
        ' make the menu read Set the Intersection Number
    celObj.Formula = "=""Set the Intersection Number"""
        ' get a reference to the Prompt Cell
    Set celObj = shpObj.Cells("Actions.Prompt")
        ' make the prompt read Set the Intersection Number
    celObj.Formula = "=""Set the Intersection Number"""
        ' call the Custom Properties Dialogue Box
    Visio.Application.DoCmd (visCmdFormatCustPropEdit)
        ' and end the routine
End Sub
```

Though you will most probably not be creating new SmartShape symbols on-the-fly, you will be manipulating existing SmartShape symbols for your application's purpose. A thorough understanding of the AddSection, AddRow, AddRows, and AddNamedRows methods of a Shape object, as well as the DeleteRow and DeleteSection methods, will give you the flexibility you need in manipulating your SmartShape symbols.

To delete a section in a SmartShape symbol's ShapeSheet, use the DeleteSection method of the Shape object. The syntax is as follows:

```
shpObj.DeleteSection <section constant>
```

In this syntax, shpObj is the valid reference to the Shape object. DeleteSection is the Delete Section method of the Shape object; <section constant> is the Visio constant for the valid and available sections in a ShapeSheet that a user can legally delete.

To delete a row from a section in a SmartShape symbol's ShapeSheet, you use the DeleteRow method of the Shape object. The syntax is as follows:

```
shpObj.DeleteRow <section constant>, <row number>
```

In this syntax, shpObj is the valid reference to the Shape object. DeleteRow is the Delete Row method of the Shape object; <section constant> is the Visio constant for the valid and available sections in a ShapeSheet that a user can legally add. The integer row number where the row in question is to be deleted is indicated by <row number>.

In the next chapter, you learn much more about getting data from SmartShape symbols. You will learn about the differing data types. You will learn how to iterate through an object collection. You will learn how to obtain page and layer information via Automation as well as object type information about any object in Visio. You will learn how to isolate and query cells as well as iterating through sections and rows in a SmartShape symbol's ShapeSheet. You will learn about the Selection object and how to use it. You will learn about obtaining window information and information about the connections between SmartShape symbols. Finally, in the next chapter you will also learn about Visio's use of Globally Unique Identifiers (GUIDs).

Getting Data from Visio Drawings

IN THIS CHAPTER

Visio diagrams are much more than "clip art" or pictures. As we have seen, they are rich repositories of data. That data may be from external sources, or held within the SmartShape symbols themselves. In this chapter, we will look at how data can be retrieved from Visio diagrams and used for any purpose the application developer wants.

Types of Visio Data

We have already discussed getting references to specific Visio SmartShape symbols' ShapeSheet cells through the `Formula` and `Result` properties of the `Cell` object. Therefore I'll not repeat that information. However, keep those concepts in mind as we go forward. You will use them time and again.

I want to spend a moment discussing the different data types in Visio and how Visio understands them. This knowledge will be of great assistance as you plan your solution, which might query Visio SmartShape symbols for their stored data.

Visio returns all real numbers as floating-point numbers with 15 significant digits. These numbers include the result of a formula, even if that formula evaluates to an integer—unless you retrieve the result with `ResultInt`. A basic axiom that you can use is that if it makes sense for a property to return any fractional or percentage value, Visio will return the value as a floating-point number. To ensure the accuracy is maintained, always assign real numbers to a double or variant data type.

Many properties return values as integers. These values are usually short integers. There are, however, a few that return long integers, such as `InstanceHandle32` and `WindowHandle32`. Any `TRUE` or `FALSE` return value returns an integer that is 0 for `FALSE` and non-zero for `TRUE`.

All strings returned by Visio are 64,000 characters or less. There are a very limited number of properties that return strings that long, however. `Text` is one property that can indeed be that large.

Under Visio 5.0 and previous versions, `Formula` properties were limited to 127 characters. Under Visio 2000, this restriction has been lifted, and the limit is now 64KB.

Names are always limited to 31 characters. NameIDs are limited to 36 characters. Prompts are limited to 255 characters. Filenames and paths are limited by the operating systems and work within the operating system's valid maximums.

Iterating Through an Object Collection

By now you have learned that you can use the `Item` property of any collection object to retrieve a reference to any item within the collection by either name or index number. You can iterate through the subject collection to perform the same operation on every member of the collection or test each member of the collection for a required validity and then, and only then, perform that action on that current item within the collection. Iteration is usually performed with a For-Next loop or a Do-While loop. IF statements are often triggers within these loops.

Most Visio collection objects are indexed at 1; that is, their member count begins with 1 and continues up to the value established with the Count property. The Count property returns the number of object items within the collection. Remember that the count that you retrieve is static. When you use the Count property, you obtain a number. If, after retrieving that value, you add or remove items from that collection, your Count number and the actual count no longer match. Should you then attempt to perform some action on each and every member of the collection, you may have unexpected, and maybe even application-crashing, results.

As an example, if your application gathered a count of the number of masters in the local masters collection, held that number, and expected to iterate through that number of masters, and your application also added a master during its execution by instancing a master from an external stencil, your expected action will miss the last master in your newly larger masters collection. As another example, if you set up a loop to iterate through a collection of shapes on the page and delete selected members, the count and the number of members of the selection will be out of sync as soon as you delete the first member of the selection. This discrepancy will cause you to fall off the end of the collection, causing an error to be raised and your application to crash.

Any time you iterate through a collection and decide to take an action other than querying the collection, you should decrement through the collection rather than increment through the collection. Here is an example of decrementing:

```
For I = shpsObj.Count To 1 Step -1
        Set shpObj = shpsObj.Item(I)
        shpObj.Delete
Next I
```

Remember that a subject collection always exists. However, that subject collection may be empty, in which case its Count property will return zero (0).

Listing 17.1 is an example of a brand new open document with one docked stencil. This application iterates through both the Documents collection and the Masters collection. A message box informs the user of the master name, the item count of that master within the collection, the document it resides in, and the item count for the document within the Documents collection.

LISTING 17.1 Iterating Through the Documents Collection

```
Public Sub WalkTheWalk_TalkTheTalk()
    Dim docsObj As Visio.Documents
    Dim docObj As Visio.Document
    Dim mastsObj As Visio.Masters
```

continues

17

GETTING DATA
FROM VISIO
DRAWINGS

LISTING 17.1 Continued

```
    Dim mastObj As Visio.Master
    Dim szObjName As String
    Dim intDocsBaseCount As Integer
    Dim intDocsCounter As Integer
    Dim intMastsBaseCount As Integer
    Dim intMastsCount As Integer
    Set docsObj = Visio.Documents
    intDocsCounter = docsObj.Count
    For intDocsBaseCount = 1 To intDocsCounter
        Set docObj = docsObj.Item(intDocsBaseCount)
        Set mastsObj = docObj.Masters
        intMastsCount = mastsObj.Count
        If intMastsCount > 0 Then
            For intMastsBaseCount = 1 To intMastsCount
                Set mastObj = mastsObj.Item(intMastsBaseCount)
                szObjName = "Document Name: " & docObj.Name & vbCrLf
                szObjName = szObjName & "Document Number: " & intDocsBaseCount
                ➥ & vbCrLf
                szObjName = szObjName & "Master Name: " & mastObj.Name & vbCrLf
                szObjName = szObjName & "Master Number: " & intMastsBaseCount
                MsgBox szObjName, vbInformation + vbOKOnly, "Iteration Demo"
            Next intMastsBaseCount
        Else
            szObjName = "Document Name: " & docObj.Name & vbCrLf
            szObjName = szObjName & "Document Number: " & intDocsBaseCount &
            ➥vbCrLf
            szObjName = szObjName & vbCrLf & "THIS DOCUMENT CONTAINS NO
            ➥MASTERS!"
            MsgBox szObjName, vbExclamation + vbOKOnly, "Iteration Demo"
        End If
    Next intDocsBaseCount
End Sub
```

Getting a Page Through Automation

You have seen that you can open an existing diagram using the Open method of the Documents collection object by using the following syntax:

```
Set docObj = docsObj.Open("fullpath")
```

Or you can use the OpenEx method of the Documents collection object:

```
Set docObj = docsObj.OpenEx("fullpath", visOpenRO)
```

Once a document is open, you can then reference it by filename by using this syntax:

```
Set docObj = docsObj.Item("filename")
```

Or you can use the following syntax to reference an open document by index:

```
Set docObj = docsObj.Item(index)
```

The following syntax provides quick access to the currently active document:

```
Set docObj = Visio.ActiveDocument
```

With a valid document reference, you can obtain a wealth of information about the document, including information retrieved by the `Masters` property, the `Pages` property, the `Styles` property, the `Fonts` property, the `Colors` property, the `Name` property, the `Fullname` property, the `Path` property, the `Creator` property, the `Description` property, the `Keywords` property, the `Subject` property, and the `Title` property. Remember that documents also are flagged as opened read-only, saved or not, or opened in-place.

Just as documents can be referenced by name, so too can pages with the following syntax:

```
Set pagObj = pagsObj.Item("pagename")
```

Pages also can be referenced by index:

```
Set pagObj = pagsObj.Item(index)
```

To quickly access the currently active page, use this syntax:

```
Set pagObj = Visio.ActivePage
```

Remember that the `ActivePage` is generally meaningless if the active window is a stencil window.

To quickly access the currently active window, use this syntax:

```
Set winObj = Visio.ActiveWindow
```

Listing 17.2 is an example of obtaining information about the currently active window, document, and page. In this example, the application posts the information to a message box.

LISTING 17.2   Querying a Visio Document, Window, and Page

```
Public Sub TellMeWinDocAndPage()
    Dim docsObj As Visio.Documents
    Dim docObj As Visio.Document
    Dim pagsObj As Visio.Pages
    Dim pagObj As Visio.Page
    Dim winsObj As Visio.Windows
```

continues

LISTING 17.2 Continued

```
    Dim winObj As Visio.Window
    Dim szInfoString As String
    Set docsObj = Visio.Documents
    Set docObj = Visio.ActiveDocument
    Set pagsObj = Visio.ActiveDocument.Pages
    Set pagObj = Visio.ActivePage
    Set winsObj = Visio.Windows
    Set winObj = Visio.ActiveWindow
    szInfoString = "The Active Window is: " & winObj.Caption & vbCrLf
    szInfoString = szInfoString & "The Window ID is: " & winObj.ID & vbCrLf
    szInfoString = szInfoString & "It is Window Number: " & winObj.Index &
➥" of " & winsObj.Count &_
        " Windows." & vbCrLf
    MsgBox szInfoString, vbInformation + vbOKOnly, "Window Information"
    szInfoString = "The Active Document is: " & docObj.Name & vbCrLf
    szInfoString = szInfoString & "It was created by: " & docObj.Creator &
➥vbCrLf
    szInfoString = szInfoString & "Company Name: " & docObj.Company & vbCrLf
    szInfoString = szInfoString & "A brief description of the document is: " &
➥docObj.Description & vbCrLf
    szInfoString = szInfoString & "It is located at: " & docObj.FullName & vbCrLf
    szInfoString = szInfoString & "It is Document Number: " & docObj.Index &
➥" of " & docsObj.Count &_
        " Open Documents." & vbCrLf
    szInfoString = szInfoString & "It will be printed on: " & docObj.PaperSize
➥ & " Sheet of Paper." & vbCrLf
    szInfoString = szInfoString & "It was created using Visio Version: " &
➥docObj.Version & vbCrLf
    MsgBox szInfoString, vbInformation + vbOKOnly, "Document Information"
    szInfoString = "The Active Page is: " & pagObj.Name & vbCrLf
    szInfoString = szInfoString & "It is Page: " & pagObj.Index & " of " &
➥pagsObj.Count & vbCrLf
    MsgBox szInfoString, vbInformation + vbOKOnly, "Page Information"
End Sub
```

Note that the .Version property returns zero until you save the drawing, at which time it will
return the proper version number.

Getting Layer Information from Pages and SmartShapes Symbols

Remember in the previous discussion of layers as they applied to SmartShape symbols and
their ShapeSheets and Visio pages and their ShapeSheets that layer names are stored in the

page's ShapeSheet, and the layer assignment indexes are stored in a given SmartShape symbol's ShapeSheet. This zero-based indexing means that an index entry in the SmartShape symbol's ShapeSheet that states "1" refers to the second row in the page's Layers section of its ShapeSheet. This process may seem confusing at first, but once you get it down, you will not have a problem.

The Layers property returns the Layers collection of the page or SmartShape symbol. A Layer object's Row property returns the corresponding row in the Layers section of the page's ShapeSheet. A SmartShape symbol object's LayerCount property returns the total number of layers to which the SmartShape symbol has been assigned.

To assign a SmartShape symbol to a layer, use the Add method of the Layer object and specify the SmartShape symbol object you want to add. To reverse the process, use the Remove method.

To add a layer to a Page or Master SmartShape symbol, use the Add method of the Layers collection object and specify the name of the layer you want to add. To reverse the process, use the Delete method.

To specify any of the attributes of a given layer, such as visibility, printability, and the attribute of being locked or being current, go directly to that attribute cell in that row of the page's PageSheet object and set a new formula for that particular attribute cell.

Listing 17.3 is an example of querying individual SmartShape symbols for their layer attributes. This application traverses the SmartShape symbols on the page and uses an Arrow Pointer SmartShape symbol to point to the Subject SmartShape symbol. It pops up a message box whose title is the name of the pointed-to symbol and whose text reveals the layer assignments for that symbol. The code is heavily commented. Read it over carefully, and you will understand how the application works. To use this code, create a new document and add some symbols. Assign layers to the symbols and then run the code against the drawing.

LISTING 17.3 Layer Query Application

```
Public Sub LayerDescriptor()
    Dim pagObj As Visio.Page
    Dim pagShpObj As Visio.Shape
    Dim celPagLayers As Visio.Cell
    Dim intNumShapes As Integer
    Dim shpObjBox As Visio.Shape
    Dim celBoxLyr As Cell
    Dim szLyrNdxStr As String
    Dim shpObjArrow As Visio.Shape
    Dim celObjPinX As Visio.Cell
    Dim celObjPinY As Visio.Cell
    Dim intCounter1 As Integer
```

continues

LISTING 17.3   Continued

```
Dim LyrNme(5) As String
Dim szLyrVerbose As String
' get page Object
Set pagObj = Visio.ActivePage
' get page sheet Object
Set pagShpObj = pagObj.PageSheet
' get and store first layer name
LyrNme(1) = Mid(pagShpObj.Cells("Layers.Name").Formula, 3,
➥Len(pagShpObj.Cells("Layers.Name").Formula) - 3)
' get and store second layer name
LyrNme(2) = Mid(pagShpObj.Cells("Layers.Name[2]").Formula, 3,
➥Len(pagShpObj.Cells("Layers.Name[2]").Formula) - 3)
' get and store third layer name
LyrNme(3) = Mid(pagShpObj.Cells("Layers.Name[3]").Formula, 3,
➥Len(pagShpObj.Cells("Layers.Name[3]").Formula) - 3)
' get and store fourth layer name
LyrNme(4) = Mid(pagShpObj.Cells("Layers.Name[4]").Formula, 3,
➥Len(pagShpObj.Cells("Layers.Name[4]").Formula) - 3)
' get arrow shape Object
Set shpObjArrow = pagObj.Shapes.Item("Arrow")
' get the arrow's PinX cell Object
Set celObjPinX = shpObjArrow.Cells("PinX")
' get the arrow's PinY cell Object
Set celObjPinY = shpObjArrow.Cells("PinY")
' find the total number of shapes on the page
intNumShapes = pagObj.Shapes.Count
' for each shape on the page...
For intCounter1 = 1 To intNumShapes
    ' assign the sequential shape to an Object variable
    Set shpObjBox = pagObj.Shapes.Item(intCounter1)
    ' get the name of the shape
    Select Case shpObjBox.Name
        ' if it is an arrow shape forget about it
        Case "Arrow"
        ' if it is the background shape forget about it
        Case "Background"
        ' if it is anything else, i.e. the box shape, then...
        Case Else
            ' initialize a string to be an empty string
            szLyrVerbose = ""
            ' get the layer member cell of the box shape
            Set celBoxLyr = shpObjBox.Cells("LayerMember")
            ' read the formula in the cell
            szLyrNdxStr = celBoxLyr.Formula
            ' show me what the cell contains...
```

```
' MsgBox "Shape Name = " & shpObjBox.Name & vbCrLf & 
➥"Layer Cell = " & szLyrNdxStr
' find out how long the string is in the cell
Select Case Len(szLyrNdxStr)
    ' if it is 3 characters long...
    Case 3
        ' get the 2nd character, read it, make it a number and
        ' add 1 to it to get the index for the right layer name
        ' from the page
        szLyrVerbose = LyrNme(Val(Mid(szLyrNdxStr, 2, 1)) + 1)
    ' if it is 5 characters long...
    Case 5
        ' get the 2nd character, read it, make it a number and
        ' add 1 to it to get the index for the right layer name
        ' from the page
        szLyrVerbose = LyrNme(Val(Mid(szLyrNdxStr, 2, 1)) + 1)
        ' get the 4th character, read it, make it a number and
        ' add 1 to it to get the index for the right layer name
        ' from the page and concatenate that with the previous

        ' layer name
        szLyrVerbose = szLyrVerbose & ", " &
        ➥LyrNme(Val(Mid(szLyrNdxStr, 4, 1)) + 1)
    ' if it is 7 characters long...
    Case 7
        ' get the 2nd character, read it, make it a number and
        ' add 1 to it to get the index for the right layer name
        ' from the page
        szLyrVerbose = LyrNme(Val(Mid(szLyrNdxStr, 2, 1)) + 1)
        ' get the 4th character, read it, make it a number and
        ' add 1 to it to get the index for the right layer name
        ' from the page and concatenate that with the previous
        ' layer name
        szLyrVerbose = szLyrVerbose & ", " &
        ➥LyrNme(Val(Mid(szLyrNdxStr, 4, 1)) + 1)
        ' get the 6th character, read it, make it a number and
        ' add 1 to it to get the index for the right layer name
        ' from the page and concatenate that with the previous
        ' layer names
        szLyrVerbose = szLyrVerbose & ", " &
        ➥LyrNme(Val(Mid(szLyrNdxStr, 6, 1)) + 1)
    ' if it is 9 characters long...
    Case 9
        ' get the 2nd character, read it, make it a number and
        ' add 1 to it to get the index for the right layer name
        ' from the page
```

17

GETTING DATA FROM VISIO DRAWINGS

continues

LISTING 17.3   Continued

```
              szLyrVerbose = LyrNme(Val(Mid(szLyrNdxStr, 2, 1)) + 1)
              ' get the 4th character, read it, make it a number and
              ' add 1 to it to get the index for the right layer name
              ' from the page and concatenate that with the previous
              ' layer name
              szLyrVerbose = szLyrVerbose & ", " &
              ➥LyrNme(Val(Mid(szLyrNdxStr, 4, 1)) + 1)
              ' get the 6th character, read it, make it a number and
              ' add 1 to it to get the index for the right layer name
              ' from the page and concatenate that with the previous
              ' layer names
              szLyrVerbose = szLyrVerbose & ", " &
              ➥LyrNme(Val(Mid(szLyrNdxStr, 6, 1)) + 1)
              ' get the 8th character, read it, make it a number and
              ' add 1 to it to get the index for the right layer name
              ' from the page and concatenate that with the previous
              ' layer names
              szLyrVerbose = szLyrVerbose & ", " &
              ➥LyrNme(Val(Mid(szLyrNdxStr, 8, 1)) + 1)
          Case Else
              ' otherwise it has no layer assignment... tell me so...
              szLyrVerbose = "None"
      ' end of layer names building
      End Select
      ' move the arrow to the right box shape in X
      celObjPinX.Formula = "=" &
      ➥Str(shpObjBox.Cells("PinX").Result("in.") - 0.5)
      ' move the arrow to the right box shape in Y
      celObjPinY.Formula = "=" &
      ➥Str(shpObjBox.Cells("PinY").Result("in.") + 0.5)
      ' finalize the output string
      szLyrVerbose = "Assigned to Layer(s): " & szLyrVerbose
      ' display the output string
      MsgBox szLyrVerbose, vbInformation + vbOKOnly, shpObjBox.Name
  ' end of shape filtering
    End Select
  ' get the next shape Object
  Next intCounter1
  ' when we are through, move the arrow back to rest in X
  celObjPinX.Formula = "=1 in."
  ' when we are through, move the arrow back to rest in Y
  celObjPinY.Formula = "= 0 in."
' end of subroutine
End Sub
```

Getting Object Type Information

When you are accessing objects in a Visio diagram through Automation you might be accessing any number of differing objects. These objects might be SmartShape symbols, they might be grouped SmartShape symbols, they might be guides, they might be imported graphics, or they might be other foreign objects. Some might be linked or embedded into a Visio diagram.

You need to understand what type of object you are dealing with when you are iterating through a collection of objects. To that end, a Shape object's Type property returns the type of object under scrutiny. Listing 17.4 allows the user to select anything on the page. It then returns the type of object selected as text in a message box. This code uses a simple Select Case method to sort through the available types.

LISTING 17.4 Visio Object Type Specifier

```
Public Sub GiveMeMyType()
    Dim winObj As Visio.Window
    Dim selObj As Visio.Selection
    Dim shpObj As Visio.Shape
    Dim szTypeString As String
    Set winObj = Visio.ActiveWindow
    Set selObj = winObj.Selection
    Set shpObj = selObj.Item(1)
    Select Case shpObj.Type
        Case visTypeBitmap
            szTypeString = " is a Bitmap."
        Case visTypeDoc
            szTypeString = " is a Document."
        Case visTypeForeignObject
            szTypeString = " is a Foreign Object."
        Case visTypeGroup
            szTypeString = " is a Group."
        Case visTypeGuide
            szTypeString = " is a Guide."
        Case visTypeIsControl
            szTypeString = " is a Control."
        Case visTypeIsEmbedded
            szTypeString = " is Embedded."
        Case visTypeIsLinked
            szTypeString = " is Linked."
        Case visTypeMetafile
            szTypeString = " is a Metafile."
        Case visTypePage
            szTypeString = " is a Page."
```

continues

LISTING 17.4 Continued

```
        Case visTypeShape
            szTypeString = " is a SmartShape Symbol."
        Case visTypeUnits
            szTypeString = " is of a Units Type."
        Case Else
            szTypeString = " is indecipherable to Visio."
    End Select
    MsgBox "The Selected Object " & szTypeString, vbExclamation + vbOKOnly,
    ➥ "Type Demonstration"
End Sub
```

Listing 17.5 is another quick example of iteration through a Shapes collection. It is a great example of using recursion in looking at the items.

The ShapesCount function is a recursive function designed to count all of the SmartShape symbols in the "root." To count all of the SmartShape symbols on a page, you call the ShapesCount function with the "root" set to the Page object. ShapesCount iterates through the Shapes collection of "root" and, if it encounters a group, calls itself to count all of the SmartShape symbols within the group (but does not include the group itself in the count). Notice the IF statement that checks shpObj.Type in Listing 17.5.

LISTING 17.5 Counting Shapes

```
Public Function ShapesCount(root As Object) As Integer
    Dim shpsObj As Visio.Shapes
    Dim shpObj As Visio.Shape
    Dim intCount As Integer
    Dim intTick As Integer
    Set shpsObj = root.Shapes
    intCount = 0
    For intTick = 1 To shpsObj.Count
        Set shpObj = shpsObj.Item(intTick)
        If shpObj.Type = visTypeGroup Then
            intCount = intCount + ShapesCount(shpObj)
        Else
            intCount = intCount + 1
        End If
    Next intTick
    ShapesCount = intCount
End Function
Public Sub UseShapesCount()
    Dim pagObj As Visio.Page
    Dim intRetValInt As Integer
```

```
      Dim szDisplayString As String
      Set pagObj = Visio.ActivePage
      intRetValInt = ShapesCount(pagObj)
      szDisplayString = "The total number of SmartShape Symbols on the page is:
      ➥ " & Str(intRetValInt)
      MsgBox szDisplayString, vbInformation + vbOKOnly, "Recursion Demonstration"
End Sub
```

Getting Cells and Querying Cells in Visio ShapeSheets

Thus far you have accessed the `Cells` property of a `Shape` object by name to obtain a reference to a specific cell. In most cases, this is the best way to accomplish this task. However, you may need to iterate through sections, rows, and cells in a given SmartShape symbol's ShapeSheet; for example, in a symbol with multiple `Geometry` sections. To accomplish this, you can use the section, row, and cell indices. Both VISCONST.BAS and the Visio Type Library viewable via the Object Browser give you full information for all of these section, row, and cell constants.

Look at the following example for a cell in a `Controls` section:

```
Set celObj = shpObj.CellsSRC(visSectionControls, visRowControl +3, visCtlX)
```

In this example, `celObj` is the reference to the `Cell` object; `shpObj` is the reference to the `Shape` object. `CellsSRC` is the `CellsSRC` function designed to access a `Cell` object by its section constant, row constant, and cell constant. The constant for the `Controls` section is `visSectionControls`; `visRowControl +3` is the fourth row in the `Controls` section (the offset `+3` is the third row offset from the first row, or the fourth row). Lastly, `visCtlX` is the `X` cell in the fourth control row of the `Controls` section.

On the companion CD, you will find a Visio diagram and accompanying VBA code called CellsSRC CH17.VSD. This diagram illustrates how to use `CellsSRC` to find a specific cell. The diagram contains a Button SmartShape symbol. Each time you double-click the symbol, the button toggles from unselected (raised) to selected (depressed). When the button is depressed, a VBA form is activated that allows the user to choose between either a user-defined section or a `Scratch` section in the Button SmartShape symbol's ShapeSheet. With the section selected, the user then selects the row of interest. Finally, with the row selected, the user selects the cell of interest. With this accomplished, the user then selects the Get the Cell Formula button, and the formula in that particular cell, retrieved via the `CellsSRC` property, will be displayed as well as the ID numbers for each of the section, row, and cell constants. Clicking the Exit the Demonstration button terminates the application. Listing 17.6 has the complete code for this application.

LISTING 17.6   Query a Shape with CellsSRC

```
Global intSectFlag As Integer
Global intRowFlag As Integer
Global intCellFlag As Integer
Global shpObj As Visio.Shape
Global celObj As Visio.Cell

Public Sub Selector()
    Set shpObj = Visio.ActiveWindow.Selection.Item(1)
    ChooseCellsSRC.Show
End Sub
Private Sub CommandButton1_Click()
Unload ChooseCellsSRC
End Sub

Private Sub CommandButton2_Click()
    Dim intS As Integer
    Dim intR As Integer
    Dim intC As Integer
    If intSectFlag > 0 Then
        If OptionButton1.Value = True Then
            intS = 1
            ' User Defined Section
            If OptionButton3.Value = True Then
                intR = 1
            ElseIf OptionButton4.Value = True Then
                intR = 2
            ElseIf OptionButton5.Value = True Then
                intR = 3
            ElseIf OptionButton6.Value = True Then
                intR = 4
            ElseIf OptionButton7.Value = True Then
                intR = 5
            End If
            If OptionButton8.Value = True Then
                intC = 1
            Else
                intC = 2
            End If
        Else
            intS = 2
            ' Scratch Section
            If OptionButton3.Value = True Then
                intR = 2
            ElseIf OptionButton4.Value = True Then
```

```
            intR = 3
        End If
        If OptionButton8.Value = True Then
            intC = 3
        ElseIf OptionButton9.Value = True Then
            intC = 4
        ElseIf OptionButton10.Value = True Then
            intC = 5
        ElseIf OptionButton11.Value = True Then
            intC = 6
        ElseIf OptionButton12.Value = True Then
            intC = 7
        ElseIf OptionButton13.Value = True Then
            intC = 8
        End If
End If
If intS = 1 Then
    intSectFlag = visSectionUser
    Select Case intR
        Case 1
            intRowFlag = visRowUser
        Case 2
            intRowFlag = visRowUser + 1
        Case 3
            intRowFlag = visRowUser + 2
        Case 4
            intRowFlag = visRowUser + 3
        Case 5
            intRowFlag = visRowUser + 4
    End Select
    Select Case intC
        Case 1
            intCellFlag = visUserValue
        Case 2
            intCellFlag = visUserPrompt
    End Select
Else
    intSectFlag = visSectionScratch
    intRowFlag = visRowScratch
    Select Case intC
        Case 3
            intCellFlag = visScratchX
        Case 4
            intCellFlag = visScratchY
        Case 5
            intCellFlag = visScratchA
```

continues

17

GETTING DATA FROM VISIO DRAWINGS

LISTING 17.6   Continued

```
                    Case 6
                        intCellFlag = visScratchB
                    Case 7
                        intCellFlag = visScratchC
                    Case 8
                        intCellFlag = visScratchD
                End Select
            End If
            TextBox1.Text = intSectFlag
            TextBox2.Text = intRowFlag
            TextBox3.Text = intCellFlag
            Set celObj = shpObj.CellsSRC(intSectFlag, intRowFlag, intCellFlag)
            TextBox4.Text = celObj.Formula
        End If
End Sub

Private Sub OptionButton1_Click()
    Me.OptionButton3.Caption = "Row_1"
    Me.OptionButton3.Visible = True
    Me.OptionButton3.Value = False
    Me.OptionButton4.Caption = "Row_2"
    Me.OptionButton4.Visible = True
    Me.OptionButton4.Value = False
    Me.OptionButton5.Caption = "Row_3"
    Me.OptionButton5.Visible = True
    Me.OptionButton5.Value = False
    Me.OptionButton6.Caption = "Row_4"
    Me.OptionButton6.Visible = True
    Me.OptionButton6.Value = False
    Me.OptionButton7.Caption = "Row_5"
    Me.OptionButton7.Visible = True
    Me.OptionButton7.Value = False
    Me.OptionButton8.Caption = "Value"
    Me.OptionButton8.Visible = True
    Me.OptionButton8.Value = False
    Me.OptionButton9.Caption = "Prompt"
    Me.OptionButton9.Visible = True
    Me.OptionButton9.Value = False
    Me.OptionButton10.Caption = ""
    Me.OptionButton10.Visible = False
    Me.OptionButton10.Value = False
    Me.OptionButton11.Caption = ""
    Me.OptionButton11.Visible = False
    Me.OptionButton11.Value = False
```

```
        Me.OptionButton12.Caption = ""
        Me.OptionButton12.Visible = False
        Me.OptionButton12.Value = False
        Me.OptionButton13.Caption = ""
        Me.OptionButton13.Visible = False
        Me.OptionButton13.Value = False
        intSectFlag = 1
        intRowFlag = 0
        intCellFlag = 0

End Sub

Private Sub OptionButton10_Click()
        intCellFlag = 1

End Sub

Private Sub OptionButton11_Click()
        intCellFlag = 1

End Sub

Private Sub OptionButton12_Click()
        intCellFlag = 1

End Sub

Private Sub OptionButton13_Click()
        intCellFlag = 1

End Sub

Private Sub OptionButton2_Click()
        Me.OptionButton3.Caption = "1"
        Me.OptionButton3.Visible = True
        Me.OptionButton3.Value = True
        Me.OptionButton4.Caption = ""
        Me.OptionButton4.Visible = False
        Me.OptionButton4.Value = False
        Me.OptionButton5.Caption = ""
        Me.OptionButton5.Visible = False
        Me.OptionButton5.Value = False
        Me.OptionButton6.Caption = ""
        Me.OptionButton6.Visible = False
        Me.OptionButton6.Value = False
        Me.OptionButton7.Caption = ""
```

continues

LISTING 17.6 Continued

```
    Me.OptionButton7.Visible = False
    Me.OptionButton7.Value = False
    Me.OptionButton8.Caption = "X"
    Me.OptionButton8.Visible = True
    Me.OptionButton8.Value = False
    Me.OptionButton9.Caption = "Y"
    Me.OptionButton9.Visible = True
    Me.OptionButton9.Value = False
    Me.OptionButton10.Caption = "A"
    Me.OptionButton10.Visible = True
    Me.OptionButton10.Value = False
    Me.OptionButton11.Caption = "B"
    Me.OptionButton11.Visible = True
    Me.OptionButton11.Value = False
    Me.OptionButton12.Caption = "C"
    Me.OptionButton12.Visible = True
    Me.OptionButton12.Value = False
    Me.OptionButton13.Caption = "D"
    Me.OptionButton13.Visible = True
    Me.OptionButton13.Value = False
    intSectFlag = 2
    intRowFlag = 1
    intCellFlag = 0

End Sub

Private Sub OptionButton3_Click()
    If intSectFlag = 1 Then
        Me.OptionButton8.Caption = "Value"
        Me.OptionButton8.Visible = True
        Me.OptionButton8.Value = False
        Me.OptionButton9.Caption = "Prompt"
        Me.OptionButton9.Visible = True
        Me.OptionButton9.Value = False
        Me.OptionButton10.Caption = ""
        Me.OptionButton10.Visible = False
        Me.OptionButton10.Value = False
        Me.OptionButton11.Caption = ""
        Me.OptionButton11.Visible = False
        Me.OptionButton11.Value = False
        Me.OptionButton12.Caption = ""
        Me.OptionButton12.Visible = False
        Me.OptionButton12.Value = False
        Me.OptionButton13.Caption = ""
        Me.OptionButton13.Visible = False
```

```
            Me.OptionButton13.Value = False
            intRowFlag = 1
            intCellFlag = 0
        ElseIf intSectFlag = 2 Then
            Me.OptionButton8.Caption = "X"
            Me.OptionButton8.Visible = True
            Me.OptionButton8.Value = False
            Me.OptionButton9.Caption = "Y"
            Me.OptionButton9.Visible = True
            Me.OptionButton9.Value = False
            Me.OptionButton10.Caption = "A"
            Me.OptionButton10.Visible = True
            Me.OptionButton10.Value = False
            Me.OptionButton11.Caption = "B"
            Me.OptionButton11.Visible = True
            Me.OptionButton11.Value = False
            Me.OptionButton12.Caption = "C"
            Me.OptionButton12.Visible = True
            Me.OptionButton12.Value = False
            Me.OptionButton13.Caption = "D"
            Me.OptionButton13.Visible = True
            Me.OptionButton13.Value = False
            intRowFlag = 1
            intCellFlag = 0
        End If
End Sub

Private Sub OptionButton4_Click()
    Me.OptionButton8.Caption = "Value"
    Me.OptionButton8.Visible = True
    Me.OptionButton8.Value = False
    Me.OptionButton9.Caption = "Prompt"
    Me.OptionButton9.Visible = True
    Me.OptionButton9.Value = False
    Me.OptionButton10.Caption = ""
    Me.OptionButton10.Visible = False
    Me.OptionButton10.Value = False
    Me.OptionButton11.Caption = ""
    Me.OptionButton11.Visible = False
    Me.OptionButton11.Value = False
    Me.OptionButton12.Caption = ""
    Me.OptionButton12.Visible = False
    Me.OptionButton12.Value = False
    Me.OptionButton13.Caption = ""
    Me.OptionButton13.Visible = False
    Me.OptionButton13.Value = False
```

continues

LISTING 17.6   Continued

```
    intSectFlag = 1
    intRowFlag = 1
    intCellFlag = 0

End Sub

Private Sub OptionButton5_Click()
    Me.OptionButton8.Caption = "Value"
    Me.OptionButton8.Visible = True
    Me.OptionButton8.Value = False
    Me.OptionButton9.Caption = "Prompt"
    Me.OptionButton9.Visible = True
    Me.OptionButton9.Value = False
    Me.OptionButton10.Caption = ""
    Me.OptionButton10.Visible = False
    Me.OptionButton10.Value = False
    Me.OptionButton11.Caption = ""
    Me.OptionButton11.Visible = False
    Me.OptionButton11.Value = False
    Me.OptionButton12.Caption = ""
    Me.OptionButton12.Visible = False
    Me.OptionButton12.Value = False
    Me.OptionButton13.Caption = ""
    Me.OptionButton13.Visible = False
    Me.OptionButton13.Value = False
    intSectFlag = 1
    intRowFlag = 1
    intCellFlag = 0

End Sub

Private Sub OptionButton6_Click()
    Me.OptionButton8.Caption = "Value"
    Me.OptionButton8.Visible = True
    Me.OptionButton8.Value = False
    Me.OptionButton9.Caption = "Prompt"
    Me.OptionButton9.Visible = True
    Me.OptionButton9.Value = False
    Me.OptionButton10.Caption = ""
    Me.OptionButton10.Visible = False
    Me.OptionButton10.Value = False
    Me.OptionButton11.Caption = ""
    Me.OptionButton11.Visible = False
    Me.OptionButton11.Value = False
    Me.OptionButton12.Caption = ""
```

```
        Me.OptionButton12.Visible = False
        Me.OptionButton12.Value = False
        Me.OptionButton13.Caption = ""
        Me.OptionButton13.Visible = False
        Me.OptionButton13.Value = False
        intSectFlag = 1
        intRowFlag = 1
        intCellFlag = 0

End Sub

Private Sub OptionButton7_Click()
        Me.OptionButton8.Caption = "Value"
        Me.OptionButton8.Visible = True
        Me.OptionButton8.Value = False
        Me.OptionButton9.Caption = "Prompt"
        Me.OptionButton9.Visible = True
        Me.OptionButton9.Value = False
        Me.OptionButton10.Caption = ""
        Me.OptionButton10.Visible = False
        Me.OptionButton10.Value = False
        Me.OptionButton11.Caption = ""
        Me.OptionButton11.Visible = False
        Me.OptionButton11.Value = False
        Me.OptionButton12.Caption = ""
        Me.OptionButton12.Visible = False
        Me.OptionButton12.Value = False
        Me.OptionButton13.Caption = ""
        Me.OptionButton13.Visible = False
        Me.OptionButton13.Value = False
        intSectFlag = 1
        intRowFlag = 1
        intCellFlag = 0

End Sub

Private Sub OptionButton8_Click()
        intCellFlag = 1

End Sub

Private Sub OptionButton9_Click()
        intCellFlag = 1

End Sub
```

continues

LISTING 17.6   Continued

```
Private Sub UserForm_Activate()
    Me.OptionButton1.Caption = "User-defined"
    Me.OptionButton1.Visible = True
    Me.OptionButton1.Value = False
    Me.OptionButton2.Caption = "Scratch"
    Me.OptionButton2.Visible = True
    Me.OptionButton2.Value = False
    Me.OptionButton3.Caption = ""
    Me.OptionButton3.Visible = False
    Me.OptionButton3.Value = False
    Me.OptionButton4.Caption = ""
    Me.OptionButton4.Visible = False
    Me.OptionButton4.Value = False
    Me.OptionButton5.Caption = ""
    Me.OptionButton5.Visible = False
    Me.OptionButton5.Value = False
    Me.OptionButton6.Caption = ""
    Me.OptionButton6.Visible = False
    Me.OptionButton6.Value = False
    Me.OptionButton7.Caption = ""
    Me.OptionButton7.Visible = False
    Me.OptionButton7.Value = False
    Me.OptionButton8.Caption = ""
    Me.OptionButton8.Visible = False
    Me.OptionButton8.Value = False
    Me.OptionButton9.Caption = ""
    Me.OptionButton9.Visible = False
    Me.OptionButton9.Value = False
    Me.OptionButton10.Caption = ""
    Me.OptionButton10.Visible = False
    Me.OptionButton10.Value = False
    Me.OptionButton11.Caption = ""
    Me.OptionButton11.Visible = False
    Me.OptionButton11.Value = False
    Me.OptionButton12.Caption = ""
    Me.OptionButton12.Visible = False
    Me.OptionButton12.Value = False
    Me.OptionButton13.Caption = ""
    Me.OptionButton13.Visible = False
    Me.OptionButton13.Value = False
    intSectFlag = 0
    intRowFlag = 0
    intCellFlag = 0
End Sub
```

Quite a bit of this code is designed to populate the three frames in the dialog box properly. This is effectively a decision tree from section, to row, to cells determining which choices to present in the dialog box. Once these choices have been made, the heart of the code that performs the CellsSRC function is quite simple.

Iterating Through Sections and Rows in Visio ShapeSheets

Just as we have seen in Listing 17.6, using CellsSRC can make locating a particular cell easier if you are not sure exactly where that cell is. Remember that the Shape object also has the SectionExists, RowExists, CellExists, and CellsSRCExists properties to assist you in determining the validity of a particular Cell object.

A Shape object also has the RowCount and RowsCellsCount properties to set limits for iteration. The following sample code fragment iterates through the Geometry1 section of a SmartShape symbol's ShapeSheet and lists each Cell object's formula in the VBS Immediate or Debug window.

```
iGeometry = visSectionFirstComponent
nRows = shpObj.RowCount(iGeometry)
For iRow = 0 To (nRows -1)
        nCells = shpObj.RowsCellCount(iGeometry, iRow)
        For iCell = 0 To (nCells - 1)
                Debug.Print shpObj.CellsSRC(iGeometry, iRow, iCell).Formula
        Next iCell
Next iRow
```

Getting a Selection Object

Using this syntax obtains the Selection object in the currently active window in Visio:

```
Set selObj = Visio.ActiveWindow.Selection
```

In this syntax, selObj is the object reference to the Shapes selection object. Visio.ActiveWindow.Selection is the concatenated object reference chain to the Shapes selection object.

Remember that the Selection property of a Window object is only valid for a drawing window. The Selection object is similar to the Shapes collection object in that it has both an Item and a Count property. The order of the Shape objects within the Selection collection object reflects the order that the Shape objects were selected in the diagram. It does not include Visio SmartShape symbols that were subselected from within a Group SmartShape symbol.

You can add or delete members of the Selection collection object using the Select, SelectAll, Cut, and Delete methods. The Selection collection does not necessarily reflect the status of items currently selected in the diagram because it is a snapshot of the selection at the given moment in time when it was called. For this reason, it is your responsibility as the programmer to keep the selection current.

Getting Window Information in Visio

The Visio Application object has a Windows Collection property. This property is the Windows collection object. It includes all windows within the Visio environment that might be open at any given time: drawing windows, ShapeSheet windows, stencil windows, and icon edit windows. Keep in mind that as the user opens and closes windows, and as the user shifts focus from one window to another, the Windows collection object's count may increase or decrease by one or more items.

You can iterate through a Windows collection in the usual way, but more often you will be interested in a particular type of window. The Window object's Type property returns the window type. If the returned window type is a drawing window, you will also want to check the SubType property. The window types are visDrawing, visSheet, visStencil, and visIcon. The subtypes are visPagWin, visMasterWin, visPageGroupWin, and visMasterGroupWin.

The syntax for the ActiveWindow object is as follows:

```
Set winObj = Visio.ActiveWindow
```

To check a window's Type property, you can use this syntax:

```
If winObj.Type <> visDrawing Then
        Debug.Print "Not a Drawing Window."
End If
```

As you iterate through the Windows collection object examining each window, you can use the Activate property of the Window object to make that particular window active. The syntax is as follows:

```
WinObj.Activate
```

You can ascertain the document associated with a given window with the Document property of the Window object. You can change the magnification of the subject window with the Window object's Zoom property. You can also get the collection of any selected SmartShape symbols selected in the subject window with the Window object's Selection property.

Here is a quick trick. You can center a selected SmartShape symbol in a zoom area with a single line of code.

```
WinObj.Zoom = WinObj.Zoom
```

If you are zoomed into the drawing and the selected SmartShape symbol is off the page, the above code will center the selection at the current zoom percentage.

Getting Information About Connections Between SmartShapes Symbols

Previously you learned how to connect (glue) SmartShape symbols via VBA's Automation interface. Whenever a connection has been established, the SmartShape symbol that is doing the gluing exposes a valid `Connect` object. Every SmartShape symbol has a `Connects` collection. If the SmartShape symbol is not glued to any other SmartShape symbol, the collection is empty.

If a symbol is glued to another symbol, as in the case of a symbol with a control handle gluing to the connection point on another symbol, the `Connects` collection contains one item (index 1). If a symbol is glued to two other symbols, as in the case of a Dynamic Connector SmartShape symbol gluing to two Process SmartShape symbols, the `Connects` collection contains two items (index 1 and 2).

You may obtain information about these connections via the various properties of the `Connects` collection object. For example, every `Connects` collection has a `Count` property to ascertain how many connections have been established.

A `Connects` collection item has the `FromSheet` and `ToSheet` properties that return the sheet identifier of the SmartShape symbol doing the gluing and the sheet identifier of the SmartShape symbol being glued. A `Connects` collection item also has the `FromPart` and `ToPart` properties that return the Visio constant for the type of part establishing the glue (plus applicable offset if valid) and the Visio constant for the type of part receiving the glue (plus applicable offset if valid). These constants are represented by the integer returns for the constants like `visControlPoint` or `visConnectionPoint`. The offset is the offset from index zero of the row within that applicable section. In addition, a `Connects` collection item has the `FromCell` and `ToCell` properties that return the name of the cell establishing the glue and the cell receiving the glue.

The following example is found on the companion CD as Connects CH17.VSD. This example allows the user to select a Dynamic Connector SmartShape symbol and, by right-clicking and selecting Check the Connection from the context menu, launch a VBA dialog box that displays all of the property information about the connections established for that Dynamic Connector SmartShape symbol (see Listing 17.7).

LISTING 17.7   Checking Connections in a Dynamic Connector

```
Public Sub RunConnProp()
    ConnProp.Show
End Sub
Private Sub CommandButton1_Click()
    Unload ConnProp
End Sub
Private Sub UserForm_Activate()
    Dim shObjConn As Visio.Shape
    Dim conObjshConn As Visio.Connects
    Dim intConnsCollCount As Integer
    Dim intBegin As Integer
    Dim intEnd As Integer
    Set shObjConn = Visio.ActiveWindow.Selection.Item(1)
    Me.ConnName.Text = shObjConn.Name
    Me.tbBPXPos.Text = shObjConn.Cells("BeginX").Result("in.") & " in."
    Me.tbBPYPos.Text = shObjConn.Cells("BeginY").Result("in.") & " in."
    Me.tbEPXPos.Text = shObjConn.Cells("EndX").Result("in.") & " in."
    Me.tbEPYPos.Text = shObjConn.Cells("EndY").Result("in.") & " in."
    Set conObjshConn = shObjConn.Connects
    intConnsCollCount = conObjshConn.Count
    Select Case intConnsCollCount
        Case 0
        Case 1
            If conObjshConn.Item(1).FromCell.Name = "BeginX" Then
                Me.tbBPFromSheet.Text = conObjshConn.Item(1).FromSheet.Name
                Me.tbBPToSheet.Text = conObjshConn.Item(1).ToSheet.Name
                Me.tbBPFromPart.Text = PartFlag(conObjshConn.Item(1).FromPart)
                Me.tbBPToPart.Text = PartFlag(conObjshConn.Item(1).ToPart)
                Me.tbBPFromCell.Text = conObjshConn.Item(1).FromCell.Name
                Me.tbBPToCell.Text = conObjshConn.Item(1).ToCell.Name
            Else
                Me.tbEPFromSheet.Text = conObjshConn.Item(1).FromSheet.Name
                Me.tbEPToSheet.Text = conObjshConn.Item(1).ToSheet.Name
                Me.tbEPFromPart.Text = PartFlag(conObjshConn.Item(1).FromPart)
                Me.tbEPToPart.Text = PartFlag(conObjshConn.Item(1).ToPart)
                Me.tbEPFromCell.Text = conObjshConn.Item(1).FromCell.Name
                Me.tbEPToCell.Text = conObjshConn.Item(1).ToCell.Name
            End If
        Case 2
            If conObjshConn.Item(1).FromCell.Name = "BeginX" Then
                intBegin = 1
                intEnd = 2
            Else
                intBegin = 2
                intEnd = 1
            End If
```

Getting Data from Visio Drawings

CHAPTER 17

349

17

GETTING DATA
FROM VISIO
DRAWINGS

```
                Me.tbBPFromSheet.Text = conObjshConn.Item(intBegin).FromSheet.Name
                Me.tbBPToSheet.Text = conObjshConn.Item(intBegin).ToSheet.Name
                Me.tbEPFromSheet.Text = conObjshConn.Item(intEnd).FromSheet.Name
                Me.tbEPToSheet.Text = conObjshConn.Item(intEnd).ToSheet.Name
                Me.tbBPFromPart.Text =
                ➥PartFlag(conObjshConn.Item(intBegin).FromPart)
                Me.tbBPToPart.Text = PartFlag(conObjshConn.Item(intBegin).ToPart)
                Me.tbEPFromPart.Text = PartFlag(conObjshConn.Item(intEnd).FromPart)
                Me.tbEPToPart.Text = PartFlag(conObjshConn.Item(intEnd).ToPart)
                Me.tbBPFromCell.Text = conObjshConn.Item(intBegin).FromCell.Name
                Me.tbBPToCell.Text = conObjshConn.Item(intBegin).ToCell.Name
                Me.tbEPFromCell.Text = conObjshConn.Item(intEnd).FromCell.Name
                Me.tbEPToCell.Text = conObjshConn.Item(intEnd).ToCell.Name
        End Select
End Sub
Private Function PartFlag(theVisCode As Integer) As String
    Dim retStr As String
    Select Case theVisCode
        Case 9
            retStr = "visBegin"
        Case 12
            retStr = "visEnd"
        Case 3
            retStr = "visSheet"
        Case Else
            retStr = "visConnectionPoint + " & Str(theVisCode - 100)
    End Select
    PartFlag = retStr
End Function
```

The subroutine RunConnProp() loads and activates the VBA form that displays the properties.
The PartFlag() function is designed to take in the integer for the FromPart or ToPart
property, ascertain the Visio constant name, offset for that integer, and return it as a string.
This function is used in sending information to the proper text box on the form. The
CommandButton1_Click() subroutine simply unloads the dialog box and ends the application.
The UserForm_Activate subroutine looks at the selected Dynamic Connector SmartShape
symbol and obtains its Connects collection. Using the Count property, it establishes how many
connections have been made and then displays the proper information based on a Select Case
statement.

Globally Unique Identifiers

Visio utilizes Globally Unique Identifiers in the same manner that Microsoft does: as a mechanism for establishing a total uniqueness for any given object. In this manner, you can establish

a reliable correspondence between a specific SmartShape symbol and an external source of data from a database. This is preferable to using sheet identifiers or symbol names.

A Globally Unique Identifier, or GUID, is stored internally as a 128-bit value and is passed as a null-terminated, 39-character string. Be aware that by default all masters have a GUID, but individual SmartShape symbols do not. If a SmartShape symbol or Master SmartShape symbol has a GUID, you may safely assume that no other SmartShape symbol or Master SmartShape symbol in the same Visio document or any other document has the same GUID. Visio generates GUIDs using the same technology that is used to generate OLE 2 GUIDs, and does not reuse them. The chances of generating duplicate GUIDs are remote, even on different systems. It is, however, possible to duplicate a GUID. For example, if you save a Visio drawing file and then make a copy of that file by any usual DOS methodology (copying in Windows Explorer, for example), the SmartShape symbols in that duplicate file are identical to the original file. If you then copy a SmartShape symbol from the copied diagram into the original diagram, you will have two SmartShape symbols with exactly the same GUID. If you copy a Master SmartShape symbol, it will have the same GUID as the original until you edit the Master SmartShape symbol and save the diagram.

A `Shape` object has one method for working with GUIDs: the `UniqueID` method. The `UniqueID` method has three possible arguments that may be passed to it: `visGetGUID`, `visGetOrMakeGUID`, and `visDeleteGUID`. To obtain a SmartShape symbol's GUID, the syntax is as follows:

```
IDstr = shpObj.UniqueID(visGetGUID)
```

In this syntax, (as in the next two examples) `IDstr` is a string variable used to hold the value; `shpObj` is the reference to the subject SmartShape symbol. `UniqueID` is the `Shape` object's method to work with the GUID; `visGetGUID` is the Visio constant to obtain the GUID of a SmartShape symbol that already has a GUID established.

To obtain or create a SmartShape symbol's GUID, the syntax is as follows:

```
IDstr = shpObj.UniqueID(visGetOrMakeGUID)
```

`UniqueID` is the `Shape` object's method to work with the GUID; `visGetOrMakeGUID` is the Visio constant to obtain the GUID of a SmartShape symbol that already has a GUID established or, if it has no GUID established, to create one.

To delete a SmartShape symbol's GUID, the syntax is as follows:

```
IDstr = shpObj.UniqueID(visDeleteGUID)
```

UniqueID is the Shape object's method to work with the GUID; visDeleteGUID is the Visio constant to destroy the GUID of a SmartShape symbol.

Be aware that some actions in Visio cause the application to automatically delete a GUID. For example, if you cut a SmartShape symbol with a GUID established to the Clipboard in Windows and then paste it multiple times, the first time you paste the SmartShape symbol, Visio preserves the GUID; subsequent pastes have the GUID deleted.

Thus far you have looked at various methodologies for obtaining data about Visio documents. In the next chapter, you will learn about event handling in Visio as well as ShapeSheet events and VBA code behind events for Visio objects. You will look at VBA behind ActiveX controls on a Visio page and study ShapeSheet cell dependencies. You will also learn about the WithEvents keyword in Visio and how to create your own event sink for Visio objects.

Event Handling in the Visio Object Model

IN THIS CHAPTER

Prior to Visio 4.1, the only mechanism for Visio to respond to user events was through the ShapeSheet, utilizing either the Event section of the ShapeSheet with any of the `TheText`, `EventXFMod`, `EventDblClick`, or `EventDrop` Cells or by using a `DependsOn()` formula to simulate event handling for a particular cell. Although these methods are still available to you as the programmer, and they are still recommended when they solve the problem sufficiently, Visio has added a more robust, programmable event mechanism.

Beginning with Visio 4.1, an event object model was added to the Visio object model. This enabled the programmer to set up event handling for a much greater set of events. In Visio, something happens as a result of a user's interaction with some aspect of Visio such as a SmartShape symbol, the page, and so on. This is an event. As a programmer, you want your application to be aware of these events so that your application can do something in response to that specific event.

VBA Code Behind Events for Visio Objects

Events in Visio are defined in the Visio type library. Due to this definition set, each Visio object obtains its own event list. These event lists are specific to the Visio objects with which they are associated. For example, a document has a DocumentOpened and a `DocumentCreated` event, while a page has a BeforeShapeDeleted event. To illustrate this, the application listed in Listing 18.1 shows an event linked to the `ShapeAdded` event of the document object. The code looks at the object just added and ascertains if it is a shape object, a group object, or any other type of object. If it is a shape object, it then analyzes it to be sure that it has a filled area. If so, it reports the filled area to the user in a message box and then enables that total to be placed as text upon the face of the symbol. If it is a group object, it drills down into each sub-shape object, sums all of the valid filled areas, reports the filled area to the user in a message box, and then enables that total to be placed as text upon the face of the group symbol. The application then creates a custom formula in the EventXFMod cell of the resultant ShapeSheet that calls a slightly different area calculation subroutine, which recalculates the filled area after any resizing of the symbol and reposts the new area to the symbol's text.

LISTING 18.1 Advanced Shape Area Calculator and Reporter

```
Private Sub Document_DocumentOpened(ByVal doc As IVDocument)
    Dim szMessageHolder As String
    szMessageHolder = "Drag out a Shape from the tools, i.e." & vbCrLf
    szMessageHolder = szMessageHolder & "Rectangle Tool, Ellipse Tool,
    ➥Freeform Tool, Line Tool, Arc Tool, Pencil Tool." & vbCrLf
    szMessageHolder = szMessageHolder & "Or drag any Master from a Stencil." &
    ➥vbCrLf
    szMessageHolder = szMessageHolder & "After the shape is instantiated,
    ➥Resize the shape or move the shape or rotate the shape." & vbCrLf
```

```
        MsgBox szMessageHolder, vbInformation + vbOKOnly, "Read Me First"
End Sub
Private Sub Document_ShapeAdded(ByVal Shape As IVShape)
    Dim szMessageHolder As String
    Dim intRetVal As Integer
    Dim dblAreaHolder As Double
    dblAreaHolder = 0#
    Dim shpObjSubShape As Visio.Shape
    Dim intSubShapeCount As Integer
    Dim celObjEventXFModCell As Visio.Cell
    If Shape.Type = visTypeShape Then
        If Shape.Cells("Height").Result("in.") > 0 And Shape.Cells
        ➥("Width").Result("in.") > 0 Then
            szMessageHolder = "The Filled Area of this Shape is: "
            szMessageHolder = szMessageHolder & Shape.AreaIU & " Sq. In." &
vbCrLf
            szMessageHolder = szMessageHolder & "Do you want to place the
            ➥value as text on the Shape?"
            intRetVal = MsgBox(szMessageHolder, vbInformation + vbYesNo,
            ➥"Demonstration")
            If intRetVal = vbYes Then
                Shape.Text = Shape.AreaIU & " Sq. In."
            End If
        ElseIf Shape.Cells("Height").Result("in.") > 0 Then
            szMessageHolder = "The new Shape has no Width." & vbCrLf
            szMessageHolder = szMessageHolder & "The Shape's Height is: "
            szMessageHolder = szMessageHolder & Shape.Cells("Height").Result
            ➥("in.") & " in."
            MsgBox szMessageHolder, vbInformation + vbOKOnly, "Demonstration"
        ElseIf Shape.Cells("Width").Result("in.") > 0 Then
            szMessageHolder = "The new Shape has no Height." & vbCrLf
            szMessageHolder = szMessageHolder & "The Shape's Width is: "
            szMessageHolder = szMessageHolder & Shape.Cells("Width").Result
            ➥("in.") & " in."
            MsgBox szMessageHolder, vbInformation + vbOKOnly, "Demonstration"
        Else
            szMessageHolder = "This Shape Seems to have no area at all!"
            MsgBox szMessageHolder, vbInformation + vbOKOnly, "Demonstration"
        End If
    ElseIf Shape.Type = visTypeGroup Then
For intSubShapeCount = 1 To Shape.Shapes.Count
            Set shObjSubShape = Shape.Shapes.Item(intSubShapeCount)
            If shObjSubShape.Type = visTypeShape Then
                If shObjSubShape.Cells("Height").Result("in.") > 0 And
shObjSubShape.Cells("Width").Result("in.") > 0 Then
                    dblAreaHolder = dblAreaHolder + shObjSubShape.AreaIU
```

continues

LISTING 18.1 Continued

```
                End If
            End If
        Next intSubShapeCount
        szMessageHolder = "The Filled Area of this Group Shape is: "
        szMessageHolder = szMessageHolder & dblAreaHolder & " Sq. In." & vbCrLf
        szMessageHolder = szMessageHolder & "Do you want to place the value as
        ➥text on the Shape?"
        intRetVal = MsgBox(szMessageHolder, vbInformation + vbYesNo,
        ➥"Demonstration")
        If intRetVal = vbYes Then
            Shape.Text = dblAreaHolder & " Sq. In."
        End If
    Else
        szMessageHolder = "The New Item Is Not A Shape" & vbCrLf & "Not Able
        ➥To Calculate A Filled Area."
        MsgBox szMessageHolder, vbExclamation + vbOKOnly, "Demonstration"
    End If
    Set celObjEventXFModCell = Shape.Cells("EventXFMod")
    celObjEventXFModCell.FormulaForce = "RUNADDON(""ReRunAreaIU"")"
End Sub
Public Sub ReRunAreaIU()
    Dim MyShape As Visio.Shape
    Dim szMessageHolder As String
    Dim intRetVal As Integer
    Dim dblAreaHolder As Double
    dblAreaHolder = 0#
    Dim shpObjSubShape As Visio.Shape
    Dim intSubShapeCount As Integer
    Dim celObjEventXFModCell As Visio.Cell
    Set MyShape = Visio.ActiveWindow.Selection.Item(1)
    If MyShape.Type = visTypeShape Then
        If MyShape.Cells("Height").Result("in.") > 0 And MyShape.Cells
        ➥("Width").Result("in.") > 0 Then
            MyShape.Text = MyShape.AreaIU & " Sq. In."
        ElseIf MyShape.Cells("Height").Result("in.") > 0 Then
            szMessageHolder = "The new Shape has no Width." & vbCrLf
            szMessageHolder = szMessageHolder & "The Shape's Height is: "
            szMessageHolder = szMessageHolder & MyShape.Cells("Height").Result
            ➥("in.") & " in."
            MsgBox szMessageHolder, vbInformation + vbOKOnly, "Demonstration"
        ElseIf MyShape.Cells("Width").Result("in.") > 0 Then
            szMessageHolder = "The new Shape has no Height." & vbCrLf
            szMessageHolder = szMessageHolder & "The Shape's Width is: "
            szMessageHolder = szMessageHolder & MyShape.Cells("Width").Result
            ➥("in.") & " in."
```

```
                MsgBox szMessageHolder, vbInformation + vbOKOnly, "Demonstration"
        Else
            szMessageHolder = "This Shape Seems to have no area at all!"
            MsgBox szMessageHolder, vbInformation + vbOKOnly, "Demonstration"
        End If
    ElseIf MyShape.Type = visTypeGroup Then
        For intSubShapeCount = 1 To MyShape.Shapes.Count
            Set shObjSubShape = MyShape.Shapes.Item(intSubShapeCount)
            If shObjSubShape.Type = visTypeShape Then
                If shObjSubShape.Cells("Height").Result("in.") > 0 And
shObjSubShape.Cells("Width").Result("in.") > 0 Then
                    dblAreaHolder = dblAreaHolder + shObjSubShape.AreaIU
                End If
            End If
        Next intSubShapeCount
        MyShape.Text = dblAreaHolder & " Sq. In."
    Else
        szMessageHolder = "The New Item Is Not A Shape" & vbCrLf & "Not Able
        ➥To Calculate A Filled Area."
        MsgBox szMessageHolder, vbExclamation + vbOKOnly, "Demonstration"
    End If
End Sub
```

Table 18.1 is a listing of all the events exposed and supported for the Document Object under Visio 2000.

TABLE 18.1 Document Events

Event	Description
BeforeDocumentClose	Triggered prior to closing a Visio document
BeforeDocumentSave	Triggered prior to saving a Visio document
BeforeDocumentSaveAs	Triggered prior to saving a Visio document under a new unique name
BeforeMasterDelete	Triggered prior to deleting a master from a stencil or local stencil
BeforePageDelete	Triggered prior to deleting a Visio document page
BeforeSelectionDelete	Triggered prior to deleting a selection on a Visio document page
BeforeShapeTextEdit	Triggered prior to a shape's text being changed
BeforeStyleDelete	Triggered prior to deleting a style from the active document
ConvertToGroupCanceled	Triggered when the request to convert to a group is canceled by the user
DesignModeEntered	Triggered when the user changes the Visio run focus to Design mode
DocumentChanged	Triggered when a Visio document has changed

continues

TABLE 18.1   Continued

Event	Description
DocumentCloseCanceled	Triggered when the request to close a document is canceled by the user
DocumentCreated	Triggered when a new Visio document is created based on a template with the event programmed
DocumentOpened	Triggered when the Visio document containing programming is opened
DocumentSaved	Triggered when the Visio document is saved
DocumentSavedAs	Triggered when the Visio document is saved under a new name
MasterAdded	Triggered when a new master is added to a stencil or local stencil
MasterChanged	Triggered when a master is changed
MasterDeleteCanceled	Triggered when the request to delete a master shape is canceled by the user
PageAdded	Triggered when a page is added to the Visio document
PageChanged	Triggered when a page is changed in the Visio document
PageDeleteCanceled	Triggered when the request to delete a page is canceled by the user
QueryCancelConvert-ToGroup	Triggered when the Automation application validates that Cancel has been triggered
QueryCancelDocument-Close	Triggered when the Automation application validates that Cancel has been triggered
QueryCancelMaster-Delete	Triggered when the Automation application validates that Cancel has been triggered
QueryCancelPageDelete	Triggered when the Automation application validates that Cancel has been triggered
QueryCancelSelection-Delete	Triggered when the Automation application validates that Cancel has been triggered
QueryCancelStyleDelete	Triggered when the Automation application validates thatCancel has been triggered
QueryCancelUngroup	Triggered when the Automation application validates thatCancel has been triggered
RunModeEntered	Triggered when the user changes the Visio run focus to Run mode
SelectionDelete-Canceled	Triggered when the request to delete a selection of shapes is canceled by the user
ShapeAdded	Triggered when a shape is added to the Visio document
ShapeExitedTextEdit	Triggered when a shape's text editing is complete in the Visio document

Event	Description
ShapeParentChanged	Triggered when a SmartShape symbol's parent shape is changed
StyleAdded	Triggered when a style is added to the Visio document
StyleChanged	Triggered when a style is changed in the Visio document
StyleDeleteCanceled	Triggered when the request to delete a style is canceled by the user
UngroupCanceled	Triggered when the Ungroup command is canceled for the selected shapes in a Visio document

Keep in mind that the "before" events are merely notifications that the event is about to happen. It does not contain any direct mechanism for prohibiting that event from taking place. Visio 2000 supports a new cueable undo model that enables you to set a marker for undo just before a particular event takes place. After that event has terminated, you can then programmatically call an undo back to that marker. Figure 18.1 is what the basic event model looks like in Visio.

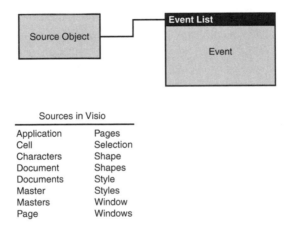

FIGURE 18.1
Visio event object model.

Any object that can serve as an event source contains an event list. The event list holds the collection of a source's event objects. An event object encapsulates an event code: action pair. When the event is triggered based on the event source or one of its subobjects, the action is performed. By default, source objects have empty event lists.

Events have a hierarchical structure. Many events are sourced by several objects. For instance Page.ShapeAdded fires when a shape is added to a page. Doc.ShapeAdded fires when a shape is added to any page in a document. App.ShapeAdded fires when a shape is added to a document open in the Visio application.

The number of times the event will fire can be very different depending upon which object you choose as the source object. For example, at the application level, the ShapeAdded event will fire any time a SmartShape symbol is added to any page in any open document in the Visio application. If the page object is used as the source object, the event fires only when a SmartShape symbol is added to that page, not when a SmartShape symbol is added to any other page in the Visio application.

Take the time to carefully review which objects source which events by using the object browser in the VBA IDE, or via Visio's online Automation reference. Make sure that you are selecting the source that makes the most sense for the context of the desired event.

You also have the ability to shut down any events from being triggered at all. This may be useful when debugging your application. This is accomplished via selecting Tools, Options, selecting the Advanced tab in the Options dialog, unchecking the Enable Automation Events checkbox, and then clicking OK to confirm your selection. This can also be accomplished via Automation programming by setting the EventsEnabled property of the Visio application: Application.EventsEnabled = FALSE.

You may probably have ascertained that you can assign procedures to the DocumentOpened event so that every time a document is opened a certain initialization of data and information is accomplished. However, while you are developing your application, it is truly an irritation to have to keep saving, closing, and re-opening the diagram to test the re-initialization of the data. It is far more convenient to attach that initialization to the RunModeEntered property of the document. When a diagram is opened, both the DocumentOpened event and the RunModeEntered event fire. To re-initialize your data, you simply need to enter Design mode and re-enter Run mode to fire the event. This is far easier than reloading the drawing time and time again.

VBA Code Behind Events for ActiveX Controls

Beginning with Visio 5.0, any page in a Visio document can host ActiveX controls. Visio is now configured with two distinct modes: a Design mode and a Run mode. To expose this feature, enable the Developer toolbar. On this toolbar you will see a button that looks like a triangle, Ruler and Pencil. This is the Design/Run mode toggle button. When the button is raised, you are in Run mode; when it is pressed, you are working in Design mode. While in Design mode, you can place ActiveX controls onto a diagram's page, reposition the control, resize the control, and set properties of the control. While in Run mode, you or your users can interact with the control just as you would with any other ActiveX Control, such as in a Visual Basic application. The diagram must be in Run mode in order for the associated events to fire and an application to have the ability to access the methods and properties of the control.

Here is a small demonstration for you to try.

1. Begin a new blank Visio diagram based on a blank document with no stencils open.
2. Open the Developer toolbar.
3. From the Developer toolbar, place the diagram in Design mode by ensuring that the button is pressed.
4. From the Developer toolbar, select the Insert Control button. This looks like a wee radio button and command button overlapping. The Insert Control listing dialog will appear.
5. Select the Microsoft Forms 2.0 CommandButton from the list.
6. Click OK to confirm your selection.
7. Reposition and resize the command button control on your diagram to suit your taste. You may interact with the button as if it were any other SmartShape symbol. Pull on the sizing handles to resize; drag to relocate.
8. Right-click the control and select from the context menu Command Button Object, Properties. Note that a Properties window appears that is similar to that within the VB/VBA IDE.
9. Set the Caption property to "Push Me…" and the Font property to 10 pt. Bold. Close the Property window.
10. Right-click the control and select from the context menu Command Button Object, View Code. You will be entered into the VBA IDE. You will also be placed in the code window for the `CommandButton1_Click` event.

Enter the code in Listing 18.2 as a subroutine.

LISTING **18.2** Code Behind the Command Button ActiveX Control

```
Private Sub CommandButton1_Click()
    Dim intRetVal As Integer
    Dim szMessageString As String
    Dim vbBoxGraphics As Integer
    szMessageString = "You have Clicked me. Are you sure you wanted to
    ➡do that?"
    vbBoxGraphics = vbQuestion + vbYesNo
    intRetVal = MsgBox(szMessageString, vbBoxGraphics, "Demonstration")
    If intRetVal = vbYes Then
        szMessageString = "Well then, Thank you so very, very much!"
        vbBoxGraphics = vbExclamation + vbOKOnly
    Else
        szMessageString = "I am terribly, terribly sorry Lad! Won't
        ➡Happen again..."
```

continues

LISTING 18.2 Continued

```
            vbBoxGraphics = vbExclamation + vbOKOnly
        End If
        MsgBox szMessageString, vbBoxGraphics, "Demonstration"
End Sub
```

11. Return to the Visio Drawing window.

12. Place the diagram into Run mode by clicking and raising the Design Mode button on the Developer toolbar.

13. Click the Command Button ActiveX control on the Visio diagram page and respond appropriately.

As you can see, ActiveX controls enable you to greatly increase the usability of your solutions by providing a user interface (UI) that assists your users in working with the requirements of your solution.

On the companion CD-ROM, you will find a Visio diagram entitled ActiveX1 CH18.VSD. This application shows how a Calendar control can be implemented in your solution. By selecting a date from the Calendar control, the application feeds the date to a SmartShape symbol in the diagram. By selecting the command button, the current time is posted to the SmartShape symbol in the diagram. The code for these two controls can be seen in Listing 18.3.

LISTING 18.3 Using an ActiveX Control to Report the Time

```
Private Sub buTimeSet_Click()
    Dim pagObjPage As Visio.Page
    Dim shObjPageSheet As Visio.Shape
    Dim celObjPropTime As Visio.Cell
    Dim varCurrentHour As Variant
    Dim szAMPM As String
    Dim varCurrentMinute As Variant
    Dim varCurrentSecond As Variant
    Dim szCurrentTime As String
    Set pagObjPage = Visio.ActivePage
    Set shObjPageSheet = pagObjPage.PageSheet
    Set celObjPropTime = shObjPageSheet.Cells("Prop.Time")
    varCurrentHour = Hour(Now)
    If varCurrentHour > 11 Then
        szAMPM = "PM"
    Else
        szAMPM = "AM"
    End If
    If varCurrentHour > 12 Then
```

```
            varCurrentHour = varCurrentHour - 12
        End If
        varCurrentMinute = Minute(Now)
        If Len(varCurrentMinute) < 2 Then
            varCurrentMinute = "0" & varCurrentMinute
        End If
        varCurrentSecond = Second(Now)
        szCurrentTime = varCurrentHour & ":" & varCurrentMinute & " " & szAMPM & "
    ➥ + " & varCurrentSecond & " sec."
        celObjPropTime.Formula = Chr(34) & szCurrentTime & Chr(34)
End Sub
Private Sub MonthView1_DateClick(ByVal DateClicked As Date)
    Dim pagObjPage As Visio.Page
    Dim shObjPageSheet As Visio.Shape
    Dim celObjPropDate As Visio.Cell
    Dim varCurrentYear As Variant
    Dim varCurrentMonth As Variant
    Dim varCurrentMonthName As Variant
    Dim varCurrentDay As Variant
    Dim varCurrentDayOfWeek As Variant
    Dim varCurrentDayOfWeekString As Variant
    Dim szCurrentDateString As String
    Set pagObjPage = Visio.ActivePage
    Set shObjPageSheet = pagObjPage.PageSheet
    Set celObjPropDate = shObjPageSheet.Cells("Prop.Date")
    varCurrentYear = MonthView1.Year
    varCurrentMonth = MonthView1.Month
    Select Case varCurrentMonth
        Case 1
            varCurrentMonthString = "January"
        Case 2
            varCurrentMonthString = "February"
        Case 3
            varCurrentMonthString = "March"
        Case 4
            varCurrentMonthString = "April"
        Case 5
            varCurrentMonthString = "May"
        Case 6
            varCurrentMonthString = "June"
        Case 7
            varCurrentMonthString = "July"
        Case 8
            varCurrentMonthString = "August"
        Case 9
            varCurrentMonthString = "September"
```

18

EVENT HANDLING
IN THE VISIO
OBJECT MODEL

continues

LISTING 18.3   Continued

```
        Case 10
            varCurrentMonthString = "October"
        Case 11
            varCurrentMonthString = "November"
        Case 12
            varCurrentMonthString = "December"
    End Select
    varCurrentDay = MonthView1.Day
    varCurrentDayOfWeek = MonthView1.DayOfWeek
    Select Case varCurrentDayOfWeek
        Case 1
            varCurrentDayOfWeekString = "Sunday"
        Case 2
            varCurrentDayOfWeekString = "Monday"
        Case 3
            varCurrentDayOfWeekString = "Tuesday"
        Case 4
            varCurrentDayOfWeekString = "Wednesday"
        Case 5
            varCurrentDayOfWeekString = "Thursday"
        Case 6
            varCurrentDayOfWeekString = "Friday"
        Case 7
            varCurrentDayOfWeekString = "Saturday"
    End Select
    szCurrentDateString = varCurrentDayOfWeekString & " " & 
➥varCurrentMonthString & " " & varCurrentDay & "," & varCurrentYear
    celObjPropDate.Formula = Chr(34) & szCurrentDateString & Chr(34)
End Sub
```

Cell Dependencies

Thus far in this chapter, we have looked at Automation-based mechanisms for handling events. We will continue with this in a moment, but it is important to remember that many events can be handled on a SmartShape symbol-by-SmartShape symbol basis using cell dependencies. As you are aware, any cell in a Visio ShapeSheet can reference any other cell in a Visio ShapeSheet through formulas. These are the inter-cell references we spoke of in the earlier portions of the book. They create inter-cell relationships or cell dependencies.

These dependencies are implied by the cell names used in the formulas. In the following example of a 1-D connector SmartShape symbol, PinY depends on BeginY and EndY. EndY, in turn, depends on a ConnectionPoint in Sheet.2. When the value of the connection point changes, the value of the EndY cell is recalculated. When the value of EndY changes, the PinY Cell is recalculated.

```
PinY = (BeginY + EndY) / 2
EndY = PAR(PNT(Sheet.2!Connections.X1, Sheet.2!Connections.Y1))
```

The dependency network that is implied here is that PinY depends on EndY, which depends on Sheet.2!Connections.X1.

The value change in Connections.X1 forces a change in the value of EndY and hence PinY.

The Visio recalculation engine does not recalculate every cell when a SmartShape symbol changes in some way. Rather, it establishes a dependency network or tree such that it only recalculates the cells that have the potential to change.

In addition to the general form of dependencies established via inter-cell references, such as we have just seen above, you can force cell dependencies by using the DependsOn function in a ShapeSheet cell. DependsOn creates a cell reference dependency on the cells specified in the list of "trigger cells". The function always returns FALSE (0) and, as such, has no effect on the final value of the cell when used in this fashion.

Here are two uses of the DependsOn function. They would typically be placed in a user-defined cell or a scratch cell:

```
=RUNADDON("string") + DependsOn(TriggerCell)
=SETF("Cell",Formula) + DependsOn(TriggerCell)
```

A typical use of the DependsOn function is to cause some action to occur whenever a cell's value changes. In the first example above, an add-on is run whenever the trigger cell's value changes. In the second example, the formula of a specified cell is set whenever the trigger cell's value changes. In these examples, the final result of the user-defined or scratch cell is irrelevant. Your use of DependsOn is, however, not limited to these types of examples.

Here is a practical example of an application of DependsOn usage. Presume that you want to construct a SmartShape symbol such that the user can set the color of the symbol's fill via a Custom Properties dialog. However, you do not want to prohibit the user from setting the fill color from normal UI menus and toolbars. Furthermore, setting the value in the Custom Properties dialog box should update the FillFormat cell, and setting the value from the UI should update the value in the dialogue as well as update the FillFormat cell. Keep in mind that a SmartShape symbol's color is kept as an integer value in the FillForegnd cell. Creating a custom property cell named Prop.Color creates a repository to store integer values for color indices. By creating two user-defined cells as follows

```
User.Row_1 -> =DEPENDSON("Prop.Color") + SETF("FillForegnd",Prop.Color)
User.Row_2 -> =DEPENDSON("FillForegnd") + SETF("Prop.Color",FillForegnd)
```

18

EVENT HANDLING
IN THE VISIO
OBJECT MODEL

you create a set of dependencies that states when the value of the custom property Prop.Color cell changes, the FillForegnd cell is updated and when the value of the FillForegnd cell changes, the Prop.Color custom property cell is updated.

Generally, Visio prohibits circular references to inhibit infinite recalculation. However, in a triggered dependency such as this, it is allowable.

WithEvents Keyword in Visio Automation

Let's return to Automation programming again. Now that you have seen how dependencies are established, you will want to use Automation interfaces to look for dependency triggers and take appropriate action based on that trigger.

You can define a class object to receive events. A class that receives events is sometimes called an event sink or a sink object. With the class definition, you can use the VBA keyword WithEvents to declare an object variable for the Visio object whose events you want to handle.

The next three examples will show three increasing levels of complexity in utilizing WithEvents.

The first example is a binding of the object defined WithEvents within the document module. This binding keeps track of any time the Connector SmartShape symbol is either glued or unglued from another SmartShape symbol. The file on the companion CD-ROM is VBA Connect Events.VSD (see Listing 18.4).

LISTING 18.4 Glue Status Events Demonstration

```
Option Explicit
' Declare a variable withevents of type Page.   This will be
' used to capture the connection events.   Remember that this
' variable needs to be bound to a real Visio object before it
' will respond to events.
Private WithEvents thePage As Visio.Page
Private Sub Document_DocumentOpened(ByVal doc As Visio.IVDocument)
    ' Bind the thePage variable to the ActivePage in Visio
    ' This will allow event handling to start to happen
Set thePage = Visio.ActivePage
End Sub
Private Sub thePage_ConnectionsAdded(ByVal Connects As Visio.IVConnects)
    ' Iterate through the connects collection passed to us
    Dim i As Integer
        For i = 1 To Connects.Count
        ' Do something with the info
        With Connects(i)
            MsgBox .FromCell.Name & " in " & .FromSheet.Name & " glued to "
```

```
              ➥ & .ToCell.Name & " in " & .ToSheet.Name, vbInformation,
                ➥"Developing Visio Solutions"
          End With
        Next
End Sub
Private Sub thePage_ConnectionsDeleted(ByVal Connects As Visio.IVConnects)
    ' Iterate through the connects collection passed to us
    Dim i As Integer
        For i = 1 To Connects.Count
          ' Do something with the info
          With Connects(i)
              MsgBox .FromCell.Name & " in " & .FromSheet.Name & " unglued from "
                ➥ & .ToCell.Name & " in " & .ToSheet.Name, vbInformation,
                ➥"Developing Visio Solutions"
          End With
        Next
End Sub
```

Listing 18.5 shows how a class definition is established. The file on the companion CD-ROM
is TestEdgeWithEvents.VSD.

LISTING 18.5 Testing Events Demonstration

```
Option Explicit
Dim mypage As New PageObject
Private Sub Document_DocumentOpened(ByVal doc As Visio.IVDocument)
    'InitPage
End Sub
Private Sub Document_RunModeEntered(ByVal doc As Visio.IVDocument)
    'MsgBox "run mode entered"
    mypage.InitPage
End Sub
Dim WithEvents pagobj As Visio.Page
Private Sub pagobj_ConnectionsAdded(ByVal Connects As Visio.IVConnects)
    Dim celobj As Visio.Cell
    Dim PosPeriod As Integer
    Dim strFromName As String
        ' MsgBox "Connection Add"
        'Get the root name of the FromSheet
    strFromName = Connects.FromSheet.Name
    PosPeriod = InStr(1, strFromName, ".")
    If PosPeriod <> 0 Then
        strFromName = Left(strFromName, PosPeriod - 1)
    End If
```

continues

LISTING 18.5 Continued

```
    If strFromName <> "Edge" Then Exit Sub
        'Determine if it is the begin or end point that is connected
    If Connects(1).FromPart = visEnd Then
        'Connection is to the End point - set Prop.To value
        Set celobj = Connects.FromSheet.Cells("Prop.To.Value")
    ElseIf Connects(1).FromPart = visBegin Then
        'Connection is to the Begin point - set Prop.From value
        Set celobj = Connects.FromSheet.Cells("Prop.From.Value")
    End If
    celobj.Formula = Chr$(34) & Connects.ToSheet.Name & Chr$(34)
End Sub
Private Sub pagobj_ConnectionsDeleted(ByVal Connects As Visio.IVConnects)
    Dim celobj As Visio.Cell
    Dim PosPeriod As Integer
    Dim strFromName As String
        ' MsgBox "Connection Delete"
        'Get the root name of the FromSheet
    strFromName = Connects.FromSheet.Name
    PosPeriod = InStr(1, strFromName, ".")
    If PosPeriod <> 0 Then
        strFromName = Left(strFromName, PosPeriod - 1)
    End If
    If strFromName <> "Edge" Then Exit Sub
'Determine if it is the begin or end point that is connected
    If Connects(1).FromPart = visEnd Then
        'Connection is to the End point - set Prop.To value
        Set celobj = Connects.FromSheet.Cells("Prop.To.Value")
    ElseIf Connects(1).FromPart = visBegin Then
        'Connection is to the Begin point - set Prop.From value
        Set celobj = Connects.FromSheet.Cells("Prop.From.Value")
    End If
    celobj.Formula = Chr$(34) & Chr$(34)
End Sub
Public Sub InitPage()
    Set pagobj = Visio.ActivePage
End Sub
```

Listing 18.6 is an example of trapping CellChanged events for any SmartShape symbol that has been added to the diagram. It utilizes the collection object defined in VBA to hold a reference to each sink object as it is created. The file on the companion CD-ROM is VBA WithEvents Sample.VSD.

LISTING 18.6 Trapping CellChanged Events

```
Option Explicit
        ' Create a collection to hold the sink objects
Dim sinks As New Collection
Private WithEvents m_shpObj As Visio.Shape
Private Sub Document_BeforeSelectionDelete(ByVal Selection As
➥Visio.IVSelection)
' This routine removes the shape(s) from the sinks collection since they are
' being deleted
        Dim i As Integer    ' Loop variable
' Loop through the selection deleting the shapes from the collection
    For i = 1 To Selection.Count
            ' Remove the sink from the sinks collection
            ' We can find the correct member using the shape's UniqueID since this
            ' was specified as the key when the sink was added
        sinks.Remove Selection(i).UniqueID(visGetGUID)
    Next i
End Sub
Private Sub Document_ShapeAdded(ByVal Shape As Visio.IVShape)
' This routine initializes a sink object with the new shape and
' ands it to the sinks collection
        Dim sinkObj As New ShapeSink
        sinkObj.InitWith Shape
' Add the sink object to the sinks collection
    ' We will need a unique identifier for the member of the collection
    ' when we delete it so use the shape UniqueID
    sinks.Add sinkObj, Shape.UniqueID(visGetOrMakeGUID)
End Sub
Public Sub InitWith(ByVal aShape As Visio.Shape)
' This routine sets the shape object contained within the ShapeSink class.
' Setting this binds the event handling to a real Visio object
    Set m_shpObj = aShape
End Sub
Private Sub m_shpObj_CellChanged(ByVal Cell As Visio.IVCell)
' This routine will be called when a cell changes in the shape
' If the Immediate Window is not visible, select View Immediate Window
' to see the output of the Debug.Print statement
        Debug.Print _
        Cell.Shape.Name & " " & Cell.Name & " changed to =" & Cell.Formula
End Sub
```

Creating an Event Sink for Visio Objects

To use the event model, you first need to create a sink object if you are going to send notifications to your add-on (see Figure 18.2). Running add-ons in response to events does not require a sink object. The event sink is an instance of a class module for which you have defined the VisEventProc method. Whether you plan to send event notifications or run add-ons, you next need to get a reference to the Visio source object and hold on to it. Usually, this reference is a global variable. If your add-on releases this reference (the Object goes out of scope), event handling will cease.

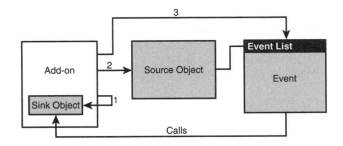

FIGURE 18.2

Event object model flow.

Besides the normal collection properties and methods (Item, Count, and so on), the EventList collection has two methods that enable you to create event objects. When the Add method is used to create an event object, the action code for the event causes the add-on to be executed when the event fires. When an AddAdvise method is used to create an event object, the action caused by the event firing is to send a notification to an event handler routine (called an event sink), which you create. The event sink receives the event code, a reference to the source object, and other data related to the event. You program the event sink to respond to the event in some appropriate manner.

Look at the following code fragment:

```
Set g_sink = New EventSink
If Not g_documents Is Nothing Then
Set evt1 = g_documents.EventList.AddAdvise (visEvtCodeDocSave, g_sink, "", "")
Set evt2 = g_documents.EventList.AddAdvise (visEvtCodeDocSaveAs, g_sink,
➥"", "")
Set evt3 = g_documents.EventList.Add (visEvtCodeBefSelDel, visActCodeRunAddon,
➥ "addon.exe", "")
```

This code fragment creates the event objects within the `EventList` object of g_documents. Assume that g_documents is a global reference to the documents collection and does not go out of scope.

g_sink is a sink object created from the VB class object `EventSink`. It contains the method `VisEventProc` and a reference to it is passed by the `AddAdvise` method when the event object is created. This enables VB to hand a pointer to the sink back to Visio so that Visio can use it as a callback to the sink.

The third event object is created by the `Add` method. Its action code is `visActCodeRunAddon` and the name of the add-on to be executed is passed to the Add method. The event sink is not called when the event `BeforeSelectionDelete` is triggered. Rather, the add-on "addon.exe" is executed.

> **CAUTION**
>
> Although event codes appear with other Visio constants in the Visio type library, some cannot be used from the library because of the way it handles large hexadecimal values. Any constant with the high bit set (that is, a constant with a hexadecimal value greater than &H7FFF or 32,767) causes a numeric overflow condition, and some Visio event codes happen to fall in this range. You can use the hexadecimal value directly in your code instead of the named constant defined in the type library.

The sample code in Listing 18.7 is a simple event handler routine. The name of the method *must* be `VisEventProc`. It simply examines the event code and takes some action for each event of which it is sent notice.

LISTING 18.7 Event Procedure

```
Public Sub VisEventProc(event As Integer, source As Object, id As Long, seq
➥As Long, subject As Object, etc As Variant)
     Dim eventStr As String
     Select Case event
            Case visEvtCodeDocSave
                   eventstr = "save: " & subject.Name
            Case visEvtCodeDocSaveAs
                   eventstr = "saveas: " & subject.Name
            Case Else
                   eventstr = "unhandled event " & event
     End Select
     Debug.Print "seq: ; seq; "id: "; id; eventstr
End Sub
```

Developers new to Visio event-handling applications tend to look at the process with some amount of trepidation and consternation. If you follow the guidelines shown in this chapter, however, you should have no difficulty in creating your own robust and powerful event-handling routines that make your application all the more powerful.

In the next chapter, you will take an in-depth look at customizing the Visio UI. You will learn what can be customized, the size and persistence of UI customizations, and how to actually make the modifications to the UI. You will learn about Visio's menu objects, its toolbar objects, and how to make use of external UI files to recall at will.

Customizing the Visio User Interface Under Automation

IN THIS CHAPTER

There will be times in developing your applications when you will need to customize the Visio user interface (UI). For example, your solution may call for a very tightly limited subset of the tools to be found on the toolbars and menus due to your users needing only three or four specific tools to accomplish a repetitive subset of tasks. It might be that your application wants to add additional menu items and toolbars to the Visio UI. Do note, however, that if your solution is to be used in conjunction with or in addition to the concurrent usage of solutions shipping with Visio right out of the box, it most probably is *not* a good idea to customize the UI, as this will cause confusion on the part of the users of the in-box solutions as well as the users of your solution.

Under Visio 2000, users have the ability to customize toolbars in much the same way that they do in Microsoft Office applications by adding and removing toolbar buttons from existing toolbars and creating their own toolbars to suit their needs. However, the ability to handle both menus and toolbars programmatically is still a function of Automation applications. This capability began with Visio 4.0 and has grown more robust with each successive release. The methodologies, however, remain the same.

So just what *can* be customized under Visio's user interface? Menus and accelerators can be fully customized. A menu is any item that appears at the topmost edge of the Visio Parent Window. By default, these are, from left to right:

File, Edit, View, Insert, Format, Tools, Shape, Window, and Help.

Certainly, each of these contains a list of menu items and often sub-menus within them.

Select the Edit menu. Notice that the copy drawing has a listing to its right that states Ctrl+C. This is an accelerator. Within the Visio UI, any of these accelerators may be customized as well.

Be aware that accelerator tables are independent of menus. Be aware also that removing a menu does not remove an associated accelerator if one exists. If you truly want to eliminate a particular function from the UI, you will want to remove it from the menus, toolbars, and accelerator tables. Finally, be aware that if you add an accelerator to the accelerators table, this does not automatically add it to the associated menu item caption.

All the Visio toolbars can be fully customized as well as new ones. The status bar at the bottom of the Visio Application window can be fully customized as well. You cannot add your own listbox controls to the toolbars or the status bar. Visio is only aware of the controls supplied with these items as they ship out of the box.

Visio has what it refers to as contexts. Notice that when you have a drawing window and a ShapeSheet window open, each time you switch the window focus between these two contexts, the menus and the toolbars change as well. This is also true of all differing window contexts: drawing, ShapeSheet, Stencil, Print Preview, and Icon Edit. Remember that right-clicking on a

SmartShape symbol brings up a context menu for the shape as well. When Visio is an embedded object in another application and it is activated, it carries with it a specific set of menus and toolbars in this context as well.

There is no direct method to customize the way the user interacts with graphic objects using the mouse. This must be accomplished by object and layer properties and through add-ons that trigger events like EventXFMod. You can trigger other events indirectly by putting the formula with the syntax

=RUNADDON(AddonName) + DEPENDSON(TriggerCell)

in the scratch or user-defined sections.

Figure 19.1 is the model of the UI objects in the Visio object model.

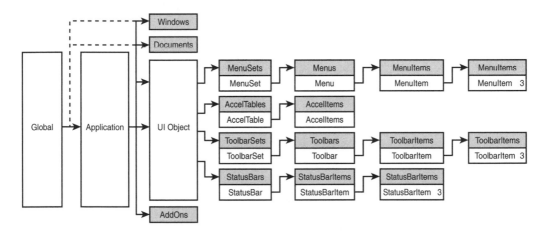

FIGURE 19.1
UI objects in the Visio object model.

There is one MenuSet per context. Each MenuSet contains a list of menus, indexed beginning at zero (0). Each menu contains a list of MenuItems, which can contain a list of MenuItems if it is hierarchical. Accelerator tables, or AccelTables, are simpler, as the same accelerator table is valid throughout the entire MenuSet.

The Size and Persistence of UI Customization

Small interface changes can be accomplished by an add-on "on the fly." Examples of this would be deleting a single menu item, adding a button to a toolbar, or adding an item to the context menu. Larger changes are certainly much more efficient when run from an external UI file. You can create this file offline, store it in a file, and then load it upon demand. The resulting UI file can be permanently bound to a file or to the application in order to create a persistent change in the UI. The UI file can be loaded and unloaded on the fly for a temporary UI change.

Here are some rules to guide you:

- Make small changes on the fly.
- Store large changes in an interface file.
- Bind permanent changes to a given document (most generally a template file), rather than the application itself.
- Make temporary changes on the fly or by loading an interface, remembering to reset or unload your changes when you are through.

Modifying the Existing UI

Here is a skeleton code framework for modifying existing menus:

```
Public Sub MakeWeeChange()
    Dim UIObj As Visio.UIObject
    Set UIObj = Visio.Application.BuiltInMenus
        ' <make modifications>
    Visio.Application.SetCustomMenus UIObj
End Sub
```

It is important that you do not forget to use the SetCustomMenus method of the application object. Failing to do so will fail to activate your changes.

Listing 19.1 is a full code example of adding a "demo" menu to the existing menu sets for the current diagram. The menu item runs a VB add-on called DispName.EXE.

LISTING 19.1   Adding a Menu to Visio

```
Sub AddAWeeDemoMenu()
        Dim appVisio       As Visio.Application
        Dim UIObj          As Visio.UIObject      'Contains the UI object
        Dim menuSetsObj    As Visio.MenuSets      'MenuSets collection
        Dim menuSetObj     As Visio.MenuSet       'A MenuSet object
        Dim menusObj       As Visio.Menus         'Menus collection
        Dim menuObj        As Visio.Menu          'A Menu object
        Dim menuItemsObj   As Visio.MenuItems     'MenuItems collection
        Dim menuItemObj    As Visio.MenuItem      'A MenuItem object
        Set appVisio = Visio.Application
        Set UIObj = appVisio.BuiltInMenus
```

```
'Set menuSetObj to the menu set for the drawing window
Set menuSetsObj = UIObj.MenuSets
Set menuSetObj = menuSetsObj.ItemAtID(visUIObjSetDrawing)
'Insert a menu just after the Tools menu
Set menusObj = menuSetObj.Menus
Set menuObj = menusObj.AddAt(6)
menuObj.Caption = "Demo"
'Add a single menu item which runs DispName.exe
Set menuItemsObj = menuObj.MenuItems
Set menuItemObj = menuItemsObj.Add
menuItemObj.Caption = "&Run Display Name"
menuItemObj.CmdNum = 0
menuItemObj.ActionText = "Run Display Name"
menuItemObj.AddOnName = "dispname.exe"
menuItemObj.MiniHelp = "Display the name of the currently selected
Âobject."
'Change the current menus to the custom one
appVisio.SetCustomMenus UIObj
End Sub
```

Menus

Figure 19.2 illustrates the structure of the menu items within Visio's object model hierarchy. You will notice that this structure is similar in concept to all of the remaining objects within the object model. Collections contain items and a property of an item is the collection below it.

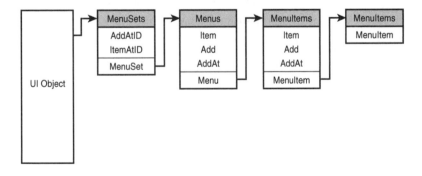

FIGURE 19.2
Menu items in the Visio object model.

Listing 19.2 is a skeleton code framework for accessing menu items.

19

CUSTOMIZING THE
VISIO USER INTERFACE
UNDER AUTOMATION

LISTING 19.2 Accessing a Menu Item

```
Public Sub AccessAWeeMenueItem()
    Dim UIObj As Visio.UIObject
    Dim MenuSetsObj As Visio.MenuSets
    Dim MenuSetObj As Visio.MenuSet
    Dim MenusObj As Visio.MenuItems
    Dim MenuObj As Visio.Menu
    Dim MenuItemObj As Visio.MenuItem
    Set UIObj = Visio.Application.BuiltInMenus
    Set MenuSetsObj = UIObj.MenuSets
    Set MenuSetObj = MenuSetsObj.ItemAtID(visUIObjSetDrawing)
    Set MenusObj = MenuSetObj.Menus
    Set MenuObj = MenusObj.Item(6)
    Set MenuItemObj = MenuObj.MenuItems.Add
        ' <make modifications>
    Visio.Application.SetCustomMenus UIObj
End Sub
```

Table 19.1 lists the properties of a menu item that may be of interest to you as a programmer. Each of these properties should be set from within your code when developing custom menus for your application.

TABLE 19.1 Properties of a MenuItem Object

Caption	Text that appears in the menu
CmdNum	The Visio constant for the command to be executed
MiniHelp	Help string for the status line
ActionText	Undo/redo string
AddonName	Name of add-on to run (optional)
AddonArgs	Arguments to pass to the add-on (optional)

Keep in mind that an empty menu will not appear even if it has a caption. It must have at least one MenuItem. If you are going to set the AddOnName, set the command number to zero (0). To create a separator in a menu, add a MenuItem with all the fields in a default state. For a MenuItem to appear and not act as a separator, either CmdNum or AddonName must be set to non-default values. Remember to use the ampersand "&" immediately prior to the subject hotkey letter to enable the hotkey for the MenuItem.

Listing 19.3 is another example of creating a context menu (right-click) for all SmartShape symbols in the current diagram:

LISTING 19.3 Creating a Context Menu

```
Sub AddAWeeContextMenueItem()
        Dim appVisio      As Visio.Application 'The current instance of Visio
        Dim UIObj         As Visio.UIObject    'Contains the UI object for this
        Âinstance of Visio
        Dim menuSetsObj   As Visio.MenuSets    'MenuSets collection
        Dim menuSetObj    As Visio.MenuSet     'A MenuSet object
        Dim menusObj      As Visio.Menus       'Menus collection
        Dim menuObj       As Visio.Menu        'A Menu object
        Dim menuItemsObj  As Visio.MenuItems   'MenuItems collection
        Dim menuItemObj   As Visio.MenuItem    'A MenuItem object
        Set appVisio = Visio.Application
        Set UIObj = appVisio.BuiltInMenus
        'Set menuSetObj to the menu set for right mouse button menu, drawing
        Âwindow, object selected
        Set menuSetsObj = UIObj.MenuSets
        Set menuSetObj = menuSetsObj.ItemAtID(visUIObjSetCntx_DrawObjSel)
        'Get the first and only menu
        Set menusObj = menuSetObj.Menus
        Set menuObj = menusObj.Item(0)
        'Add a single menu item which opens the Shapesheet
        Set menuItemsObj = menuObj.MenuItems
        Set menuItemObj = menuItemsObj.AddAt(0)
        menuItemObj.Caption = "Open Shapesheet"
        menuItemObj.CmdNum = visCmdWindowShowShapeSheet
        'Add another empty menu item at index 1 to create a spacer.
        Set menuItemObj = menuItemsObj.AddAt(1)
        'Change the current menus to the custom one
        appVisio.SetCustomMenus UIObj
End Sub
```

Table 19.2 lists the properties of a toolbar item that may be of interest to you as a programmer. Each of these properties should be set from within your code when developing custom toolbars for your application.

A toolbar object has the following properties of interest:

TABLE 19.2 Properties of a Toolbar Object

CntrlType	visCtrlTypeBUTTON
CntrlID	visCtrlIDNew
IconFileName	"simple.ico"
CmdNum	0
AddOnName	"simple.exe"

19

Note that the IconFileName is a method and its syntax is

```
ToolBarItemObj.IconFileName("simple.ico")
```

Visio 2000 adds the ability to use a .DLL/.VSL filename as the argument to IconFileName. Like this

```
Tb.IconFileName("myaddon.vsl,3")
```

Notice the ,3 after the name of the file. This tells Visio to use the third icon defined in the .VSL as its icon file.

Toolbars

In many ways, toolbars are highly similar to menus. Figure 19.3 is the object model for the toolbars.

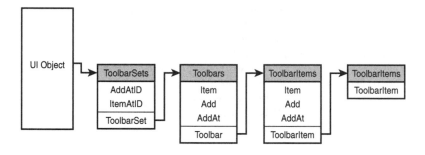

FIGURE 19.3

Toolbars in the Visio object model.

The important distinction to keep in mind here is that the set of IDs used to index ToolBarSets is different than that for MenuSets.

Listing 19.4 is a skeleton code framework for accessing toolbar items:

LISTING 19.4 Accessing a Toolbar Item

```
Public Sub AccessAWeeToolbarItem()
    Dim UIObj As Visio.UIObject
    Dim ToolbarSetsObj As Visio.ToolbarSets
    Dim ToolbarSetObj As Visio.ToolbarSet
    Dim ToolbarObj As Visio.Toolbar
    Dim ToolbarItemObj As Visio.ToolbarItem
    Set ToolbarSetsObj = UIObj.ToolbarSets
    Set ToolbarSetObj = ToolbarSetsObj.ItemAtID(visUIObjSetDrawing)
```

```
        Set ToolbarObj = ToolbarSetObj.Toolbars.Item(0)
        Set ToolbarItemObj = ToolbarObj.ToolbarItems.Add
            ' <make modifications>
        Visio.Application.SetCustomMenus UIObj
    End Sub
```

This is a thoroughly commented example of a minimalist UI context that is bound to the Visio application. This creates a single menu, the File menu, with two menu items only, Open and Exit, with a separator between them. It additionally creates a minimalist toolbar with three buttons: a single button to launch the simple.exe application and a paired state button set that toggles between the Pencil tool and the Pointer tool.

> ## CAUTION
>
> Read through and study the example in Listing 19.5, but *do not run it*. It binds this minimalist environment to the Visio application. To rid yourself of this environment, you will need to run the ClearUI.EXE application *and* delete the external UI file.

LISTING 19.5   Binding a Menu File to Visio the Application

```
Option Explicit
Sub JustReadDoNotExecute()
'Exercise 3: add a toolbar button.
Dim UIObj        As Visio.UIObject        'contains the UI object for this
⮞instance of Visio
Dim appVisio     As Visio.Application      'The instance of Visio created by
⮞this program
Dim MenuSetsObj  As Visio.MenuSets         'MenuSets collection
Dim MenuSetObj   As Visio.MenuSet          'A MenuSet object
Dim MenusObj     As Visio.Menus            'Menus collection
Dim MenuObj      As Visio.Menu             'A Menu object
Dim MenuItemsObj As Visio.MenuItems        'MenuItems collection
Dim MenuItemObj  As Visio.MenuItem         'A MenuItem object
Dim ToolbarSetsObj  As Visio.ToolbarSets   'ToolbarSets collection
Dim ToolbarSetObj   As Visio.ToolbarSet    'A ToolbarSet object
Dim ToolbarsObj     As Visio.Toolbars      'Toolbars collection
Dim ToolbarObj      As Visio.Toolbar       'A Toolbar object
Dim ToolbarItemsObj As Visio.ToolbarItems  'ToolbarItems collection
Dim ToolbarItemObj  As Visio.ToolbarItem   'A ToolbarItem object
'Create a UI object outside of Visio
    Set UIObj = CreateObject("Visio.UIobject")
'Add one menu set for the drawing context.
```

continues

LISTING 19.5 Continued

```
    UIObj.Name = "Visio Custom Menus"
'Put a single menu into this set, with caption "&File"
    Set MenuSetsObj = UIObj.MenuSets
    Set MenuSetObj = MenuSetsObj.AddAtID(visUIObjSetDrawing)
    Set MenusObj = MenuSetObj.Menus
    Set MenuObj = MenusObj.Add
    MenuObj.Caption = "&File"
'Insert three menu items: &Open..., separator, and  E&xit.
    Set MenuItemsObj = MenuObj.MenuItems
'the template for adding an individual item is:
'    Set MenuItemObj = MenuItemsObj.Add
'    MenuItemObj.Caption = "<text for menu item>"
'    MenuItemObj.CmdNum = <cmd constant from visconst.bas>
'    MenuItemObj.MiniHelp = "<text for minihelp>"
'    MenuItemObj.ActionText = "<text for undo/redo>"
'Set the CmdNum to 0 to get a separator.
Set MenuItemObj = MenuItemsObj.Add
    MenuItemObj.Caption = "&Open..."
    MenuItemObj.CmdNum = visCmdFileOpen
    MenuItemObj.MiniHelp = "Open an existing document."
    MenuItemObj.ActionText = "Open"
'Add a menuitem with CmdNum = 0 as a separator
    Set MenuItemObj = MenuItemsObj.Add
    MenuItemObj.CmdNum = 0
Set MenuItemObj = MenuItemsObj.Add
    MenuItemObj.Caption = "E&xit"
    MenuItemObj.CmdNum = visCmdFileExit
    MenuItemObj.MiniHelp = "Quit Visio."
'Add an empty toolbar set to the drawing context.
    Set ToolbarSetsObj = UIObj.ToolbarSets
    Set ToolbarSetObj = ToolbarSetsObj.AddAtID(visUIObjSetDrawing)
'Add one toolbar to the set
    Set ToolbarsObj = ToolbarSetObj.Toolbars
    Set ToolbarObj = ToolbarsObj.Add
'Add a button which will run simple.exe, use "simple.ico"
    Set ToolbarItemsObj = ToolbarObj.ToolbarItems
    Set ToolbarItemObj = ToolbarItemsObj.Add
    ToolbarItemObj.CntrlType = visCtrlTypeBUTTON
    ToolbarItemObj.CntrlID = visCtrlIDNEW
    ToolbarItemObj.IconFileName (ActiveDocument.Path & "add-ons\simple.ico")
    ToolbarItemObj.CmdNum = 0
    ToolbarItemObj.AddOnName = "Simple.exe"
    ToolbarItemObj.ActionText = "Run simple"
'Add a state button which will allow the user to draw with the pencil tool
'Put it in the same group as the next button to allow the user to choose
```

```
' either the pencil tool or the pointer tool
    Set ToolbarItemObj = ToolbarItemsObj.Add
    ToolbarItemObj.CntrlType = visCtrlTypeSTATE_BUTTON
    ToolbarItemObj.CntrlID = visCtrlIDPENCILTOOL
    ToolbarItemObj.CmdNum = visCmdDRPencilTool
'For a STATE_BUTTON, TypeSpecific1 contains the visIconIX value
    ToolbarItemObj.TypeSpecific1 = visIconIXPENCILTOOL
    ToolbarItemObj.TypeSpecific2 = 2
    ToolbarItemObj.Spacing = visCtrlSpacingFIXED_BEFORE
'Add a state button which will allow the user to use the pointer tool.
'Put it in the same group as the pencil tool button.
    Set ToolbarItemObj = ToolbarItemsObj.Add
    ToolbarItemObj.CntrlType = visCtrlTypeSTATE_BUTTON
    ToolbarItemObj.CntrlID = visCtrlIDPOINTERTOOL
    ToolbarItemObj.CmdNum = visCmdDRPointerTool
'For a BUTTON, TypeSpecific1 contains the visIconIX value
    ToolbarItemObj.TypeSpecific1 = visIconIXPOINTERTOOL
    ToolbarItemObj.TypeSpecific2 = 2
'Save the UIObj to a file.
    UIObj.SaveToFile ("c:\minmenus.vsu")
'Attach the UI to Visio, quit Visio.
    Set appVisio = Visio.Application
    appVisio.CustomMenusFile = "c:\minmenus.vsu"
    appVisio.CustomToolbarsFile = "c:\minmenus.vsu"
End Sub
```

Using External UI Files

Now that you are concerned about binding to the application object, let's take a moment to discuss how different bindings work and how you can create, save, and load external interface files.

To create a UI object outside of Visio, use the following:

```
Dim UIObj As Object
```

```
Set UIObj = CreateObject("Visio.UIObject")
```

This creates an EMPTY UIObject. This is a good way to build minimal UIs.

Saving a UI object to a file is accomplished by the following:

```
UIObj.SaveToFile("c:\visio\solutions\mymenues.vsu")
```

Loading a UI object from a file is done by

```
UIObj.LoadFromFile("c:\visio\solutions\mymenues.vsu")
```

Binding a UI object to the Visio application is done by

```
AppVisio.CustomToolbarsFile = "c:\visio\solutions\mytools.vsu"
```

Binding a UI object to a Visio document is done by

```
docObj.CustomToolbarsFile = "c:\visio\solutions\mytools.vsu"
```

The binding designations are stored in the Windows registry file. As stated before, if you bind to the application, you may have to run the ClearUI.EXE application *and* delete the external UI file, as well as delete the applicable entry in the Windows registry file. Keep in mind that Windows 95 has a nasty habit of caching the registry settings it creates. You may need to reboot to be sure that all is clear.

The Visio UI is indeed fully customizable. You are free to create your own UI at any point in time. Keep in mind that your users may be using not only *your* solution, but may well be using Visio to create many other diagram types. Consider your users first when making decisions on customizing the user interface.

In the next chapter, you will begin to look at using ActiveX automation to create interactions between Visio and other COM/ActiveX-enabled applications. You will also read about other automation and object models. Objects, properties, methods, and events will be discussed further, as will the VBA integrated development environment and browsing an object model. All of this is a precursor to learning about Visio's interaction with Microsoft Office applications in Chapters 21 through 26.

Visio Development with Microsoft Office 2000 and other VBA-Enabled Applications

IN THIS PART

Using Visio to Interact with VBA-Enabled Applications

IN THIS CHAPTER

As I have stated before, the key to automation programming is working with an application's object model. VBA is a programming language, and as such, it can be written to perform mathematical calculations, manipulate strings, and make logic decisions and iterations. But without an object model to operate against an automation language, be it C, C++, or VB, VBA does little more than calculations and the displaying of dialog boxes. It is only when VBA begins to manipulate an application's objects that you begin to sense the sheer power and elegance of automation application programming.

What then is an object model? An object model is a hierarchical structure of the objects within an application. It is a "tree," if you will (see Figure 20.1). The root of the tree is most generally the application object or sometimes the global object accessible via the application object. One of the properties of the application object is the documents collection object (in the case of Multiple Document Interface (MDI) applications), or the document object (in the case of Single Document Interface (SDI) applications). In an object model, this is the first "branch" of the tree. If the application is an MDI application, as are all of the Microsoft Office applications, the documents collection object then itself has a property that is the document object property. An additional property could be the count property. The document object would be the next branch of the tree, as it cascades out from the root.

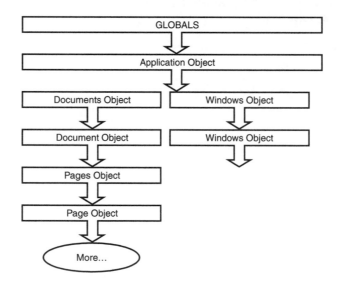

FIGURE 20.1
An object hierarchy tree.

By traversing the object model, looking at the objects in the model and understanding each object's properties, methods, and events as they apply to the application itself, you can begin to understand how the automation interface can be programmed. As if you might not have already figured this out, another basic (excuse the pun) requirement for automation application programming is a solid understanding of how to actually use the application. For example, if you understand how to use your mouse to select a range of cells in Excel, apply a particular formatting to them, select another range of cells, and then sum them to generate a total formula for the cells, either to the right or below that range, you will have a much easier time working with an automation application that seeks to imitate the same functionality via accessing the application's objects and their inherent properties, methods, and events.

Objects, Properties, Methods, and Events

What then is an object? Numerous definitions have been proffered as to the meaning of an object. One I recently read stated that "An object is a named unit within a program that possesses both data and code that acts on that data. An object is said to encapsulate the data and the related code." This is a wee bit like stating that an object is an object. It is true, but it certainly does not assist you in gaining any understanding.

Let's try a different approach. Begin by thinking of yourself as an object. I know that in today's politically correct climate you are not supposed to objectify anyone, but you can make an exception this one time. As an object, you have properties, which are those things that describe you. You have eyes. Those eyes are blue. See? You just traversed an object model here. The root object is you the person.

A property of the person is the eyes collection object. A property of the eyes collection object is the item property and another is the count property. For each item in the eyes collection is a valid count of 1 to 2. The eye object has properties as well. A property of the eye is color. In this case, the color property has a value of blue. Other notable properties of you, the person object, are the hair collection object, the legs collection object, the arms collection object, the ears collection object... you get the point. A property is some feature of an object that can be queried and, in many cases, changed, such as in the case of hair color in the hair collection object of the person object.

A method of the person object might be walk. The walk method is called via the application and is then executed. A person object has many methods such as look, hear, see, smell, and touch. A method is an action that the application can perform when called by your automation application program.

An event is something that happens to the object and that sends out a notification that this event is either about to happen or that it just happened. In the case of our person object, an event might be the fall event. The fall event might actually be broken down (sub-classed) into two differing types of fall events: the BeforeFallOccurs event and the IveFallen event. In the case of the BeforeFallOccurs event, the person object may call an ExtendArm method. In the case of the IveFallenEvent, the person object may call some form of vocalization method, passing it the string "Ouch."

I believe you get the point here. An object is a member of an object model, a hierarchical tree of objects. Each object has properties, methods, and events that are associated with it. An automation application program makes use of these objects, properties, methods, and events to manipulate the application and automate its functionality, as well as enable it to pass information to and receive information from other applications that are automation-enabled.

The VBA Integrated Development Environment

When applications first began to expose methodologies for automating themselves, each had its own proprietary programming or "macro" language. Some were at least fairly robust; some were all but abysmal. A programmer had to learn each separate language to manipulate each application. Finally, Microsoft introduced a true viable VBA, Visual Basic for Applications. This brought about not only a common programming language, but, equally as important, a common programming interface. The Visual Basic for Applications Integrated Development Environment (VBA IDE) is a unified programming environment shared by every VBA-enabled application. This is important because once you have learned how to navigate about in the IDE for any one application, you can immediately go to any other application's VBA IDE and be instantly productive. The only things you will need to master to automate that application is an understanding of what that application does and the structure of that application's object model.

Browsing an Object Model

When you are within an application's VBA IDE (usually launched by pressing Alt+F11) and you press F2, you launch the object browser. In the upper-right corner of the object browser window, you will find a drop-down list. This is the Project/Library list box. By default, this lists <All Libraries> as the selection. This means that the information shown in the Classes list at the left of the object browser and the Members of Class list at the right of the object browser are from all attached libraries and object models, as set in the References dialog box. To begin understanding the object model for any given VBA-enabled application, you should limit the listing to that application's object model. This is done by selecting that object model from the Project/Library list box.

The Classes list will now display only the objects for that application. As you select an object, say, the application object, you will see members of that particular class object displayed. Selecting a member of that class will display details about that member in the details pane at the bottom of the object browser. This shows you whether it is a property (the small hand holding a property sheet), a method (a smell green brick being thrown), or an event (a small yellow lightning bolt). Additional items include constants and classes. The details pane shows you the syntax for that item's usage as well as of which class it is a member. To obtain help about that particular item, press F1 and a help browser will be launched to give you full assistance in understanding that item. This help is contingent upon the software author's help implementation. Both Visio and Microsoft have taken great care to create quality, robust, and example-rich help for all items in their help systems.

Right-clicking any item in the Members of Class area will also enable you to copy that item to the clipboard. You can then return to your code window and paste that item in it. Because it details the framework and syntax, it should be much easier and far less prone to typos in your code.

The next series of chapters are designed to show you how to write applications that enable Visio to communicate with Microsoft Office applications.

In the next chapter, you will learn how to contact Excel from Visio. You will learn how to send data from Visio to Excel and retrieve information from Excel to use in Visio. You will also learn how to query Excel for use in your Visio-based application and learn how to sever the connection when you are finished with the communication.

Visio Automation and Microsoft Excel 2000 Interaction

IN THIS CHAPTER

As we saw with Visio earlier, there are three methods for contacting Excel from within Visio: `GetObject()`, `CreateObject()`, and `New`. The first of these presumes that Excel is already up and running. The second and third assume nothing and will launch a new copy of Excel, even if it is already running. Listing 21.1 is the syntax.

LISTING 21.1 Accessing the Excel Application

```
Public Sub RunExcel1()
        Dim excelApp As Excel.Application
        Set excelApp = GetObject("Excel.Application")
        excelObj.Visable = True
End Sub
Public Sub RunExcel2()
        Dim excelApp As Excel.Application
        Set excelApp = CreateObject("Excel.Application")
        excelObj.Visable = True
End Sub
Public Sub RunExcel3()
        Dim excelApp As New Excel.Application
        Set excelApp = Excel.Application
        excelObj.Visable = True
End Sub
```

Again, as with Visio, you may want to test if Excel is already running and which Workbook is open prior to launching a new instance if you want to access the current one. Use the proper syntax for currently running or not yet running as applicable.

Sending Data to Excel

Once you have a reference to the Excel application, you need to get a reference to the Workbooks collection object.

```
Dim xlObjBooks As Excel.Workbooks
Set xlObjBooks = excelApp.Workbooks
```

With that accomplished, you need to get a reference to the Workbook object. This will differ depending upon if Excel is already running or if you launched a new instance. If Excel is already running, you can get a reference to the Workbook object by naming the workbook as in

```
Dim xlObjBook As Excel.Workbook
Set xlObjBook = xlObjBooks. Item("TestCase.XLS")
```

or you can get a reference to the Workbook object by referencing the workbook by its index as in

```
Dim xlObjBook As Excel.Workbook
Set xlObjBook = xlObjBooks. Item(1)
```

Visio Automation and Microsoft Excel 2000 Interaction

CHAPTER 21

395

21

VISIO AUTOMATION
AND MICROSOFT
EXCEL 2000
INTERACTION

If Excel is not already running, you can get a reference to the Workbook object by using the Add method of the Workbooks collection object as in

```
Dim xlObjBook As Excel.Workbook
Set xlObjBook = xlObjBooks.Add
```

Now that you have a reference to the workbook, you can obtain a reference to the Worksheet object by name or index as in

```
Dim xlObjSheet As Excel.Worksheet
Set xlObjSheet = xlObjBook.Worksheets.Item("Sheet1")
```

or

```
Dim xlObjSheet As Excel.Worksheet
Set xlObjSheet = xlObjBook.Worksheets.Item(1)
```

Now that you have a reference to the subject Worksheet, you can obtain a reference to any cell and send it data as follows:

```
Dim xlObjCell As Excel.Range
Set xlObjCell = xlObjSheet.Range("C3")
xlObjCell.Select
```

Then send the information to the cell as follows:

```
xlObjCell. FormulaR1C1 = "Some text"
```

or

```
xlObjCell. Value = 32.75
```

You can also use a larger range to format, for example, by specifying the entire range as follows:

```
Set xlObjCell = xlObjSheet.Range("A2:D2")
xlObjCell.Select
```

Getting Data from Excel

To access the information in an Excel cell, use the Value property of the cell object and store the result in a variable or pass it directly to Visio as in Listing 21.2.

LISTING 21.2 Getting an Excel Cell's Value

```
Public Sub GrabFromExcel()
    Dim shpObj As Visio.Shape
    Dim celObj As Visio.Cell
    Dim xlObjApp As Excel.Application
    Dim xlObjBook As Excel.Workbook
```

continues

LISTING 21.2 Continued

```
    Dim xlObjSheet As Excel.Worksheet
    Dim xlObjCell As Excel.Range
    Set shpObj = Visio.ActiveWindow.Selection.Item(1)
    Set celObj = shpObj.Cells("Prop.Duration")
    Set xlObjApp = GetObject(, "Excel.Application")
    Set xlObjBook = xlObjApp.Workbooks.Item("TestCase.XLS")
    Set xlObjSheet = xlObjBook.Worksheets.Item("Sheet1")
    Set xlObjCell = xlObjSheet.Range("C3")
    xlObjCell.Select
    celObj.Formula = xlObjCell.Value
End Sub
```

Querying Excel for Visio's Use

Here is an example of sending information to an Excel spreadsheet that is an inventory of all
the furnishings in an executive office. Each Visio SmartShape symbol used as a furniture item
has a custom property "Inventory." Only those items that have this property are passed to
Excel. The application is launched via an ActiveX control on the Visio page. This example can
be found on the companion CD-ROM as OfficeExcel Ch21,VSD.

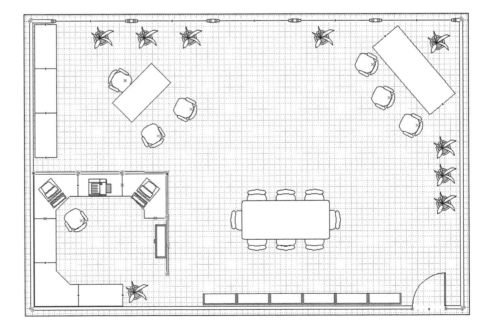

FIGURE 21.1
Executive office drawing.

LISTING 21.3 Passing Data to Excel

```
Private Sub CommandButton1_Click()
    Call RunInventoryToExcel
End Sub
Public Sub RunInventoryToExcel()
    Dim szMessageString As String
    Dim intMessageFlags As Integer
    Dim intRetVal As Integer
    szMessageString = "Do you want to Inventory this Executive Office in
Excel?"
    intMessageFlags = vbQuestion + vbYesNo
    intRetVal = MsgBox(szMessageString, intMessageFlags, "Demonstration")

    If intRetVal = vbYes Then
    'declare variables and data type them
    Dim pagObj As Visio.Page
    Dim colObj As Visio.Shapes
    Dim intTotSymbols As Integer
    Dim intCounter As Integer
    Dim shpObjItem As Visio.Shape
    Dim intRowCounter As Integer
    Dim intColCounter As Integer
    Dim celObjPropInventory As Visio.Cell
    Dim celObjPropOwner As Visio.Cell
    Dim celObjPropCost As Visio.Cell
    Dim ExcelApp As Excel.Application
    Dim ExcelWorkbook As Excel.Workbook
    Dim ExcelSheet As Excel.Worksheet
    Dim szExcelRangeStr As String
    ' find the total number of symbols on the page
    Set pagObj = Visio.ActivePage
    Set colObj = pagObj.Shapes
    intTotSymbols = colObj.Count
    'launch Excel and get active worksheet
    Set ExcelApp = CreateObject("Excel.Application")
    ExcelApp.Application.Visible = True
    Set ExcelWorkbook = ExcelApp.Workbooks.Add
    Set ExcelSheet = ExcelWorkbook.Worksheets("Sheet1")
    'do the pretty work for the headers
    Excel.ActiveCell.FormulaR1C1 = "Executive Office Inventory"
    Range("A2").Select
    ActiveCell.FormulaR1C1 = "Item Name"
    Range("B2").Select
    ActiveCell.FormulaR1C1 = "Inventory Number"
    Range("C2").Select
    ActiveCell.FormulaR1C1 = "Owner"
```

continues

LISTING 21.3 Continued

```
Range("D2").Select
ActiveCell.FormulaR1C1 = "Item Cost"
Range("A2:D2").Select
With Selection
    .HorizontalAlignment = xlCenter
    .VerticalAlignment = xlCenter
    .WrapText = False
    .Orientation = 0
    .ShrinkToFit = False
    .MergeCells = False
End With
With Selection.Font
    .Name = "Arial"
    .FontStyle = "Bold"
    .Size = 12
    .Strikethrough = False
    .Superscript = False
    .Subscript = False
    .OutlineFont = False
    .Shadow = False
    .Underline = xlUnderlineStyleNone
    .ColorIndex = 2
End With
Selection.Borders(xlDiagonalDown).LineStyle = xlNone
Selection.Borders(xlDiagonalUp).LineStyle = xlNone
Selection.Borders(xlEdgeLeft).LineStyle = xlNone
Selection.Borders(xlEdgeTop).LineStyle = xlNone
With Selection.Borders(xlEdgeBottom)
    .LineStyle = xlContinuous
    .Weight = xlThin
    .ColorIndex = xlAutomatic
End With
Selection.Borders(xlEdgeRight).LineStyle = xlNone
Selection.Borders(xlInsideVertical).LineStyle = xlNone
With Selection.Interior
    .ColorIndex = 25
    .Pattern = xlSolid
    .PatternColorIndex = xlAutomatic
End With
Selection.Columns.AutoFit
Range("A1:D1").Select
With Selection
    .HorizontalAlignment = xlCenterAcrossSelection
    .VerticalAlignment = xlTop
    .WrapText = False
```

Visio Automation and Microsoft Excel 2000 Interaction

CHAPTER 21

399

21

VISIO AUTOMATION
AND MICROSOFT
EXCEL 2000
INTERACTION

```
        .Orientation = 0
        .ShrinkToFit = False
        .MergeCells = False
End With
With Selection.Font
        .Name = "Arial"
        .FontStyle = "Bold"
        .Size = 18
        .Strikethrough = False
        .Superscript = False
        .Subscript = False
        .OutlineFont = False
        .Shadow = False
        .Underline = xlUnderlineStyleNone
        .ColorIndex = xlAutomatic
End With
'Check the data in Visio and hand off to Excel
intRowCounter = 1
For intCounter = 1 To intTotSymbols
        Set shpObjItem = colObj.Item(intCounter)
        If shpObjItem.CellExists("Prop.Inventory", 0) = True Then
                Set celObjPropInventory = shpObjItem.Cells("Prop.Inventory")
                Set celObjPropOwner = shpObjItem.Cells("Prop.Owner")
                Set celObjPropCost = shpObjItem.Cells("Prop.Cost")
                ExcelSheet.Cells(intRowCounter + 2, 1).Value = shpObjItem.Name
                ExcelSheet.Cells(intRowCounter + 2, 2).Value =
                ➥celObjPropInventory.Formula
                ExcelSheet.Cells(intRowCounter + 2, 3).Value =
                ➥celObjPropOwner.Formula
                ExcelSheet.Cells(intRowCounter + 2, 4).Value =
                ➥celObjPropCost.Result(visNumber)
                intRowCounter = intRowCounter + 1
        End If
Next intCounter
'format Cost column for currency
szExcelRangeStr = "D3:D" & intRowCounter + 4
Range(szExcelRangeStr).Select
Selection.NumberFormat = "$#,##0.00"
'Sum the Cost of the Inventory
szExcelRangeStr = "D" & intRowCounter + 2
Range(szExcelRangeStr).Select
szExcelRangeStr = "=SUM(R[-" & intRowCounter & "]C:R[-1]C)"
ActiveCell.FormulaR1C1 = szExcelRangeStr
With Selection.Font
        .Name = "Arial"
        .FontStyle = "Bold"
```

continues

LISTING 21.3   Continued

```
            .Size = 11
            .Strikethrough = False
            .Superscript = False
            .Subscript = False
            .OutlineFont = False
            .Shadow = False
            .Underline = xlUnderlineStyleNone
            .ColorIndex = 30
        End With
        Selection.Borders(xlDiagonalDown).LineStyle = xlNone
        Selection.Borders(xlDiagonalUp).LineStyle = xlNone
        Selection.Borders(xlEdgeLeft).LineStyle = xlNone
        With Selection.Borders(xlEdgeTop)
            .LineStyle = xlContinuous
            .Weight = xlThin
            .ColorIndex = xlAutomatic
        End With
        Selection.Borders(xlEdgeBottom).LineStyle = xlNone
        Selection.Borders(xlEdgeRight).LineStyle = xlNone
        ' finally fit the widths properly
        szExcelRangeStr = "A2:D" & intRowCounter + 4
        Range(szExcelRangeStr).Select
        Selection.Columns.AutoFit
            Else
            szMessageString = "Visio Will Not Inventory this Executive Office in
            ➥ Excel as this time."
            MsgBox szMessageString, vbInformation, "Demonstration"
        End If
End Sub
```

A lot of what you see in the above code is there only to format the Excel cells and make the Excel worksheet prettier. Additionally, you will see that a summation of the cost cells has been accomplished and that summation cell is formatted as well.

Severing the Connection

To terminate the connection between Visio and Excel, you simply need to quit Excel as in

```
xlObjApplication.Quit
Set xlObjApplication = Nothing
```

The final line ensures that the Excel application object goes out of scope and is removed from memory as well as all objects under the application object

In the next chapter, you will learn how to contact Access from Visio. You will learn how to send data from Visio to Access and retrieve information from Access to use in Visio. You will also learn how to query Access for use in your Visio-based application and learn how to sever the connection when you are finished with the communication.

21

VISIO AUTOMATION
AND MICROSOFT
EXCEL 2000
INTERACTION

Visio Automation and Microsoft Access 2000 Interaction

IN THIS CHAPTER

As we saw with Visio earlier, contacting Access from within Visio can be done using `GetObject()`, `CreateObject()`, and `New`. The first of these presumes that Access is already up and running. The second and third assume nothing and will launch a new copy of Access, even if it is already running. Listing 22.1 shows the syntax.

LISTING 22.1   Launching Access

```
Public Sub RunAccess1()
        Dim accessApp As Access.Application
        Set accessApp = GetObject(,"Access.Application")
        accessObj.Visable = True
End Sub
Public Sub RunAccess2()
        Dim accessApp As Access.Application
        Set accessApp = CreateObject("Access.Application")
        accessObj.Visable = True
End Sub
Public Sub RunAccess3()
        Dim accessApp As New Access.Application
        Set accessApp = Access.Application
        accessObj.Visable = True
End Sub
```

Again, as with Visio, you may want to test if Access is already running and which database is open prior to launching a new instance if you want to access the current one. Use the proper syntax for currently running or not yet running as applicable.

Though this methodology will give you an entrance to Access itself, there is a faster and more direct entrance to the data that resides in an Access database. That methodology is through the Data Access Object (DAO) and this is the route I will describe in this chapter. Keep in mind that the code examples that follow are all very much dependent upon one another and should not be run as separate bits without the assistance of the others. Please refer to the entire code structure as developed in the ProOfficeEquip.VST file on the companion CD-ROM.

To open a communications channel to an already established Access database through DAO so that you can begin accessing the data in the database's tables, records, and fields, you need to use the OpenDatabase method of the DatabaseEngine object.

```
Public g_dbsMyDatabase As DAO.Database
Public g_szDBFileName As String
Public Sub GoAheadAndOpenTheDatabase()
        'Open the database non-exclusive
        g_szDBFileName = "c:\somedirectory\somedatabase.mdb"
        Set g_dbsMyDatabase = dbEngine.OpenDatabase(g_szDBFileName, False)
End Sub
```

You may choose to use the Windows Common dialog box for files to enable the user to select the database to reference. Binding the return from this search to a global variable typed as a string will make it accessible to your application for the opening process.

If the database you want to interact with has not yet been created, you will need to create the database, create the table and field definitions, and then re-open the database to access the data. This is done as follows in Listing 22.2.

LISTING 22.2   Creating a Database Using DAO

```
Public g_dbsMyDatabase As DAO.Database
Public g_szDBFileName As String
Global Const g_szDefFileName$ = "c:\somedirectory\somedatabase.mdb"
Global Const g_szFieldGUID$ = "ItemID"
Global Const g_szIndexName$ = "ItemIndex"
Public Sub GoAheadAndCreateTheDatabase()
        'Table definition
        Dim tdfsMyTableDefs As DAO.TableDefs 'The tables in the new database
        Dim tdfMyTableDef As DAO.TableDef   'A table in the new database
        Dim fldsMyFields As DAO.Fields      'The fields in the table
        Dim fldMyField As DAO.Field         'A field in the fields collection
        Dim idxMyIndex As DAO.Index         'An index for tdfMyTableDef
        Dim fldMyIndexField As DAO.Field    'A field in the index
        'Create the database
        Set g_dbsMyDatabase = dbEngine.CreateDatabase(g_szDBFileName,
        ➡dbLangGeneral)
        Set tdfsMyTableDefs = g_dbsMyDatabase.TableDefs
        'Create the table
        Set tdfMyTableDef = g_dbsMyDatabase.CreateTableDef(g_szTableName)
        Set fldsMyFields = tdfMyTableDef.Fields
        'Add the ItemID field
        Set fldMyField = tdfMyTableDef.CreateField(g_szFieldGUID, dbText, 50)
        fldMyField.AllowZeroLength = False
        fldMyField.Required = True
        fldsMyFields.Append fldMyField
        'Create an index & make ItemID the primary key
        Set idxMyIndex = tdfMyTableDef.CreateIndex(g_szIndexName)
        Set fldMyIndexField = idxMyIndex.CreateField(g_szFieldGUID)
        idxMyIndex.Fields.Append fldMyIndexField
        idxMyIndex.Primary = True
        idxMyIndex.Required = True
        idxMyIndex.Unique = True
        tdfMyTableDef.Indexes.Append idxMyIndex
        tdfsMyTableDefs.Append tdfMyTableDef
        'Close the database & open it non-exclusive so we can show it next
```

continues

22

VISIO AUTOMATION
AND MICROSOFT
ACCESS 2000
INTERACTION

LISTING 22.2   Continued

```
        'to our Visio diagram
        g_dbsMyDatabase.Close
        Set g_dbsMyDatabase = dbEngine.OpenDatabase(g_szDBFileName, False)
End Sub
```

Sending Data to Access

With the communication channel now open to the database, you can now send data from a Visio diagram to an Access database via the channel using DAO as in Listing 22.3.

LISTING 22.3   Sending Data from a Diagram to Acess via DAO

```
Public g_dbsMyDatabase As DAO.Database
Public g_szDBFileName As String
Public g_bTrack As Boolean
Global Const g_szDefFileName$ = "d:\MyDatabase.mdb"
Global Const g_nFileNotFound% = &HFFFFFFFF
Global Const g_szTableName$ = "Item"
Global Const g_szFieldCost$ = "ItemCost"
Global Const g_szFieldName$ = "ItemName"
Global Const g_szFieldGUID$ = "ItemID"
Global Const g_szUserFileName$ = "User.DBFileName"
Global Const g_szUserTrack$ = "User.Track"
Global Const g_szPropTrack$ = "Prop.Track"
Global Const g_szPropName$ = "Prop.Name"
Global Const g_szPropCost$ = "Prop.Cost"
Global Const g_szIndexName$ = "ItemIndex"
'   Event:  Shape Added
'   Action: Add a record to the database representing this shape
Private Sub Document_ShapeAdded(ByVal vShape As Visio.IVShape)
        Dim vCell As Visio.Cell 'A cell in the new shape
        Dim szGUID As String    'The unique identifier of the new shape
        Dim szName As String    'The name of the item the shape represents
        Dim cyCost As Currency  'The cost of the item the shape represents
        Dim rstMyRecordset As DAO.Recordset 'A record in the tracking table
        'Add a new record
        Set rstMyRecordset = g_dbsMyDatabase.OpenRecordset(g_szTableName)
        rstMyRecordset.AddNew
        'Set the ItemID
        szGUID = vShape.UniqueID(visGetOrMakeGUID)
        rstMyRecordset(g_szFieldGUID) = szGUID
        'Set the ItemName
        Set vCell = vShape.Cells(g_szPropName)
```

```
        szName = vCell.Formula
        'Strip quotes
        szName = Mid(szName, 2, (Len(szName) - 2))
        rstMyRecordset(g_szFieldName) = szName
        'Set the ItemCost
        Set vCell = vShape.Cells(g_szPropCost)
        cyCost = vCell.Result(visCurrency)
        rstMyRecordset(g_szFieldCost) = cyCost
        rstMyRecordset.Update
        rstMyRecordset.Close
End Sub
```

Note here that the AddNew method of the Recordset object has been called to add the new item. A simple assignment then passes the data to the appropriate field in the record from the Visio data. The Update method of the Recordset object, followed by the Close method of the Recordset object, is very important. Unless the Update method is called, any changes will not be recorded, and unless the Close method is called, no further access to that Recordset object is allowed.

Getting Data from Access

The process of retrieving information from a given Recordset is almost identical to sending it to the Recordset. The change is in the line

```
rstMyRecordset(g_szFieldName) = szName
```

where it then needs to be assigned in the opposite direction as

```
SzName = rstMyRecordset(g_szFieldName)
```

Querying Access for Visio's Use

Listing 22.4 shows a deletion process when items are deleted in Visio and they need to have the corresponding record deleted in the Access database.

LISTING 22.4   Deleting Database Records by Deleting Shapes in a Visio Diagram

```
Public g_dbsMyDatabase As DAO.Database
Public g_szDBFileName As String
Public g_bTrack As Boolean
Global Const g_szDefFileName$ = "d:\MyDatabase.mdb"
Global Const g_nFileNotFound% = &HFFFFFFFF
Global Const g_szTableName$ = "Item"
Global Const g_szFieldCost$ = "ItemCost"
```

continues

LISTING 22.4   Continued

```
Global Const g_szFieldName$ = "ItemName"
Global Const g_szFieldGUID$ = "ItemID"
Global Const g_szUserFileName$ = "User.DBFileName"
Global Const g_szUserTrack$ = "User.Track"
Global Const g_szPropTrack$ = "Prop.Track"
Global Const g_szPropName$ = "Prop.Name"
Global Const g_szPropCost$ = "Prop.Cost"
Global Const g_szIndexName$ = "ItemIndex"
'   Event:  Before Selection Delete
'   Action: Remove any references to the selected shape(s) in the database
Private Sub Document_BeforeSelectionDelete(ByVal vSelection As
➥Visio.IVSelection)
        Dim nCt As Integer                   'Total items in selection
        Dim nCur As Integer                  'Current item in selection
        Dim vShape As Visio.Shape            'A selected shape
        Dim szGUID As String                 'The selected shape's GUID
        Dim rstMyRecordset As DAO.Recordset  'A record in the database
        Set rstMyRecordset = g_dbsMyDatabase.OpenRecordset(g_szTableName)
        rstMyRecordset.Index = g_szIndexName
        nCt = vSelection.Count
        'Walk each item in the selection & delete any database references it
        For nCur = 1 To nCt Step 1
                Set vShape = vSelection.Item(nCur)
                szGUID = vShape.UniqueID(visGetGUID)
                If szGUID <> "" Then
                rstMyRecordset.Seek "=", szGUID
                If Not rstMyRecordset.NoMatch Then
                rstMyRecordset.Delete
                        End If
                End If
        Next
rstMyRecordset.Close
End Sub
```

Listing 22.5 shows the complete interaction between Visio and an Access database through DAO. In this example, when a new Visio diagram is created based upon the associated template, the OnDocumentCreate event triggers the creation of a new Access database. The OnDocumentOpen event opens the Access database through DAO to write records. The ShapeAdded event writes records for each Visio SmartShape symbol that has a User.Track cell set to a value of 1 for "trackable." Each time a shape is deleted, the BeforeSelectionDelete event looks to see if the SmartShape symbol is trackable, and if it is, the associated record in the database is deleted as well.

LISTING 22.5 Asset Tracking: Visio Diagram and Access Database Communication

```
Option Explicit

Public g_dbsMyDatabase As DAO.Database
Public g_szDBFileName As String
Public g_bTrack As Boolean

Global Const g_szDefFileName$ = "d:\MyDatabase.mdb"
Global Const g_nFileNotFound% = &HFFFFFFFF
Global Const g_szTableName$ = "Item"
Global Const g_szFieldCost$ = "ItemCost"
Global Const g_szFieldName$ = "ItemName"
Global Const g_szFieldGUID$ = "ItemID"
Global Const g_szUserFileName$ = "User.DBFileName"
Global Const g_szUserTrack$ = "User.Track"
Global Const g_szPropTrack$ = "Prop.Track"
Global Const g_szPropName$ = "Prop.Name"
Global Const g_szPropCost$ = "Prop.Cost"
Global Const g_szIndexName$ = "ItemIndex"
'''''''''''''''''''''''''''''
'   Event:  Click on "Browse..." button
'   Action: Show the OpenFile common dialog & get a file name
Private Sub Browse_Click()
OpenFile.Flags = cdlOFNPathMustExist
OpenFile.ShowOpen
FileName.Text = OpenFile.FileName
End Sub
'''''''''''''''''''''''''''''
'   Event:  Click on "Cancel" button
'   Action: Set the global track flag false & exit the dialog
Private Sub Cancel_Click()
g_bTrack = False
AccessFileDialog.Hide
End Sub
'''''''''''''''''''''''''''''
'   Event:  Click on "OK" button
'   Action: Set the global track flag true, set the global filename &
'           exit the dialog
Private Sub OK_Click()
g_bTrack = True
g_szDBFileName = FileName.Text
AccessFileDialog.Hide
End Sub
'''''''''''''''''''''''''''''
'   Event:  Before Selection Delete
```

22

VISIO AUTOMATION
AND MICROSOFT
ACCESS 2000
INTERACTION

continues

LISTING 22.5   Continued

```
'   Action: Remove any references to the selected shape(s) in the database
Private Sub Document_BeforeSelectionDelete(ByVal vSelection As
Visio.IVSelection)
Dim nCt As Integer                'Total items in selection
Dim nCur As Integer               'Current item in selection
Dim vShape As Visio.Shape         'A selected shape
Dim szGUID As String              'The selected shape's GUID
Dim rstMyRecordset As DAO.Recordset 'A record in the database

'Exit if we aren't tracking equipment
If g_bTrack = False Then
    Exit Sub
End If

Set rstMyRecordset = g_dbsMyDatabase.OpenRecordset(g_szTableName)
rstMyRecordset.Index = g_szIndexName

nCt = vSelection.Count

'Walk each item in the selection & delete any database references it
For nCur = 1 To nCt Step 1
    Set vShape = vSelection.Item(nCur)
    szGUID = vShape.UniqueID(visGetGUID)
    If szGUID <> "" Then
        rstMyRecordset.Seek "=", szGUID
        If Not rstMyRecordset.NoMatch Then
            rstMyRecordset.Delete
        End If
    End If
Next

rstMyRecordset.Close

End Sub


''''''''''''''''''''''''''''''''
'   Event:  Document Created
'   Action: Create a new database & store its name in a cell in the document
Private Sub Document_DocumentCreated(ByVal vDoc As Visio.IVDocument)
Dim vPages As Visio.Pages          'The pages in the new document
Dim vPage As Visio.Page            'The first page in the new document
Dim vSheet As Visio.Shape          'The page sheet
Dim vCell As Visio.Cell            'A cell in the page sheet
    'Table definition
```

```
Dim tdfsMyTableDefs As DAO.TableDefs 'The tables in the new dataabse
Dim tdfMyTableDef As DAO.TableDef    'A table in the new database
Dim fldsMyFields As DAO.Fields       'The fields in the table
Dim fldMyField As DAO.Field          'A field in the fields collection
Dim idxMyIndex As DAO.Index          'An index for tdfMyTableDef
Dim fldMyIndexField As DAO.Field     'A field in the index

'Get the Access file name from the user
AccessFileDialog.Show

'If the user canceled don't track equipment
Set vPages = vDoc.Pages
Set vPage = vPages.Item(1)
Set vSheet = vPage.PageSheet
Set vCell = vSheet.Cells(g_szUserTrack)
vCell.Result(visNumber) = g_bTrack

If g_bTrack = False Then
    Exit Sub
End If

'Save the filename in a user defined cell in the document
Set vCell = vSheet.Cells(g_szUserFileName)
'Add quotes & set the formula
vCell.Formula = "=" + """" + g_szDBFileName + """"

'Create the database
Set g_dbsMyDatabase = dbEngine.CreateDatabase(g_szDBFileName, dbLangGeneral)
Set tdfsMyTableDefs = g_dbsMyDatabase.TableDefs

'Create the table
Set tdfMyTableDef = g_dbsMyDatabase.CreateTableDef(g_szTableName)
Set fldsMyFields = tdfMyTableDef.Fields

'Add the ItemID field
Set fldMyField = tdfMyTableDef.CreateField(g_szFieldGUID, dbText, 50)
fldMyField.AllowZeroLength = False
fldMyField.Required = True
fldsMyFields.Append fldMyField

'Add the ItemName field
Set fldMyField = tdfMyTableDef.CreateField(g_szFieldName, dbText, 50)
fldsMyFields.Append fldMyField

'Add the ItemCost field
Set fldMyField = tdfMyTableDef.CreateField(g_szFieldCost, dbCurrency, 50)
```

continues

LISTING 22.5 Continued

```
fldsMyFields.Append fldMyField

'Create an index & make ItemID the primary key
Set idxMyIndex = tdfMyTableDef.CreateIndex(g_szIndexName)
Set fldMyIndexField = idxMyIndex.CreateField(g_szFieldGUID)
idxMyIndex.Fields.Append fldMyIndexField
idxMyIndex.Primary = True
idxMyIndex.Required = True
idxMyIndex.Unique = True
tdfMyTableDef.Indexes.Append idxMyIndex

tdfsMyTableDefs.Append tdfMyTableDef

'Close the database & open it non-exclusively so we can show it next
'to our Visio diagram
g_dbsMyDatabase.Close
Set g_dbsMyDatabase = dbEngine.OpenDatabase(g_szDBFileName, False)

End Sub
''''''''''''''''''''''''''''''''
'   Event:  Document Opened
'   Action: Open the database associated with this document
Private Sub Document_DocumentOpened(ByVal vDoc As Visio.IVDocument)
Dim vPages As Visio.Pages    'The pages in this document
Dim vPage As Visio.Page      'The first page in this document
Dim vSheet As Visio.Shape    'The page sheet
Dim vCell As Visio.Cell      'A cell in the page sheet

'See if we're tracking equipment
Set vPages = vDoc.Pages
Set vPage = vPages.Item(1)
Set vSheet = vPage.PageSheet
Set vCell = vSheet.Cells(g_szUserTrack)
g_bTrack = vCell.Result(visNumber)

'Exit if we aren't tracking equipment
If g_bTrack = False Then
    Exit Sub
End If

'Get the Access file name
Set vCell = vSheet.Cells(g_szUserFileName)
g_szDBFileName = vCell.Formula
'If there is no file name we have nothing to track
If g_szDBFileName = "" Then
```

```
        g_bTrack = False
        Exit Sub
End If
'Strip quotes from the formula, this is our file name
g_szDBFileName = Mid(g_szDBFileName, 2, (Len(g_szDBFileName) - 2))


'Open the database non-exclusive
Set g_dbsMyDatabase = dbEngine.OpenDatabase(g_szDBFileName, False)


End Sub
''''''''''''''''''''''''''''''
'   Event:  Shape Added
'   Action: Add a record to the database representing this shape
Private Sub Document_ShapeAdded(ByVal vShape As Visio.IVShape)
Dim vCell As Visio.Cell 'A cell in the new shape
Dim szGUID As String     'The unique identifier of the new shape
Dim szName As String     'The name of the item the shape represents
Dim cyCost As Currency  'The cost of the item the shape represents
Dim rstMyRecordset As DAO.Recordset 'A record in the tracking table


'Exit if we aren't tracking equipment
If g_bTrack = False Then
    Exit Sub
End If


'If the Track property is true for this shape add it to the database
If vShape.CellExists(g_szPropTrack, False) Then
    Set vCell = vShape.Cells(g_szPropTrack)
    If vCell.ResultInt(visNumber, 1) Then
        'Add a new record
        Set rstMyRecordset = g_dbsMyDatabase.OpenRecordset(g_szTableName)
        rstMyRecordset.AddNew

        'Set the ItemID
        szGUID = vShape.UniqueID(visGetOrMakeGUID)
        rstMyRecordset(g_szFieldGUID) = szGUID

        'Set the ItemName
        Set vCell = vShape.Cells(g_szPropName)
        szName = vCell.Formula
        'Strip quotes
        szName = Mid(szName, 2, (Len(szName) - 2))
        rstMyRecordset(g_szFieldName) = szName

        'Set the ItemCost
        Set vCell = vShape.Cells(g_szPropCost)
```

continues

LISTING 22.5 Continued

```
        cyCost = vCell.Result(visCurrency)
        rstMyRecordset(g_szFieldCost) = cyCost

        rstMyRecordset.Update
        rstMyRecordset.Close
    End If
End If

End Sub
```

Severing the Connection

To close the DAO connection between Visio and the Access database, simply close the database object as in

```
g_dbsMyDatabase.Close
```

To terminate the connection between Visio and Access, you simply must quit Access:

```
accessObjApplication.Quit
Set accessObjApplication = Nothing
```

The final line ensures that the Access application object goes out of scope and is removed from memory as well as from all objects under the Application object.

In the next chapter, you will learn how to contact Word from Visio. You will also see how to send data from Visio to Word and retrieve information from Word to use in Visio. You will be shown how to query Word for use in your Visio-based application and learn how to sever the connection when you are finished with the communication.

Visio Automation and Microsoft Word 2000 Interaction

IN THIS CHAPTER

As you have seen earlier, contacting Word within Visio can be done using one of three methods: GetObject(), CreateObject(), and New. The first of these presumes that Word is already up and running. The second and third assume nothing and will launch a new copy of Word, even if it is already running. Listing 23.1 shows the syntax of each.

LISTING 23.1 The Syntax for GetObject, CreateObject, and New

```
Public Sub RunWord1()
        Dim wordApp As Word.Application
        Set wordApp = GetObject(,"Word.Application")
        wordApp. Visible= True
End Sub
Public Sub RunWord2()
        Dim wordApp As Word.Application
        Set wordApp = CreateObject("Word.Application")
        wordApp. Visible= True
End Sub
Public Sub RunWord3()
        Dim wordApp As New Word.Application
        Set wordApp = Word.Application
        wordApp. Visible= True
End Sub
```

Again, as with Visio, you may want to test to see if Word is already running and which document is open prior to launching a new instance if you want to access the current one. Use the proper syntax for currently running or not yet running as applicable.

After you have a running instance of Word, you need to obtain a reference to the document object. This can be done by creating a new document, as in

```
' Add a new document to the Word application
    Set wrdDocObj = wordApp.Documents.Add("Normal.dot")
```

or by referencing an existing document as in

```
' Reference an existing document in Word
    Set wrdDocObj = wordApp.Documents.Item("MyDissertation.DOC")
```

Sending Data to Word

Sending data to Word is a matter of obtaining a selection object and then using the TypeText method of the selection object to pass Word the text you want included in your document:

```
' Add some text
    Set wrdObjsel = wrdDocObj.ActiveWindow.Selection
    wrdObjsel.Style = wrdDocObj.Styles("Heading 1")
```

```
wrdObjsel.TypeText Text:="Now is the time for all good men to come to the
➥ aid of their party."
wrdObjsel.TypeParagraph
```

Notice how you can format the text by providing a paragraph style prior to handing off the text. Notice also how the `TypeParagraph` method of the selection object begins a new paragraph.

Getting Data from Word

Obtaining text from Word to pass back to Visio is a matter of collecting the text you want and assigning it to a string variable. Then you can pass that reference to the text property of the subject's Visio SmartShape symbol. You can select the entire document's text as in

```
Selection.WholeStory
    Selection.Copy
```

Or if text has already been selected:

```
Selection.Copy
```

To programmatically select text in a Word document, you will need to make use of both the selection object and the range object.

Here is an example of selecting the first paragraph of the document:

```
ActiveDocument.Paragraphs(1).Range.Select
```

Here is another example in which you select the character count from a specific point within the document to an ending point:

```
ActiveDocument.Range(Start:=10, End:=20).Select
```

Bind the selection to a variable and pass this to the symbol in Visio as in

```
MySelectionVar = ActiveDocument.Range(Start:=10, End:=20).Select
```

Listing 23.2 is an example of launching Word, opening a document, reading the first of many paragraphs, and passing the collected text to the text of a Visio SmartShape symbol. This code is available on WalrusDoc CH23.VSD on the companion CD.

LISTING 23.2 Passing Information from Word to Visio

```
Public Sub MakeAPoem()
    Dim pagObj As Visio.Page
    Dim shpObj As Visio.Shape
    Dim wrdObjApp As Word.Application
    Dim wrdObjDoc As Word.Document
    Dim wrdObjRange As Word.Range
```

23

VISIO AUTOMATION
AND MICROSOFT
WORD 2000
INTERACTION

continues

LISTING 23.2   Continued

```
    Dim szTextCollector As String
    Dim intCounter As Integer
    Set pagObj = Visio.ActivePage
    Set shpObj = pagObj.DrawRectangle(0.5, 10.5, 8, 0.5)
    Set wrdObjApp = CreateObject("Word.Application")
    wrdObjApp.Visible = True
    Set wrdObjDoc = wrdObjApp.Documents.Open("d:\Book-Macmillan\The Walrus
    ➥ And The Carpenter.DOC")
    szTextCollector = ""
    For intCounter = 1 To 10
        szTextCollector = szTextCollector & wrdObjDoc.Paragraphs(intCounter)
        ➥.Range & vbCrLf
    Next intCounter
    shpObj.Text = szTextCollector
    wrdObjApp.Quit
    Set wrdObjApp = Nothing
End Sub
```

Querying Word for Visio's Use

Listing 23.3 is another example of collecting information in Visio SmartShape symbols and passing them to Word to generate a full report about the business process in the business process diagram. This code can be found in Process CH32.VSD on the companion CD.

LISTING 23.3   Passing Data from Visio to Word

```
Private Sub btnReportToWord_Click()
    Call MakeWordReport
End Sub
Global intStepIndex As Integer
Global intDirtyFlag As Integer
Global shpObjSubjectStep As Visio.Shape
Public Sub ShowNotes()
    If Visio.ActiveWindow.Selection.Count = 1 Then
        If Visio.ActiveWindow.Selection.Item(1).CellExists("Prop.Cost", 0)
        ➥ = True Then
            Set shpObjSubjectStep = Visio.ActiveWindow.Selection.Item(1)
            frmNotes.Show
        End If
    End If
End Sub
Private Sub buAccept_Click()
```

```
        shpObjSubjectStep.Data1 = Me.tbNoteText.Text
        intDirtyFlag = 0
End Sub

Private Sub buCxl_Click()
    If intDirtyFlag = 1 Then
        Dim intRetVal As Integer
        intRetVal = MsgBox("Save Note Text Changes to Shape?", vbQuestion +
        ➥vbYesNo, "Unsaved Changes")
        If intRetVal = vbYes Then
            shpObjSubjectStep.Data1 = Me.tbNoteText.Text
        End If
        Unload frmNotes
    Else
        Unload frmNotes
    End If
End Sub

Private Sub buNext_Click()
    Dim collObjShapes As Visio.Shapes
    Dim shpObjTempShape As Visio.Shape
    Dim intShapeCounter As Integer
    Dim intRetVal As Integer
    Dim selObj As Visio.Selection
    If intDirtyFlag = 1 Then
        intRetVal = MsgBox("Save Note Text Changes to Shape?", vbQuestion +
        ➥vbYesNo, "Unsaved Changes")
        If intRetVal = vbYes Then
            shpObjSubjectStep.Data1 = Me.tbNoteText.Text
        End If
        intDirtyFlag = 0
    End If
    Set collObjShapes = Visio.ActivePage.Shapes
    For intShapeCounter = 1 To collObjShapes.Count
        Set shpObjTempShape = collObjShapes.Item(intShapeCounter)
        If shpObjTempShape.CellExists("Prop.Cost", 0) = True Then
            If Val(shpObjTempShape.Cells("Comment").Result(visNumber)) =
            ➥intStepIndex + 1 Then
                Set shpObjSubjectStep = shpObjTempShape
                Set selObj = Visio.ActiveWindow.Selection
                selObj.Select shpObjSubjectStep, visSelect + visDeselectAll
                intStepIndex = intStepIndex + 1
                intShapeCounter = collObjShapes.Count
                Me.tbNoteText.Text = shpObjSubjectStep.Data1
                intDirtyFlag = 0
```

continues

LISTING 23.3 Continued

```
                    Me.Caption = "Visio Dynamic Notes. Shape: " &
                    ➡shpObjSubjectStep.Name
                    If Val(shpObjTempShape.Cells("Comment").Result(visNumber)) =
                    ➡9 Then
                        MsgBox "End Of Process Steps Reached", vbExclamation +
                        ➡vbOKOnly, "No Further Process Steps Available"
                    End If
                End If
            End If
        Next intShapeCounter
End Sub

Private Sub buOK_Click()
    shpObjSubjectStep.Data1 = Me.tbNoteText.Text
    Unload frmNotes
End Sub

Private Sub buPrev_Click()
    Dim collObjShapes As Visio.Shapes
    Dim shpObjTempShape As Visio.Shape
    Dim intShapeCounter As Integer
    Dim intRetVal As Integer
    Dim selObj As Visio.Selection
    If intDirtyFlag = 1 Then
        intRetVal = MsgBox("Save Note Text Changes to Shape?", vbQuestion +
        ➡vbYesNo, "Unsaved Changes")
        If intRetVal = vbYes Then
            shpObjSubjectStep.Data1 = Me.tbNoteText.Text
        End If
        intDirtyFlag = 0
    End If
    Set collObjShapes = Visio.ActivePage.Shapes
    For intShapeCounter = 1 To collObjShapes.Count
        Set shpObjTempShape = collObjShapes.Item(intShapeCounter)
        If shpObjTempShape.CellExists("Prop.Cost", 0) = True Then
            If Val(shpObjTempShape.Cells("Comment").Result(visNumber)) =
            ➡intStepIndex - 1 Then
                Set shpObjSubjectStep = shpObjTempShape
                Set selObj = Visio.ActiveWindow.Selection
                selObj.Select shpObjSubjectStep, visSelect + visDeselectAll
                intStepIndex = intStepIndex - 1
                intShapeCounter = collObjShapes.Count
                Me.tbNoteText.Text = shpObjSubjectStep.Data1
                intDirtyFlag = 0
```

```
                Me.Caption = "Visio Dynamic Notes. Shape: " &
                ➥shpObjSubjectStep.Name
                If Val(shpObjTempShape.Cells("Comment").Result(visNumber)) =
                ➥ 1 Then
                    MsgBox "Beginning Of Process Steps Reached", vbExclamation
                    ➥ + vbOKOnly, "No Previous Process Steps Available"
                End If
            End If
        End If
    Next intShapeCounter
End Sub


Private Sub Frame1_Click()

End Sub


Private Sub tbNoteText_Change()
    intDirtyFlag = 1
End Sub


Private Sub UserForm_Activate()
    intStepIndex = Val(shpObjSubjectStep.Cells("Comment").Result(visNumber))
    Me.tbNoteText.Text = shpObjSubjectStep.Data1
    intDirtyFlag = 0
    Me.Caption = "Visio Dynamic Notes. Shape: " & shpObjSubjectStep.Name
End Sub
Public Sub MakeWordReport()
    Dim wrdDocObj As Word.Document
    Dim intTick As Integer
    Dim intInnerTick As Integer
    Dim wrdObjsel As Word.Selection
    Dim wrdApp As Word.Application
    Dim intPathCount As Integer
    Dim strProps As String
    Dim dblResTot As Double
    Dim dblResTemp As Double
    Dim dblDurTot As Double
    Dim dblCostTot As Double
    Dim dblCPRUTot As Double


    ' create a new instance of Word
    Set wrdApp = CreateObject("Word.Application")
    wrdApp.Visible = True

    ' Add a new document to the Word application
```

continues

LISTING 23.3 Continued

```
Set wrdDocObj = wrdApp.Documents.Add("Normal.dot")

' Add some title text
Set wrdObjsel = wrdDocObj.ActiveWindow.Selection
wrdObjsel.Style = wrdDocObj.Styles("Heading 1")
wrdObjsel.TypeText Text:="Process Flow Diagramme"
wrdObjsel.TypeParagraph

wrdObjsel.Style = wrdDocObj.Styles("Heading 2")
wrdObjsel.TypeText Text:="Business Procedures"
wrdObjsel.TypeParagraph


' Select all the flowchart stuff in the drawing
' Start by deselecting everything
Visio.ActiveWindow.DeselectAll

' Step through the shapes and look for cost property, assume
➥flowchart shape
For intTick = 1 To ActivePage.Shapes.Count
    With ActivePage.Shapes(intTick)
        If .CellExists("Prop.Cost", 0) = True Then
            ' Select the shape
            ActiveWindow.Select ActivePage.Shapes(intTick), visSelect
        ElseIf .CellExists("EndX", 0) = True Then
            ActiveWindow.Select ActivePage.Shapes(intTick), visSelect
        End If
    End With
Next intTick
' Copy to Clipboard
ActiveWindow.Copy

' Paste diagram into Word
wrdObjsel.Paste
wrdObjsel.InsertBreak wdPageBreak

' Print out a detailed report of each process node in Word

wrdObjsel.Style = wrdDocObj.Styles("Heading 2")
wrdObjsel.TypeText Text:="Business Procedures Flow Details"
wrdObjsel.TypeParagraph

' Step through all the process steps and print out the notes
dblResTot = 0
dblDurTot = 0
```

```
dblCostTot = 0
dblCPRU = 0
dblResTemp = 0
For intTick = 1 To ActivePage.Shapes.Count
    With ActivePage.Shapes(intTick)
        ' If the cost property exists, assume process shape
        If .CellExists("Prop.Cost", 0) Then
            ' put title of system in
            wrdObjsel.Style = wrdDocObj.Styles("Heading 3")

            ' Print out shape detail

            wrdObjsel.TypeText Text:=.Text & vbCrLf
            wrdObjsel.Style = wrdDocObj.Styles("Normal")
            strProps = .Data1 & vbCrLf
            dblCostTot = dblCostTot + .Cells("Prop.Cost").Result
            ➡(visNumber)
            strProps = strProps & .Cells("Prop.Cost").ResultStr("usd")
            ➡ & vbCrLf
            dblDurTot = dblDurTot + .Cells("Prop.Duration").Result
            ➡(visNumber)
            strProps = strProps & .Cells("Prop.Duration").Result
            ➡(visNumber) & " Person Hour(s)" & vbCrLf
            dblResTemp = Val(.Cells("Prop.Resources").ResultStr(""))
            If dblResTemp > dblResTot Then
                dblResTot = dblResTemp
            End If
            strProps = strProps & .Cells("Prop.Resources")
            ➡.ResultStr("") & vbCrLf
            dblCPRUTot = dblCPRUTot + (.Cells("Prop.Duration")
            ➡.Result(visNumber) *
            ➡Val(.Cells("Prop.Resources").ResultStr("")))
            wrdObjsel.TypeText strProps
        End If
    End With
Next intTick
wrdObjsel.Style = wrdDocObj.Styles("Heading 2")
wrdObjsel.TypeText Text:="Business Procedures Flow Totals"
wrdObjsel.TypeParagraph
wrdObjsel.Style = wrdDocObj.Styles("Heading 3")
wrdObjsel.TypeText Text:="Total Business Procedures Cost"
wrdObjsel.TypeParagraph
wrdObjsel.Style = wrdDocObj.Styles("Normal")
wrdObjsel.TypeText Text:=FormatCurrency(dblCostTot, 2)
wrdObjsel.TypeParagraph
wrdObjsel.Style = wrdDocObj.Styles("Heading 3")
```

23

VISIO AUTOMATION AND MICROSOFT WORD 2000 INTERACTION

continues

LISTING 23.3   Continued

```
wrdObjsel.TypeText Text:="Total Business Procedures Duration"
wrdObjsel.TypeParagraph
wrdObjsel.Style = wrdDocObj.Styles("Normal")
wrdObjsel.TypeText Text:=Str(dblDurTot) & " Person Hours"
wrdObjsel.TypeParagraph
wrdObjsel.Style = wrdDocObj.Styles("Heading 3")
wrdObjsel.TypeText Text:="Total Business Procedures Resources"
wrdObjsel.TypeParagraph
wrdObjsel.Style = wrdDocObj.Styles("Normal")
wrdObjsel.TypeText Text:=Str(dblResTot) & " Persons"
wrdObjsel.TypeParagraph
wrdObjsel.Style = wrdDocObj.Styles("Heading 3")
wrdObjsel.TypeText Text:="Calculated Cost Per Resource Unit Figure"
wrdObjsel.TypeParagraph
wrdObjsel.Style = wrdDocObj.Styles("Normal")
wrdObjsel.TypeText Text:=FormatCurrency((dblCostTot / dblCPRUTot), 2)
wrdObjsel.TypeParagraph

    Visio.ActiveWindow.DeselectAll

End Sub
```

Severing the Connection

To terminate the connection between Visio and Word, you simply need to quit Word as in

```
wordObjApplication.Quit
Set wordObjApplication = Nothing
```

The final line ensures that the Word application object goes out of scope and is removed from memory as well as all objects under the application object.

In the next chapter, you will learn how to contact PowerPoint from Visio. You will also learn how to send data from Visio to PowerPoint and retrieve information from PowerPoint to use in Visio. The chapter will also cover how to query PowerPoint for use in your Visio-based application and learn how to sever the connection when you are finished with the communication.

Visio Automation and Microsoft PowerPoint 2000 Interaction

IN THIS CHAPTER

As we saw with Visio earlier, there are three methods of contacting PowerPoint, the application from within Visio: GetObject(), CreateObject(), and New. The first of these presumes that PowerPoint is already up and running. The second and third assume nothing and will launch a new copy of PowerPoint even if it is already running. Listing 24.1 is the syntax.

LISTING 24.1   Launching the PowerPoint Application from Code

```
Public Sub RunPowerPoint1()
        Dim pptApp As PowerPoint.Application
        Set pptApp = GetObject(,"PowerPoint.Application")
        pptApp.Visible = True
End Sub
Public Sub RunPowerPoint2()
        Dim pptApp As PowerPoint.Application
        Set pptApp = CreateObject("PowerPoint.Application")
        pptApp.Visible = True
End Sub
Public Sub RunPowerPoint3()
        Dim pptApp As New PowerPoint.Application
        Set pptApp = PowerPoint.Application
        pptApp.Visible = True
End Sub
```

Again, as with Visio, you may want to test if PowerPoint is already running and what Presentation is open prior to launching a new instance if you want to access the current one. Use the proper syntax for currently running or not yet running as applicable.

Sending Data to PowerPoint

You may wonder why you would want to send data to PowerPoint. If you say that you can place charts in PowerPoint, someone may argue that Excel charts do very well in PowerPoint. In fact, some may argue that Microsoft provides its own charting object to build charts in presentations. Why then *would* you place a Visio diagram in a PowerPoint presentation? Certain types of charts, most especially graphical symbol charts akin to those you see in *USA Today*, are not available within Excel or the Microsoft Graph applet. Visio does a brilliant job of creating these chart types and furthermore these chart types can be linked to external data sources such that the data in the external source controls the charting objects in Visio. The inclusion of one of these chart types in a PowerPoint presentation is highly beneficial. Additionally, Visio diagram types, such as floor plans and process flow diagrams, are highly useful as topic points in PowerPoint presentations. Listing 24.2 illustrates taking a specialized chart type and dropping it into a PowerPoint slide. Notice that it utilizes the Windows clipboard to accomplish this transfer.

LISTING 24.2 Sending Visio Graphics to PowerPoint

```
Public Sub SendOffToPowerPoint()
    Dim winObjVisioWindow As Visio.Window
    Dim pptObjApplication As PowerPoint.Application
    Set winObjVisioWindow = Visio.ActiveWindow
    winObjVisioWindow.DeselectAll
    winObjVisioWindow.SelectAll
    winObjVisioWindow.Copy
    Set pptObjApplication = CreateObject("PowerPoint.Application")
    pptObjApplication.Visible = True
    pptObjApplication.Presentations.Add.Slides.Add(1, ppLayoutBlank)
    ➥.Shapes.Paste
End Sub
```

Getting Data from PowerPoint

It is possible to take information from a PowerPoint document and use it to build a Visio diagram. The example below looks at an existing PowerPoint presentation and counts the number of slides. For each slide, it takes the title and bullet text and uses them to pass to Visio. Visio receives them and creates a new shape for each, sizing each appropriately, based on the quantity of text. Visio then connects each SmartShape symbol to create a flow diagram of the PowerPoint presentation (see Listing 24.3).

LISTING 24.3 Analyzing a PowerPoint Presentation as a Visio Flowchart

```
Public Sub PowerPointAnalysis()
    Dim pagObj As Visio.Page
    Dim shpObj As Visio.Shape
    Dim shpObjPast As Visio.Shape
    Dim shpObjConn As Visio.Shape
    Dim celObj As Visio.Cell
    Dim pptObjApp As PowerPoint.Application
    Dim pptObjPres As PowerPoint.Presentation
    Dim intPptSlideCount As Integer
    Dim pptObjPptSlide As PowerPoint.Slide
    Dim intPptShapeCount As Integer
    Dim pptObjSlideShp As PowerPoint.Shape
    Dim szTextHolder As String
    Dim intFirstFlag As Integer
    intFirstFlag = 1
    Set pagObj = Visio.ActivePage
    Set pptObjApp = CreateObject("PowerPoint.Application")
    pptObjApp.Visible = msoTrue
```

24

VISIO AUTOMATION
AND MICROSOFT
POWERPOINT 2000
INTERACTION

continues

LISTING 24.3   Continued

```
Set pptObjPres = pptObjApp.Presentations.Open("d:\Book-Macmillan\
➥History.PPT")
For intPptSlideCount = 1 To pptObjPres.Slides.Count
    Set pptObjPptSlide = pptObjPres.Slides(intPptSlideCount)
    szTextHolder = ""
    For intPptShapeCount = 1 To pptObjPptSlide.Shapes.Count
        Set pptObjSlideShp = pptObjPptSlide.Shapes(intPptShapeCount)
        If pptObjSlideShp.Type = msoPlaceholder Then
            szTextHolder = szTextHolder & pptObjSlideShp.TextFrame
            ➥.TextRange & vbCrLf
        End If
    Next intPptShapeCount
    If intFirstFlag = 1 Then
        Debug.Print "first Time through"
    Else
        Set shpObjPast = shpObj
    End If
    Set shpObj = pagObj.DrawRectangle((pagObj.PageSheet.Cells("PageWidth")
    ➥.Result(visNumber) / 2) - 1, (pagObj.PageSheet.Cells("PageHeight")
    ➥.Result(visNumber) / 2) + 1, (pagObj.PageSheet.Cells("PageWidth")
    ➥.Result(visNumber) / 2) + 1, (pagObj.PageSheet.Cells("PageHeight"
    ➥).Result(visNumber) / 2) - 1)
    shpObj.Text = szTextHolder
    Set celObj = shpObj.Cells("Width")
    celObj.Formula = "=GUARD(TEXTWIDTH(TheText))"
    Set celObj = shpObj.Cells("Height")
    celObj.Formula = "=GUARD(TEXTHEIGHT(TheText, Width))"
    shpObj.AddNamedRow visSectionConnectionPts, visRowConnectionPts, 0
    Set celObj = shpObj.CellsSRC(visSectionConnectionPts,
    ➥visRowConnectionPts, visCnnctX)
    celObj.Formula = "=Width*0.5"
    Set celObj = shpObj.CellsSRC(visSectionConnectionPts,
    ➥visRowConnectionPts, visCnnctY)
    celObj.Formula = "=Height*1"
    shpObj.AddNamedRow visSectionConnectionPts, visRowConnectionPts + 1, 0
    Set celObj = shpObj.CellsSRC(visSectionConnectionPts,
    ➥visRowConnectionPts + 1, visCnnctX)
    celObj.Formula = "=Width*0.5"
    Set celObj = shpObj.CellsSRC(visSectionConnectionPts,
    ➥visRowConnectionPts + 1, visCnnctY)
    celObj.Formula = "=Height*0"
    Set celObj = shpObj.Cells("LocPinY")
    celObj.Formula = "=Height*1"
    Set celObj = shpObj.Cells("PinY")
    If intFirstFlag = 1 Then
```

```
            celObj.Formula = pagObj.PageSheet.Cells("PageHeight")
            ➥.Result(visNumber) - 1
        Else
            celObj.Formula = shpObjPast.Cells("PinY").Result(visNumber) -
(shpObjPast.Cells("Height").Result(visNumber) + 1)
            Set shpObjConn = pagObj.DrawLine(1, 2, 1, 1)
            Set celObj = shpObjConn.Cells("BeginX")
            celObj.GlueTo shpObjPast.Cells("Connections.X2")
            Set celObj = shpObjConn.Cells("EndX")
            celObj.GlueTo shpObj.Cells("Connections.X1")
        End If
        intFirstFlag = 0
    Next intPptSlideCount
    Visio.ActiveWindow.Selection.DeselectAll
End Sub
```

Querying PowerPoint for Visio's Use

Because PowerPoint is a presentation tool, there is probably not a huge amount of data that will be queried. However, the presentation object contains a lot of information (read properties) about who created the presentation, when it was created, and much more. This can be used in Visio timeline applications, business process diagrams, critical path methodologies, and other diagram types. The above example should help get you started.

Severing the Connection

To terminate the connection between Visio and PowerPoint, you simply need to quit PowerPoint as in

```
pptApp.Quit
Set pptApp = Nothing
```

The final line ensures that the PowerPoint application object goes out of scope and is removed from memory as well as all objects under the application object.

In the next chapter, you will learn how to contact Outlook from Visio. You will learn how to send data from Visio to Outlook and retrieve information from Outlook to use in Visio. You will learn how to query Outlook for use in your Visio-based application and learn how to sever the connection when you are finished with the communication.

Visio Automation and Microsoft Outlook 2000 Interaction

IN THIS CHAPTER

As we saw earlier, contacting Outlook from within Visio can be done using one of three methods: GetObject(), CreateObject(), and New. The first of these presumes that Outlook is already up and running. The second and third assume nothing and will launch a new copy of Outlook, even if it is already running. Listing 25.1 is the syntax.

LISTING 25.1   Launching Outlook from Code

```
Public Sub RunOutlook1()
        Dim otlkApp As Outlook.Application
        Set otlkApp = GetObject(,"Outlook.Application")
        otlkApp.Visible = True
End Sub
Public Sub RunOutlook2()
        Dim otlkApp As Outlook.Application
        Set otlkApp = CreateObject("Outlook.Application")
        otlkApp.Visible= True
End Sub
Public Sub RunOutlook3()
        Dim otlkApp As New Outlook.Application
        Set otlkApp = Outlook.Application
        otlkApp.Visible= True
End Sub
```

Again, as with Visio, you may want to see if Outlook is already running and if Mailbox, Calendar, To Do List, and Contacts Manager are open prior to launching a new instance if you want to access the current one. Use the proper syntax for currently running or not yet running as applicable.

After you have a reference to the application itself, you will need to obtain a reference to a NameSpace. This is unique to Outlook. The NameSpace object is used to log on and out of Outlook itself. Here is the syntax:

```
Set nmspObj = otlkApp.NameSpace("MAPI")
```

Note that the MAPI argument is mandatory and the only valid argument to the NameSpace property.

After the NameSpace object has been secured, you can then actually log on to Outlook in order to establish a MAPI session. This is done by invoking the Logon method of the NameSpace object. The syntax is

```
nmspObj.Logon(Profile, Password, ShowDialog, NewSession)
```

where

- *Profile* is the name of the Outlook profile to use in the MAPI session.

- *Password* is the name of the password associated with this profile.
- *ShowDialog* is a Boolean TRUE or FALSE that determines whether or not Outlook displays the Logon dialog box. Set this value to TRUE to obtain the dialog box.
- *NewSession* is a Boolean TRUE or FALSE that determines whether or not Outlook creates a new MAPI session. Set this value to TRUE to start a new session and FALSE to log on to the current session.

Presuming that a Mr. Bill Ding has a user profile of "BillD" and that his password is "lumber," a valid Logon to Outlook without the need for a dialog would be

```
nmspObj.Logon("BillD", "lumber", FALSE, TRUE)
```

Sending Data to Outlook

Listing 25.2 illustrates how a Visio organizational chart diagram containing Visio SmartShape symbols with a Prop.eMail Custom Property cell can be iterated through and an email message that is sent to each of the persons, who are represented by the SmartShape symbols. After you obtain a reference to the folder object in Outlook, you use the CreateItem method of the Outlook application object and then use the .Recipients property to pass the Custom property from Visio to the message object. Additionally, you use the .Subject and the .Body properties to add the required information prior to using the .Send method to send off the message to the designated recipient. This code is in ToOutlook2000 CH25.vsd on the companion CD.

LISTING 25.2 Mailing to a Visio Recipient Listing Using Outlook

```
Global g_MailItem As Object
Public Sub MailIntoHistory()
    Dim pagObjVis As Visio.Page
    Dim shpObjVis As Visio.Shape
    Dim celObjVis As Visio.Cell
    Dim intCounter As Integer
    Dim otlkObjApp As Outlook.Application
    Dim otlkObjNmeSpc As Outlook.NameSpace
    Dim otlkObjFolder As MAPIFolder
    Set otlkObjApp = CreateObject("Outlook.Application")
    Set otlkObjNmeSpc = otlkObjApp.GetNamespace("MAPI")
    otlkObjNmeSpc.Logon
    Set otlkObjFolder = otlkObjNmeSpc.GetDefaultFolder(olFolderInbox)
    Set pagObjVis = Visio.ActivePage
    For intCounter = 1 To pagObjVis.Shapes.Count
        Set shpObjVis = pagObjVis.Shapes.Item(intCounter)
        If shpObjVis.CellExists("Prop.eMail", 0) Then
            Set celObjVis = shpObjVis.Cells("Prop.eMail")
            If Len(celObjVis.ResultStr("")) > 0 Then
```

25

VISIO AUTOMATION
AND MICROSOFT
OUTLOOK 2000
INTERACTION

continues

LISTING 25.2 Continued

```
                Set g_MailItem = otlkObjApp.CreateItem(olMailItem)
                With g_MailItem
                    . Recipients.Add celObjVis.ResultStr("")
                    .Subject = "Psssst... 2007 is just about here."
                    .Body = "Come on back and join the celebration!"
                    .Send
                End With
            End If
        End If
    Next intCounter
End Sub
```

Getting Data from Outlook

Listing 25.3 illustrates how, subsequent to obtaining a reference to the MAPI folder object, you can read information about each message in the subject inbox. This information includes the sender's name, the subject, the message size in bytes, the time the message was received, and the entire message contents. With this information, you can then construct a process diagram based on Visio's organizational charting to display all the information about the messages in the inbox. The code is in FromOutlook2000 CH25.vsd on the companion CD.

LISTING 25.3 Building an Organizational Chart from Outlook Data

```
Public Sub FromOutlook2000()
    Dim pagObjVis As Visio.Page
    Dim shpObjVisThisShape1 As Visio.Shape
    Dim shpObjVisThisShape2 As Visio.Shape
    Dim stnObjVis As Visio.Document
    Dim mastObjVis As Visio.Master
    Dim otlkObkApp As Outlook.Application
    Dim otlkObjNmeSpc As Outlook.NameSpace
    Dim otlkObjFolder As Outlook.MAPIFolder
    Dim intCounter As Integer
    Dim intFirstTrigger As Integer
    Dim dblHeightSpacing As Double
    Dim dblDropX As Double
    Dim dblDropY As Double
    Dim szShapeText As String
    Dim celObjVis As Visio.Cell
    intFirstTrigger = 1
    Set pagObjVis = Visio.ActivePage
    Set stnObjVis = Visio.Documents.Item("Organization Chart Shapes.VSS")
    Set otlkObjApp = CreateObject("Outlook.Application")
```

```
    Set otlkObjNmeSpc = otlkObjApp.GetNamespace("MAPI")
    otlkObjNmeSpc.Logon
    Set otlkObjFolder = otlkObjNmeSpc.GetDefaultFolder(olFolderInbox)
    dblHeightSpacing = 0
    For intCounter = 1 To otlkObjFolder.Items.Count
     szShapeText = ""
     With otlkObjFolder.Items(intCount)
         dblDropX = pagObjVis.PageSheet.Cells("PageWidth").Result(visNumber) / 2
          dblDropY = pagObjVis.PageSheet.Cells("PageHeight").Result(visNumber)
         Set mastObjVis = stnObjVis.Masters.Item("Executive")
          Set shpObjVisThisShape1 = pagObjVis.Drop(mastObjVis, dblDropX,
          ➥dblDropY - (dblHeightSpacing + 0.25))
          dblHeightSpacing =
shpObjVisThisShape1.Cells("Height").Result(visNumber)
          shpObjVisThisShape1.Text = "Message Number: " & Str(intCounter)
          Set mastObjVis = stnObjVis.Masters.Item("Staff")
          dblDropY = shpObjVisThisShape1.Cells("PinY").Result(visNumber)
          Set shpObjVisThisShape2 = pagObjVis.Drop(mastObjVis, dblDropX - 1,
          ➥dblDropY - dblHeightSpacing)
          szShapeText = "Sender Name: " & .SenderName
         shpObjVisThisShape2.Text = szShapeText
          Set celObjVis = shpObjVisThisShape2.Cells("Controls.X1")
          celObjVis.GlueToPos shpObjVisThisShape1, 0.5, 0#
          Set shpObjVisThisShape2 = pagObjVis.Drop(mastObjVis, dblDropX - 1,
          ➥dblDropY - (dblHeightSpacing + 0.25))
          szShapeText = "Subject: " & .Subject
         shpObjVisThisShape2.Text = szShapeText
          Set celObjVis = shpObjVisThisShape2.Cells("Controls.X1")
          celObjVis.GlueToPos shpObjVisThisShape1, 0.5, 0#
          Set shpObjVisThisShape2 = pagObjVis.Drop(mastObjVis, dblDropX - 1,
          ➥dblDropY - (dblHeightSpacing + 0.5))
          szShapeText = "Size: " & .Size
         shpObjVisThisShape2.Text = szShapeText
          Set celObjVis = shpObjVisThisShape2.Cells("Controls.X1")
          celObjVis.GlueToPos shpObjVisThisShape1, 0.5, 0#
          Set shpObjVisThisShape2 = pagObjVis.Drop(mastObjVis, dblDropX - 1,
          ➥dblDropY - (dblHeightSpacing + 0.75))
          szShapeText = "Received Time: " & .ReceivedTime
         shpObjVisThisShape2.Text = szShapeText
          Set celObjVis = shpObjVisThisShape2.Cells("Controls.X1")
          celObjVis.GlueToPos shpObjVisThisShape1, 0.5, 0#
          Set mastObjVis = stnObjVis.Masters.Item("Position")
          Set shpObjVisThisShape2 = pagObjVis.Drop(mastObjVis, dblDropX + 1,
          ➥dblDropY - (dblHeightSpacing + 0.75))
          szShapeText = "Message Text: " & vbCrLf & .Body
         shpObjVisThisShape2.Text = szShapeText
```

continues

LISTING 25.3   Continued

```
        Set celObjVis = shpObjVisThisShape2.Cells("Controls.X1")
        celObjVis.GlueToPos shpObjVisThisShape1, 0.5, 0#
        dblHeightSpacing = dblHeightSpacing + shpObjVisThisShape2
    ➥.Cells("Height").Result(visNumber)
    Next intCounter
End Sub
```

Querying Outlook for Visio's Use

After you have obtained a reference to any given message in an Outlook mail folder, you can query the MailItem object for any one or more of the numerous properties of the object. Some of these are

MailItem.Body	The body of the message
MailItem.CC	The display name of the person listed on the CC line
MailItem.DeferredDeliveryTime	The deferred delivery time of the message
MailItem.DeleteAfterSubmit	True if the MailItem will not be saved after being sent
MailItem.ExpiryTime	The date and time the message expires
MailItem.FlagDueBy	The due date flag for the message
MailItem.FlagRequest	The action to be taken if the .FlagStatus is set to olFlagMarked
MailItem.FlagStatus	The flag status for the mail item. To set the flag, use olFlagMarked to set a flag's status to "complete;" use olFlagComplete to remove the flag and set the flag's status to olNoFlag
MailItem.HTMLBody	Sets the body type as HTML
MailItem.Importance	The importance level of the message
MailItem.ReadReceiptRequested	A return receipt is requested
MailItem.ReceivedTime	The date and time of the message receipt
MailItem.Recipients	The recipients object for all of the intended recipients
MailItem.SaveSentMessageFolder	The MAPI folder object
MailItem.SenderName	The sender's name
MailItem.Sensitivity	The sensitivity level for the message
MailItem.SentOn	The date and time the message was sent

MailItem.Size	The size in bytes of the message
MailItem.Subject	The text of the subject line of the message
MailItem.UnRead	Whether or not the message has been read
MailItems.VotingOptions	The voting options for the message
MailItem.VotingResponse	The voting response for the message

You should be aware that there is no direct way to retrieve the actual email address of the sender. To overcome this difficulty, here is a workaround. This involves sending a temporary reply to the message, which creates a new `MailItem` object. With that `MailObject` referenced, you can access the `To` property of the MailItem. The code is as follows in Listing 25.4.

LISTING 25.4 Workaround: Retrieving Email Addresses from Outlook

```
Function GetSenderAddress(otlkObjMsg As Object) As String
    Dim otlkObjReplyItem As Outlook.MailItem
    Dim szSenderAddress As String
    Set otlkObjReplyItem = otlkObjMsg.Reply
    GetSenderAddress = otlkObjReplyItem.To
    Set otlkReplyItem = Nothing
End Function


' to use this function…
Public Sub TestTheSenderAddress()
    Dim otlkObjNmeSpc As Outlook.NameSpace
    Dim otlkObjFolder As MAPIFolder
    Set otlkObjApp = GetObject(, "Outlook.Application")
    Set otlkObjNmeSpc = otlkObjApp.GetNamespace("MAPI")
    otlkObjNmeSpc.Logon
    Set otlkObjFolder = otlkObjNmeSpc.GetDefaultFolder(olFolderInbox)
    MsgBox GetSenderAddress(otlkObjFolder.Items(1))
End Sub
```

Severing the Connection

Prior to terminating any connection between Visio and Outlook, you need to ensure that you have logged off of Outlook. This is accomplished by using the Logoff method of the NameSpace object. The syntax is

```
OtlkObjNmeSpc.Logoff
```

To terminate the connection between Visio and Outlook, you simply need to quit Outlook as in

```
otlkObjApplication.Quit
Set otlkObjApplication = Nothing
```

The final line ensures that the Outlook application object goes out of scope and is removed from memory as well as all objects under the application object.

In the next chapter, you will learn about the packaging and deployment of Visio solutions. You will learn about the installation considerations, about Visio as an active document, and how Visio diagrams can be viewed over the Internet. You will learn how to ascertain which files to include with your solution as well as how to update your solution as you revise, fix bugs, and incrementally upgrade your solution. You will also learn about the maintenance of Visio solutions.

Packaging and Deploying Visio Automation Solutions

IN THIS CHAPTER

After you have created the ultimate Visio solution and have determined that you are ready to deploy it, you need to consider how the solution will be installed on the users' systems. If you own a copy of Microsoft Visual Studio, you have a fully adequate toolkit for deployment of your solution. You can build a Visual Basic installer and collect all the required source material into one or more .CAB files. The VB application can then be burned onto a CD-ROM and duplicated for each user. Alternately, you could place the installation system on your network server and direct your users to it. They then could run the installation application from the server. It is also possible to create an HTML page for your intranet that enables the user to perform the install.

Keep in mind that your users are most generally using Visio first and then are adding your solution on top of Visio. This means that your users will expect that whenever they are not working with your solution yet are still using Visio, Visio will behave as it always has, prior to the installation of your solution. As you now know, if a solution is placed in a directory beneath the \Visio\Solutions directory, when Visio is launched, it will recache the solutions structure and your users will be able to see the solution listed as part of the Visio system. This is grand, but if the user upgrades to a new version of Visio, your system could be jeopardized. It is preferable to place your solution in its own directory structure and then add your solution to the solutions directory structure. This can be done manually via the Tools, Options dialog box under the File Paths tab. This can also be accomplished programmatically via the StartUpPaths property of the Visio application object. With this mechanism, you can test for the existence of your solution in the path structure, add to it as necessary, or modify it as required.

My strongest recommendation is that you do not alter the behavior structure of Visio, save for the addition of your solution to the paths structure and the behavior of any documents created based upon the templates you provide. Keep in mind that your code may reside in a template and that the template code may provide the user with exactly the menu systems, toolbar systems, stencils, and user interface (UI) behavior that you want them to experience while they use your solution. However, even in the same running session of Visio, if the user chooses to begin a diagram based on one of Visio's shipping solutions or modify a diagram based on any other template, the user's experience should be as if your solution is not present at all.

Web-Based Document Viewing and Interaction

Most users, and many developers as well, are not aware that Visio is an active document application. This means that Visio diagrams may be both viewed and edited across the Internet based upon some specific criteria. Presume that you have a Web server located in Koala Lumpur. That Web server has public access to a directory containing a Visio diagram. Presume also that you are located in Minot, North Dakota and you are using Microsoft Internet Explorer

Packaging and Deploying Visio Automation Solutions

CHAPTER 26

441

26

PACKAGING AND
DEPLOYING VISIO
AUTOMATION
SOLUTIONS

4.0 or greater as your Web browser. Additionally presume that you have a copy of Visio 5.0 or higher installed on your desktop. You do not even need to be aware that Visio is installed locally; it simply resides there.

When you are actively working within IE 4.0 or greater and browsing Web pages, if you access the Visio diagram located on the Web server, you can open that diagram and actively run code against it, modify it, query information about it, print it, and generally work with the diagram as if it were residing on your local machine (subject to connectivity speeds, of course). Other individuals will be able to view the diagram at the same time; however, the first one to open it has the edit rights and the others will be able to view and interact with it as it existed at its last saved state. Because they have read-only access, any changes they make will be lost when they exit the diagram.

This far underutilized capability is not to be dismissed rapidly. This capability means that a utility diagram showing the location of every power vault in a service can be posted to a Web server, maintained by a dispatcher remotely, and queried by the field service technicians at locations all through the service area by utilizing mobile Web access. By incorporating interaction with Microsoft Outlook, as we have seen before, the dispatcher can receive notification of updated maintenance information and update the diagram accordingly. Reloading the page, which is shown in the diagram, would relay the updated information to all field sources.

Files to Include

What files should you include as part of your solution? This generally depends upon how extensive your solution is as you design it. Minimally, your solution should include one Visio template file. All new diagrams based on this template should behave accordingly. This template can utilize just the existing Visio stencil files, and therefore the one file would be sufficient. Your template could utilize one or more custom stencils that you create. This entails the shipping of these stencil files along with the template file.

Should your solution include highly customized toolbars with your own specific iconography on the button faces, make sure that your code knows where these .ICO files are located. Also include a mechanism for tracking any changes in their location as well as a "fallback" icon file, should the proper file be destroyed, deleted, or otherwise missing in action.

Your solution may include code solution items created in C++ as Visio .VSL files, or items created in Visual Basic as Visio additive .EXE executable files. This means that these files must be included as well. Remember the caveat about isolating your solution to its own directory structure. This will make your solution *much* easier to maintain. Additionally, as you design your solution, keep in mind where any permanent or temporary files will be stored. Do not rely upon the Windows temporary directory as a default. Users have a habit of deleting files from it as well as having enough clutter there to render the space unusable, due to a lack of available disk space. When you write out temporary files, check available disk space. When you write out permanent files, place them in a pre-designated location accessible via some set-up mechanism that is easily modifiable, or use the Windows Common dialog box feature to allow your users to decide where they would like to store the files.

Updating Your Solution

It is rare that any solution that goes out in "one-point-oh" format is never altered or updated. To this end, it is important to consider how you will plan to update your solution. It would be easy to say that you will simply burn a new CD and overwrite any previous files with newer versions of them upon installation of your updated solution. This might work for any .VSL or .EXE files, but you need to keep in mind something you learned early on in this book. When a user drags out a master from a stencil onto a drawing page, Visio makes a local copy of that master in the drawing's local stencil. From that point on, that diagram never looks back to the external stencil for information about that master. If you delete the master from the local stencil, it does not re-read it from the external; rather, it severs the connection from the master to the individual instances, rendering them incapable of inheritance and increasing their size as well.

As you have seen earlier, it is possible to generate a SmartShape symbol on the fly. This means that you can actually use code to modify the geometry and properties of the master. However, this would require a rather large body of code to validate and that you change every aspect of each master on a stencil, whether external or local.

Remember that code associated with a template becomes part of the document the moment it is created. Any changes to the template subsequently are never seen by the document. It is true that you can use VBE (which differs slightly from VBA in that VBE is used to modify VBA code and the VBA environment) to alter the code already associated with a document. However, like attempting to use code to fully recreate a SmartShape symbol master on a local stencil, using VBE to modify existing code in a document is painful at best and generally discouraging.

A better solution is to maintain your code in a Visio stencil file. If you update your code, simply ship a new stencil, and each time the code is called, it is called from the updated version in the associated stencil. However, the stencil must be open and usable with every diagram that needs that code. You may need some mechanism that ensures that your document based on your solution's template with that stencil is opened each time.

Solutions Maintenance

Just as you have learned about deploying your solution via many mechanisms, your solutions maintenance can be delivered in the same way. By attaching a C++ or VB executable as well as any new stencils, icons, templates, and so on, the executable can call VBA functionality from within Outlook to extract the attached, required files and install them properly. The user would simply need to receive the email message and double-click on the update executable; your updating code could then run properly. However, you are as aware as I am that most large corporate information systems (IS) managers would lose 7 to 10 years of their lives should this type of non-secure solution be implemented. In a large corporate environment, it is far preferable to ship an update CD, let the IS folks install the changes to a corporate server, and then have individuals run an update routine from there.

Deployment, installation, maintenance and updating are all unique tasks and highly subject to the rules, regulations, and requirements of the client you are servicing. Work within their parameters to develop a schema that works for both them as users and you as the developer.

INDEX

MTS Programming with Visual Basic

Scot Hillier
0-672-31425-8
$29.99 USA/$44.95 CAN

Building Enterprise Solutions with Visual Studio 6

G.A. SULLIVAN
0-672-31489-4
$49.99 USA/$74.95 CAN

Palm Programming

Glenn Bachmann
0-672-31493-2
$29.99 USA/$44.95 CAN

Other Related Titles

Microsoft Windows DNA Exposed
Louis Storms IV; Scott Peterson
0-672-31561-0
$29.99 USA/$44.95 CAN

Roger Jennings' Database Developer's Guide with Visual Basic 6
Roger Jennings
0-672-31063-5
$59.99 USA/$89.95 CAN

Sams Teach Yourself Database Programming with Visual Basic 6 in 21 Days
Curtis Smith and Mike Amundsen
0-672-31308-1
$45.00 USA/$64.95 CAN

Sams Teach Yourself Database Programming with Visual C++ 6 in 21 Days
Lyn Robison
0-672-31350-2
$34.99 USA/$52.95 CAN

Sams Teach Yourself SQL in Days, Second Edition
Ryan K. Stephens, Ronald R. Plew, Bryan Morgan and Jeff Perkins
0-672-31110-0
$39.99 USA/$57.95 CAN

Sams Teach Yourself UML in 24 Hours
Joseph Schmuller
0-672-31636-6
$24.99 USA/$37.95 CAN

SAMS

www.samspublishing.com

All prices are subject to change.

CD-ROM INSTALLATION

WINDOWS 95/NT INSTALLATION INSTRUCTIONS

1. Insert the CD-ROM disc into your CD-ROM drive.

2. From the Windows 95/NT desktop, double-click the My Computer icon. Some features may be accessible by right-clicking the CD icon from your My Computer menu.

3. Double-click the icon representing your CD-ROM drive.

4. Double-click the icon titled START.EXE to run the CD-ROM interface.

NOTE

If Windows 95/NT is installed on your computer, and you have the AutoPlay feature enabled, the START.EXE program starts automatically whenever you insert the disc into your CD-ROM drive.